Narrative, Social Myth, and Reality in Contemporary Scottish and Irish Women's Writing

Narrative, Social Myth, and Reality in Contemporary Scottish and Irish Women's Writing: Kennedy, Lochhead, Bourke, Ní Dhuibhne, and Carr

By

Tudor Balinisteanu

CAMBRIDGE SCHOLARS

PUBLISHING

Narrative, Social Myth, and Reality in Contemporary Scottish and Irish Women's Writing:
Kennedy, Lochhead, Bourke, Ní Dhuibhne, and Carr,
by Tudor Balinisteanu

This book first published 2009

Cambridge Scholars Publishing

12 Back Chapman Street, Newcastle upon Tyne, NE6 2XX, UK

British Library Cataloguing in Publication Data
A catalogue record for this book is available from the British Library

ISBN (10): 1-4438-1127-0, ISBN (13): 978-1-4438-1127-9

TABLE OF CONTENTS

ACKNOWLEDGEMENTS

Dr Alice Jenkins (University of Glasgow) read many drafts of this study. Her comments proved invaluable in strengthening my argument. Prof Susan Rowland (University of Greenwich) and Dr John Coyle (University of Glasgow) offered extremely useful suggestions in the final stages. A significant part of this study was shaped in the welcoming atmosphere of the teaching teams lead by Dr Donald Mackenzie, the convener of the "Writing and Ideology" course, and Dr Elwira Grossman, the convener of the Comparative Literature Programme (University of Glasgow).

I owe a special debt of gratitude to Laura Manea for encouragement and inspiration throughout the stages of this project.

This book is for Eldalie.

Some of the material used in this book was previously published as follows: "States of Fancy. The Role of Fantasy and Narrative in Constructing Social Worlds" in *Angelaki Journal of the Theoretical Humanities*, Vol. 13, No. 3 (2008), and "Elements of the Eden Myth in A.L. Kennedy's 'Original Bliss'" in the *Journal of Gender Studies*, Vol. 18, No. 3 (2009). They are reprinted here in revised form with the permission of Taylor & Francis Ltd. "Tangled Up in Blue. Liz Lochhead's Grimm Sisters Tales" first appeared in *Marvels & Tales: Journal of Fairy-Tale Studies*, Vol. 23, No. 2 (2009). It is used here with the permission of Wayne State University Press. "The Land of Witch's Heart's Desire. Ontological Flickers in Marina Carr's *By the Bog of Cats...*" was originally published in the *Irish Feminist Review*, Vol. 3 (2007); "Otherworldly Women and Neurotic Fairies. The Cultural Construction of Women in Angela Bourke's Writing" in the *Irish University Review*, Vol. 37, No. 2 (2007); "My Words Should Catch Your Words: Myth, Writing and Social Ritual in A. L. Kennedy's *Everything You Need*" in the *International Review of Scottish Studies*, Vol. 32 (2007). They are used here with the editors' permission. "The Persephone Figure in Eavan Boland's 'The Pomegranate' and Liz Lochhead's 'Lucy's Diary'" was first published in *From Word to Canvas: Appropriations of Myth in Women's Aesthetic Production* (Cambridge Scholars Publishing 2009) edited by Sanja Bahun-Radunović and V.G. Julie Rajan.

PREFACE

This book is concerned with narrative constructions of women's identities in texts by contemporary Scottish and Irish women writers.[1] The theoretical framework of my analysis has been inspired by the writers' concerns with the relationship between narrative and reality. A. L. Kennedy has compared voice with a river that collects affluents (others' voices).[2] On another occasion, reading for the *Aye Write!* Festival in Glasgow, she spoke about her experiences as a student of drama who had to cite another's voice. Kennedy showed her conviction that using another's voice (the specific example was acting roles from Shakespeare's plays) "unleashes a force that transforms the actor as well as the members of the audience."[3] This view, expressed by Kennedy on numerous occasions of readings and speeches that I attended between 2004-2007, has suggested the main line of investigation of this study: an examination of how narratives in which we inevitably cite others' voices influence our presentations of ourselves to ourselves and to others in discursive interaction.

I endeavoured to undertake this investigation by following two threads. The main thread is an analysis of how the influence of narratives in shaping identities is reflected upon in the very narratives of the writers whose works form the interest of this study. In this framework, the focus is on the characters' identities. These characters, within the fictional realms where they abide, are shown as having to deal with issues of authority wielded through other narratives to which the texts refer. On the other hand, I have found that the texts that depict these characters' situations may themselves influence the texts' readers. Thus, a secondary venue of investigation opened up, enticing me to reflect on the extent to which our

---

[1] Generally, I adopt Mieke Bal's terminology: "A *narrative text* is a text in which an agent relates ('tells') a story in a particular medium, such as language ... . A *story* is a fabula that is presented in a certain manner. A *fabula* is a series of logically and chronologically related events that are caused or experienced by actors." Mieke Bal, *Narratology: Introduction to the Theory of Narrative* (Toronto: University of Toronto Press, 1997), 5, original italics.

[2] Personal conversation with A. L. Kennedy, University of Glasgow, May 2004.

[3] Approximate quotation. A. L. Kennedy, *Aye Write!* Festival reading, Mitchell Library Theatre, Glasgow, 19 February 2007.

identities as real individuals are shaped through the texts we read. My analysis will therefore also provide reflections on how texts shape identities of individuals inhabiting metatextual worlds.

The theoretical argument of this book can be summarised as follows, with a degree of generalisation. Identities are fantasised in the recesses of the mind. In order to express these fantasies, and thus flesh out our social identity, we cite, to an extent, from others' narratives. These acts of citation shape our perceptions of ourselves and of others as we negotiate, helped by these narratives, subjective identities and acceptable socialisation scenarios. These negotiations can only take place in social interaction where we become acquainted with voices that we can cite. In this view, reading is also a form of social interaction, a dialogue with the voice of the text that joins ours as we read.

Thus, others' voices have power over us and influence our identities and socialisation. We, in turn, have power over others when we express our fantasies of their identities and invite them to inhabit the subject positions we set forth when we address them. Not only the authority of voice is relevant here, that is, not only is it important to be aware that who speaks "louder" silences others; but also the power of fantasies set forth through the "louder" speech steers others as they seep into their own fantasies, permeating through voices joined in dialogue or in reading—a silent "invasion". Our fantasies, remote as they may seem in relation to the real world, nevertheless affect reality in significant ways. A vision of how this happens is suggested in Kennedy's novella "Original Bliss", which explores the idea of a cybernetics of the imagination understood as the way one is steered from the inside: "our interior lives have seismic effects on our exterior world."[4] In order to theorise the role of the imagination envisioned in "Original Bliss", so that this vision can be developed into instruments of theoretical analysis, I have used concepts of fantasy and fantasising. The analysis of these concepts offered incentives for examining how they fit with theorisations of the relationship between narrative and (inner as well as outer) reality. This examination led me to the argument that if how and what we fantasise is influenced by narratives, stories steer readers and audiences.

But if stories steer readers and audiences, the latter may also revise and reconfigure stories, staking claims on authorship and on the power it engenders. I found that this effort of reconfiguration is characteristic of Liz Lochhead's reconstructions of Grimms' fairy tales, the fabula of

---

[4] A. L. Kennedy, "Original Bliss", *Original Bliss* (London: Vintage, 1998), 151-311, 154.

Persephone's myth, and Dracula's story.[5] The analysis of Lochhead's texts provided cues for further developing the main argument of this study, and for defining its focuses. It determined this book's concern with the disciplinary effects of corpuses of narratives derived from myths, that perpetuate them or engender new myths. Addressing this concern, it has become necessary to assess the social value of corpuses of narratives that engender disciplining discourses.

Illustrative examples of such corpuses of narratives can be found in the folk and fairy-tale traditions. I endeavoured to asses the social value of the disciplining effects of narratives in relation to the varied forms of manifestation of disciplinary power engendered with folk and fairy tales, so as to provide a blueprint for analyses of other kinds of corpuses of narratives. The importance of fairy tales in shaping social attitudes is discussed in Angela Bourke's study of Bridget Cleary's murder.[6] This study, as well as some of Bourke's short stories, emphasise that physical bodies and landscapes are imbricated with a community's body-social or official body politic. From the analysis of Bourke's writing, I retained a concern with how corpuses drawn upon in narratives, such as those of the folk and fairy-tale tradition, discipline audiences while at the same time legitimating social order and dictating patterns of socialisation.

Sharing similar concerns with Bourke's writing, Éilís Ní Dhuibhne's narratives are more directly preoccupied with the imbrication between verbal and material textures that stifles women's voices. Indeed, throughout the texts analysed in this book, the main concerns tend to be women's voices as well as the ways in which women's bodies are disciplined through the fantasies upon which representations of the body are based. However, the exploration of these disciplinary effects of fantasy and voice could not be undertaken without addressing issues of masculine identity. The stifling effects of narrative traditions can be seen as marking both masculine and feminine identities.

Marina Carr's discursive strategies foreground heteroglossia as a means to undermine the power of subjection exercised through stories. Never frozen within subject positions, the protagonists of Carr's plays explore the potential of heteroglossia in their attempts to find ways of exercising agency within the constraints of traditions that limit one's

---

[5] Liz Lochhead, *The Grimm Sisters, Dreaming Frankenstein & Collected Poems* (Edinburgh: Polygon, 1986), 69-104; Liz Lochhead, "Lucy's Diary", *Bagpipe Muzak* (London: Penguin, 1991), 60-62; Liz Lochhead, *Dracula, Mary Queen of Scots Got Her Head Chopped Off* and *Dracula* (London: Penguin, 1989), 69-147.
[6] Angela Bourke, *The Burning of Bridget Cleary: A True Story* (London: Pimlico, 1999).

possibilities of fantasising identity. The analysis of Carr's work suggested the idea to examine also the texts of the other writers with a view to their interest in forms of heteroglossic intervention that undermine monoglossic discursive regimes.

Thus, the analysis of the relationship between narrative and reality called for by these writers' works had to be interdisciplinary, involving elements of narratology theory, linguistics, philosophy, anthropology, and social theory. However, it was not my purpose to offer an exhaustive critical analysis of the texts from within each of these disciplines. I have used primarily the tools of literary criticism to find out how the texts envision narrative as developing from, and affecting, reality. But at the same time, I attempted to define an interdisciplinary theoretical framework that is useful in studying the relationship between narrative and reality in broader contexts. This theoretical framework will be presented in the first part of the book, but I emphasise that many of its elements have been derived from analyses of the texts. Thus, each analysis of an author's work, having yielded some, not all, of the elements of the overall critical framework, will highlight various facets of this framework. At the same time, the theoretical framework has been continuously reshaped to respond to the visions that emerged from close readings of the texts. I have then used it to reinterpret the texts in order to define their common ground. For instance, the vision of how a discourse's heteroglossia can be used to deconstruct oppressive subjection, suggested by Carr's plays, has not only served the chapters concerned with this playwright's work, which are the last chapters of the book, but I have also used this vision to reflect on the other writers' work, in order to see how their texts use the decentralising power of heteroglossia.

From these movements between a specific textual analysis and an overarching perspective, there emerged the third major term in the overall architecture of this study. I have spoken of the relationship between narrative and reality. From now on I will refer to a triad instead of a dyad when speaking about the main focus of this study, which is the relationship between narrative, reality, and myth.

All the writers whose works are examined here share a concern with myths of femininity and with familiar mythic themes that influence perceptions of femininity. There exists a strong tradition developed by women writers of rethinking and rewriting stories derived from myths. I will discuss the importance of this tradition in the introductory chapter of Part I. At this point, I am satisfied to simply signal the existence of a need for rewritings of stories derived from myths through Marina Warner's comments:

Myths offer a lens which can be used to see human identity in its social and cultural context—they can lock us up in stock reactions, bigotry and fear, but they're not immutable, and by unpicking them, the stories can lead to others. Myths convey values and expectations which are always evolving, in the process of being formed, but—and this is fortunate—never set so hard they cannot be changed again, and newly told stories can be more helpful than repeating old ones.[7]

In my analyses a central concern is the influence of myth in constructing our identities in social reality, but I am equally concerned with the ways in which acts of citation of stories can lead to productive mutations that help us imagine new identities and social worlds.

Most of the texts examined in this book engage, to various extents, with stories derived from myths in order to re-signify the myths. Although grounded in the specificities of Scotland or Ireland, the treatment of mythic themes in these texts has wider relevance. Some of the texts focus on the specific manifestation in Scottish and Irish culture of elements of myths that are encountered in most Western traditions. Other texts deal with elements of myths that are specific to Scottish and Irish cultures, in a manner that shows their cross-cultural value. My focus on Scottish and Irish writers is partly determined by the fact that their work continues to offer fertile ground for critical exploration. My study is intended as an addition to the work already undertaken on these authors, expanding this work. On the other hand, the texts studied in this book answer questions of interest for worldwide audiences in original ways, and my focus on Scotland and Ireland should not be understood as an endorsement of understandings of these cultures as cultures that deserve to be "redeemed" through further study. The non-parochial character of contemporary Scottish and Irish writing has been substantially documented in critical arguments that show how Scottish and Irish writers respond to questions of international interest.[8]

---

[7] Marina Warner, *Managing Monsters: Six Myths of Our Time (The 1994 Reith Lectures)* (London: Vintage, 1994), 14.

[8] Douglas Gifford, "At Last—the Real Scottish Literary Renaissance?", *Books in Scotland* 34 (1990): 1-4, 2; Alison Lumsden, "Scottish Women's Short Stories: 'Repositories of Life Swiftly Apprehended'", *Contemporary Scottish Women Writers*, eds. Aileen Christianson and Alison Lumsden (Edinburgh: Edinburgh University Press, 2000), 156-69, 168. Gerry Smyth, *The Novel and the Nation: Studies in the New Irish Fiction* (London: Pluto, 1997), 47; Edna Longley, "From Cathleen to Anorexia: The Breakdown of Irelands", *The Living Stream: Literature and Revisionism in Ireland* (Newcastle-upon-Tyne: Bloodaxe, 1994), 173-95, 194-5. Alison Lumsden and Aileen Christianson, "Introduction", *Contemporary*

In Chapter 4 I will examine in more detail definitions of the concept of myth, explaining how this concept will be used in my analysis. For now it will suffice to highlight Bruce Lincoln's argument that *mythos* is "an assertive discourse of power and authority that represents itself as something to be believed and obeyed."[9] In this understanding, the discourse of myth is not necessarily tied up with a specific genre, historical period, theme, etc. Rather, Lincoln's argument suggests that manifestations of authority through discourse justify the suspicion that a myth may be employed in the service of authority. In this sense, some of the myths explored in the writings analysed in this study are: the vampire myth, the Persephone myth, and myth as folk and fairy tale (Lochhead); myths of Irishness derived from the masculine cultural canon (Carr); myths reiterated in various folk-tales that legitimate male-dominated gender regimes (Ní Dhuibhne); and Enlightenment myths that emphasise the organic contiguity of feminine bodies with a powerful body of nature seen as needing to be tamed and governed by a masculine elite, lest the alliance between women and nature should threaten the legitimate masculine body politic (Bourke).[10] I will argue that narratives derived from these myths can influence how feminine bodies are socialised. Kennedy's writing will be examined not so much for its use of elements of myths (for instance of the Grail myth in the novel *Everything You Need*) as for its emphasis on the mythologizing effects of the stories through which we fantasise ourselves and those with whom we interact.[11]

As noted, my methodology has been influenced by the very texts which I analyse in this study. However, a methodology suited to the task of critical analysis could not have been entirely reliant on the visions on the role of fantasy and fantasising, on the social value of myth, on the effects of reiterating stories, or on heteroglossia that I derived from these texts. I sought to develop these visions using critical theory. My

---

Scottish Women Writers, 1-7, 2; Margery McCulloch, "Scottish Women's Poetry 1972-1999: Transforming Traditions", *Contemporary Scottish Women Writers*, 11-26, 25.

[9] Bruce Lincoln, *Theorizing Myth: Narrative, Ideology and Scholarship* (Chicago: University of Chicago Press, 1999), 17.

[10] The concept of "gender regime" used here is derived from Sylvia Walby, *Gender Transformations* (London: Routledge, 1997), 6. Walby identifies six interrelated structures (household production, paid employment, the state, violence, sexuality and cultural representation in various media) that sustain a gender regime in the domestic and public spheres.

[11] A. L. Kennedy, *Everything You Need* (London: Vintage, 2000). The novel was first published by Cape in 1999.

methodology is heavily indebted to theories developed by Jacques Derrida and Judith Butler. I have already mentioned Kennedy's point that voice is like a river that collects affluents. This vision has suggested a Derridean approach to narrative as an act of citation. This approach allowed me to conceive subjectivity as unstable and amenable to change through reiteration, and to think of subjects as always incomplete; there would always exist a supplement that hinders claims of subjects' immutable identity, while at the same time preconditioning any possible identity.

Thinking of myth as a discourse of authority, I sought to establish possibilities of theorising myth that take into account the subject's alterity. I have found that Judith Butler's theories, which work with Derridean concepts, are crucial in developing such theorisation. From Butler's work, I retain as a cornerstone of my theoretical framework the concepts of repudiation and abjection. Legitimate subjects are constituted through casting away in domains of abjection that which is fantasised as illegitimate. The repetition of such constitutive acts that presuppose repudiation creates, in time, norms. I will argue that a myth is the expression of such norms at a given point in time. In turn, myths permeate discursive interaction, prescribing and scripting the ways in which subjects are constituted. It would not be feasible at this point to explain how the use of these two theorists have influenced the development of my methodology through reference to theories of narrative, discourse, materiality, social interaction, and psychoanalysis. These will be revealed at length in the first part of the book, which is heavily theoretical, while the second part focuses on close readings of texts. And, it is important to remember at the outset that what follows is not an attempt to fit the material analysed into pre-existing theoretical frameworks, but rather an attempt to find a critical angle that responds to the perspective developed in the texts on what literature does, or can do to readers and audiences as individuals or groups engaged in social interaction.

Another use of terminology must be clarified before we can proceed. I acknowledge that the texts studied can be approached from many angles. However, my focus will be on constructions of femininity in these texts, and on the ways in which they reflect processes of femininity construction. According to Doreen Massey, "deeply internalized dualisms ... structure personal identities" through "structuring the operation of social relations and social dynamics, and ... derive their masculine feminine coding from the deep socio-philosophical underpinnings of western society."[12] In my

---

[12] Doreen Massey, "Masculinity, Dualisms and High Technology", *Transactions of the Institute of British Geographers* 20 (1995): 487-99, 492.

analysis I will emphasise that masculine/feminine coding is derived from
narratives that are underpinned by socio-philosophical factors that
maintain dualist understandings of masculinity and femininity. Indeed, the
narrators analysed here cannot avoid engaging with these dualisms,
working as they are in the continuation of a masculine tradition whose
social myths legitimate these dualisms. However, when I use the term
"femininity" I do not have a static definition in mind, but rather a fluid
understanding of negotiable characteristics attributable to women at a
given point in time, and within a given tradition. I will often engage with
the dualisms that structure femininity/masculinity in Western society,
using "femininity" to refer to traditional Western understandings of it as
one of the binary terms of a duality. But I do not endorse that duality, even
though I acknowledge it as reference in relation to which one should
negotiate critically meanings of femininity.

PART I

THEORIES OF NARRATIVE, SOCIAL MYTH, AND THE BODY

INTRODUCTION TO PART I: CONTEXTS

In this chapter I will define my analysis framework in relation to wider theoretical contexts and trends. This will help me to clarify how the theoretical framework at first sketched in the following chapter, then developed at length in consequent chapters, is situated in critical traditions the goals and vision of which I share. I will first define my position in relation to a thread in Irish Studies that takes in the modernist writers. After that, I will define my position in relation to contemporary feminist work.

Perhaps a characteristic concern of modernist writers is their interest in the otherness which permeates our experience of the past through memory, our experience of socialisation through the conscious mind, and our experience of language as proof that we exist in the here and now. The analyses developed in this study focus on contemporary writers, but they answer in part concerns raised by modernist writers, or rather, they answer questions that contemporary writers have inherited from the tradition of modernist thought: does memory bind us to a constraining social world by reminding us the traditions of a "truer self"? Or does it free us by stealing into our experience clues that help us to discover a different, if "less human" in being an-other, identity? Is our conscious mind paralysed by social norms and conventions, or can it be awoken to reality through epiphanies that cast reality anew in the otherness of a lightening flash? Is the "I" in the language we use our own or does this "I" also belong to another? If the latter is true, is this other owned in the "I", even while it is estranged from the self proclaimed through the "I"?

As one may readily infer, my formulation of these questions has been inspired by texts of the Irish writers W. B. Yeats, James Joyce, and Samuel Beckett. These texts provide excellent examples of modernist engagement with the otherness which permeates our experience of memory, of social reality, and of language. Although these writers explore, to varying degrees and with different emphases, all three kinds of experiences, a highly provisional classification could ascribe the province of social reality to Joyce, that of language to Beckett, and that of memory to Yeats. It would be a task beyond the scope of a single book to show extensively how these writers' ideas and their rich literary expression affect the themes, narrative techniques, and preoccupations of contemporary writers concerned with the bearings of memory, language, and social identity in today's world. But, taking into account the main focus of this study, it is important to comment at least on an example of how one of these dimensions of experience has been treated by a major figure of the past and passing world of literary modernism. Yeats's exploration of the realm of memory is relevant for my analysis framework because it concerns the ways in which we deal with a past harboured in myth in order to define our social identity in the present. I am especially interested in Yeats's take on how the imagination stirs the realms of myth, and on how myth stirs the realm of memory, so that the social self is governed by the three powers of imagination, myth, and memory.

Yeats's infatuation with Celtic myths is well known, as is the fact that he joined the efforts of other Irish groups and individuals attempting to forge a Gaelic consciousness in which might abide a truly Irish social identity. We may use the two famous metaphors of "stone" and "living stream", through which Yeats explored the complexities of perceptions of embedded fixity and change ("How can we know the dancer from the dance?")[1], to comment on John Unterecker's assessment of the role of the mythological figure of Cuchulain, a favourite of Yeats's, in the culture of the Irish Revival. Unterecker's assessment captures the dynamics of the social reality born at the confluence of myth, imagination, and memory:

> Yeats's audience saw in Cuchulain a figure half way between myth and allegory, an embodiment of dreams familiar to themselves as well as to Yeats. The more Yeats wrote, the more useful the figure became. Gradually, the wish-fulfilment projection took on new roles, sometimes a figure celebrated, sometimes satirized, finally humanized; for in the character's long career … Cuchulain had become as much a part of Yeats's world (and his audience's) as Maud Gonne or Lady Gregory.[2]

Unterecker's comments suggest that a figure drawn from myth may gain life not only metaphorically, in the texts that reiterate its being and its actions, but also quite literally, as it enters the fantasies of real individuals and from there governs the imagination through which social identities are fashioned. In my analyses, I will investigate to what extent elements of

---

[1] W. B. Yeats, "Among School Children", *The Collected Works of W. B. Yeats, Volume I: The Poems*, ed. Richard Finneran (New York: Simon & Schuster, 1997), 219-21, 221.

[2] John Unterecker, "Introduction", *Yeats: A Collection of Critical Essays*, ed. John Unterecker (Englewood Cliffs, NJ: Prentice Hall, 1963), 1-6, 2-3.

myths may shape the lives of real individuals in the social world. But acknowledging this shaping force of myth does not mean that we are merely prey to the myths and the narratives derived from them, imprisoned in the subject positions to which they may bind us. For, as Yeats advocated, we should remain mindful of the living stream of the imagination lest we should become enchanted to frozen, stone-like stances. In his poem "Easter, 1916" Yeats wrote

> Hearts with one purpose alone
> Through summer and winter seem
> Enchanted to a stone
> To trouble the living stream.[3]

Using the central metaphors of these lines, the main argument of my study can be phrased thus: social myths yield identities that can be compared to the identity of statues fashioned out of stone; but the living stream of the imagination is a powerful force that can reshape the statue-like identities we may acquire through inhabiting the subject positions derived from myths.

Yeats's metaphors of "stone" and "living stream" refer to interconnected states of stasis and change. Stasis ("the stone") binds the alterity of the living stream of change; the living stream of change shapes and polishes the contour of figures seemingly possessing the durability of engraved figures "writ in stone". Yeats's understanding of the social value of the reciprocal conditioning of stasis and change, "stone" and "living stream", is highlighted by Edna Longley thus:

> This is no simple antithesis between obsession and flux. The stone actively 'troubles' the stream in the sense of political turbulence and conceptual challenge. Years before reinventing Cathleen ni Houlihan as Medusa, Yeats had associated stone with opinion, abstraction and his own temptations thereto. ... In the context of Irish Nationalism Yeats came to identify himself, the natural world and poetry with the female principle, and Maud Gonne (Cathleen), mechanism and opinion with the male.[4]

In my analyses, myths will be regarded as being the effect of a certain kind of obsession, the kind that compels us to reiterate legitimate stories, and which troubles the flux of the imagination, "enchanting it to a stone". But this enchantment will also be seen as a conceptual challenge: the writers

---

[3] W. B. Yeats, "Easter, 1916", *Collected Works*, 182-3, 182.
[4] Edna Longley, "Introduction: Revising 'Irish Literature'", *The Living Stream*, 1-68, 63.

whose texts will be examined deal with this challenge and register the political and strategic value of the turbulence created by the myths turning reality into stone. This value is connected to the possibility of using stories to change opinion, and to breath new life into the identity constructs that, having been reiterated and consecrated as myths, become abstractions in the etymological sense of the word: identities that have been dragged away from the reality of experience with a certain kind of violence and which convict and imprison us, as if we were turned to stone by a witch's or wizard's magic wand.

I will also engage with the kind of identifications Longley discerns as Yeats's, even though my analyses will not be guided by Yeatsean paradigms except in a very broad sense. The texts I will examine do problematise identifications of the natural world with the feminine and cast a critical eye on the mechanisms of male-dominated social worlds. However, although such problematics did not escape Yeats's own thoughts, in this respect my analyses will be heavily indebted to contemporary feminist theorists.

Exploring the possibilities of feminist postmodernist criticism from political sciences perspectives in late 1980s, Jane Flax proposed that

> Feminist theorists are faced with a fourfold task. We need to (1) articulate feminist viewpoints of/within the social worlds in which we live; (2) think about how we are affected by these worlds; (3) consider the ways in which how we think about them may be implicated in existing power/knowledge relationships; and (4) imagine ways in which these worlds ought to and can be transformed.[5]

The formulation of goals of feminist criticism as requiring an assessment of the reciprocal influence of social and personal realities, which emphasises that social and individual worlds are thoroughly imbricated, is representative of the priorities that informed the work of feminist critics across disciplines, not only in the seventies and the eighties, but also in the decades leading up to the present. Examples abound. From work in the history of science by Donna Haraway, Evelyn Fox Keller, or Katherine Hayles to research in queer theory by Judith Butler, or in film studies by Barbara Creed, feminist theorists have examined how the social worlds in which we live affect our identities, how current power/knowledge

---

[5] Jane Flax, "Postmodernism and Gender Relations in Feminist Theory", *Feminism/Postmodernism*, ed. Linda Nicholson (New York: Routledge, 1990), 39-62, 55.

relationships that shape identities are engendered in these worlds, and possibilities of transforming these worlds.[6]

The critical assessment of the dynamic interaction between social worlds, narrative, and constructions of identities has not been the exclusive preserve of critics and theorists. Along with, and inspiring, feminist analyses of naturalised cultural identities, many women writers and artists have used various mediums of fiction to explore critically the ways in which male-generated texts shape feminine and masculine identities, as well as the ways in which constraining identities can be subverted. Texts of fiction reconsidering the social value of identities hitherto perceived as legitimate are of many kinds: films, theatre productions, literary texts, art installations etc.

As regards literary texts, an excellent example is Angela Carter's work. One of the most widely studied authors, Carter has perhaps been canonised, to use Lorna Sage's words, as "a figure identified with 'fantasy', Gothic, otherness". However, Sage notes, Carter "had always taken the line that fantasy was not the shadow-side of a binary opposition, but had a real life history. Being was marinated in magic, and (conversely), imaginary monsters had no separate sphere."[7] This perception of an interpenetration of realms of fantasy and "real life history" informs the writer's interest in how mythologies affect identities and social roles. Carter's literary work revises a wide-ranging stock of established cultural constructs, transmitted in narratives of various genres from fairy tales to romance and Gothic. This revisionist work is underlain by a recurrent critical take on the mythologizing effects of narratives.

Carter's interest in revisiting and reconstructing established and normative male-generated traditions is echoed in Flax's recommendation that "we need to recover and write the histories of women and our activities into the accounts and stories that cultures tell about themselves."[8]

---

[6] See for instance Donna Haraway, *Simians, Cyborgs and Women: The Reinvention of Nature* (London: Free Association, 1991); Evelyn Fox Keller, *Reflections on Gender and Science* (New Haven, CT: Yale University Press, 1985); Katherine Hayles, *How We Became Posthuman: Virtual Bodies in Cybernetics, Literature, and Informatics* (Chicago: University of Chicago Press, 1999); Judith Butler, *Gender Trouble: Feminism and the Subversion of Identity* (New York: Routledge, 1990);   Judith Butler, *Bodies That Matter: On the Discursive Limits of "Sex"* (New York: Routledge, 1993). Barbara Creed, *The Monstrous Feminine: Film, Feminism, Psychoanalysis* (London: Routledge, 1993).
[7] Lorna Sage, "Introduction", *Flesh and the Mirror: Essays on the Art of Angela Carter*, ed. Lorna Sage (London: Virago, 1994), 1-23, 1.
[8] Flax, 55.

Carter's concern with how male-dominated traditions generate disempowering women's identities and social roles can be compared with Flax's assertion that "we need to recover and explore the aspects of social relations that have been suppressed, unarticulated, or denied within dominant (male) viewpoints."[9] That Carter and Flax share a similar vision is not due to a direct relation between them. Instead, it can be seen as signalling a general need among feminists (but not only) for reconsiderations of naturalised perspectives, attitudes, and social rituals that, in their unchallenged reiteration of what counts as legitimate identities, consecrate myths whose power extends not only over realms of fantasies, but also over social realms in which we enact those fantasies.

Jack Zipes offers an extensive list of rewritings of fairy tales by feminist authors, of which perhaps the most suggestive title is *Kissing the Witch: Old Tales in New Skins*, by Emma Donoghue.[10] Referring to these texts, Zipes underlines that

> Almost all the rewritings of traditional fairy tales have a greater awareness of the complexities of sexuality and gender roles and have sought to explore traditional fairy tales with a social consciousness and awareness in keeping with our changing times.[11]

Zipes' comments again highlight the social value of these rewritings. It is with a view to the interactive dimension of such rewritings that I approach the texts analysed in this book: how do presentations of ourselves and of others fare in the social worlds in which we live? To echo Flax, how do these stories help us to imagine ways in which these social worlds can be transformed by transforming the ossified identities traditionally regarded as legitimate? In order to examine such possibilities of transformation I will develop the concept of fantasy and fantasising as means to create one's identity. In order to connect this process of identity construction with narrative, I will focus on the extent to which these fantasies are narratable. The concept of narratable fantasies will help us to examine the processes whereby identities are constituted through stories that circulate in social spaces.

Perhaps most commonly circulated are stories derived from or exploiting the traditional fairy-tale ethos. However, my interests are not

---

[9] Ibid.

[10] Jack Zipes, *Why Fairy Tales Stick: The Evolution and Relevance of a Genre* (New York: Routledge, 2006), 103-4. Emma Donoghue, *Kissing the Witch: Old Tales in New Skins* (New York: Harper, 1997).

[11] Zipes, *Why Fairy Tales Stick*, 103.

limited to rewritings of fairy tales. Indeed, the re-evaluations of traditionally legitimate identities in literary fiction do not work only with stories from the fairy-tale stock, but have also tackled motifs and themes from ancient and contemporary myths. Jay Clayton, for instance, notes that

> [Alice] Walker dedicates a novel to the Spirit (*The Color Purple* [1982]); [Toni] Morrison opens several texts with an allusion to ritual (*Sula* [1974] and *Song of Solomon* [1977]); other writers make healers, voodoo figures, or conjure women the presiding spirits of their novels (Bambara's *Salt Eater*, Ntozake Shange's *Sassafrass, Cypress and Indigo* [1982], Paule Marshall's *Praisesong for the Widow* [1983], and Gloria Naylor's *Mama Day* [1988]).[12]

Another example is Christine Crow's *Miss X or the Wolf Woman*, which Susan Sellers regards as a text that

> encompasses many of the classical, biblical, literary and even psychoanalytic myths that have constituted Western culture, unravelling and representing these to demonstrate the ways they obliterate or falsely distort women's experiences.[13]

The texts I will discuss always offer opportunities for tackling a network of myths, rather than a single theme, tale, or motif derived from myths. In analysing how these networks of myths construct identities through distorting representations of women's experiences we will come across different kinds of texts, the roots of which are entangled with myths in ways that resist easy categorisation or systematisation. Classical myths such as that of Persephone have been transmitted through different channels and may be detected in different layers of cultural memory than myths constituted in more recent times, for instance the Dracula myth. A flexible concept of "myth" is required if we are to define an interpretative framework that can accommodate a complex network of cultural themes. That is why I will be working with a wider concept of myth which allows us to conceive that any narrative can be elevated to the status of myth at any given point in time, under specific circumstances.

---

[12] Jay Clayton, "The Narrative Turn in Minority Fiction", *Narrative and Culture*, eds. Janice Carlisle and Daniel Schwarz (Athens: University of Georgia Press, 1994), 58-76, 66, first names in brackets added.
[13] Susan Sellers, *Myth and Fairy Tale in Contemporary Women's Fiction* (Houndmills: Palgrave, 2001), 52; Christine Crow, *Miss X or the Wolf Woman* (London: Women's Press, 1990).

In widening the concept of myth, the question arises of how is myth different from ideology and why should we speak of myth and not of ideologies or ideological functions of myth. I have found that the concept of "ideology" can be too rigid to cope with the diversity presented by the socio-cultural networks in which our identities are constituted. "Ideology" seems less fruitful a concept for dealing with the ground zero whence myths take off. I have therefore defined a distinction between ideology and myth by examining the roots of stories that may become myths. Stories may become myths through challenging other myths in the social circles where stories are at first used to think about existing power/knowledge relationships. The already existing power/knowledge relationships are legitimated through other stories that have come to script social identities and roles. A story used to think about one's place in the social world by devising alternative stories of legitimate social worlds may itself come to convey myths, through its reiteration in a monoglossic discursive regime that may dominate a social space. These myths born out of social interaction may be called social myths to emphasise the social value of their centralising tendency and their heteroglossia.

Having sketched my goals and interests in reference to existing critical contexts, I will now define my theoretical framework in more detail. This will form the first part of this study. The second part will offer textual analyses within the outlined theoretical framework as well as explanations of how they helped me to define this framework.

CHAPTER ONE

FANTASY, NARRATIVE, AND SOCIAL WORLDS

I will begin with a sketch of a theoretical framework for defining the relationship between narratives and socialisation, postponing for now the analysis of their relationship to myth. My main argument at this stage is that our modes of socialisation are steered by fantasies derived from narratives. Thus, I will first clarify my use of the concepts of fantasy and fantasising. I will then explain how fantasies help construct subjectivity. I will mainly use theories developed by Judith Butler and Jacques Derrida, whose work is of central importance in my arguments. The theoretical analysis of fantasy and fantasising will be exemplified with close readings in the chapter examining Kennedy's novel *Everything You Need* and her novella "Original Bliss". Issues of subjectivity construction will be explored throughout the close readings of the second part of this study, with the Derridean perspective more emphatically used in the analysis of Bourke's and Ní Dhuibhne's writings.

Pierre Bourdieu comments that one's bodily feelings and experiences are created through repeatedly enacting complexes of words, bodily postures, and gestures:

> there is no better image of the logic of socialization, which treats the body as a 'memory-jogger', than those complexes of gestures, postures and words—simple interjections or favourite clichés—which only have to be slipped into, like a theatrical costume, to awaken, by the evocative power of bodily mimesis, a universe of ready-made feelings and experiences.[1]

In my textual analyses I will focus on the role of complexes of words which constitute narratives in determining bodily feelings and experiences, and on the role of fantasies in mediating translations of narrative "realities" into the reality of experience.

---

[1] Pierre Bourdieu, *Distinction: A Social Critique of the Judgement of Taste*, trans. Richard Nice (London: Routledge, 1984), 474.

My understanding of the concepts of "fantasy" and "fantasising" draws heavily on Judith Butler's argument in "Gender Trouble, Feminist Theory, and Psychoanalytic Discourse". Butler uses Roy Schaffer's argument that "when identifications [in a psychoanalytic sense] are understood as internalizations, they imply a trope of inner psychic space that is ontologically insupportable."[2] Butler notes Schaffer's suggestions that "internalization is understood better not as a process but as a fantasy" and challenges the psychoanalytic view of the self as an inner core or essence.[3] Rather than identifying oneself as an individual with certain attributes (such as gender), one fantasises that s/he is that individual: "fantasies constitutive of identifications are not part of the set of properties that a subject might be said to have, but they constitute the genealogy of that embodied/psychic identity, the mechanism of its construction. ... [T]hese fantasies are themselves disciplinary productions of grounding cultural sanctions and taboos ... ."[4] The difference between identifications and fantasising is important, because in the latter case it is conceivable that one's identity changes according to one's imagination of what is desirable for him/her to be, whereas in the former case, one cannot be but a certain individual with certain attributes; if s/he does not become that individual, s/he is branded psychotic. Butler's argument can be used to explain how the configuration of the self may be changed with the changes in one's fantasies that challenge cultural sanctions and taboos.

Jean Laplanche and J. B. Pontalis argue that fantasy is not "the object of desire, but its setting. In fantasy the subject does not pursue the object or its sign: he appears caught up himself in the sequence of images."[5] As in Butler's argument, in Laplanche and Pontalis' view the self is imagined as an inner site in which one sees oneself with a certain identity. Both arguments show that the fantasy of the self is constitutive of the subject, expressing the self's identity in sequences of images. Elizabeth Cowie extends the applicability of Laplanche and Pontalis' argument from individual private fantasising to fantasising based on texts.[6] Thus, the

---

[2] Judith Butler, "Gender Trouble, Feminist Theory, and Psychoanalytic Discourse", *Feminism/Postmodernism*, ed. Linda J. Nicholson (New York: Routledge, 1990), 324-40, 333, brackets mine. See also Roy Schaffer, *A New Language for Psychoanalysis* (New Haven, CT: Yale University Press, 1976).

[3] Butler, "Gender Trouble", 333.

[4] Ibid., 334.

[5] Jean Laplanche and Jean-Bertrand Pontalis, "Fantasy and the Origins of Sexuality", *Formations of Fantasy*, ed. Victor Burgin et al (London and New York: Routledge, 1986), 5-34, 26.

[6] Elizabeth Cowie, "Fantasia", *m/f* 9 (1984): 70-105.

sequences of images which constitute the self can be regarded as narrative sequences, not just as events of the imagination. Using narratological terminology, it can be said that for Laplanche and Pontalis fantasies are like fabulas (series of events), whereas for Cowie they are like stories (fantasies are narratable). Thus, one may suspect two-way traffic between fantasies and narratives: if "internal" fantasies are narratable, then "external" narratives can influence one's fantasising.

Laplanche and Pontalis argue that "the subject, although always present in the fantasy, may be so in a desubjectivized form, that is to say, in the very syntax of the sequence in question."[7] In this perspective, it is difficult to distinguish between one's image of one's self as a character (or subject) and the realm one figures as an eventful space that his/her self inhabits (the scenario one fantasises for the subject through which s/he consents to be signified). These fantasies are rather like texts signed (in the Derridean sense) with the indelible mark of the self. According to Derrida,

> In the form of the whole name, the inscription of the signature plays strangely with the frame, with the border of the text, sometimes inside, sometimes outside, sometimes included, sometimes overthrown. But it is still included when thrown overboard and always eminent when drunk in by the surface of the text.[8]

The inscription of the self as a subject in a fantasy "plays strangely" with the frame and border of its domain. The self is drunk in by the texture of fantasies. Even when thrown overboard, it can still be summoned and made amenable to rules governing its medium of expression; thus being amenable to cultural sanctions and taboos, to subjection. If, through using narratives, one's fantasising of a given scenario and subjective constitution is repeated, then, in time, one's body learns to be awakened to ways of feeling and experiencing that these narratives make available. One will then enact complexes of gestures, bodily postures, and words that one has grown accustomed to fantasising as one's own.

One always participates in discourse in one way or another in social interaction. Thus, one's identity is always derived to an extent from a narrative whose subject is fantasised as being of one's self. One lives socially through fantasising in this sense. However, the performance of these fantasies, that is, the production of a social persona one sets out and steers in the social world, is not simply an enactment of ready-made

---

[7] Laplanche and Pontalis, 26.
[8] Jacques Derrida, *Signéponge/Signsponge*, trans. Richard Rand (New York: Columbia University Press, 1984), 120.

narrative constructs. This performance depends not only on an individual's subjection to a pre-existing text in his/her discursive presentation of him/herself to the world; but also on his/her interaction with other individuals whose discourses affect one's fantasy script through heteroglossic interference.[9] In order to examine how discursive interaction alters the participants' fantasy scripts, it is necessary to examine the conditions in which such a script may remain stable or may be destabilised. This examination can be undertaken using Derrida's and Butler's theories, which demonstrate that narrative iterations provide opportunities for re-creating subject positions in new configurations.[10]

Let us postpone this examination for a short while in order to sum up the main argument so far: the events of the imagination in which we figure our selves can be said to be derived, to an extent, from stories. At the same time, our fantasies are narratable. The self is constituted at the intersection between fantasies and stories as an "I". On the one hand, this "I" is amenable to cultural sanctions and taboos that govern its narrative expression, and guide its presentation as social persona. On the other, this "I" is always amenable to change because, as is argued in deconstruction theory, the "I" of narration and of social scenarios is not unitary and stable.

In order to explore the instability and incompleteness of the narrative "I" I will focus on Derrida's essay "Signature Event Context", in which he challenges the premises of J. L. Austin's theory of performatives.[11] Derrida focuses on Austin's qualification of performative utterances said by actors on stage, introduced in a poem or spoken in soliloquy as parasitical, non-serious, and non-ordinary. Derrida regards this qualification as an exclusion of acts of citation that helps Austin to "pass off as ordinary

---

[9] By "fantasy script" I understand a scenario of social interaction that one fantasises as suitable for oneself based on scripts derived from narrative "acquaintance" with the world, i.e. based on the schemata of social interaction offered in narratives that make sense of (signify) the world.

[10] The concept of "iterability" is used by Derrida throughout his work but see for instance Jacques Derrida, "'This strange institution called literature': An Interview with Jacques Derrida", *Jacques Derrida: Acts of Literature*, trans. Nicholas Royle, ed. Derek Attridge (London: Routledge, 1992), 33-75, 62; and Jacques Derrida, *Limited Inc*, ed. Gerald Graff (Evanston, IL: Northwestern University Press, 1988). Judith Butler's understanding of iterability and reiteration is developed in the context of her theory of performativity in Butler, *Gender Trouble*, esp. 140, 145, 226; and Butler, *Bodies That Matter*, esp. 1-29, 124-40, and 187-9.

[11] Jacques Derrida, "Signature Event Context", *Limited Inc*, 1-21. See also John Langshaw Austin, *How to Do Things with Words*, eds. James Urmson and Marina Sbisà (Cambridge: Harvard University Press, 1975).

an ethical and teleological determination of the utterance."[12] The subject expressed through Austin's ordinary utterances remains "'at home,' by and in itself, in the shelter of its essence or *telos*".[13] Derrida insists that the parasitism which Austin repudiates in order to purify speech is rather "its internal and positive condition of possibility".[14] By demonstrating that every utterance is impure, because it is to an extent a citation or iteration, Derrida shows that every narrative is "parasitical", and therefore the subject is not ordinarily unitary and stable, but its configuration is constantly renegotiated through (con)textual (re)positioning. Therefore, the configuration of the subject through which we express our identity in social interaction is never fully complete; this configuration is endlessly worked out in discursive interaction. A unitary subject can only exist through the exclusion of its alterity.[15]

Judith Butler argues that constructions of the subject operate "through *exclusionary* means, such that the human is not only produced over and against the inhuman, but through a set of foreclosures, radical erasures, that are, strictly speaking, refused the possibility of cultural articulation."[16] However, as Butler argues, fantasies of legitimate subjectivities may be subverted through the rearticulation of what has been hitherto repudiated as abject. Butler's argument applies not only to gender, but to all kinds of normative constructions of identity. Thus, subjective identity is shaped through a continuous process in which one fantasises his/her identities, rather than being formed through a pre-determined cast one must become, or else one is seen as psychotic or abject.

Constructions of the subject affect one's personal, physiological, and social space. They can be regarded as products of "semiotic technologies", to use Donna Haraway's words. Semiotic technologies cannot be divorced from material and social technologies. It is always through a collaboration of the three that "what will count as nature and as matters of fact get constituted."[17] Thus, I regard narratives also as tools for crafting minds and bodies.

The argument of this chapter can be summarised thus: fantasies are narratable and inform subjectivity constructions. But every subject is constituted through citing legitimate subjects in narrative presentations of

[12] Derrida, "Signature Event Context", 17.
[13] Ibid.
[14] Ibid.
[15] Ibid., 9, 18.
[16] Butler, *Bodies That Matter*, 8, original italics.
[17] Donna Haraway, *Modest_Witness@Second_Millenium: FemaleMan©_Meets_OncoMouse™* (London: Routledge, 1997), 50.

the self. Through this citation, fantasies of the self's identity can be governed. This process of government engenders the exclusion of those fantasies that threaten its prescribed stability. Once excluded, such fantasies become illegitimate. Their alterity is ungovernable. However, such ungovernable fantasies can be readmitted in discourse, permitting reconstructions of the subject. This dialectic relationship between fantasy and subjectivity informs narrative presentations of one's self in social interaction and thus affects the configuration of one's personal, physiological, and social space, i.e. one's bodily identity and social persona which together form what one refers to as one's "I".

These theorisations of narrative and of its functioning suggest that texts can be regarded as platforms for developing relationships between writing, subjectivity, and socialisation, enticing us to explore writing as a process through which it is possible to engage social myths. As I will argue, social myths are the manifestation in narratives of certain worldviews that guide and constrain the shaping of fabulas into stories. Because these stories play an important role in scripting individuals' identities, it is important to examine whether the visions derived from social myths that guide the narrative presentation of ourselves to ourselves and others, and our fantasising our identities, are constraining or empowering, that is, to what extent they distort and/or falsify our experiences of self and other.

In the following I will define my methodological perspective in three chapters. The first explains the relationships between narrative, subjectivity, and fantasy; the second deals primarily with the relationships between ideology, social myth, and social reality; and the third focuses on the relationships between narrative, materiality, and constructions of bodies.

CHAPTER TWO

NARRATIVE REPRESENTATION

Narrative and Subjectivity

In the first section of this chapter I will focus on relations of reciprocal determination and conditioning between narratives and subjectivity. While acknowledging that narratives place constraints on subjects' agency, I will argue that subjects may recover agency to an extent by exploiting a texts' heteroglossic dimension. I understand subjectivity as the expression of an individual's identity in three overlapping worlds of narrative, through which an individual places him/herself in various locales (i.e. bodies and social spaces) and thus makes sense of objects and environments of the material reality. The three worlds of narrative are: the fictional world of texts, the fantasy world of the self, and the social world of discourse. This analysis will be used in all the close readings of the second part of this study, but it informs especially the interpretations of Carr's plays.

As Steven Cohan and Linda Shires point out, a reader enters the fictional world of a text by identifying textual inscriptions which provide him/her with "a position towards the story that is not value-free but, on the contrary, is bound by a particular set of values."[1] To borrow from Cohan and Shires' analysis, the reader who recognises him/herself in the subject of narration, and adopts the position of subject offered by a text, "gains the pleasure of being signified as a coherent subject, but loses … autonomy from the discourse" in which the reader's identity is signified as subject.[2] In other words, texts offer the means to fantasise oneself as the actor of a

---

[1] Steven Cohan and Linda Shires, *Telling Stories: A Theoretical Analysis of Narrative Fiction* (London: Routledge, 1988), 97. Smyth argues that "every example of human discourse" "has an addressee of some sort encoded into its discourse, an ideal reading subject whom the text, as it were, brings into being. When we read novels, therefore, we are also being read by them in terms of their authorial intentions and expectations." Smyth, *The Novel and the Nation*, 44.

[2] Cohan and Shires, 153. See also Italo Calvino, *If on a winter's night a traveller*, trans. William Weaver (Orlando, Florida: Harcourt, 1981).

narrative scenario; but through this fantasising, the reader adopts a particular set of values that undercuts the range of choices s/he may use to construct his/her identity. Subjectivity is gained at the expense of agency. But having said that, I must emphasise that neither does there exist a "pure" subject, obtained through the sublimation of an individual in text, nor shall we ever meet an individual who is not, to some extent, bound by identities established in relation to texts.[3]

Thus, the reader is not refined out of existence by being signified as subject; in fact, I would argue, the reader is endowed with a certain kind of agency. This agency is gained through what Gérard Genette identifies as the relationship between "discourse and the act that produces it, actually … or fictively."[4] Genette discusses here, as he puts it, narrative in its oldest meaning, as that which refers "to an event: not, however, the event that is recounted, but the event that consists of someone recounting something: the act of narrating taken in itself."[5] In this perspective, Genette understands narrating or recitation as "the producing narrative action and, by extension, the whole of the real or fictional situation in which that action takes place."[6] Genette's position suggests that, although we may claim that an individual's identity is acquired by exchanging autonomy for a subject position, this exchange is ultimately a matter of consent to participating in producing and generating subjectivity.[7] Agency is wielded when we present ourselves to ourselves and to others using discourse; not only are we interpellated or hailed by others, but we in turn interpellate and hail those around us, seeking to enrol their consent to one

---

[3] This view is expressed suggestively by Paul de Man when he remarks that while no one in his right mind would try to grow grapes by the light of the word "day", it would be very difficult "not to conceive the pattern of one's past and future existence as in accordance with temporal and spatial schemes that belong to fictional narratives and not to the world." Paul de Man, *The Resistance to Theory* (Minneapolis: University of Minnesota Press, 1986), 11.

[4] Gérard Genette, *Narrative Discourse: An Essay in Method*, trans. Jane Lewin (Ithaca: Cornell University Press, 1980), 27.

[5] Ibid., 26.

[6] Ibid., 27.

[7] According to Butler, "the reconceptualization of identity as an *effect*, that is, as *produced* or *generated*, opens up possibilities of 'agency' that are insidiously foreclosed by positions that take identity categories as foundational and fixed." Butler, *Gender Trouble*, 147, original italics.

or another version of ourselves and them, or rather, of ourselves with them as a social group with a legitimate identity.[8]

Questions related to the manifestation of agency in discourse are also raised in Emile Benveniste's research. Emphasising the importance of deixis, Benveniste defines discourse as "utterance assuming a speaker and a hearer, and in the speaker, the intention of influencing the other in some way."[9] Occupying in turn the position of the teller, the participants in discourse acquire subjectivity and negotiate in dialogue their place in a world which is, through this negotiation, constituted around an "I" amongst others.[10]

Benveniste's position suggests that the agency of the speaker, derived from occupying a text's positions of narrating agency, is wielded through the discourse's deictic force. The linguists Juergen Weissenborn and Wolfgang Klein argue that "deixis is the domain par excellence where language and reality meet."[11] Paraphrasing, we may argue that narrative fiction and reality meet through the translation of the deictic force of narrative in a speech event or performance event in social interaction.

The deictic force of discourse also permits renegotiations of subjectivity, because deixis involves contextual reference. Stephen Levinson defines deixis as concerning "the ways in which languages encode or grammaticalize

---

[8] Louis Althusser, "Ideology and Ideological State Apparatuses (Notes towards an Investigation)", *Lenin and Philosophy and Other Essays*, trans. Ben Brewster (New York: Monthly Review Press, 1978), 127-87, 172-5.

[9] Emile Benveniste, *Problems in General Linguistics*, trans. Mary Meek (Coral Gables: University of Miami Press, 1971), 209.

[10] According to Benveniste, "*I* can only be identified by the instance of discourse that contains it and by that alone. It has no value except in the instance in which it is produced. But in the same way it is also as an instance of form that *I* must be taken; the form of *I* has no linguistic existence except in the act of speaking in which it is uttered." However, as Derrida's powerful argument restated in *Limited Inc* demonstrates, it can be agued that this *I* does have a linguistic existence beyond the act of speaking. This existence is implied by the iterability of narrative. Benveniste asserts that "in saying 'I,' I cannot *not* be speaking of myself." However, I acknowledge in line with Derrida's argument, that it is possible that in saying "I", I may be citing an "I" that is not necessarily myself, but it overtakes myself within its forcing coherence. I will discuss problematics associated with the issue of agency in relation to a subject that is regarded as constituted through citation in my analysis of Carr's play *By the Bog of Cats...*. Benveniste, 218, 197; Marina Carr, *By the Bog of Cats...*, *Plays One* (London: Faber, 1999), 256-341.

[11] Juergen Weissenborn and Wolfgang Klein, "Introduction", *Here and There: Cross-linguistic Studies on Deixis and Demonstration (Pragmatics& Beyond III: 2-3)*, eds. Juergen Weissenborn and Wolfgang Klein (Amsterdam: John Benjamins, 1982), 3.

features of the context of utterance or speech event and thus also concerns ways in which the interpretation of utterances depends on the analysis of that context of utterance."[12] The reference to context may involve reference to collocutors but also to other discourses to which a narrative refers intertextually. Deixis thus opens up a text to heteroglossia.

At the same time, I acknowledge that the deictic force of discourse draws its strength from a citational chain. I subscribe to Derrida's view that the formulation of an utterance in speech/discourse repeats a "'coded' or iterable utterance" and it is thus "identifiable as *conforming* with an iterable model", "identifiable in some way as a 'citation'."[13] In this view, a citation's deixis points to an iterable model, to an anterior version of the present narration (that cites that version). Thus, the manifestation of deixis as citational force of discourse tends to foreclose alterity by centring discourse on the repetition of the same, and can be compared to a centripetal force. But deixis also works towards re-creating a story in new and surprising configurations, by allowing a collocutor to vary the tendency of the citational chain to stabilise a text as monoglossic; this manifestation of deictic force can be compared to a centrifugal force.[14]

We may summarise the main points of the discussion offered in this section thus: readers and audiences consent to being signified as subjects in the narratives they use to present themselves to themselves and to others. This "surrendering" to narrative can be seen as a means of exercising agency, because it offers readers and audiences the opportunity to manipulate the deictic force of discourses. The deictic force of discourses is amplified by the citational chain that centres discourses on the repetition of the same; pointing to an iterable model, a discourse's deixis can be normative and constraining. However, a discourse's deixis can be manipulated to open up a text to heteroglossia. This is achieved by resituating a text in relation to contexts, and by exploring how a text sits in different ways in the voices of different speakers. The opening of narrative to heteroglossia allows us to explore these differences. This exploration may reveal new possibilities of interpreting bodies and material environments, by inviting subjects to renegotiate their social persona, which in turn implies a re-evaluation of the significance of one's bodily presence and of the body's relation to material environments.

---

[12] Stephen Levinson, *Pragmatics* (Cambridge: Cambridge University Press, 1983), 54.

[13] Derrida, "Signature Event Context", 18, original italics.

[14] In fact, as Butler insists, "reiterations are never simply replicas of the same." Butler, *Bodies That Matter*, 226.

Narrative and Normative Constructions of Subjects

In this section I will focus on the fantasy world of the self, adopting the view that it is to an important extent affected by narrative, so that one may speak of a narrative world of the self which coexists with the fantasy world of the self. I also take the view that the narrative world of the self is not, as in Lacanian psychoanalysis, an inescapable domain of phallic authority.[15] Instead, I regard it as a socially constructed world that can be dissolved and remade, as for instance Judith Butler argues.

In her work on the categories of gender, Butler argues that the "reiterative power of discourse" produces "the phenomena that it regulates and constrains."[16] Discursive reiteration naturalises forms of self-presentation. These naturalised forms of self-presentation become prescriptive as regards the fantasy in which an individual manifests subjective identity. Thus, identity is knowledge that, in being reiterated over and over again, becomes "natural" and normative. Yet with each reiteration the naturalised norms of knowledge instantiated in a text can be jostled against the norms of another text (a con-text) reiterating similar or competing norms. This jostling is the occasion of settling, resettling or unsettling norms of knowledge and therefore also the legitimacy of the identities the norms configure. According to Butler, echoing Derrida, "the analysis of subjection is always double, tracing the conditions of subject formation and tracing the turn against those conditions, for the subject, 'to emerge'".[17] By making visible competing forms of subjective experience, which have been repudiated in the dominant narratives constructing the legitimate subject, the constraining force of citational chains is challenged. I will explore how this challenge is brought in all my textual analyses, but especially in my readings of Lochhead's revision of Dracula's story and of traditional fairy tales and of Ní Dhuibhne's revision of tales from Irish folklore. The process of making competing forms of subjective experience visible involves citing norms but altering the deictic vectors of the discourse whence the norms derive. All the texts which I will analyse can be seen as citing normative discourses that prescribe women's identities and social roles, in order to re-create these identities in new configurations.

---

[15] See for instance Jacques Lacan, "The Function and Field of Speech and Language in Psychoanalysis", *Écrits: A Selection*, trans. Bruce Fink et al. (New York: Norton, 2004), 31-106, 65-7.

[16] Butler, *Bodies That Matter*, 2.

[17] Judith Butler, *The Psychic Life of Power* (Stanford, CA: Stanford University Press, 1997), 21.

The recontextualisation of a citation by uprooting it from a legitimating context at once transforms the scene of (narrative) presentation into a carnival scene; not in a pejorative sense, but in the sense of carnivalesque as productive of new identities through heteroglossia.[18] This may initiate a "chain reaction" in the expression of one's fantasy in social interaction that subverts the forms of expression naturalised through a citational chain, and steers others (collocutors or individuals engaged in embodied communication) toward "alternative domains of cultural ... possibilities".[19]

The search for alternative domains of cultural possibilities is a characteristic of the texts analysed in this book. Often, these alternative domains lie in the margin of the realm of signification perceived as a realm of masculine authority. Psychoanalytic theory, especially that developed by Lacan, has been par excellence concerned with the realm of signification as a realm of masculine authority. Applied in, and popularised through, practice psychoanalysis has influenced greatly how one conceives one's social identity as legitimate. In Lacanian theory the Law of the Father allows an individual to express his individuality by acknowledging the break with the Real, understood as a realm of the mother's body. An individual thus internalises the gap between signifier and signified, and enters the realm of the Symbolic. The signifier carries the power of the Law of the Father, through which is constructed one's social self and social imaginary. The signified belongs to the Real in which one longs to find himself, but should never succeed since merging with the Real would threaten the "emerged" subject with psychotic dissolution. One would no longer be able to inhabit the realm of intelligibility, of signification, since the gap, guarded by the Father, that makes possible the tension between signifier and signified in which self-expression is born, would no longer exist. For Lacan, one's ties with the Real should remain foreclosed, cast away.[20]

In "Gender Trouble", Butler's analysis of the normative character of heterosexuality develops a critique of the psychoanalytic interpretations of sociality to point out that their models of socialisation through

---

[18] As Mikhail Bakhtin puts it, "People who in life are separated by impenetrable hierarchical barriers enter into free familiar contact on the carnival square. ... Carnival is the place for working out ... a *new mode of interrelationship between individuals* ... ." Mikhail Bakhtin, *Problems of Dostoevsky's Poetics*, ed. Caryl Emerson (Minneapolis: University of Minnesota Press, 1984), 123, original italics.

[19] Butler, *Gender Trouble*, 145.

[20] See Jacques Lacan, *The Seminar of Jacques Lacan, Book III: The Psychoses 1955-1956*, ed. Jacques-Allain Miller, trans. Russell Grigg (New York: Norton, 1993), esp. 161-230.

identifications manifested discursively can be seen as themselves tributary to discursive constructions. Intelligible discourse does not exist at the expense of the Real; rather, the Real is itself an effect of discourse. In Butler's terms, the Law of the Father is not a precondition of discourse, but merely a discursive construction among others. Butler argues that

> if [the reality of the gendered body] is fabricated as an interior essence, that very interiority is a function of a decidedly public and social discourse, the public regulation of fantasy through the surface politics of the body. In other words, acts and gestures articulate and enacted desires create the illusion of an interior and organizing gender core, an illusion discursively maintained ... .[21]

In Butler's terms, Lacanian psychoanalysis can be seen as conceiving the outside of the Symbolic order "as the locus of subversion", but this outside is in fact "a construction within the terms of that constitutive discourse".[22] "The 'unthinkable' is thus fully within culture but excluded from *dominant* culture" through abjection.[23] The abject is not beyond signification, but it is rather a realm of the imagination from which one is steered away through narrations that constitute one's subjectivity. The jerking away of the subject from zones of uninhabitability ensures the possibility of masculine authority that prescribes what fantasies are legitimate. The narrations derived from, and prescribing such fantasies reiterate scripts that constrain the performance of social personae. Rather than understanding subjectivity and social reality in psychoanalytic terms, I am compelled to seek to understand them in relation to language as social phenomena.

Narrative and Social Reality

In the following I will explore how narratives shape social reality by helping to construct social identity; at the same time, I will argue, narratives are being shaped by pre-existing social identities, and by elements of social reality, in reciprocal inter-conditioning. This theoretical analysis will be used throughout my close readings of texts, but especially in my readings of Bourke's study of Bridget Cleary's murder and of Ní Dhuibhne's stories that explore the relationship between narrative and the configuration of the body-social.

---

[21] Butler, "Gender Trouble", 336-7.

[22] Butler, *Gender Trouble*, 77.

[23] Ibid., original italics.

The circulation of narrative constructions of identity between discourse participants has been theorised convincingly as an event in which sociality is born(e). According to sociologists Nelson Phillips and Cynthia Hardy:

> The things that make up the social world—including our very identities—appear out of discourse. To put it another way, our talk, and what we are, are one and the same. ... Without discourse, there is no social reality, and without understanding discourse, we cannot understand our reality, our experiences, or ourselves.[24]

Another sociologist, Gunther Kress, emphasises that "texts are the sites of the emergence of complexes of social meanings" that record "in partial ways" the power relations between discourse participants, language, social system, and social institutions, thus offering "a partial history of the language and the social system".[25] Referring in particular to gender, geographer Linda McDowell points out that social practices and "ways of thinking about and representing place/gender are interconnected and mutually constituted"; our acts in social reality are guided by "our intentions and beliefs, which are always culturally shaped and historically and spatially positioned."[26] Thus, narratives are always embedded within, and themselves embed, forms of socialisation. In this framework, an analysis emphasising the elements that ground narratives in the reality of social experience has the advantage of pointing out, as Susan Sellers reminds us, "the role of narrative in enabling us to undergo, shape and survive those experiences." According to Sellers

> stories play a formative part in creating who we are since they present a medium through which we can organise, communicate and remember our experiences, proffering ready-made schemata that equip us to understand and evaluate our lives by connecting what happens to us to a wider community and other points of view.[27]

Stories always offer ways of showing ourselves to ourselves in the fantasies they inspire. Through stories, we make sense of ourselves as part

---

[24] Nelson Phillips and Cynthia Hardy, *Discourse Analysis: Investigating Processes of Social Construction* (Thousands Oaks: Sage, 2002), 2.

[25] Gunther Kress, "The Social Production of Language: History and Structures of Domination", *Discourse in Society: Systemic Functional Perspectives*, eds. Peter Fries and Michael Gregory (Norwood, NJ: Ablex, 1995), 115-40, 122.

[26] Linda McDowell, *Gender, Identity and Place: Understanding Feminist Geographies* (Cambridge: Polity, 2005), 7.

[27] Sellers, vii.

of a social circle and of the realms within and without it. We use stories to create our social personae in social worlds. These social personae and social worlds have a fictional dimension because they are fantasised. However, the act of fantasising has material effects because fantasies may be materialised in actual performances of individuals in the material world.

This materialisation can occur because texts make available a range of social personae and scenarios of social performance, and entice readers to fantasise their identities accordingly. But discursive reiterations of legitimate constructions of the social self and socialisation scenarios constrain these fantasies through the normative requirements the reiterations create. These norms define what counts as legitimate, what seems "real" because it has been naturalised as such. Because of that, the process of fantasising governed by norms lends realness to readers as subjects in discourse. This realness is transformed into reality when readers enact fantasised identities in the social world. To use Butler's words, "the matter of bodies" is "the effect of a dynamic of power" that indissolubly ties the matter of bodies with "the regulatory norms that govern their materialization and the signification of those material effects".[28] Thus, it will seem appropriate to speculate regarding what kind of materiality is woven for a subject adopting social personae/socialisation scenarios made available through texts.

The texts selected for analysis in this study focus especially on women's identities that are constructed and legitimated through narratives derived from myths. My analyses will show that in these texts women's narrated voices entice women readers, who narrate these voices in their reading, to imagine empowering socialisation scenarios. However, this confidently optimistic conclusion will have been drawn after much deliberation. In her analysis of the individual experience of one's relationship to norms, regarded as being established also through narrative reiterations, Butler shows that

> sometimes the very conditions for conforming to the norm are the same as the conditions for resisting it. When the norm appears at once to guarantee and threaten social survival (it is what you need to live; it is that which, if you live it, it will threaten to efface you), then conforming and resisting become a compounded and paradoxical relation to the norm, a form of suffering and a potential site for politicization. The question of how to

---

[28] Butler, *Bodies That Matter*, 2.

embody the norm is thus very often linked to the question of survival, of whether life itself will be possible.[29]

I interpret Butler's insight as offering two important cautionary notes to the analyst of the relationship between narrative constructions of women and social reality: one concerns the very analysis of the effects of narrative in social reality; the other concerns the feminist politics such an analysis might endorse. As regards the former, one is warned that the analyst's extrapolations of individual performances in social reality, seen as based on fantasies derived from narratives, will be entangled in the double dealing with the norms that Butler highlights. Adapting Butler's insight to my concern here, the analyst's efforts of clarifying what real individuals may achieve in their relationship with narrative will be resisted by the requirement that what can be said about those individuals remains, in the last instance, only true about an abstract individual whom the analyst imagines; yet another character after all.

As regards the feminist politics my analysis endorses, I hope to demonstrate that the narratives I will examine do offer opportunities for women's empowerment, but that this empowerment is also "a form of suffering".[30] Analyses of women's writing work through difficult and labyrinthine mazes of texts that sometimes idealise, at other times abject women; that highlight both the pleasure and security of conformism to norms, and the different kind of pleasure and confidence that comes from recognising difference by seeing it from afar, from the realms of abjection.

Stories create the illusion of a unified and coherent self endowed with the skill to re-establish itself in dialogue with an other. This citation of the legitimate self (to oneself and to others) in a social group forecloses "complexity and indeterminacy" and constitutes group identity "only through the exclusion of some part of the constituency that it simultaneously seeks to represent."[31] Thus, the subject offered in tales is never quite a match for the identity of individuals who partly recognise themselves through its imaginary identity; there is always a residue around which a different subject may coagulate, an other whose credibility must be constantly undermined, if the social norms that yield legitimate identities are to remain unchallenged. Or, if these norms should be challenged, this other must be summoned to the social stage and given due credit in terms of social legitimacy.

---

[29] Judith Butler, *Undoing Gender* (New York: Routledge, 2004), 217.

[30] Ibid.

[31] Butler, *Gender Trouble*, 14.

In order to see what forces the other comes up against in this process, I will now turn to analyses of how myth functions, arguing in favour of an understanding of myth as a corpus of normative stories, that have become normative through narrative reiterations of the same social identities and socialisation scenarios.

CHAPTER THREE

SOCIAL MYTH, IDEOLOGY,
AND SOCIAL REALITY

In the sections of this chapter I will focus on the manifestation of myth in narrative, and on the influence of myth on subjective identity. The concept of myth has often been tied up with a vision of the role of narrative. According to Jean-Pierre Vernant, for the ancient Greeks myth was defined "through the setting up of an opposition between *muthos* and *logos*, henceforth seen as separate and contrasting terms."[1] Exploring the earliest attestations of the meanings of *mythos* and *logos*, the myth theorist Bruce Lincoln argues that initially

> *logos* denoted not rational argumentation but rather shady speech acts: those of seduction, beguilement, and deception, through which structural inferiors outwitted those who held power over them. *Mythos*, in contrast, was the speech of the preeminent, above all poets and kings, a genre (like them) possessed of high authority, having the capacity to advance powerful truth claims, and backed by physical force.[2]

Lincoln's argument suggests that what has come to pass as rational representation of reality (*logos*) as well as its contrasting other, fictional representations of reality, can only be considered as authoritative in relation to institutionalised social, cultural, and material practices. But perhaps most relevant to my analysis is one of the conclusions of Lincoln's study, where he points out that sometimes "myths are the product and reflection of a people who tell stories in which they

---

[1] Jean-Pierre Vernant, *Myth and Society in Ancient Greece* (London: Methuen, 1982), 187.

[2] Lincoln, x. Both words *muthos* and *mythos* can be translated as "something told (as/during a ritual act)". In ancient Greek "y" was pronounced as [u]; when *muthos* (spelled with "y" in Greek, with the "y" pronounced as [u]) was adopted in Latin, the "y" lacked an exact phonetic equivalent in Latin, and was pronounced as [i]. Hence the difference in spelling *muthos* and *mythos*. I will adopt the spelling *mythos* instead of *muthos* from here on.

effectively narrate themselves." However, as Lincoln underlines, at other times "myths are stories in which some people narrate others, and at times the existence of those others is itself the product of mythic discourse."[3] In this chapter, I will begin with a brief review of the most important aspects of theorisations of myth that bear upon the conception of myth which I will employ in my analysis. I will argue that myth is the effect of acts of citation that reiterate representations of subjective identities and scenarios for the subject's social acts. These reiterations, that constitute myth, establish normative constraints that affect one's fantasising one's identity and one's presentation in social reality. After a brief and selective survey of theories of myth I will define my understanding of the concept of "social myth" by contrasting myth and ideology. And finally, I will examine aspects of the relationship between social myth and social reality.

Theories of Myth

In this section I will offer a brief survey of nineteenth and mid-twentieth-century concepts of myth in order to sketch a genealogy of the concept of social myth that I will be using throughout my analysis. In this way I am also preparing the ground for an analysis of the relationship between myth and ideology, through which I will define my understanding of social myth.

The Romantics often understood myth as an underlying force shaping the experience of consciousness that could usher men into realms of absolutes mystically located in a transcendental relationship with the time and space of mundane life.[4] They professed that the arts, especially poetry, may offer the key to the gate opening onto this heavenly absolute.[5] Unjustly simplifying the Romantic conception of myth, we may say that it offers an idealised (and often exotic) other; through this offering it may

---

[3] Lincoln, 211.

[4] See for instance René Wellek, *Concepts of Criticism* (New Haven, CT: Yale University Press, 1963), 220; Tsvetan Todorov, *Theories of the Symbol*, trans. Catherine Porter (Ithaca: Cornell University Press, 1982), 206-7; Marilyn Butler, *Romantic, Rebels and Reactionaries: English Literature and Its Background 1760-1830* (Oxford: Oxford University Press, 1982), 184.

[5] According to Jerome McGann, "the idea that poetry, or even consciousness, can set one free of the ruins of history and culture is the grand illusion of every Romantic poet." Jerome McGann, *Romantic Ideology: A Critical Investigation* (Chicago: University of Chicago Press, 1983), 91. See also Friedrich Schelling, *System of Transcendentalism*, trans. Peter Heath (Charlottesville: University of Virginia Press, 1978), 232.

mobilise social forces for political purposes; and it creates the possibility of conceiving literature and its makers as an enlightened elite, keepers of the key to otherworldly bliss. These Romantic features of concepts of myth have persisted into the late nineteenth century and well into the twentieth century, strengthening and legitimating, like the myth narratives the Romantics reinterpreted (sometimes selectively), discourses of masculine authority.

The mutual corroboration of myths and discourses of masculine authority, rooted in Romantic understandings of myth, can be exemplified with discourses that harnessed myth to nationalist causes, affecting constructions of identity in Irish narratives; other examples include psychoanalytic discourses that used myth to extend masculine authority over the realm of signification; and discourses of folk and fairy tales that transformed myths to legitimate male-dominated gender regimes. In the following I will first comment briefly on the importance of the relationship between myth and psychoanalysis. I will then trace conceptions of the relationship between myth and society that stand behind the vision of one of the great theorists of the twentieth century, Northrop Frye. This will allow me to pursue aspects of these theories that are useful for defining the relationship between myth and society in ways that respond to complexities of contemporary theory, while also allowing me to highlight critically their limitations. I will proceed from Andrew Von Hendy's position on the influence of Romantic theories of myth on twentieth-century re-workings of the concept.

In his analysis of the modern construction of myth, Von Hendy argues that "two major tenets of the Romantic construction of myth" ground two very different conceptions of myth in the twentieth century. The first tenet is that

> mythology belongs to an unconscious, teleological process that is ultimately outside of human time and history, though humans experience its effects from inside. The second tenet, however, is that, as Vico discovered, humans make their social world, and mythopeia, broadly understood, is constitutive of culture.[6]

The first tenet can be seen as the root of theories of myth that emphasise the psychological dimension of mythic experience. The second tenet can

---

[6] Andrew Von Hendy, *The Modern Construction of Myth* (Bloomington: Indiana University Press, 2002), 39.

be seen as having inspired the ritual school of myth.[7]

The first tenet entices us to explore the relationship between myth and psychoanalysis. Michelle Massé, summarising theories of the relationship between psychoanalysis and Gothic literature, points out some critics' belief that because "psychoanalysis grows from the same cultural unease as the Gothic", "it is itself a socio-cultural symptom, with no more explanatory force than any novel."[8] In Hélène Cixous's feminist analyses, psychoanalysis is suspected of being a myth used to corroborate male-dominated gender regimes through corroborating the authority of the Father.[9] Similarly, Gayle Rubin argues that "the Oedipal complex is a machine which fashions the appropriate forms of sexual individuals" with women constructed as objects of exchange between men.[10] In my analysis I regard the categories with which psychoanalysis operates as discursive constructions; their realness derives from their reiteration in institutionalised settings. I accept the view that psychoanalysis functions in similar ways to myths that corroborate visions of social order.

The second Romantic tenet identified by Von Hendy as a root of conceptions of myth, developed from late nineteenth century and well into the twentieth century, yields the belief that "humans make their social world, and mythopeia, broadly understood, is constitutive of culture."[11] We find this belief amongst theorists who derive their views from the ritual school of myth. The school's most inspiring scholar, James Frazer, regarded myth as derived from ritual, and universalised the cyclical patterns of the regeneration motif as the basic pattern of most myths.[12] Close to the myth and ritual school, Lord Raglan argued that myth

---

[7] The ideas vehiculated in the ritual school and in psychoanalysis often share common views. As Von Hendy indicates, J. G. Frazer's concept of "savagery" anticipates psychoanalytic perspectives. Von Hendy notes that for Frazer "'savagery' is no longer an abandoned cultural zone, safely confined to the past; we carry it within us, a 'solid layer' repressed and 'slumbering' volcanically beneath a 'thin crust' of civilization." Von Hendy, 96.

[8] Michelle Massé, "Psychoanalysis and the Gothic", *A Companion to the Gothic*, ed. David Punter (Oxford: Blackwell, 2000), 229-41, 230; see also 231.

[9] Hélène Cixous, "Sorties: Out and Out: Attacks/Ways Out/Forays", *The Newly Born Woman*, with Catherine Clément, trans. Betsy Wing (London: Tauris, 1996), 63-132, 101.

[10] Gayle Rubin, "The Traffic in Women: Notes on the Political Economy of Sex", *Toward an Anthropology of Women*, ed. Rayna Reiter (New York: Monthly Review Press, 1975), 157-210, 189; see also 192.

[11] Von Hendy, 39.

[12] James Frazer, *The Golden Bough: A Study in Magic and Religion* (Hertfordshire: Wordsworth, 1993).

narratives are descriptions of rituals meant to remind the members of a social community authorised socialisation patterns and can be traced back to the rituals' dramatic performances.[13] In the context of ideas derived from the ritual school, John Gray suggests a distinction between myth and social myth. A text narrating a myth is not simply an aesthetic exercise, but serves "a practical purpose in the community where it [is] current, to achieve some desired end or to conserve certain accepted values ... [S]ocial customs and institutions [are] conserved by their insertion into myth", thus yielding a social myth.[14] Gray argues that a social myth is one that helps materially to preserve the *social* order, while other kinds of myth express the need to preserve a *cosmic*, or *natural*, order.

Thus, the treatment of myth in the ritual school and in theories derived from it helps to define a conception of myth suitable for the analysis of myths' social value. This conceptualisation of myth allows us to examine how narratives may become vehicles of myths, carrying incentives for audiences to legitimate (or contest) social order. In fact, most narratives, whether or not explicitly dealing with myths, can be seen as having what Gray calls "a mythical aspect, its function being to articulate and so conserve features thought to be vital to the social life."[15]

Mid-twentieth-century theorisations of myth continue to develop an interest in the narrative aspects of myth.[16] In order to define my concerns in relation to the spirit of mid-twentieth-century theories of myth, I will explore in more detail some of Northrop Frye's work. Frye argues that a society's symbolic practices and forms of expression stem from, and are clustered around, a central myth of concern, i.e. the core beliefs shared,

---

[13] Lord Raglan, "Myth and Ritual" (1955), *Myth: A Symposium*, ed. Thomas Sebeok (Bloomington: Indiana University Press, 1965), 122-35, 122, 124-5. See also Stanley Hyman's discussion of Raglan's work. Stanley Hyman, "The Ritual View of Myth and the Mythic", *Myth: A Symposium*, 136-53, esp. 150.

[14] John Gray, *The Krt Text in the Literature of Ras Shamra: A Social Myth of Ancient Canaan* (Leiden: Brill, 1964), 2-6.

[15] Ibid., 9.

[16] For instance, Claude Lévi-Strauss argues that myth offers universal patterns in which we express the relationship between culture and nature. According to Lévi-Strauss, these patterns are transcendental, but may be glimpsed through analysing the structure of stories derived from myths. The great myth theorist Mircea Eliade defines an opposition between the realms of the sacred and of the profane, arguing that the former can only be accessed through epiphanic revelation. For Eliade, narrations of myth may provoke epiphanies. Claude Lévi-Strauss, *Structural Anthropology*, trans. Monique Layton, 2 vols. (Chicago: University of Chicago Press, 1976). Mircea Eliade, *The Sacred and the Profane: The Nature of Religion*, trans. Willard Trask (New York: Harcourt, 1957).

cherished, and defended by society. Literature, in maintaining a critical attitude towards the myth of concern, and making available alternative worlds of possibility, helps maintain a myth of freedom.[17] Frye's conceptualisation of the myth of freedom is broadly similar to the concept of social myth that I develop in the following sections, and which emphasises a discourse's entropy, its heteroglossic function that makes available the possibility of alterity.[18] On the other hand, the myth of concern fulfils the function of a social myth turned into ideology: it is normative and static, helping to maintain a social order. As Frye explains:

> The myth of concern exists to hold society together, so far as words can help to do this. For it, truth and reality are not directly connected with reasoning or evidence, but are socially established. What is true, for concern, is what society does and believes in response to authority, and a belief, so far as a belief is verbalized, is a statement of willingness to participate in a myth of concern.[19]

Frye's insight is useful for understanding how myths help maintain the cohesion of society through mobilising the society's members' consent to an ordering vision: "The anxiety of society, when it urges the authority of a myth and the necessity of believing it seems to be less to proclaim its truth than to prevent anyone from questioning it. It aims at consent … rather than conviction."[20] His argument suggests the investigation of narrative as means to change the social myths that draw individuals' consent to a constraining socio-cultural order.

However, placed in the wider context of his work, Frye's arguments reveal yet another Romantic thrust for ideals. For Frye the myth of

---

[17] Northrop Frye, *The Critical Path: An Essay on the Social Context of Literary Criticism* (Bloomington: Indiana University Press, 1971), 44. Frye's view of literature as maintaining a myth of freedom also promotes an elite whose faith is engendered by Enlightenment values. See for instance Jean O'Grady, "Northrop Frye at Home and Abroad", *Northrop Frye Newsletter* 8 (1999): 22-32, 27. Also see Northrop Frye, *Myth and Metaphor: Selected Essays, 1974-1988*, ed. Robert Denham (Charlottesville: University of Virginia Press, 1990).
[18] In the perspective developed by Frye, this heteroglossia would be confined to a predetermined framework of discourses that evince "objectivity, suspension of judgement, tolerance, and respect for the individual". Frye, *The Critical Path*, 44. These values derived from the Enlightenment have been examined critically in feminist theory, as is well known. See for instance *Feminism/Postmodernism*.
[19] Frye, *The Critical Path*, 36-7.
[20] Northrop Frye, *The Secular Scripture: A Study of the Structure of Romance* (Cambridge, Massachusetts: Harvard University Press, 1976), 16.

concern derives from the narratives of the Judeo-Christian myth.[21] According to him, above "the Christian fallen world" "is a world which ..., related by analogy to the intelligible world of the philosopher and scientist, the imaginable world of the poet, and the revealed world of religion, is increasingly referred to ... by the term 'model'."[22] For Frye, the narratives that fulfil the myth of freedom would question the meanings legitimated by the myth of concern, but such questioning can only yield the revelation of an archetypal pattern, which for those under the spell of the myth of concern remains invisible. In the context of my analysis, the significance of archetypal myth theory lies in highlighting the fact that the repetition of a narrative pattern will engender a normative vision of self, sociality, and the cosmos (what Frye calls a "model") for those engaged in discursive interaction. But this normative model is not immutable, nor transcendental.

A brief summary of late nineteenth and mid-twentieth-century conceptions of myth should note that in Romantic conceptions myth is often seen as offering symbols that must be revelatory of a wholesome mystery invested socially when it locates truth within the "mystical brotherhood" of a cultural elite. In modernist conceptions, myths are often seen as making available a transcendental pattern of socialisation, which only the initiated may decipher, and which determines one's identity as member of a social group or of a society. This is generally true also of psychoanalysis, even though the set of discourses that define this discipline are not widely regarded as myths. With significant variations, in both Romantic and modernist concepts of myth, as well as in cases when these concepts feed into each other, myth fulfils a social function of making available to the members of a society a compelling vision of a coherent social and cosmic Universe. From this vision are derived socialisation scripts and identity. Thus, a connection between myth and ideology with its various idealising or rationalising programmes seems inevitable.

---

[21] Frye, *The Critical Path*, 36-7. Frye uses the term "social mythology" to define a tension in the consciousness between two "polarized ... mythical conceptions, the conception of the social contract and the conception of the Utopia or ideal state. These two principles ... descend historically, as myths, from their Christian predecessors, the alienation myth of the fall of man and the fulfilment myth of the City of God." Frye, *The Critical Path*, 158. Also see: Northrop Frye, *Words with Power: Being a Second Study of The Bible and Literature* (New York: Harcourt, 1990).

[22] Frye, *The Critical Path*, 30-2. Also see: Northrop Frye, *Anatomy of Criticism: Four Essays* (Princeton: Princeton University Press, 1957).

Myth and Ideology

In this section I will focus on the contrast between myth and ideology. I will emphasise the monoglossic character of ideologic discourse, regarding the latter as an ossification of social myth. I will offer a definition of social myth as discourse that can be located in a continuum between the frozen stances of monoglossic discourse and the fluid discursive stances of heteroglossic meltdown.[23] The distinction between myth and ideology is often difficult to make because the terms have been used interchangeably within similar contexts. I will argue that ideology is the monoglossic discourse of an elite, proclaimed from top down, while social myth is the heteroglossic discourse of social interaction that can become ideological if it is elevated and accorded prestige by an elite that uses it to legitimate its interests.

Louis Althusser defines ideology as "a matter of the *lived* relation between men and their world" in which they express "not the relation between them and their conditions of existence, but *the way* they live the relation between them and their conditions of existence: this presupposes both a real relation and an '*imaginary*' '*lived*' relation."[24] According to Althusser "the bourgeoisie *lives* in the ideology of *freedom* the relations between it and its conditions of existence: that is, *its* real relation (the law of liberal capitalist economy), but *invested in an imaginary relation* (all men are free, including the free labourers)."[25] Althusser's perspective suggests that everyone is born into ideology through language, which affords only a distorting apprehension of the real status of material conditions.

However, a narrative carrying the interpellating power of the ideological law may be used subversively. Butler argues in Derridean vein that "the call by the law which seeks to produce a lawful subject, produces a set of consequences that exceed and confound what appears to be the disciplining intention motivating the law".[26] Thus, "the law might not only be refused, but it might also be ruptured, forced into a rearticulation that calls into question the monotheistic force of its own unilateral operation."[27] A

---

[23] A view based on Bakhtin's essays on the dialogic imagination. Mikhail Bakhtin, *The Dialogic Imagination*, ed. M. Holquist, trans. C. Emerson and M. Holquist (Austin: University of Texas Press, 1981).

[24] Louis Althusser, "Marxism and Humanism", *For Marx*, trans. Ben Brewster (London: Allen Lane, 1969), 219-47, 233, original italics.

[25] Ibid., 234.

[26] Butler, *Bodies That Matter*, 122.

[27] Ibid.

narrative that achieves this would be difficult to identify as ideological on Althusser's terms. This narrative would not be conducive of a distorted apprehension of the reality of experience in the same way in which a dominant narrative would be, because it would represent a manifestation of precisely that fantasy or imagination which must remain unthinkable in order for ideology to dominate. Because of that, it would threaten to expose the constructed nature of ideology, as well as the possibility of its reconstruction. I regard such a narrative as one kind of narrative instantiation of social myth, placing more weight on its social dimension than on its mythologizing function, since the most important thing about this narrative is that it involves social interaction at "grassroots" level. By contrast, a dominant narrative would be ideological, serving the interests of an elite capable of enforcing the dominance of the norms the narrative legitimates. This ideological narrative would have a strong mythologizing function, being less conducive of the kind of dialogue that happens in social interaction. The heteroglossic character of the latter would threaten the authority of ideological narrative, which fosters monoglossic discursive regimes.

Thus, an ideology is the narrative expression of the lived relation between the members of an elite and the world, that legitimates as real and justified this relation only, in its definitive configuration; this narrative interpellates others, as Althusser argues, with the power of law, seeking to persuade them to consent to its legitimacy.[28] But, as Butler points out, Althusser "does not consider the range of *disobedience* that such an interpellating law might produce." Butler argues that

> the "I" who would oppose its construction is in some sense drawing from that construction to articulate its opposition; further, the "I" draws what is called "agency" in part through being implicated in the very relations of power it seeks to oppose.[29]

The "I" who opposes the norms of the dominant narrative uses the norm against itself by transforming the dominant monoglossic narrative in dialogic discourse where the norm is made to compete with another version of itself. The contestation and reworking of the norm presupposes participation in dialogue through which new affinities of dissenting voices are found and therefore a form of solidarity emerges that quickly transforms the reworked narration into a "proto"-myth. In my terms, this is one of the forms in which social myth is born. Because it is not yet the

---

[28] Althusser, "Marxism and Humanism", 235.
[29] Butler, *Bodies That Matter*, 122-3, original italics.

story of an elite, the narrative of a social myth is not yet ideological. But it can become ideological once the means are created for consolidating it and promoting it as *the* story.

In *Mythologies* (1957), Roland Barthes argues that myth is a "second-order semiological system" which establishes correspondences between complexes of signifier-signified relations, naturalised through language use, and concepts of myth, via language.[30] A complex connecting signifiers to signifieds constitutes the signifier of the second order mythological concept. Thus, within the meaning systems of language nestles the metalanguage of myth. We become, sometimes against ourselves, mindful of a world that arises surreptitiously from discourses that hijack the sense-making power of language in order to legitimate a myth. For Barthes, myths and ideologies are synonymous to the extent that they mask their origins, their socio-historical genealogy.

In this context, I take note of Terry Eagleton's comments on the difficulties of distinguishing between myth and ideology. For Eagleton "some ideological discourses may harness bodies of myth to their purposes." He also speaks of "aspects of ideologies which are mythical" as opposed to those which are not.[31] Eagleton defines myth as "a particular *register* of ideology, which elevates certain meanings to numinous status".[32] His argument emphasises a conscious consent to the fictionality of myth, whereas one is not immediately aware of the fictionality of ideology. These blurred boundaries can be more clearly defined if we premise the distinction between ideology and myth on the distinction between dominant and heteroglossic narrative. In this case we would not speak of a myth as a narrative aspiring to hand over a numinous reality, but we would emphasise the value of myth in socialisation in circles that contest and reconstruct the norms of dominant ideology; while on the other hand we would recognise the potency of myth to structure our reality and identity when it is turned into dominant narrative, i.e. ideology. This distinction would be in many ways parallel to the distinction between monoglossia and heteroglossia developed by Bakhtin. While monoglossia would be a characteristic of ideological narrative, heteroglossia would be a characteristic of social myth. The "social" would refer to the carnival of voices through which the norms of dominant ideology are contested and reconstructed; "myth" would refer to the possibility, highlighted by Bakhtin,

---

[30] Roland Barthes, *Mythologies*, trans. Annette Lavers (New York: Hill and Wang, 1983), 114-123.
[31] Terry Eagleton, *Ideology: An Introduction* (London: Verso, 1991), 188.
[32] Ibid., 189.

> to imagine and postulate a unified truth that requires a plurality of consciousnesses, one that cannot in principle be fitted into the bounds of a single consciousness, one that is, so to speak, by its very nature *full of event potential* and is born at a point of contact among various consciousnesses.[33]

However, we would accept the possibility that such a unified truth may once again become ideological when various modes of consciousness would be forced to merge into one through reiterations that dry it of its event potential, that is, to force a paraphrase in Derridean terms, of its amenability to alterity.

Summing up the argument so far yields my definition of "social myth": a narrative structure that reflects an illegitimate or legitimate vision of social order, which, in the former case, accommodates heteroglossia but, in the latter case, is susceptible of becoming monoglossic through reiterations that naturalise identities and socialisation scenarios (in which case it expresses an ideology).

Having defined my understanding of "social myth" by contrasting it with ideology, I will now explain the mechanisms through which social myths influence the acquisition of identity. The way social myth functions can be best explained by using the concept of "social imaginaries". The contemporary understanding of the concept can be seen as developed from Jacques Lacan's theory of the mirror stage, and its implications for the individual's interaction with the symbolic order.[34] This is the stage in the development of identity when the infant acquires a socially constructed sense of self by misrecognising him/herself as the image of him/herself s/he receives from the society. Lacan's theory proposes that social imaginaries frame an individual's fantasy of his/her identity. One can only arrive at certain social imaginaries in fathoming his/her identity. This deterministic view has been challenged. Cornelius Castoriadis, for instance, in contrast to Lacan's view, emphasises on the issue of agency in the construction of the social imaginaries through which the members of society institute social order.[35] Castoriadis posits that social imaginaries current in a society can be reconstructed to correspond to emerging needs and desires, rather than being regarded as sanctioned by external authority.

---

[33] Bakhtin, *Problems of Dostoevsky's Poetics*, 81, original italics.

[34] Jacques Lacan, "The Mirror Stage as Formative of the *I* Function, as Revealed in Psychoanalytic Experience", *Écrits*, 3-9.

[35] Cornelius Castoriadis, *The Imaginary Institution of Society* (Michigan: MIT, 1998), 165-373.

I share Moira Gatens's view, which has more in common with Castoriadis's than with Lacan's. Discussing the meaning of "ideology", Gatens argues that there exists not just one social imaginary, but rather multiple social imaginaries. Therefore, the term "ideology" does not cover the whole complex of relationships in which the identity of the subject is gained. As Gatens puts it,

> To acknowledge the diversity in, and dynamism of, our social imaginaries allows one to focus on those aspects of present social imaginaries which are contradictory or paradoxical. This, in turn, allows one to see that the system of linked social imaginaries is constantly being transfigured and refigured.[36]

According to Gatens, there exist "multiple and historically specific social imaginaries".[37] This vision can be used to understand "the system of linked social imaginaries"[38] as a continuum of transformation stages in a narrative's status as it develops from social myth into ideology. Social myths have degrees of fluidity, according to the degree to which they remain open to heteroglossia. Indeed, an ossified social myth has become an ideology. By using the term "ossification" to refer to the process of turning social myth into ideology, I hope to point out two important aspects of the process. First, social myth becomes ideology if it is promoted to the status of "official story", the story that is reiterated as the valid narrative expression of a social reality and which can be regenerated only over long periods of time. Second, social myth turned into ideology ceases to be a heteroglossic narrative, whose meanings can be negotiated, but forms the skeleton structure in whose logocentric cultural frame society's members acquire identity.

The distinction between social myth and ideology may be further clarified through an analogy with Jack Zipes' distinction between myth and folk/fairy tale. Social myths fulfil a similar function to folktales as narratives through which "common folk" devise social identity and scenarios for social interaction in non-institutional fields, while ideology is more akin to fairy tales as narratives produced by a cultural elite, that corroborate this elite's authority in the institutions it controls. One notes the possibility that a social myth is hijacked into ideological discourse, in

---

[36] Moira Gatens, *Imaginary Bodies: Ethics, Power and Corporeality* (London: Routledge, 1996), ix.

[37] Ibid., x.

[38] Ibid., ix.

the same way that in Zipes' perspective a folk/fairy tale may be elevated to the status of myth (functioning as ideology).[39]

The distinction between social myth and ideology is relevant to my textual analyses because it permits us to view narratives challenging ideologies as working within the latter's constraints, in the continuation of a citational chain that prescribes currently legitimate identities and socialisation patterns. The concept of social myth defined above allows us to avoid an understanding of ideology as monolithic: it is always the case that a network of social myths prescribes our identities and modes of socialisation, but it is also always true that new social myths can be born(e) into this network, changing its configuration. Bakhtin, speaking of a variety of discourses that may anchor an ideological network, asserts:

> It is our conviction that there never was a strictly straightforward genre, no single type of direct discourse—artistic, rhetorical, philosophical, religious, ordinary everyday—that did not have its own parodying and travestying double, its own comic-ironic *contre-partie*. What is more, these parodic doubles and laughing reflections of the direct word were, in some cases, just as sanctioned by tradition and just as canonized as their elevated models.[40]

In my analysis, the *contre-partie* Bakhtin invokes will be ironic in a very wide sense, involving an exploitation of the incongruity between ideological, official or otherwise legitimated discourse and marginalised discursive realities, that is evidence of an alterity of the discourse, an alterity which may deconstruct it. Ideological discourse requires dialogue to the extent that it can foster its aim of achieving consent, foreclosing alterity. The ideological declaration of social myth in narrative is sufficient in itself; it does not require creative, but merely consenting, collocution.

But every narrating of social myth, enabling a dialogical space, also creates the possibility for hearing dissenting voices. The dissenters may bring different understandings of the myth to bear on the institutionalised version. Both the institutionalised version of the tale corroborating a social myth and the dissenting version "make common sense", but in divergent ways. The sense-making meanings proposed by dissenting voices differ from the meanings enshrined by an elite. The narrative deployment of a social myth creates the conditions for ideological homology, because the myth may be used for ideological purposes. To borrow Bakhtin's words to

---

[39] Jack Zipes, *Fairy Tales and the Art of Subversion* (New York: Routledge, 1991), 6-11.

[40] Bakhtin, *The Dialogic Imagination*, 53.

express my point, social myths may be "sanctioned by tradition and just as canonized as their elevated models" which they challenge.[41] But the narrative deployment of social myth can also exploit a discourse's propensity towards heteroglossia.[42]

Summarising the discussion of the relationship between ideology and social myth offered in this section, I would admit that ideology and social myth are two sides of the same coin and cannot be separated entirely. A social myth can be elevated to the status of ideology, becoming the property of an elite and serving to define the institutional fields the elite controls. On the other hand, a social myth may escape ideological control and dissolve into heteroglossia characteristic of non-institutional fields. When beyond ideological control, the narrative of social myth can accommodate subversive voices. These propose alternative meanings to the ones operating in legitimate institutional fields and would temporarily coexist with the latter, competing with them. Thus, a social myth may offer a counter-narrative to ideological proclamation. However, such reconstructions may themselves be turned into ideological narratives. Because of my emphasis on the dynamics of social imaginaries through which one fantasises his/her identity in social interaction, I will use the term "social myth", rather than "ideology", throughout my analysis. I wish thus to emphasise the provisional character of any dominant narrative as well as its vulnerability to heteroglossic intervention, even while admitting that social myths share with ideologies the power to constrain our fantasising the identity of ourselves and others, and therefore constrain our acts in the social realm.

---

[41] Ibid., 115.

[42] The distinction between ideology and social myth can be compared to Bakhtin's distinction between primary and secondary (ideological) genres. Bakhtin argues that "[e]ach separate utterance is individual, of course, but each sphere in which language is used develops its own *relatively stable types* of these utterances [which] we may call *speech genres*." For Bakhtin, secondary speech genres are institutionalised forms of discourse, vehicles of ideologies. Primary speech genres, which in my terms are discourses whence social myths take off, are utterances of non-institutionalised discourses. But, as Bakhtin points out, the two speech genres feed off each other: "Secondary (complex) speech genres ... arise in ... highly developed and organized communication (primarily written) that is artistic, scientific, sociopolitical, and so on. During the process of their formation, they absorb and digest various primary (simple) genres that have taken form in unmediated speech communion. These primary genres are altered and assume a special character when they enter into complex ones." Mikhail Bakhtin, *Speech Genres and Other Late Essays*, trans. Vern McGee, eds. Caryl Emerson and Michael Holquist (Austin: University of Texas Press, 1986), 60, 62, original italics.

Social Myth, Narrative, and Social Reality

In the following, I examine the impact myth can have on reality, highlighting ways of changing social reality by working with narrative deployments of the myths that script our identities. The material effects of myths are more tangible than it might seem. For, as Kenneth Burke puts it,

> 'Myths' ... are our basic psychological tools for working together. A hammer is a carpenter's tool; a wrench is a mechanic's tool; and a 'myth' is the social tool for welding the sense of interrelationship by which the carpenter and the mechanic, though differently occupied, can work together for common social ends. In this sense a myth that works well is as real as food, tools, and shelter are.[43]

Adopting a similar perspective, I regard the narrating of stories (or, in different terms, the actualisation of stories' texts in discourse) as always implying a sharing of expressions of identity and agency. Narratives are "tools" for "working together" that, in welding a sense of social interrelationship, affect the material reality wherein stories are circulated between the members of a social community. Narrations of certain identities and modes of agency can be repeated, cited over and over again until, having become dominant stories, they shape identity and agency for most of those engaged in locution and collocution in specific settings, and thus contribute to maintaining the material, tangible reality in a certain state of order.[44] The stories that convey dominant expressions of identity and agency thus become the vehicles of social myths, and may become ideologies through ossification. A social myth consists of templates for identity and agency, forged in the reiteration of their narrative expression and continuing to forge the citational chain of discourse inspiring individuals to act in certain ways in the material reality.

---

[43] Kenneth Burke, "Revolutionary Symbolism in America" (1935), *The Legacy of Kenneth Burke*, eds. Herbert Simons and Trevor Melia (Madison: University of Wisconsin Press, 1989), 267-8.

[44] Social sciences research methodology can be used to identify such dominant narrations through empirical studies. See for instance *Narrative and Social Control: Critical Perspectives*, ed. Dennis Mumby (Newbury Park: Sage, 1993). According to Phillips and Hardy, this collection focuses on how various narrative genres "contribute to the construction of the social reality that constitutes the lived world of social actors. By portraying and conveying identities, stories help to 'linguistically objectify' a social order." Phillips and Hardy, 29-30.

According to the sociologist Randall Collins, the social world is born through communication that can become ritualised by repetition.[45] And, as David Boje, also a sociologist, emphasises, stories discipline by "defining characters, sequencing plots, and scripting actions".[46] Thus, what can be narrated in social interaction is to an extent determined by the ensembles of characters and plots that narratives are made of, and through which individuals fantasise their identity as they speak. Expressing a similar position, Catherine Belsey argues that: "Texts address readers. They urge us into position, invite us to take up attitudes, call on us to believe their analyses and promises."[47] The reiteration of a story prescribes social roles and provides socialisation scripts.

One of the reasons why stories can function in this way is that stories can serve as vehicles for social myths. But precisely because of that, stories distort and falsify: they constitute the expression of the self according to a mythic vision of order pitched against a vision of disorder which calls for the myth's ordering operation. That is why, as Belsey points out, "it's good to unmask the values [texts] promote, but it's better still to see that they can't do it without also enlisting us in the contradictions it is their aim to suppress, or without betraying the existence of something unnameable that escapes their mastery."[48] Thus, it is important to emphasise that each reiteration of socialisation scripts, in which social roles and social order are given anew, is also the occasion of glimpsing a realm of disorder and alterity that may be engaged with productively. Narratives thus provide the opportunity to revise the social value of myth. This revision may help to change the material practices in which the social roles and scripts derived from myths are enacted.

One of the most immediate material places affected by narratives derived from social myths is the place of the body. In the following chapter I will focus on the interaction between stories and bodies.

---

[45] Randall Collins, "On the Microfoundations of Macrosociology", *American Journal of Sociology*, 86 (1981): 984-1013.

[46] David Boje, "Stories of the Storytelling Organization: A Postmodern Analysis of Disney as 'Tamara-Land'", *Academy of Management Journal*, 38 (1994): 997-1035, 1000.

[47] Catherine Belsey and Neil Badmington, "From *Critical Practice* to Cultural Criticism: An Interview with Catherine Belsey", *Textual Practice*, 19 (2005): 1-12, 3.

[48] Ibid., 3.

CHAPTER FOUR

THE BODY

In this chapter I will focus on constructions of bodily identity, since the body is the most immediate material place in relation to which surrounding places are constituted in perception as material environments, under the spell of social myths. I will first examine issues of bodies' materialisation. I define materialisation as the act of presenting the body as an object amongst others in social reality. I will then argue that this presentation is influenced by narrative representations of bodies, explaining how this influence is exercised, and how narratives derived from, or enshrining, social myths affect materiality. I will conclude by placing my argument in the context of definitions of femininity derived from the dichotomy mind/body, which has affected constructions of feminine identity since the dawn of the modern age. The analyses of this section will be exemplified in the second part of this book, especially in my interpretation of Angela Bourke's study of Bridget Cleary's murder, in my readings of Ní Dhuibhne's writing, and in my analysis of the Dracula myth.

Narrative, Social Myth, and the Body

I will begin by focusing on aspects of what Elizabeth Grosz calls "discursive positioning", that is, "a complex relation between the corporeality of the author, the author's textual residues or traces, the text's materiality, and its effects in marking the bodies of the author and readers, and the corporeality and productivity of readers."[1] I am particularly interested in the texts' effects in marking the bodies of readers, because it is partly through this marking that bodies acquire material identity.

The socialisation scenarios readers derive from narratives may be actualised in their bodies' performance in social spaces. The prescriptive

---

[1] Elizabeth Grosz, "Sexual Signatures: Feminism After the Death of the Author", *Space, Time, and Perversion: Essays on the Politics of Bodies* (New York: Routledge, 1995), 9-24, 18.

power of scenarios internalised through narratives derived from social myths affects men and women differently: most current social myths compel women's socialisation in ways that maintain the legitimacy of masculine gender regimes. In this study, I hope to demonstrate that the narratives I will analyse are geared to achieve a shift in the material practices through which gender regimes are maintained; and that this shift could be achieved by questioning, challenging, and reconstructing the normative knowledge of self and body naturalised through narratives derived from social myths.

In this subchapter I focus especially on normative knowledge of the body which influences bodies' materialisation, and on how the normativity of such knowledge can be challenged. I will emphasise that a challenge to normative knowledge of the body involves a critical examination of the relationship between discourse, subjectivity, and cultural norms through which bodies are materialised. The importance of this relationship is highlighted in Judith Butler's analysis of the concept of "sex". Butler links the "process of 'assuming' a sex with the question of *identification*, and with the discursive means by which the heterosexual imperative enables certain sexed identifications and forecloses and/or disavows other identifications."[2] In my analysis I will explore to what extent Butler's argument can be extended in order to be used to investigate the signifying power wielded through social myths. Social myths can be seen as providing discursive means that enable certain identifications and foreclose others. These identifications and disavowals do not affect only one's "sex" but bodily attributes in general. Furthermore, using Linda McDowell's comments on definitions of spaces, we may argue that the signifying power of social myths, engendering identifications and disavowals of materiality attributes, constitutes not only the realness and materiality of the body, but also the realness and materiality of the places the body inhabits legitimately or illegitimately.

McDowell argues that

> places are contested, fluid and uncertain. It is socio-spatial practices that define places and these practices result in overlapping and intersecting places with multiple and changing boundaries, constituted and maintained by social relations of power and exclusion ... . These boundaries are both social and spatial—they define who belongs to a place and who may be excluded, as well as the location or site of the experience.[3]

---

[2] Butler, *Bodies That Matter*, 3, original italics.
[3] McDowell, 4.

In this view, social myths can be seen as conferring morphological stability to all kinds of material places, including the place of the body. When I refer to "the place of the body" I refer to the body as place as well as to the body as an object amongst others, located in space in ways that give it social value: the body is "put in its (proper) place". In my analysis of the texts in the second part of this study, I will explore to what extent a challenge to narratives reiterating women's identities implies a challenge to the morphological stability that social myths confer upon women's bodies, seeking to reveal how this challenge affects the social value of discursive practices as constitutive of the materiality of places including the place of the body. Such challenges affect the process of subjective fantasising through which an individual acquires the "I" made available through discursive subjectivity constructions.

The texts I will analyse in the second part of the book engage with discourses that bear the semiotic markings of paradigms that hold social myths. In Derridean terms, these markings can be understood as the signature of authority of social myths. In resignifying discourses bearing (and enacting, when read or narrated) this signature of authority, the texts challenge social myths ossified into ideologies. Derrida argues that:

> In order to function, that is, to be readable, a signature must have a repeatable, iterable, imitable form; it must be able to be detached from the present and singular intention of its production. It is its sameness which, by corrupting its identity and its singularity, divides its seal [*sceau*].[4]

In the context of my analysis, the condition of authority wielded through narratives derived from social myths is their iterability. But the monoglossic regime based on the sameness of the story repeated in dialogical exchanges or solitary reading cannot last, precisely because in its reiteration, the identity and singularity of the story's signature of authority is altered, and thus the story becomes amenable to heteroglossic intervention.

In Chapter One I explained that my understanding of "realms of fantasy" derives from Judith Butler's interpretation of fantasy as a means of figuring an individual's interiority whereby the individual gains a sense of self.[5] This sense of self forms the background to an individual's construction as subject. The legitimacy of the subject is established by fantasising, under the pressure of norms, a socially undesirable subject which is repudiated, rather than being inhabited as a means to contest the

---

[4] Derrida, "Signature Event Context", 20.
[5] Butler, "Gender Trouble", 333.

norms. The legitimate subject is materialised in the social acts scripted by narratives that repeat (differently) the repudiation of the illegitimate, abject vision of the uninhabitable self. Thus, a fantasised subject is legitimated and comes across as "reality".[6] Fantasising, narratives, and social acts are inextricably linked. Their imbrication makes possible the configuration of identity in a space of the mind sensed as "interiority", which accommodates subject positions derived from discourses. Subjective identity in turn influences how one presents oneself to others in social interaction. Discourses are thus materialised; they lend their marks to performances of the body in the social arena.

I note here the objections made to a theory of discourse that seems to disregard the potency of the material body, and of institutions empowered to act physically on individuals' bodies, in shaping one's identity.[7] I hope to answer such concerns by emphasising the intersubjective character of identity construction in discourse, and the role of deictic force in discursive interaction. These concepts allow us to treat the discursive formation of identity as indissolubly connected to individuals' interaction in the material institutional settings in which they "wear" their bodies. One's embodied presence in the world does entail a presentation of the body attuned to the image of the body that is shown in a fantasy as belonging to oneself; but this fantasy is inextricably linked to the material reality and the body, to which it constantly refers through the deictic force of the fantasy's underlying narrative script. The image of one's body is shaped by narrations that compel one to think one's body as a certain kind of material object. Obviously, the object presented as one's body in fantasising is immaterial. But one's social persona is not; we assume that it has a material substrate.[8] The fantasy used to construct one's social

---

[6] See Butler, *Bodies That Matter*, 1-23.

[7] For objections to Butler's theory, and generally to theories reducing material reality to the reality formed through discourse, see for instance Anne McClintock's arguments. For McClintock "the planned institutional violence of armies and law courts, prisons and state machinery", although backing up discourse, "is not reducible to the 'violence of the letter'". And, according to Biddy Martin, body and psyche are not reducible to the effects of power enacted discursively. Anne McClintock, *Imperial Leather: Race, Gender and Sexuality in the Colonial Contest* (London: Routledge, 1995), 16; and Biddy Martin, "Sexuality without Gender and Other Queer Utopias", *Diacritics* 24 (1994): 104-121, 119.

[8] Or, to phrase this point in psychology terminology, one assumes that one's body image is underlain by one's body schema. John Campbell proposes that one's representations of one's body "might be used only in mediating one's own perceptions and actions, in which case I will speak of a body schema. Or the representation might also be used in registering the impact of one's behavior on

persona obscures the material body in order to claim its materiality. That is, the matter of the body is absorbed into one's social persona, which thus gains materiality while at the same time masking one's body.

In this subchapter I clarified my understanding of the relationship between discursive subjectivity and one's perceptions of one's body, focusing on how these perceptions are influenced by the narratives which we use to understand ourselves and others. In the following section I will focus on understandings of the relationship between nature and culture through dichotomies that establish relationships of government of the body, seen as contiguous with nature, through discourse, seen as a tool for rationalising experiences of embodiment. This will help us to understand the effects of disciplinary cultural discourses on bodies. These effects are important concerns in all the texts studied here, but the analysis of the constructed dichotomy mind:culture/body:nature is especially relevant in my interpretation of Lochhead's play *Dracula*, Bourke's study *The Burning of Bridget Cleary*, and Ní Dhuibhne's novel *The Dancers Dancing*.[9] Although the traditional equation of bodies with women/femininity will be discussed, my arguments will refer to bodies in general, men's or women's.

Nature, Discourse, and Bodies

It has been widely noted in feminist criticism that various discourse networks construct dichotomised arrangements that place nature (organic bodies, women, feminine corporeality) in opposition to culture (reason, spiritual faith, incorporeal masculinity), with the first posited as subject to/of government by the latter. For instance, Evelyn Fox Keller's analysis of Enlightenment rationalism concludes that discourses on science and nature transfer the power associated with women, nature, and life from God to nature. This transfer transforms the language of secrets of creation from a sacred language to a mundane (and profane) language whose

---

other people, in which case I will speak of a body image." In my analysis, the fantasising of one's identity through using narrative in discursive interaction yields a body image. Yet the location produced by discursive deixis also interferes with one's body schema, with his/her sense of belonging to a material environment. John Campbell, "The Body Image and Self-Consciousness", *The Body and the Self*, eds. José Bermúdez et al. (Cambridge, Massachusetts: MIT, 2001), 29-42, 33-4.

[9] Éilís Ní Dhuibhne, *The Dancers Dancing* (Belfast: Blackstaff, 1999).

semiotic domain is nature and women.[10] Thus, femininity is associated with nature whose secrets must be gained so that it may be governed.

Another important example of critical examinations of constructions of femininity through associations between women and nature is Hélène Cixous's writing that focuses on male-generated psychoanalytic theory. Cixous explores gender hierarchies derived from visions of nature as a dark continent to be subordinated to masculine logos and faith. She especially criticises the role of Freudian and Lacanian psychoanalysis in legitimating these hierarchies. In the first note to her essay "The Laugh of the Medusa" she argues:

> Men still have everything to say about their sexuality, and everything to write. For what they have said so far, for the most part, stems from the opposition activity/passivity from the power relation between a fantasized obligatory virility meant to invade, to colonize, and the consequential phantasm of woman as a 'dark continent' to penetrate and to 'pacify.' ... Conquering her, they've made haste to depart from her borders, to get out of sight, out of body.[11]

Cixous's argument offers an analysis of how the male-generated perception of the relationship between nature and culture is gendered, and of how this gendering, underpinning social practices, especially the practice of psychoanalysis, serves to subordinate women.

Moira Gatens points out the importance of the connection between psychoanalysis, fantasy, myth, and social order to show that in the field of psychoanalysis the management of the body serves the legitimation of the masculine body politic. In her view, the

> masculine image of unity and independence from women and nature has strong resonances in psychoanalytic accounts of infantile anxieties and the fantasies created to cope with them. The image of artificial man, the body politic, perfectly mirrors the infantile wish for independence from the maternal body. It is a fantasy that can be found in mythology too.[12]

---

[10] Evelyn Fox Keller, "Secrets of God, Nature, and Life", *The Gender/Sexuality Reader: Culture, History, Political Economy*, eds. Roger Lancaster and Micaela di Leonardo (New York: Routledge, 1997), 209-218, 211, 214-5.
[11] Hélène Cixous, "The Laugh of the Medusa", *Feminisms: An Anthology of Literary Theory and Criticism*, eds. Robin Warhol and Diane Herndl (New Brunswick: Rutgers University Press, 1997), 347-62, 362.
[12] Gatens, 22.

A psychoanalytic understanding of the self, disseminated through accounts of the formation of self identity as an ego that transcends the body, condemns women to a subjectivity that can find only masculine subject positions in discourse, and therefore finds its femininity in a realm beyond discourse. This schism, between masculine subjectivity made for women to inhabit as their own, and feminine subjectivity as otherness, derives from women's association with nature simultaneously with their dissociation from culture, from the domain of the symbolic.

Julia Kristeva's re-evaluation of psychoanalysis proposes that the realm beyond discourse is a realm of the abject, a realm of maternal authority that must be repelled in order for paternal laws to take over authority of the body, and thus socialise the body. The abject "disturbs identity, system, order."[13] Kristeva distinguishes between the semiotic and the symbolic. The language of the semiotic is the irrational language of poetry, a language of bodily rhythms associated with maternal *chora*, which, through the authority of the mother, "shapes the body into a territory having areas, orifices, points and lines, surfaces and hollows."[14] The language of the symbolic is the language of masculine socialisation, the language of any rational discourse. In my terms, every discourse (including poetry and body language) is a realm of the symbolic, in which the fantasies through which bodies are socialised are expressed. Perhaps what Kristeva calls the semiotic is best referred to in my analysis as body schema, the non/pre-conscious awareness of one's body. But, in the same terms, my main concern is with the body image, i.e. with the social persona formed through fantasising identities derived from stories vehiculated in social interaction. However, following Kristeva through Butler's theory of the abject, I regard the abject as representable and as constitutive of the legitimate subject: the abject is invoked in order to be repudiated.

The arguments referred to in this section help us to understand that discursive constructions of subjects are implicated in one's perceptions of one's body to the point that they may govern the body by rationalising it. This rationalisation can be seen to amount to a writing of the body as a certain kind of object. In Elizabeth Grosz's terms, the body becomes a surface of inscription:

> The body can be regarded as a kind of *hinge* or threshold: it is placed between a psychic or lived interiority and a more sociopolitical exteriority

---

[13] Julia Kristeva, *Powers of Horror: An Essay on Abjection*, trans. Leon Roudiez (New York: Columbia University Press, 1982), 4.
[14] Ibid., 71-2.

that produces interiority through the *inscription* of the body's outer surface. Where psychoanalysis and phenomenology focus on the body as it is experienced and rendered meaningful, the inscriptive model is more concerned with the processes by which the subject is marked, scarred, transformed, and written upon or constructed by the various regimes of institutional, discursive, and nondiscursive power as a particular kind of body.[15]

Grosz's argument summarises the concerns raised in theories dealing critically with the government of the body through discourse. It also emphasises that government of the body is not strictly achieved through discourse, but also through the institutions that discourses legitimate.

Before concluding this section I will briefly outline the main points of my theoretical framework. Constructions of the subject presuppose a psychic interiority that, as Butler points out, can be fantasised as inhabitable or uninhabitable, according to the repudiations that constructions of the subject enact. The body will be disciplined according to the body image that is seen as belonging to the legitimate subject. This body is subordinated to the subject through relationships of government established through various discourses, with different effects for men and women. Such discourses include psychoanalysis, science or discourses of the legitimate body politic. The body thus becomes a threshold between one's fantasised identity and socio-political demands, and its material surface will be marked accordingly.

Narratives are means of marking bodies. But while heteroglossic narratives, being conducive of a play of differences, destabilise normative constructions of subjects, narratives derived from ossified social myths serve to stabilise them. The scenarios presented in the latter repeatedly show the range of legitimate actions and identities for subjects. These scenarios become the bearers and the support of what Butler calls "regulatory norms" that "work in a performative fashion to constitute the materiality of bodies" and "to materialize" the bodies' attributes.[16] Butler argues, referring in particular to gender, that

In this sense, what constitutes the fixity of the body, its contours, its movements, will be fully material, but materiality will be rethought as the effect of power, as power's most productive effect. And there will be no way to understand 'gender' as a cultural construct which is imposed upon the surface of matter, understood either as 'the body' or its given sex.

---

[15] Elizabeth Grosz, "Bodies and Knowledges: Feminism and the Crisis of Reason", *Space, Time, and Perversion*, 25-43, 33, original italics.
[16] Butler, *Bodies That Matter*, 2.

Rather, ... the materiality of the body will not be thinkable apart from the materialization of that regulatory norm.[17]

For Butler, "sex" is "one of the norms by which the 'one' becomes viable at all, that which qualifies a body for life within the domain of cultural intelligibility."[18] But, as she points out in a note to this statement, "Clearly, sex is not the only such norm by which bodies become materialized, and it is unclear whether 'sex' can operate as a norm apart from other normative requirements on bodies."[19]

Butler's analysis of materialisation is helpful in examining the process in which the reiteration of narratives affects the presentation of bodies in social reality. This process can be outlined thus: the fantasies inspired by narratives derived from social myths are shaped according to the norms enshrined by the myths. The normative requirements on bodies are thus implicated in the constitution of bodies as entities endowed with the attribute of materiality. These normative requirements constrain the range of possible occurrences of the body. But narratives that reflect on their normative character can ease these constraints, thus offering opportunities of empowering rematerialisation of bodies.

---

[17] Ibid.
[18] Ibid.
[19] Ibid., 243.

CONCLUSION

My methodology of analysis is developed through corroborating visions of the relationship between narrative and reality offered in the texts studied, and analyses of this relationship in linguistics, anthropology, narratology, and social theory. In the first part of this study I focused on theoretical studies addressing the relationship between narrative and reality. In the second part I will show how the texts that form the interest of this study have suggested recourse to the theories, and how they inspired my methodological decisions. The works of each author discussed require different theoretical emphases and therefore different aspects of the theoretical framework developed in the first part will inform the analysis in each chapter. At the same time, the discussion of the texts in the second part of the book will show how they support and illustrate aspects of the theoretical framework outlined in the first part.

However, this theoretical framework can be used for analyses of any literary texts. In general terms, my theoretical vision centres on the argument that the world of the imagination is a realm of fantasy where one acquires identity. The ways in which we fantasise identity are in part derived from narratives. Every literary text influences the ways in which readers fantasise identity. How this influence is exercised cannot be fully explained theoretically as literary texts always also appeal to the infinite realms of emotion, memory or intuition. What can be explained is how texts shape subjectivity and reflect on the ways in which subjectivity is constituted. I argued that subjectivity is amenable to myths, which I defined as ossified or emerging discourses of authority. Legitimate subjectivity is constituted through acts of citation that reiterate discourses of authority ossifying social myths. Illegitimate subjectivity can be traced to what has been repudiated in order to construct legitimate subjects. Given narrative expression, illegitimate subjectivities enter the domains of legitimacy and may crystallise emerging social myths. Through reiteration, these subjectivities may acquire normative character. The naturalisation of these subjectivities as legitimate may yield ossified social myths that fulfil the functions of ideologies.

Narratives, as one of the means through which we negotiate identities and adequate socialisation scenarios, may become oppressive when they coalesce into discourses of authority that create myths. However, narratives are also means of exploring the regenerative potential of the identities we can derive from myths. All of the texts engaged with in the second part of this study investigate, from different angles, the tension between the oppressive and the regenerative potential of myths. Narrative (reiterative) citations of discourses of authority may consolidate social myths, but reiterations of certain myths can also become subversive. When the reiteration of a myth foregrounds what has been repudiated in the discourses which consecrate the myth, it brings into light new cultural possibilities of conceiving identities. The texts studied in this book perform this kind of narrative reiteration, and entice readers to reflect on the possibilities it offers. In doing so, the texts explore the potential for productive heteroglossia. The narrative development of this potential counteracts the stifling disciplinary force of myths that compels the repetition of the same, a force which creates normative constraints for the subjects it seeks to shape.

Narratives derived from myths help construct ideological monoglossic regimes, casting away what heteroglossia might allow in. The texts I will discuss engage with such narratives that coalesce to form disciplining traditions, lighting up their cast of shadows. Enticing us to participate in this engagement, they may steer us toward new ways of fantasising identities, helping us to find new ways of presenting ourselves to others, to whom we make ourselves known as subjects with a certain identity by communicating ourselves in discourse. That is, these texts might affect our presence in social reality. Our fantasies become material once we substantiate them in our bodily acts in social reality by wearing the identity make-ups they provide and by adopting the postures offered by their scripts. In my analyses I will explore to what extent the texts that form the interest of this study, while helping us to redefine our social identities, also help us to re-conceive bodily identity and to redefine the materiality of bodies.

Thus, my analyses will show how texts by Scottish and Irish women writers challenge the social fictions through which social and bodily identities are constituted. A significant amount of critical work explores how such challenges are made in texts by British and American writers. Although Scottish and Irish texts have also benefited of sustained analysis in this respect, most explorations of their concerns with the constitution of identities and social worlds through myths have been integrated in criticism with a different main focus. The texts I will analyse have not been studied extensively as texts that deal with social myths, although the ways in which these texts challenge confining social norms has been explored in significant detail. This study adds to existing scholarship an explanation of how social norms derive from myths, of how myths function, and of how myths can be challenged, an explanation based on Scottish and Irish writers' specific visions of the role of narrative in conveying constraining traditions that enshrine social worlds and socialisation scenarios.

Some of the texts analysed here have been less explored in the existing critical literature; others, that have received significant critical attention, will be investigated from new angles. For instance, Kennedy's novel *Everything You Need* received mixed reviews and sporadic critical attention; the role of fantasy envisioned in Kennedy's novella "Original Bliss" has not been explored; analyses of Lochhead's play *Dracula* have not regarded Dracula's story as having generated a myth; Ní Dhuibhne's work has received extremely little critical attention; studies of Carr's plays have not focused sufficiently on her particular vision of a subject's agency. Studied here for the first time together, these writers' works offer new opportunities for analysing narratives as tools for continually negotiating our identities, social worlds, and socialisation scenarios.

My analyses will use feminist theory and research to focus on constructions of feminine bodies and identities and on the social myths that shape them. I acknowledge the difficulties entailed by my position as a male writing a feminist critique of social myths bearing the marks of masculine authority. According to Stephen Heath, "men's relation to feminism is an impossible one" because while "women are the subjects of feminism, its initiators, its makers, its force", men are "the objects", "agents" and "carriers of the patriarchal mode"; men's desire to be feminist "is then only the last feint in the long history of [women's] colonization [by men]."[1] On the other hand, Joseph Boone recommends a focus on "the *possibilities* (rather than impossibilities) inherent in the conjunction of men *and* feminism."[2] I subscribe to Boone's position. Constructions of feminine bodies and identities are relevant to men as much as constructions of masculine bodies and identities are relevant to women. For instance, speaking as a man about the organic body, one cannot avoid speaking about femininity and its constructed associations

---

[1] Stephen Heath, "Male Feminism", *Men in Feminism*, eds. Alice Jardine and Paul Smith (New York: Methuen, 1987), 1-32, 1, brackets mine.

[2] Joseph Allen Boone, "Of Me(n) and Feminism: Who(se) is the Sex That Writes?", *Engendering Men: The Question of Male Feminist Criticism*, eds. Joseph Boone and Michael Cadden (New York: Routledge, 1990), 11-25, 12, original italics.

with organicity.[3] In my analyses, rather than speaking from an appropriated feminist position, I speak with the awareness that every individual, man or woman, must work out the identity of her/his incorporeal social persona and corporeal fleshly organism and how these are compelled to coexist in his/her body's social figure, in reference to traditional definitions of what counts as masculine and feminine.

---

[3] A summary of the problematic construction of femininity through association with bodily organicity is offered in Rachel Alsop et al., *Theorizing Gender* (Cambridge: Polity, 2002), 16-22. This summary highlights the fact that in the tradition of Western thought masculinity was constructed "in terms of an aspirational ideal which characterized what men should be" while "being female was treated more as a biological kind." But, it is underlined, many men were not able to live up to the standard of legitimate masculinity, for instance "slaves, non-Europeans and members of the lower classes" who were regarded as "anchored in the sensuous and unable to rise above their animal natures." Alsop et al., 17.

PART II

NARRATIVE, SOCIAL MYTH, AND REALITY IN TEXTS BY A. L. KENNEDY, LIZ LOCHHEAD, MARINA CARR, ÉILÍS NÍ DHUIBHNE, AND ANGELA BOURKE

PREFACE

The chapters in the second part of this study focus on narrative constructions of women's identities in selected texts by A. L. Kennedy, Liz Lochhead, Marina Carr, Éilís Ní Dhuibhne, and Angela Bourke. The overarching vision that guides my analyses, which employ the theoretical framework outlined in the first part, is circumscribed by a wider horizon. These writers' narratives can be set next to other texts by women writers which revisit and revise discourses whose reiteration has solidified and naturalised normative and constraining worldviews. This revisioning is performed in ways that engage readers' inertial yielding into subject positions to which they are bound through normative discourses. Summarising work by Alice Walker, Toni Morrison, and other "minority" writers, Jay Clayton points out that for these writers narrative has a "transformative capacity" as it

> possesses a performative dimension; it enacts as well as means. Just as the ritual process can have a transformative effect on its participants, so stories can change the person who becomes caught up in their charm.[1]

Adopting a similar perspective, I emphasise that my analyses will focus both on how stories mean and on how they compel readers to enact subject positions. When Clayton refers to "ritual process" he has in mind the rituals that may accompany oral storytelling, the techniques of which are employed by American "minority" writers. Some of the texts I will examine fit well this comparison with ritual processes, especially works by Lochhead, Bourke, and Ní Dhuibhne which engage with folk and fairy-tale traditions in order to re-create their ethos from women's perspective. In Carr's plays, ritual is implied by her themes drawn from Greek myths and Ireland's own ritualised revival drama, ritualised in the sense of sharing the desiderate of socio-political change which it seeks to effect through reiterating conventionalised scenarios. By resignifying these scenarios, Carr's plays entice readers to rethink the value of social interaction and the boundaries within which myths confine women's subjectivities. As regards Kennedy, her texts are less concerned with ritual than with what it

---

[1] Clayton, 66.

means for someone to become caught up in a story's charm, and with what it means to have the authority to cast or break this spell. These writers' concerns justify their placing along with American writers such as Walker and Morrison, keeping in mind however that "minority", a term I disavow when applied to women's writing, but nevertheless use temporarily for the sake of the argument, would have very different connotations if applied to Scottish and Irish white women.

But perhaps the most apt description of what the texts analysed in this study do can be offered using Angela Carter's words: each of these texts offers from different angles an "investigation of the social fictions that regulate our lives."[2] In my analysis I regard these social fictions as being derived from a network of discourses that include the literary tradition as well as folk and fairy tales as vehicle of myths, but also discourses that mythologize such as discourses about science, or discourses that found disciplines, such as psychoanalysis.

In the first chapter I examine two texts by A. L. Kennedy. Kennedy's concerns about the power of voice are explored in her novel *Everything You Need*. The novel is an account of the initiation of a writer's daughter as a writer. The narrator focuses on her relationship to the kind of power words wield. The power of words to shape identity has been a constant preoccupation in feminist thought. While noting that Kennedy does not describe herself as a feminist, one also notes how fittingly her vision of the relationship between words and authority in *Everything You Need* answers feminist concerns such as those expressed by Adrienne Rich. Rich believes that

> words *can* help us move or keep us paralysed, and that our choices of language and verbal tone have something—a great deal—to do with how we live our lives and whom we end up speaking with and hearing; and that we can deflect words, by trivialisation, of course, but also by ritualised respect, or we can let them enter our souls and mix with the juices of our minds.[3]

My analysis of *Everything You Need* as a text that works to swerve the power of words focuses on Kennedy's vision that voices do not belong to anyone, but they are vehicles of others' voices from the past or from around us. Thus, we are steered in our narrations of ourselves by these

---

[2] Angela Carter, "Notes from the Front Line", *Shaking a Leg: Collected Journalism and Writings* (London: Vintage, 1998), 36-43, 38.

[3] Adrienne Rich, "Toward a More Feminist Criticism", *Gender*, ed. Anna Tripp (Houndmills: Palgrave, 2000), 42-50, 45, original italics.

voices. The ways in which stories steer individuals to act in the social reality are explored in Kennedy's novella "Original Bliss" from the collection with the same title, which reflects on the role of fantasy in the relationship between narrative, identity, and reality. Based on this novella, I will develop further the concepts of voice and authority examined through the analysis of *Everything You Need*.

The following three chapters focus on Liz Lochhead's work, extending the analysis of the relationship between storytelling voices and various narrative traditions to include fairy tales, classical myths, and modern day myths. In his analysis of the oral and the feminist properties of Lochhead's work, Robert Crawford points out that Lochhead's verse can be fruitfully contextualised with Liz Yorke's assessment of subversive strategies in contemporary women's poetry:

> *Anywhere that experience, memory, fantasy or dream can be retrieved, whether in words or images, it may be revalued, and re-presented. This effort of retrieval may permit different textures, colours, aspects, lights and shadings to be heard, seen and felt: such feminist transvaluation is a continual re-processing.*[4]

My analysis of Lochhead's texts will focus on her reprocessing of elements of male-generated cultural memory and realms of fantasy, which I regard as also a process of repossessing tradition. I begin by comparing Eavan Boland's "The Pomegranate" and Liz Lochhead's "Lucy's Diary", and their relationship to the story of Persephone as rendered in Classical Greek culture.[5] This analysis allows us to explore how the Persephone myth defines social roles of women as wives and lovers through scripting rituals of erotic encounters in terms of enchantment, abduction, and temptation. The next chapter follows up with an analysis of Liz Lochhead's full-length reinterpretation of Bram Stoker's *Dracula* (1897).[6] Highlighting the polyphony of Stoker's narrative, I nevertheless conclude that his gentlemen of spirit and taste are members of a brotherhood elite whose identity is constituted through envisioning relationships in which

---

[4] Liz Yorke, *Impertinent Voices: Subversive Strategies in Contemporary Women's Poetry* (London: Routledge, 1991), 23. Cited in Robert Crawford, "The Two-faced Language of Lochhead's Poetry", *Liz Lochhead's Voices*, eds. Robert Crawford and Anne Varty (Edinburgh: Edinburgh University Press, 1993), 57-74, 62, original italics.

[5] Eavan Boland, "The Pomegranate", *In a Time of Violence* (Manchester: Carcanet, 1994), 20-21.

[6] Bram Stoker, *Dracula*, eds. Nina Auerbach and David Skal (New York: Norton, 1997).

they govern nature, the passions of the body and thus the passions of women, and, by metaphorical extension, the passions of the body politic. Lochhead uses Stoker's text to create an intertext which foregrounds women's voices excluded by his story, investigating the possibilities of using Dracula's myth to envision a social space wherein women circulate alternative stories about bodies and feminine sexuality. In the next chapter I examine poems from Lochhead's collection *The Grimm Sisters* (1981), which challenges the ways in which the Grimms' fairy tales construct women's identities. The poems create an awareness of stories as tools for challenging the sense of social interrelationships established in masculine gender regimes. Lochhead's storytellers reconstruct the realms of fairy-tale fantasy, proposing disjunctive stories that rematerialise empowering women's identities.

The following chapter is concerned with the treatment of the relationship between stories and social reality in Angela Bourke's writing. In her study of Bridget Cleary's case, Bourke shows that the fantasies associating women with nature in Irish folktales are correlated with a mythical geography in which holy wells, fairy raths, and burial mounds represent metaphorically points of access into the inner realms of the body of nature.[7] In this context, Bourke highlights the sinuous trajectories of abjection and idealisation of women, examining also their role in representations of the body politic, produced in the interaction between Irish rural culture and British metropolitan culture.

The next chapter is an examination of issues of embodiment and subjectivity in Éilís Ní Dhuibhne's novel *The Dancers Dancing* (1999). Ní Dhuibhne's novel focuses on the transformations, accompanied by negotiations of social imaginaries, through which young girls acquire cognitive maps of femininity and corresponding structures of emotional affects. The main character of the novel, Orla, reads her body as feminine through representing to herself its alliance with an ungovernable body of nature in ways that suggest possibilities of recuperating authority over her body and the social spaces it inhabits. Another chapter is concerned with Éilís Ní Dhuibhne's short stories. I examine Ní Dhuibhne's explorations of constructions of women's identities through figurations of their bodies' materiality on masculine terms. These stories deal with the imbrication of bodies' materiality with the materiality of social spaces, and with the social rituals through which the body is transubstantiated into the body-social.

---

[7] Bourke, *The Burning of Bridget Cleary*, 24.

The last two chapters focus on Marina Carr's plays. First, I examine Carr's plays *Low in the Dark* (1990), *The Mai* (1995), and *Portia Coughlan* (1996).[8] Carr's plays focus on the effects of myths enshrined in the Irish cultural canon in the realms of family and personal relationships. I will show that Carr's plays develop heteroglossic voices in order to reconstruct the myths with a view to steering social relationships in order to create new maps for social encounters and landscapes. Carr's plays too can be seen as rewritings of tradition and canonical myths and stories, even though her dialogue with the past is more emphatically marked by ontological questions about how subjectivity arises from the past and about the constitution of the subject through discourses from the past that haunt us in the present. In an essay that highlights Carr's concerns with what it means to be an authentic subject, Clare Wallace concludes that

> With regard to the plays especially since *The Mai*, the term 'authentic reproduction' though ripe with paradox seems particularly appropriate to the ways in which Carr draws upon different traditions and stereotypes. The replication of aspects of various dramatic traditions provides a legitimizing connection with moral values and dilemmas, which might be understood as inevitable and authentic. ... Within the plays, however, the duplicities of nostalgia are critically present and identity, amidst a plethora of fantasy and false memory, is structured by the failure to locate any ontological plenitude.[9]

These concerns with failure to attain ontological plenitude are explored in Carr's play *By the Bog of Cats...* (1998) which I examine in the last chapter of this study. The play depicts the characters' struggle to find a "home". This is also a struggle to settle ontological domains through competing definitions of "home", as ideas of belonging are rendered in superimposed discursive registers used to express tenuous intersections of mythic realities. If Lochhead's and Ní Dhuibhne's writings can be placed in context with Angela Carter's demystified and resignified myths, Carr's and Kennedy's texts compare better with works by the American authors Alice Walker and Toni Morrison. Bourke's study of the Cleary case belongs to a different kind of discourse, that of academia, and can be understood as developing the ethos these writers have legitimised as subject of academic enquiry.

---

[8] Marina Carr, *Low in the Dark*, *Plays One* (London: Faber, 1999), 1-99; *The Mai*, *Plays One*, 101-186; *Portia Coughlan*, *Plays One*, 187-255.

[9] Clare Wallace, "Authentic Reproductions: Marina Carr and the Inevitable", *The Theatre of Marina Carr: "before rules was made"*, eds. Cathy Leeney and Anna McMullan (Dublin: Carysfort, 2003), 43-64, 63-4.

My analyses of the selected texts show that they are concerned with the socialisation scenarios derived from narratives that may be actualised (i.e. transformed into acts) in women's performance of their bodily presence in social spaces. The texts undermine the prescriptive power of scenarios internalised through stories derived from social myths, through which social myths compel women's socialisation in ways that maintain the legitimacy of masculine gender regimes. Because of these features, these texts can be said to extend the revisionist work begun by other women writers, such as Angela Carter, Alice Walker, and Toni Morrison, who engage with the male-generated literary, philosophical, and humanist tradition.

My analysis will proceed in the order outlined above, beginning with Kennedy's work. This order follows that of the theoretical presentation in the first part of this study, beginning with a focus on fantasy and fantasising, then moving on to texts that explore more emphatically the relationship between narrative and subjectivity in reference to literary, mythological, socio-cultural, and political traditions. When reaching this stage I will focus more strongly on constructions of feminine bodies and of their inhabitability. The last chapters will examine more closely issues of the inhabitability of subjective identity. However, my analyses of these questions will not fit neatly into this order; various chapters will trigger analyses of these questions, which cannot be treated as strictly separated issues. It is the narratives' stronger emphasis on some of these issues rather than on the others that justifies this merely orientative separation.

CHAPTER FIVE

LIVING UP TO WRITING.
NARRATIVE VOICE AND FANTASISING
IN A. L. KENNEDY'S WRITING

In this chapter I focus on examples of Kennedy's writing that explore the relationship between narrative voice and authority, and the role of fantasy in this relationship. I will begin by examining Kennedy's novel *Everything You Need*, first published by Cape in 1999, because it offers a concept of narrative voice that is useful in analysing not only Kennedy's other texts, but generally texts preoccupied with defining narrating agency as a field of multiple, intersecting voices. In *Everything You Need* one's narrative voice is envisioned as inevitably accommodating others' voices that speak through it. This understanding of voice poses questions regarding manifestations of authority and control of narrating agency. Who else tells our story when we define our subjective identity through it? Similar questions, but with a focus on the power of fantasising through which the characters discipline one another, had been dealt with in Kennedy's preceding text, "Original Bliss". I will analyse passages from this novella in the second part of this chapter. I will argue that the two texts taken together offer a complete vision of the process whereby fantasies, inflected by disciplining discourses, become narratable, and condition the stories through which we acquire identity. In other words, identity is conditioned by the authority that filters into the language through which one narrates oneself to oneself in his/her fantasies.

This argument is important for the analyses of the following chapters, where the authority that filters into one's fantasies will be defined in relation to myths. But in this chapter, unlike in the chapters that follow, I will be less concerned with myth as a corpus of disciplinary narratives. This is because Kennedy's writing does not dwell on myth, but rather on the mythologizing effects of narrative. It allows us to explore how narrative may become a vehicle of myth, a vision that we will retain for the chapters that follow.

But having said that I note that references to mythological traditions that emphasise the power of words do come up in Kennedy's work, particularly in *Everything You Need*, although, as one reviewer put it, it is a "vaguely defined mystical tradition" that the main characters in this novel relate to.[1] I will comment on references to myth when they are relevant to the main argument: various fantasies coalesce in the voices that flow in the stories, legitimating the authority through which we steer ourselves and others in social interaction.

My Words Should Catch Your Words: Narrative Voice and Authority in A. L. Kennedy's *Everything You Need*

The plot of *Everything You Need* is developed from several intersecting stories. Although each character is devoted extensive space in this lengthy novel, the main story relates the stages of a young woman's becoming a writer, intertwined with the story relating her father's recuperation of creative power.

Mary Lamb becomes one of the seven writers on Foal Island, an island off the coast of Wales, where she is offered a writing fellowship when still a novice. There, she is mentored by Nathan. He is Mary's father, but for most of the novel he does not reveal this to Mary, who was a child at the time of Nathan's separation from his wife Maura, which also separated him from Mary. Nathan had not produced a literary novel for a long time, thriving instead, gracelessly, on genre fiction. Nathan's and Mary's story are intertwined, as they draw strength from each other in their efforts to find what the leader of the writers' guild on Foal Island, Joe, terms their own "piece of the Grail".[2]

Sarah Dunnigan notes that "*Everything You Need* explicitly uses the medieval romance metaphor of the Grail" to embody the specificity of "love's saving grace" "as rooted in a quest structure".[3] The references to the Grail myths in Kennedy's novel do not suggest a preoccupation with the disciplining effects of this particular corpus of myths, but rather an artful exploitation of its ethos. For Mary, the quest for her "piece of the Grail" is the adventure of becoming a writer. While Mary gets acquainted with the power of words, Nathan struggles with it like a Grail knight who

---

[1] Ron Charles, "No Man—or Writer—Is an Island", *Christian Science Monitor* 93, no. 164 (19 July 2001): 18-19, 18.
[2] Kennedy, *Everything You Need*, 449.
[3] Sarah Dunnigan, "A. L. Kennedy's Longer Fiction: Articulate Grace", *Contemporary Scottish Women Writers*, 144-55, 154.

fails to ask the question that heals.[4] The Grail question, "Whom does the Grail serve?", is rephrased in Kennedy's text by Joe as "Whom does the word serve?".[5] As is the fate of Grail knights, it is only when Nathan finds an answer to this question that he is healed of his graceless longing for redemption. In the process, Nathan understands that words should not be used to subject others, which is also what the novel seeks to reveal to its readers.

The reviews of *Everything You Need* show mixed responses to Kennedy's third novel. Val McDermid, reviewing for *Los Angeles Times*, notes that the novel "stretches the suspension of disbelief almost beyond the breaking point" but nevertheless praises it "as another distinctive monument in the landscape of contemporary Scottish writing", "truthful, surprising and visceral". McDermid also notes the novel's preoccupation with "the impossibility of escaping the vocation of words."[6] In the *New Statesman*, Toby Mundy notes the dreariness of the novel, complaining that "the unremitting scatology, the obsessions with pain, desperate sex, wounds and death bludgeon us, and become dull and dulling." The plausibility of the plot and the narrative construction of the story are also criticised: "More often than not, she leaves questions of motive open: thoughts and actions slip and slide into each other, while characters fumble

---

[4] In Chrètien de Troyes' *Conte du Graal*, the first known Grail story, Perceval is chided for not having asked who is served from the Grail. The story is unfinished and does not explain Perceval's perceived foolishness. Joseph Goering, summarising Wolfram von Eschenbach's *Parzival*, emphasises that the king Anfortas, who is served from the Grail, is cured of an illness that lasted for years when the knight asks what ails him. Chrètien de Troyes, *The Complete Romances of Chrètien de Troyes*, trans. David Stains (Bloomington: University of Indiana Press, 1990), ll. 6364-6433, 416-7; Joseph Goering, *The Virgin and the Grail: Origins of a Legend* (New Haven, CT: Yale University Press, 2005), 35.
[5] Kennedy, *Everything You Need*, 555. In his analysis of the origins of the Grail story Joseph Goering shows how the power of the Grail is connected with the power of words: "no surviving book containing 'Celtic marvels' or descriptions of a pagan or Christian ritual or relic" fits the source specifications given by Chrètien de Troyes in his *Conte du Graal*. Chrètien de Troyes claims that his romance tale is based on a book offered by Philip of Alsace, Count of Flanders, and does not clarify what the Grail is (he never uses a synonym for the word "graal"). The power of this enigma has haunted writers ever since, enticing them to fantasise histories and meanings of the Grail. In this sense, the power of the Grail stems entirely from the power of words. Goering, esp. 4-15.
[6] Val McDermid, "The Sorcerer's Apprentice", *Los Angeles Times* (26 August 2001): 5.

and flap at crucial moments."[7] Ron Charles too notices these shortcomings in his review for the *Christian Science Monitor*, but he believes that they are attributable, and to some extent justified by, Kennedy's "syncopated style that's perpetually surprising, mingling her own voice with the internal and spoken voices of her characters. (Even Nathan's big-hearted dog jumps into the mix now and then.)"[8] *The Spectator*'s Katie Grant criticises the novel for its unsubtle and excessive scenes of graphic sex, and for its inability to control the multitude of themes it approaches, of which "none is brought to completion."[9] In *Women's Review of Books*, Pamela Petro's praises are almost unreserved; she finds that the two main stories and the satellite stories are well integrated, with the latter helpful in defining the main characters.[10] On the contrary, Mona Knapp, writing for *World Literature Today*, again deplores Kennedy's use of profanity and the novel's implausible plot, while nevertheless conceding that "A. L. Kennedy wields a forceful pen. In syntactically sophisticated sentences that almost snap with emotional intensity, she weaves her characters' complex perceptions into riveting narration, commanding the reader's full attention."[11] As these reviews indicate, leaving aside the criticism of Kennedy's liberal use of language and plot construction, the novel evinces a preoccupation with intersecting and competing narrative planes and stories. It is this intersection of voices melting into each other or running in parallel streams that concerns me here, and not so much the question of whether or not these voices and the stories they tell are sufficiently tightened in a balanced narrative structure. Perhaps the narrative itself is an effort of making sense of the writer's own insecurities at a crucial point in her career, as a narrated interview by Yvonne Nolan suggests, and therefore its importance lies more in its sense-making effort than in the plausibility of the events it relates.[12]

That the novel reflects a need for using narrative to order the reality of experience is noted in Mundy's review as a point of general human

---

[7] Toby Mundy, "Novel of the Week", *New Statesman* 128, no. 4437 (24 May 1999): 49.

[8] Ron Charles, 19.

[9] Katie Grant, "More Four-Letter Words Than You Need", *Spectator* 282, no. 8912 (29 May 1999): 40-1, 41.

[10] Pamela Petro, "School of Wales", *Women's Review of Books* 18, nos. 10-11 (July 2001): 30.

[11] Mona Knapp, Review of *Everything You Need*, by A. L. Kennedy, *World Literature Today* 76, no. 2 (spring 2002): 151.

[12] A. L. Kennedy and Yvonne Nolan, "A Dream Not Her Own", *Publishers Weekly* 248, no. 30 (23 July 2001): 43, 46.

interest: "Kennedy is terrifyingly alive to the human need to make sense of the recalcitrant world, and to the fallacies, sops and delusions that fleetingly transform chaos into order."[13] In my analysis, I will explore Kennedy's narrators' vision of how this need is satisfied through using the ordering power of narrative. Nolan points out that the novel is almost a "how to do" guide for the creative writing process. Charles also wrote in his review that "as a story about a life of words, *Everything You Need* is literally everything you need."[14] Indeed, Kennedy's novel engages in manifold ways with questions of what it means to tell a story, although it may be difficult sometimes to distinguish whose story is told by whom: various myths are invoked throughout the novel in reference to the power of storytelling by characters who themselves may be associated with the myths' characters, the past is shown as taking off from the experience of the present, and one's voice is home to voices come from the past that may speak against one's will. However, I will argue that *Everything You Need* contains the clearest presentation of Kennedy's concept of narrative voice and of the effects of its power. It is this concept that is of interest for the overall argument of this book, and it is what we need to take forward as a basis for the analyses of the following chapters.

When Sarah Dunnigan argues that "the complex, haunting constellations of memory … are a constant theme in Kennedy's work", she illustrates her argument with a quotation from *Everything You Need*: memories haunt as ghosts "with a time past restoring."[15] In my analysis I connect this haunting with the authority one exercises through discourse. The ghost referred to in the above passage is a Nathan-created Maura, the ghost of his estranged wife. Her ghostliness is due to the fact that for Nathan, who does not realise it at first, she is also a kind of mythological creature that he has fantasised and to whom he has given identity through writing. But Maura herself rejected the identity scenarios Nathan created for her, which is to say that she refused to be disciplined by the discourses (Nathan's writing) that convey these scenarios. Maura refused to be subjected to Nathan's fantasies, because she realised that her realness to him was an effect of acts of narrating. To clothe herself in that realness would have meant, for Maura, to change *her* reality, i.e. the identity which she designed for herself. This subplot of *Everything You Need* allows us to organise the analysis around the main issues it deals with: the issue of what haunts one's voice, and the issue of how one's voice affects the

---

[13] Mundy, 49.
[14] Ron Charles, 19.
[15] Dunnigan, 145; Kennedy, *Everything You Need*, 5.

social reality of human interaction and relationships. In the following, I will examine each of these issues in turn, beginning with the former.

In *Everything You Need*, the ability to create or change reality using words is shown as an integral part and defining characteristic of what it is to be human. As Nathan puts it,

> **we've** lost the way it should be. You know the Aztecs thought paper was sacred? *Amatl*—it was an offering for the gods. And in ancient Egypt, the word was the deed, it was powerful in itself. The naming of life, it's in the Bible, it was man's first duty. All this was ours and we lost it. The life we lived in ourselves, the power of that, the way we made it speak, it was taken away. … But *real* fantasy, *real* fiction—the kind with power, the kind we're born with, that's our right—we're not supposed to want that anymore—we have to be helped with our minds, we have to be prevented from letting them go too far.[16]

The passage suggests that the power implied in voicing stories should be reclaimed by individual people. Kennedy's novel, to put it all too simply, tells the story of such reclamations. However, each individual's way of reclaiming word power is different as this power is slippery and can easily become ungovernable: it is also wielded by those whom our stories cannot avoid evoking. Joe defines this power thus:

> our words are for the dead, all of the dead: the dead who made us and the dead we loved; the dead moments passed from time; the dead passions spent; and all of the dead possibilities, the things that never were. We make them live and speak, we have that privilege.[17]

Mary learns throughout her seven years fellowship, together with her father and mentor, that words can help one think the world into being, rather than helping them to own the world; that is, stories shouldn't be used to subject reality and people, but to add to reality the voices that speak in one's voice, to bring the dead to life.

From the very beginning of her training, Mary Lamb is concerned with how writing can be used to add to reality, rather than to subject it. Soon after her arrival on Foal Island, Mary gains a vision of what the purpose of writing might be:

---

[16] Kennedy, *Everything You Need*, 274, original italics and bold. The words in bold indicate Nathan's realisation that not only he, but all of us have lost "the way it should be". He had begun by saying "I've lost" but corrects himself.

[17] Kennedy, *Everything You Need*, 555.

> She had begun to make meanings and patterns and sequences that she
> liked, that she wanted to give to the people she cared about. She wanted to
> speak out loud but inside other people: inside, the loudest place of all.[18]

Thus, Mary is not only interested in creating texts. She wishes her voice to
become part of a dialogical exchange whereby she may occur "inside other
people", whereby she may inhabit their reality. The embodied self is seen
as a forum, a chamber where intersecting voices offer multiple "meanings
and patterns and sequences". Mary's reflections suggest her early intuition
that the voice in which we express ourselves could also be intertwined
with others' voices.

A similar understanding of voice is expressed by other characters at
various points in the story of *Everything You Need*.[19] It also comes up in
other texts by Kennedy. One of Kennedy's beliefs seems to be that in the
absence of others' voices one is truly lonely, as is the case with Jennifer,
the main character of an earlier novel, *So I am Glad*, first published by
Cape in 1995.[20] Dunnigan notes Jennifer's "sense of herself as a *tabula
rasa*, a blank sheet of canvas on which to be written", when Jennifer
confesses that "I can dig down as deep as there is to dig inside me and
truly there is nothing there, not a squeak."[21] Jennifer only acquires a viable
social self through her (imagined?) dialogues with a miraculously
embodied Cyrano de Bergerac. In *Everything You Need* Nathan and Mary
too can only become "whole" through each other's stories that they spin
together. The novel endorses a vision of the role of the writer as someone
who works with the awareness of the fact that the position of telling
inscribed in discourse cannot be owned solely by the storyteller, but it is
created also through citations of stories that have ceased to be an author's
own.

Having introduced the topic of how the novel envisions the
relationship between stories and inner reality through a concept of voice
that implies the acceptance of heteroglossia, of the possibility that others'
voices speak through one's voice, I will now explore how the novel
envisions the relationship between voice and the outer, social reality. A
few comments on Kennedy's short story "The Role of Notable Silences in
Scottish History", first published in *Bête Noir* 8/9, republished in the
collection *Night Geometry and the Garscadden Trains*, may serve as a

---

[18] Ibid., 110.

[19] See for instance Kennedy, *Everything You Need*, 88, 295.

[20] My references are to the Vintage edition: A. L. Kennedy, *So I am Glad* (London:
Vintage, 1996).

[21] Dunnigan, 147. Kennedy, *So I am Glad*, 7.

suitable introduction to my readings.[22] The story contains Kennedy's clearest affirmation of the conviction that social reality is constructed through stories. Susanne Hagemann analyses this story in order to show that it evinces faith in the belief that "existence" "is textual", even though "significantly, textuality does not imply truth." As Hagemann indicates, for the narrator of this story "what matters is the text, which produces reality—in so far as reality can be said to exist at all". Hagemann underlines the narrator's vision that "the stories, once written, can be rewritten at will" and that "no aspect of any text can be regarded as permanent", which is why "identity, basically consists in nothing but the ability to 'make up your past as you go along'."[23]

A similar vision is expressed in less derogatory terms in *Everything You Need*, for instance when Nathan shows his conviction that

> writing is like wishing. … [W]hat you choose to write about will come and seek you out. What chooses your fiction can choose your reality, too. … Quickly or slowly, coincidences will happen: faces, phrases, tricks of speech, foreign cities, accidents—you'll see what you dreamed, what you thought out of nothing, what you wrote.[24]

The passage suggests that what one fantasises, "dreams out of nothing", ends up organising the reality one inhabits, governing one's awareness of reality. We note that the unspecified agency of the power that chooses one's fiction and reality reinforces the idea expressed throughout the novel that one is never the sole owner of the stories through which s/he gets acquainted with the world, even though one chooses to write those stories.

Throughout the text, Nathan is given a prominent role as capable wielder of word power. However, he often uses the words' power for myth-making in ways that affect the reality of social relationships. Nathan is the writer who in the social realm acts, however unconsciously, as creator of worlds in a God-like manner. His way of writing reality affects adversely the women in his life, and indeed himself. Dunnigan observes, in relation to Nathan's suicide attempts and Lynda's morbid psycho-sexual

---

[22] The first edition of the collection was published by Polygon in 1990. I refer to the 1993 Phoenix edition: A. L. Kennedy, "The Role of Notable Silences in Scottish History", *Night Geometry and the Garscadden Trains* (London: Phoenix, 1993), 62-72.

[23] Susanne Hagemann, "Women and Nation", *A History of Scottish Women's Writing*, eds. Douglas Gifford and Dorothy McMillan (Edinburgh: Edinburgh University Press, 1997), 316-28, 325-6. Kennedy, "The Role of Notable Silences", 64.

[24] Kennedy, *Everything You Need*, 162.

tendencies (she is another writer of the guild), that the novel "draws correspondences between writing and mutilation, a creative act which can also be self-destructive."[25] In my reading, the idea that writing can be self-destructive is connected with the authority gained through stories designed to subject others. This connection is explored in *Everything You Need* through the relationship that ties Nathan to his wife Maura and to his daughter Mary.

Nathan is at first shown as someone who uses this authority to subject his wife and his daughter. In the first chapters of the book he is writing, Maura and Mary are represented through the landmarks of a psycho-mythological territory. Nathan's first account of Mary as a child occurs in a chapter entitled '*New Found Land*'.[26] There she is understood as a landscape Nathan surveys:

> She'd uncovered herself, my daughter, and was sprawled, expansive and relaxed, out for any count, for any spark. I ... sat on the floor by her head, watching ... the rush of different lights across her.[27]

Nathan's daughter is shown as an otherworldly realm, a "sprawled", "expansive" landscape across which "rush" "different lights". Maura witnesses Nathan's contemplative stance and understands his subjection of Mary. She indicts it: "*you're always feeding off people. Always taking notes. You make me tired.*"[28] Rejected by Maura, Nathan symbolically leaves "Maura's land", wherein he was no longer "known", for "Mary's land", and crosses from an envisioned otherworld into another:

> Sleep caught me on the brink of morning and I dreamed of somersaulting into skies filled with raging shadow and twisting light. And I landed, chill and giddy, in an unforgiving country where I was not known. Then my daughter woke me, crying, and I went to her.[29]

Maura is imagined as an "unforgiving country" and her child, Mary, as an alternative realm Nathan could master through using the signifying power of words.

Other Nathan-authored representations of Maura contribute to rendering her an almost mythical goddess. Nathan recounts their togetherness as

---

[25] Dunnigan, 149.

[26] Kennedy, *Everything You Need*, 63, original italics, underline, and font.

[27] Ibid., 71, original italics and font.

[28] Ibid., 72, original italics and font.

[29] Ibid.

otherworldly, again mystically each other's, in a "subtly alien" reality: "*I could just feel her there, shining into me ... . Two Celts together, wanting to be together, on a subtly, subtly alien train.*"[30] Maura's inaccessibility is frequently hinted at ("the weight of the unobtainable rushed in at him from every side—Maura, completely wanted and completely out of reach"[31]) and most expressively in the following rendition of Nathan's thoughts: "His own imagination was performing a type of well-informed rape: penetrating him painstakingly with a ghost, with a time past restoring, an unreachable skin."[32] The Maura Nathan remembers is a "ghost" that inhabits a mythical time "past restoring": an unreachable way of being in one's flesh that ambivalently sanctions both Maura's ever receding physicality and Nathan's own possibility of physically existing in the myth about Maura that he has created. The landscape of myth and the landscape of social reality remain separated in Nathan's mind, although this separation clearly affects Maura's social identity. For him, the landscape of myth is a realm of the sacred, only accessible through the power of a writer's words to trigger epiphanic revelation. But for the real Maura, the Maura of social reality, this realm is inaccessible because in the realm of myth she is ghostly, refined out of existence through Nathan's myth-making.[33]

Nathan will eventually transcend his addiction to word power, a process that culminates with his visit to Maura in London, many years after they broke apart: he finds out that she has started a new life with someone else. Nathan's goddess is clearly demystified as the otherworldly Maura finally appears to be just a worldly woman. Yet this is a woman who had the power to leave an unsatisfying relationship and regenerate her social life on her own terms. Maura refuses to play the part of mythical inspirer of poets that Nathan assigns her in his idealisations. While disempowered as a mythical goddess and muse, she is empowered as a real woman, as an individual who inhabits a recognisable social space and not a transcendental space of myth disconnected from the social reality of individual needs for recognition and personal fulfilment.

The vision of the relationship between narrative and reality proposed in *Everything You Need* regards narrative as an important means of organising reality and of finding one's place in it. Mary Lamb and Nathan

---

[30] Ibid., 116, original italics and bold.

[31] Ibid., 119.

[32] Ibid., 5.

[33] The distinction between the realm of myth and of social reality is developed through the distinction between the sacred and the profane in Eliade's *The Sacred and the Profane*.

Staples both realise that setting forth stories moulds not only their own subjective identity but also that of those with whom they interact and who are figured in one's fantasising identity. This is especially clear in Nathan's construction of reality as a psycho-mythological territory wherein Mary and Maura are assigned identities they will disavow. The novel instructs writers and readers to beware of such mythologizing that silences others' voices rather than adding them to reality by recognising their legitimacy.

This places Kennedy's novel in context with literary works that, as Clayton puts it, make "explicit claims about the power of narrative".[34] Throughout Kennedy's novel, words are trusted with the power "to let *Life* speak", as Nathan emphasises, although not knowing at that point what this means in relation to Mary and Maura.[35] Indeed, he literally brings Joe's daughter to life through word power. Having just rescued her from drowning, Joe and Nathan attempt to resuscitate Sophie's body back to life. While Joe performs the CPR basic steps, Nathan continually speaks to her. He tells her:

'My father and my mother uttered my name, and they hid it in my body when I was born, so that none of those who would use against me words of power might succeed in making enchantments to have dominion over me,' which was Egyptian, but he couldn't think what, and   that was when she moved her head and coughed.[36]

Nathan's speaking to a seemingly dead body leads to his fulfilling the myth of the story he tells: he "hides" his words in Sophie's body so that she can be born again. By restoring word power to Sophie, he brings her back into being: the being through a story, or rather, the being through the flux of words that animate her consciousness, a flux not necessarily her own, but passing through her and reconnecting her to a community of people and to the traditions they use to represent themselves to themselves and to others.[37] The passage relating Sophie's reanimation through using the power of words entices us to read *Everything You Need* as condoning the role of narrative theorised through the concept of "surfiction".

---

[34] Clayton, 58. See also Marcel Cornis-Pope, "Narrative Innovation and Cultural Rewriting: The Pynchon-Morrison-Sukenick Connection", *Narrative and Culture*, 216-37, 225.

[35] Kennedy, *Everything You Need*, 138, original italics.

[36] Ibid., 461, original editing.

[37] Dunnigan interprets the passage as a "fable of loss and restoration" that is metaphorically related to the main narrative "of daughter-father love which refuses silence." Dunnigan, 151.

Surfiction is fiction that "[r]ather than serving as a mirror or redoubling on itself, [it] adds itself to the world, creating a meaningful 'reality' that did not previously exist. Fiction is artifice but not artificial."[38] In this context, *Everything You Need* can be read on the one hand as a text that reflects on the power words have to add fictional worlds to the world of reality, thereby changing the latter meaningfully. On the other hand, the text can be seen as adding itself to the reality which readers inhabit in ways that make them reflect on the meanings that emerge through this addition. The passage relating Sophie's bringing back to life is but one instance through which readers are called upon to ponder whom the stories serve. Elsewhere such calls for reflection are made in a more straightforward manner, for instance when Nathan says:

> Anyone can steal words, forget them, remould them, deny them, but their shadow and the way to make them is still here, a part of me. ... I like to recall, now and then, that language belongs to me, to the individual, to each and every individual—that everyone who tries to *own* it is trying to own *me*.[39]

However, there are elements in the construction of the novel that warn against the dangers of claiming too much word power. Nathan's position is initially self-centred: his statement does not indict *his* attempt to possess other people's language, to appropriate their own versions of their stories—the means through which they present themselves to themselves and to others,—thus appropriating their identities. As Maura explains to Mary, it was precisely because she had become a "real fantasy" that she had to leave Nathan:

> And then there was that whole thing of being the professional man's wife. Not myself. I lost my name. ... As if I was someone that he was imagining. ... The things he *loved* had to be his, absolutely his. ... It can feel very good to be wanted so much. Feeling *owned*, that's different. That stops you being a person anymore. ... Have you ever made love to a man and been absolutely sure he wasn't thinking of you? Better than that, have you been completely certain that he was comparing you to a woman who didn't

---

[38] Sukenick quoted in Cornis-Pope, 225. See also Ronald Sukenick, *In Form: Digressions on the Act of Fiction* (Carbondale: Southern Illinois University Press, 1985), 31-2; Raymond Federman, "Surfiction—Four Propositions in Form of an Introduction" in *Surfiction: Fiction Now...and Tomorrow*, ed. Raymond Federman (Chicago: Swallow, 1975), 5-15.

[39] Kennedy, *Everything You Need*, 294-5, original italics.

exist, a woman he'd made to please himself, a woman he spent every day with?[40]

Maura left because she refused to fulfil the fantasy roles Nathan assigned her, however real that made her to him. Nathan's possibilities of redemption imply the understanding that the hold words have on reality cannot be used to possess it. As Mary put it, inside is "the loudest place of all" where other voices speak too, and they must be listened to.[41]

Nathan's "piece of the Grail" is a mythic Maura, yet he eventually understands that he cannot replace reality with the dominion of words. This leads to the seventh rule he lays down for the writer Mary:

> Here's one last rule for you: Rule Seven. I think that I have tried to follow it and not done well, but I do still believe this to be the most useful and beautiful Rule of all, the one that is most true: *do it for love*.[42]

It is love that fuels, as Dunnigan put it, Nathan's desire "to change the narrative, 'his story', to efface its pain by the wilful act of 'editing out' or resorting to fictive inventiveness".[43] The love that inspires Mary's writing is also presented as a force that should hold sway over the reality storytellers set forth through their stories. Mary is able to speak "inching her words forward, picking them to carry tenderness and weight" and works "to build a proper fabric of sense, to set out love."[44] In relation to the novel as a whole we may understand Nathan's seventh rule as also implying caring for the voices that speak through one's voice.

In her review of *Everything You Need*, Mona Knapp compares the novel with the earlier novella "Original Bliss", arguing that both devote their narrative focus "to an eccentric, often patently dislikable protagonist in the throes of self-abasement."[45] Knapp refers to the male protagonists of the two texts. Indeed, it is through their relationships with the central women characters that the texts explore questions of authority and of the force of narrative to affect the material reality. Both texts begin with the male characters holding sway over the women's realms of imagination. But by the end of these stories Mary and Maura in *Everything You Need* and Helen Brindle in "Original Bliss" will have recuperated the power to

---

[40] Ibid., 332-7, original italics.
[41] Ibid., 110.
[42] Ibid., 567, original italics and font.
[43] Dunnigan, 149. See also 150.
[44] Kennedy, *Everything You Need*, 37.
[45] Knapp, 151.

govern imagination and fantasy manifested through one's voice. Whereas in *Everything You Need* the emphasis is on the act of narrating, in "Original Bliss" it is on the act of fantasising. As I have argued in the first part of the book, narrating and fantasising are stages of the process whereby one acquires identity through discourse. I will then turn to "Original Bliss" in order to complete my analysis of this process as it is conceived in Kennedy's writing. This analysis will help us in the chapters that follow, which focus on the discourses through which one acquires identity as discourses derived from, and in turn establishing, myths.

Narrative, Fantasy, and Reality in A.L. Kennedy's "Original Bliss"

Dream not of other worlds, what creatures there
Live, in what state, condition or degree,
Contented that thus far hath been revealed
Not of earth only but of highest heaven.
—John Milton, *Paradise Lost* VIII, ll. 175-8[46]

The analysis of Kennedy's "Original Bliss" allows us to integrate the concepts of fantasising and of voice dealt with in the previous section, while also allowing us to consider their implications further. The authority that permeates the realms of fantasising and of one's voice produces effects in the social reality because it affects the constitution of one's social persona. I will explore how such constitutive acts are treated in "Original Bliss".

"Original Bliss" was published both as a novel and as the lengthiest piece of a collection of short stories bearing its title.[47] Teresa Waugh, reviewing the collection, finds a "haunting, tantalising strangeness" "in almost all the stories which are generally concerned with love, sex, desire, attaining and not attaining." Waugh argues that of all the stories, "Original Bliss" offers the most insightful treatment of these themes and characterises the novella as "violent, disgusting, perverted, creepy, frightening, funny, extraordinarily romantic and touchingly optimistic."[48] In her *New Statesman* review, Amanda Craig finds that Kennedy "conforms to the female canon

---

[46] John Milton, *Paradise Lost*, ed. Alastair Fowler (London: Longman, 1998), 439.

[47] A. L. Kennedy, *Original Bliss* (New York: Knopf, 1999); A. L. Kennedy, *Original Bliss* (London: Jonathan Cape, 1997). I am using the Vintage edition published in 1998.

[48] Teresa Waugh, "This Small Masterpiece", *Spectator* 278, no. 8790 (18 January 1997): 35-6.

in writing exclusively about love and sex" and praises the novella "Original Bliss" as worthy of Jane Gardam or Francis King, and as effective in constructing a female fiction canon as Jeanette Winterson's writing.[49] Eamonn Wall, writing for the *Review of Contemporary Fiction*, notes that "Original Bliss" focuses on the relationships through which the characters discipline one another. He compares the novella with Barbara Pym's and Roddy Doyle's writing, and concludes that "in the end we are left with a finely rounded portrait of both the abusers and the abused with light cast on the forces that drive and manipulate human beings".[50] The question of manipulation, raised by these reviewers, through the deployment of fantasies derived from religious and pornography discourses in social interaction and the attempt to turn them into reality, will be a central concern in this section. In "Original Bliss", as in *Everything You Need*, there is a strong emphasis on the mythologizing effects of words, although here it is fantasising that is the main concern. In terms of the overall preoccupation with myth in my study, the analysis of the novella will help us to understand how telling a story affects the tellers and their collocutors by affecting how they fantasise themselves, thus providing useful insight for the analysis, in the following chapters, of narratives that convey myths and their power.

Kennedy's novella tells the story of a married woman, Mrs Brindle, who has lost her religious faith and thus the will to live. She finds love outside marriage, but her affair with a famous professor soon becomes "a monumental slew of moral and emotional dilemmas" that leads to complex re-evaluations of Mrs Brindle's body, sexuality, and religious faith.[51] Exploring these, I want to argue that Helen Brindle's story is an investigation of her subjection through various discourses and practices deriving, however deviously, from the myth of Adam and Eve. Throughout Western cultural history, re-creations and literary treatments of the myth have triggered discussion on how it affects social actors. Milton's *Paradise Lost* (first printed in 1667) is an illustrative example, and I will explore the relevance of Milton's text with reference to the diachronic dimension of the myth's manifestation. However, my main focus will be on how Kennedy's novella offers new angles for examining the contemporary performativity of the myth of Adam and Eve by

---

[49] Amanda Craig, "Passion & Physics", *New Statesman* 10, no. 435 (10 January 1997): 47.

[50] Eamonn Wall, Review of *Original Bliss*, by A. L. Kennedy, *Review of Contemporary Fiction* 19, no. 3 (fall 1999): 161.

[51] Kennedy, "Original Bliss", 154.

exploring its culturally synchronic interweaving with popular understandings of Biblical discourses and pornography.

At narrative level, the synchronic dimension of the myth is that of its realisation as text through which one may choose to signify oneself. Enabled by signification and powered by imagination and fantasy, the existence of a two-way traffic between material and fictional realities raises questions regarding "the materiality of texts and the relations between this materiality and the materiality that comprises subjects", to borrow Elizabeth Grosz's words.[52] "Original Bliss" explores the relations between bodies and words in order to understand the material effects of fantasising. It explores the significance of its characters' fantasising social personae for themselves and for those with whom they come in contact, and how fantasising affects the central protagonist's bearing in the social world by affecting how she perceives and expresses the materiality of her body and its desires. While much has been written about female bodies as text in critical analyses and literary works, Kennedy's novella offers a fresh treatment of this concept by focusing on fantasising as a process that mediates passage between the worlds of discourse and material/ social reality. "Original Bliss" shows how Mrs Brindle finds liberation by performing herself in the way of others' oppressive fantasies of feminine identity derived from the Judeo-Christian tradition, from norms of women's social role, and pornography. The novella shows how these fantasies melt into the vessel of Mrs Brindle's body, stirring in the body's physicality. As a result, Mrs Brindle, who had avoided dealing with her body's sensuality for much of her life, re-creates her Judeo-Christian religion in physical terms in ways that accommodate both sensuality and spirituality. Her trials recall the use of Eve's figure in the Western tradition to decant physicality and faith in order to repudiate the former (Milton's Eve is a case in point). Kennedy's novella shows how Mrs Brindle regains her faith precisely by recuperating her body's physicality, on her own terms, enticing us to reflect on possibilities of defining an alternative ethos of the Biblical Eve.

In "Original Bliss", Helen Brindle's body is shown as a site of two different masculine projections: one claims it through the promise of women's appropriation carried in Biblical discourse, the other envisions it as an automaton for practicing sex. The title of the novella is of course a pun on the phrase "original sin". Helen's husband abuses her systematically as punishment for what he perceives as her devious religious ecstasy: although an atheist himself, his abuse can be seen as

---

[52] Grosz, "Sexual Signatures", 11.

perpetrated through social power lines grounded in the Judeo-Christian tradition. On the other hand, Helen becomes involved with a famous scientist in an erotic partnership outside marriage. At first, because of his addiction to pornography, Professor Gluck regards Helen's body as sex object. His voyeurism suggests an Adam pleased to see not only Eve's nakedness but also her repeated re-enactment of Eden's corruption through sexual lust. This, and her own continuous reliance on Christian religious faith for empowerment, position Mrs Brindle as actor at the intersection of sinuous divergences and convergences of stories of the sinning woman.

As Eamonn Wall observed in his review, Kennedy "examines not only the surfaces of addiction—to violence, denial, and pornography—but also the mangled roots which allow these to grow."[53] The oppressive male characters of husband and lover claim the power of myths over women's submissiveness as channelled by the Christian tradition, and by pornography respectively, to subject Mrs Brindle. Her subjection through these strangely converging cultural constructions of women allows the narrator to explore the socialisation of the sinful body as the effect of heterogeneous discourses and practices that mark Mrs Brindle as sinner. The choice of Mrs Brindle's name reflects this concern. The word "brindle" refers to distinctive marking on skin. Mrs Brindle's husband and her lover require that she bears the marks of submissive femininity on the surface of her body and in the postures and styles of its presentation.

The degree of Mrs Brindle's sexual and emotional submission to her husband can be measured by her bruises after he beats her and is visible in the presence of her body as available for sex or domestic labour; his construction of Mrs Brindle's identity reflects that of an Eve that requires punishment for her sin. For Gluck, the degree to which Mrs Brindle impersonates the woman he wants can be measured by the extent to which she displays her nakedness in the same way as the women subjects of pornographic material; his construction of Mrs Brindle's identity reflects that of an Eve defined by her sexual appetite. However, the narrator of "Original Bliss" does not allow us to claim that Mrs Brindle's identity as sinning woman is simply the result of patriarchal machinations. Mrs Brindle herself intuits her body's sexuality as a kind of illegitimate but desired ecstasy, a "desirable" sin, and, fearing the implications, tries to accept the role of submissive wife in an attempt to rationalise that intuition. Again, the choice of her name mars any attempt to construct Mrs Brindle as some kind of pure sacrificial victim, suggesting the mixedness of her identity. Eventually, Mrs Brindle will use the very requirement of

---

[53] Wall, 161.

wearing visible marks of imposed femininity to challenge her husband's fantasies, to transform those of her lover, and, by testing God's patience, to regain not only spiritual, but also sensual bliss.

Thus, Kennedy's narrator is concerned with how the "original sin" becomes, through various ways of fantasising it, a marker of the female body. I understand this process of fantasising in the sense suggested by Judith Butler where she challenges psychoanalytic definitions of identity as formed through internalisations. According to Butler, "it is not possible to attribute some kind of ontological meaning to the spatial internality of internalizations, for they are only fantasied as internal" in a language of psychoanalysis "that regularly figures interior psychic locations of various kinds, a language, in other words, that not only produces that fantasy but then redescribes that figuration within an uncritically accepted topographical discourse."[54] In Butler's theorisation, psychoanalysis presupposes the existence of an interior space that is ontologically meaningless, unless one also presupposes that this space is itself a fantasy amenable to cultural norms, such as those within which psychoanalysis operates. For Butler, the fantasy of interiority is derived from psychoanalytic discourse, but psychoanalysis does not reflect on its role in the production of these figurations through the disciplinary norms in which it operates; it rather accepts uncritically the topography it has created. Butler's analysis allows us to perceive how interior psychic spaces only exist as fantasies of domains of the self. These realms are projective spaces where one idealises an image of oneself and of one's relationship to others, and then recognises this image as "the self" without questioning the norms that have produced the makeup of that "I". In Butler's words, one may find a figure of the "I" without being aware that the fantasies that figure this "I", its interiority, "are themselves disciplinary productions of grounding cultural sanctions and taboos ... ."[55]

In this sense, in "Original Bliss" both Professor Gluck and Mr Brindle are shown to fantasise locales where they can imagine Mrs Brindle's body as lustfully ecstatic (sinning Eve) and submissively non-ecstatic (corrected lustful Eve) respectively. In these locales, to apply Butler's words, "the corporeal styles that constitute bodily significations" attributed to Mrs Brindle define her as woman whose role is to please men sexually and to be a submissive wife respectively.[56] Mrs Brindle becomes acquainted with these fantasies through interacting with the two men, and, recognising

---

[54] Butler, "Gender Trouble", 333.
[55] Ibid., 334.
[56] Ibid.

herself in these fantasies, must negotiate her identity through inhabiting the subject positions these fantasies construct.

Thus, when Mrs Brindle, having deserted her husband to live with Gluck, decides to return to Mr Brindle, "[s]he had come here to submit and Mr Brindle would do God's will to her, even though he was an atheist."[57] God's will, however, may be such will as Mr Brindle recollects from myths of marriage developed from the Judeo-Christian fabula in his social circle, although he doesn't acknowledge this connection. Helen intuits it, knowing

> that tomorrow Mr Brindle might consult with the men he worked beside, or ask opinions at his pub on what he should do and how he should feel about his wife. The influence of like minds could very often make him angry with her, even if she had not.[58]

Thus, Mrs Brindle's body is caught in the net of male-generated fantasies that seek to discipline it according to idiosyncratic or socially accepted normative visions. But this is not a simple case of female submission to male fantasies. Mrs Brindle herself is shown as fantasising a locale for an experience of ecstasy that is problematic in terms of the Christian faith. As we shall see, her position in relation to the Biblical ethos is more like that of the female lover from the Song of Songs, whose sensuality has always posed a challenge to religious interpretations of Biblical discourse.

Having given a broad overview of how the main concerns of the novella relate to fantasising, I will now analyse how the novella relates fantasising to its effects in the social reality. The narrator of "Original Bliss" offers a vision regarding the use of the imagination in shaping stories that steer others. In Kennedy's view, storytelling is like cybernetics in the etymological sense of the word: it is an act of steering. The novella opens with a reflection on the relationship between fantasy and reality which focuses on how that which exists at first only in the mind becomes fact and lived experience. Mrs Brindle is half-attentive to an Open University broadcast debating the etiquette of masturbation:

> 'we are highly likely to make imaginary use,' the voice was soft, jovially clandestine, ... 'Of someone with whom we intend to be intimate.' ... 'The closer the two of us get, the more acceptable our fantasies become, until they grow up into facts and instead of the dreams that kept us company, we

---

[57] Kennedy, "Original Bliss", 286.
[58] Ibid., 287.

have memories—to say nothing of a real live partner with whom we may have decided to be in love.'[59]

The narrator thus announces that the story is about the management of desire through fantasy. On the other hand, the narrator entices us to think that the very story we read, as a form of fantasy, could inform the meta-narrative reality of its readers. The closer reader and writer get, the more acceptable their shared fantasies become, "until they grow up into facts" and "memories". "Making imaginary use" of the facts of reality, stories can add to reality by disseminating, nourishing, disassembling, and reassembling fancy until it grows into "a real live partner".[60]

The narrator is aware of the performativity of representation. The interviewee in the Open University programme asserts his point thus:

> this is all one huge demonstration of how the mind affects reality and reality affects the mind. I indulge in a spot of libidinous mental cartooning and what happens? A very demonstrable physical result. Not to mention a monumental slew of moral and emotional dilemmas, all of which may very well feed back to those realities I first drew upon to stimulate my mind, and around and around and around we go and where we'll stop, we do not know.[61]

The passage offers a key to interpreting the story. Not only is the narrative about representations ("mental cartooning") of the sexual partner's body but also about the range of behaviours representation engenders (its "demonstrable physical result"). This subjective constitution of identities "may very well feed back to those realities" whence it originally proceeded to form and reform by repetition what is a sexual partnership. Extrapolating, one may see this circular trajectory through which the realities of the mind are disseminated into those of material reality, and then reabsorbed in the configuration of the self, as shaping any aspect of experience: "around and around and around we go and where we'll stop, we do not know."

"Original Bliss" focuses on how female identity is constituted as, in Butler's terms, a "*fabrication* manufactured and sustained" through the deployment in the narratable syntax of male fantasies of a fictional feminine subject whose "corporeal signs" serve to identify legitimate or illegitimate enactments of the body.[62] As the narrator of "Original Bliss"

---

[59] Ibid., 154.
[60] Ibid.
[61] Ibid.
[62] Butler, "Gender Trouble", 336, original italics.

insists through Professor Gluck's voice, this circulation of meaning
"around and around" between outer reality and the reality of the mind
crucially involves a kind of cybernetics of socialisation:

> 'That around and around is what I mean by Cybernetics. Don't believe a
> soul who tells you different—particularly if they're engineers. *This* is
> Cybernetics—literally, it means nothing more than steering. The way I
> steer me, the way you steer you. From the inside. Our interior lives have
> seismic effects on our exterior world. We have to wake up and think about
> that if we want to be really alive.'[63]

Within the story, Mrs Brindle, her husband, and her lover steer themselves
and one another through the fantasies in which they understand each other,
and which the narrator makes visible to readers. But this act of making
visible is an act that in turn may steer the readers (on a meta-narrative
level) by affecting how they socialise. The novella engages with social
myths derived from myths about Adam and Eve and the Garden of Eden,
which, it is suggested, are repeated in different ways in curiously
converging tales of popular wisdom derived from the Bible and erotic
stories. By such repetition in different kinds of discourse, social myths
come to constitute both the social stage and the range of possible scripts
for socialisation that the stage can accommodate.

In order to explain the social value of this constitutive process and its
disciplining effects, I will now analyse several passages of the novella to
show that they suggest that Helen Brindle finds it difficult to represent in
words her intuition of religious ecstasy as also encompassing the
sensuality of the (sexual) body. In order to understand this difficulty, we
must begin by addressing the issue of agency in fantasising one's identity,
which the novella discusses through presenting Helen Brindle's
relationship with religion as wife and as adulterous woman.

The morning after she listens to the Open University programme we
find Mrs Brindle pursuing an ambiguous kind of comfort:

> She steeped real coffee in the miniature cafetière that held exactly enough
> for one and tried not to remember the space in her morning routine. Mrs
> Brindle tried not to think, 'This is when you would have prayed. This is
> when you would have started your day by knowing the shape of your
> life.'[64]

---

[63] Kennedy, "Original Bliss", 154, original italics.
[64] Ibid., 155.

The passage anticipates Mrs Brindle's struggle to overcome a sense of loneliness and pointlessness: a numbing comfort that makes "the shape of her life" impossible to figure. Steeped in a space that holds exactly enough for one, Mrs Brindle finds it difficult to hold on to this space and to hold herself within it. She avoids thinking that in the space opened up because of her husband's absence and because of her cessation of prayer she could own herself. The possibility of owning herself instead of being owned in the subject positions of wife and religious woman makes her feel guilty.

However, this possibility haunts her. Remembering the speaker of the Open University programme, Mrs Brindle purchases his book and, reading it, is somewhat surprised to find that he "personally assured her that she was *the miracle which makes itself*."[65] Mrs Brindle reacts to this empowering suggestion by recounting her past religious experiences: "This was a start, a nice thing to know, but rather lonely. Before, Something Else had made her and looked upon her and seen that she was good."[66] Mrs Brindle finds it difficult to accept agency. It makes her lonely, a loneliness she thinks of as a "misunderstanding of nature", "easily remedied" through prayer. Mrs Brindle regards her being outwith the Judeo-Christian myth as a mistake and thus reinforces the legitimacy of Christian discourses' prescriptions of being in the flesh: for her, God "had been always, absolutely, perpetually *there*: God. Her God. Infinitely accessible and a comfort in her flesh, He'd been her best kind of love."[67] However, Mrs Brindle's recounting of her religious fervour contains a suggestion that should be noted here, and to which I will return throughout this analysis: the God she speaks about is emphatically noted as "her God", which implies that she is in fact exercising agency in creating Him as such, but disavows this agency. It is *her* God before whom Mrs Brindle

> had knelt and closed her eyes and then felt her head turn in to lean against the hot Heart of it all. The Heart had given round her, given her everything, lifted her, rocked her, drawn off unease and left her beautiful. Mrs Brindle had been beautiful with faultless regularity.[68]

The narrator pitches this paradisal image against a dreary image of normality as "existence in the real world" that is "both repetitive and meaningless." Mrs Brindle's social identity is defined through the routine activities to which her social role as housewife condemns her. In an

---

[65] Ibid., 162, original italics.
[66] Ibid.
[67] Ibid., original italics.
[68] Ibid.

appraisal of Luce Irigaray's thoughts on the male-generated construction of a woman's body as a man's dwelling place, which he inhabits as his own material place, but which he may leave at will, Grosz comments that

> The containment of women within a dwelling that they did not build, nor was even built *for* them, can only amount to a homelessness within the very home itself: it becomes the space of duty, of endless and infinitely repeatable chores that have no social value or recognition, the space of the affirmation and replenishment of others at the expense and erasure of the self, the space of domestic violence and abuse, the space that harms as much as it isolates women.[69]

Mrs Brindle's dwelling in her body is affected by her dwelling in her home as wife.

It is the routine of endless and repeatable chores that had smothered Mrs Brindle's ecstatic "original bliss", for in this life "Ecstasy was neither usual nor useful because of its tendency to distract, or even to produce dependency. Her original bliss had meant she was unbalanced, but now she had the chance to be steady and properly well."[70] Mrs Brindle regards as betrayal her uneasily consenting participation in the repetitive practices that set her up as proper housewife. Having tried "to seem contented in her suddenly normal life and to be adaptable for her new world" she finds that everything she touches is "hard and cold" because she "allowed herself to betray what she had lost by ceasing to long for it."[71] Thus Mrs Brindle's character is constructed at the intersection of two kinds of repetitive social acts (that become social rituals): on the one hand, there is the religious ritual through which Mrs Brindle had been able to define a paradise of her own; on the other, there are the social norms of housewifery which she finds stifling. Yet these norms derive, after all, also from the Judeo-Christian tradition that enshrines the sanctity of marriage.

Mrs Brindle's faith in a personal God seems empowering, because it allows her a degree of personal fulfilment. But the narrator shows that this faith is problematic. Both for Mrs Brindle the faithful believer, and for Mrs Brindle the wife, "the shape" of life has been determined through external agency. This agency either belongs to God (even though to a God of Mrs Brindle's making) or is manifested through the force of social

---

[69] Elizabeth Grosz, "Women, *Chora*, Dwelling", *Space, Time, and Perversion*, 111-124, 122, original italics. Luce Irigaray, *Elemental Passions*, trans. Joanne Collie and Judith Still (New York: Routledge, 1992), 49.
[70] Kennedy, "Original Bliss", 162-3.
[71] Ibid., 163.

norms constructing her role as housewife. The first case poses a paradox: Mrs Brindle's placing agency in the hands of God may be seen as itself an act of exercising agency, especially when it means removing it from the impersonal forces that have pushed her into a routine social life. Placing herself in the hands of a God of *her* making helps Mrs Brindle to free herself from her husband, whose repudiated God nevertheless works through the norms of marriage derived from the Judeo-Christian tradition which Mr Brindle uses to dominate his wife.

Mrs Brindle's memory of her lost faith evokes an Eve that had been held in Paradise through her faith; as long as she felt she was beholding God, Mrs Brindle could fantasise a reality like that of Eden for her being in the here and now. However, although Mrs Brindle has the power to configure the Judeo-Christian myth of Eden in order to define her self and to evaluate her social experience, such power also belongs to anyone else. The myth as such does not belong to Mrs Brindle but to society at large. Indeed, it is because of the different ways in which elements of the Judeo-Christian tradition are used to construct identities, for instance, by her husband, that Mrs Brindle experiences alienation, loneliness, and physical abuse. It is then necessary to examine the ways in which elements of the Judeo-Christian myth are used in heterogeneous ways in society.

I have suggested that having lost "her original bliss", Helen Brindle may be an Eve who has lost paradise. Examined in this key, "Original Bliss" retells Eve's fabula to an extent. But, unlike Eve, Mrs Brindle does not find redemption in marriage; on the contrary, her loss of the ability to experience unity with the Heart is clearly indicated as being connected to the meaningless patterns of living socially as a wife.[72] The narrative of "Original Bliss" thus registers a contrast between the promise of social fulfilment through monogamous partnership that the Christian tradition enshrines, and the possibilities of using this model of marriage to set up meaning of personal value. This contrast can be explored by comparing Mrs Brindle's identity as housewife and the identity of woman as man's partner derived from the Bible. In order to discuss the latter, I will use passages from Milton's version of the myth of Eden given in *Paradise Lost*, not because I aim to analyse Milton's understanding of the myth in these passages, but because they offer an illustrative rendering of accepted Christian socialisation guidelines. In *Paradise Lost*, Adam, addressing Eve, comments on woman's duty thus:

> nothing lovelier can be found
> In woman, than to study household good,

---

[72] Ibid., 163.

And good works in her husband to promote. IX, ll. 232-4[73]

But for Mrs Brindle her role as "associate sole" (IX, l. 227)[74] of man is perceived as "bloody and bloody and then more bloody again".[75] In Milton's text, the Christian forbiddance of carnal pleasure is thus proclaimed by Raphael in his advice to Adam concerning the qualities Adam should praise in the love that binds Eve to him:

> In loving thou dost well, in passion not,
> Wherein true love consists not; love refines
> The thoughts, and heart enlarges, hath his seat
> In reason, and is judicious, is the scale
> By which to heavenly love thou mayst ascend,
> Not sunk in carnal pleasure, for which cause
> Among the beasts no mate for thee was found. VIII, ll. 588-94[76]

However, Mrs Brindle's husband not only punishes the sexual woman he suspects to have "sunk in carnal pleasure", but also the woman whose spiritual ecstasy cannot be harnessed to the social purposes of marriage, as he understands them: the availability of the wife's body for domestic labour and sex. The woman whose practice of Christian faith does not serve the institution of marriage in this way, Mr Brindle thinks, is also a harlot. Judging his wife's loss of her ability to experience religious ecstasy, he tells her:

> You came to your senses. Creeping round here like Mrs Fucking Jesus... I didn't marry that. ... I saw the way you were, home from your piss-hole bloody church. ... You only ever went there for a come. Sweating with your eyes shut, kneeling—you were having a fucking come. ... Then God couldn't get it up any more so you left him.[77]

Thus, even though the ecstasy Mrs Brindle is seeking is pure in Christian terms (God had been "her best kind of love"), she is made guilty as invariably a sinning woman who must pay the price of Eve's sin. For her husband, Mrs Brindle's "affair" with God is adulterous and she must be disciplined: "Her original bliss had meant she was unbalanced" but now,

---

[73] Milton, 483.

[74] Ibid.

[75] Kennedy, "Original Bliss", 163.

[76] Milton, 461.

[77] Kennedy, "Original Bliss", 224.

as wife, "she had the chance to be steady and properly well."[78] This paradox exposes the Christian tradition as also an instrument for constructing social relations of dominance: sinful or not, that is, driven by the ecstasy of lustful sexual intimacy or of purely spiritual communion, Mrs Brindle receives social correction.[79] This suggests that it is perhaps the ecstatic woman as such that is repudiated in the Christian tradition, with the story of sin produced in order to legitimate this repudiation. The correction of the sinning woman through modes of socialisation scripted in the Christian model of love and marriage can be seen not only as directed against lustful sexual women, but against ecstatic women, perhaps because this implies a communion with God hitherto exclusively reserved for men, or worse, implies a connection between carnal and spiritual desire that threatens the law of the abstract Father.[80]

The first part of "Original Bliss" shows a Mrs Brindle who denies that sexual desire is connected to what she perceives as the desirable kind of ecstasy. Gradually, as the narration unfolds Mrs Brindle's growing awareness of her sexuality, it also begins to address it more directly. Earlier on this growing awareness is glimpsed obliquely. This is how the narrator presents Mrs Brindle making the choice to travel and meet the

---

[78] Ibid., 162-3.

[79] The paradox stems from the contradiction between Christian understandings of (original) bliss as spiritual love for God and Mrs Brindle's intuition that this love could be both sensual and pure. The possible truth the paradox foregrounds is that spiritual love may not necessarily exclude sensual love, but the acceptance of this truth would lead to the deconstruction of the hierarchies whereby the body must be governed through faith, and implicitly of the hierarchies of domestic relations through which "spiritual" men govern women's bodies' sensuality.

[80] Mrs Brindle's predicament evokes the fate of visionary women in the Modern Age, including in Milton's own time. Although Mrs Brindle cannot be easily compared with, for instance, Lady Eleanor Davies, she deals with the same kind of prejudices against the possibility of a women's relationship with God that liberates them from relationships of subordination to men. In her analysis of the history of women prophets in seventeenth-century England, Phyllis Mack wrote: "When a seventeenth-century Englishman was confronted by the shocking spectacle of a woman who prophesied in public, what did he see and hear? 'A woman clothed with the sun,' 'a base slut,' 'a Jezebel,' 'a silly old woman,' 'a goat rough and hairy,' 'a woman to make your heart to tremble,' 'an old trot.'" One imagines that had Mr Brindle lived in the seventeenth-century England, he would have been the kind of man who shouted such invectives. Phyllis Mack, *Visionary Women: Ecstatic Prophecy in Seventeenth-Century England* (Berkeley: University of California Press, 1992), 17.

Open University speaker, "the prominent and fast becoming really rather fashionable Professor Edward E. Gluck":

> Having read Gluck as thoroughly as she could, Mrs Brindle knew about obsession, its causes and signs. She was well equipped to consider whether she was currently obsessing over Gluck.
> Certainly she was close to his mind, which might cause her to assume other kinds of proximity. Obsessive behaviour would read almost any meaning into even the most random collision of objects and incidents. Chance could be mistaken for Providence. ... [She] could be sure she was a person most unlikely to obsess. She had never intended to seek out Gluck, she had simply kept turning on through her life and finding he was there.[81]

We may re-evaluate the question of absence of sexual desire from the kind of ecstasy Mrs Brindle is seeking in light of this passage. Mrs Brindle understands that being close to Gluck's mind "might cause her to assume other kinds of proximity". In other words, the spiritual ecstasy she believes it is possible to achieve through intellectual communion might cause "kinds of proximity" that, one may infer, lead to sexual ecstasy. This connection is reinforced in the association of "closeness to Gluck's mind" and "other kinds of proximity" with Providence, God's granting of the sensual shape of her life. Thus, while Mrs Brindle's "turning on through her life" may have been caused by a mind-altering, ecstatic faith in God's embodiment in every shape her life had taken, it may be that such turning on presupposes a dangerous sensuality of the body (like Eve's).

Although not directly naming it as such, the narrator suggests the possibility that a kind of desire akin to sexual desire runs in the undercurrents of Mrs Brindle's vision of spiritual ecstasy. However, Mrs Brindle quickly represses this intuition, worrying that it may be an obsessive reading of her own (sexual?) desires into random events. And she concludes that "she had never intended to seek out Gluck", a denial of the undercurrents of her desire.

The question of agency in fantasising identity is again implied in this passage. The clause "she had simply kept turning on through her life" sums up Mrs Brindle's denial of responsibility for her desire: while she found Professor Gluck, his being there for her to find seems to be the effect of some other agency, not hers, perhaps the agency of God or Providence. On the other hand, Mrs Brindle didn't just *find* Gluck, she has been *finding* him, which suggests the continuity of a whirl of desire the

---

[81] Kennedy, "Original Bliss", 164-5.

centre of which would have always been a God sized down to a man, the bearer of God's lost wisdom, Adam, someone with whom Paradise may be regained. After her first meetings with Gluck, Mrs Brindle fantasises in her dreams a locale of Eden where her body is caught in a dialectics of negation and legitimation that involves a sensual call on God to become incarnated as a male lover. The description of this fantasising deserves extended quoting:

> She was alone in a sunlit space now, with something like a fountain for company and a figure far off, but walking towards her and holding yellow papers in his hand. Helen couldn't think why he seemed familiar—he had no tell-tale points to give a clue—still, she knew him. She recognised him in her sleep. ... Her dream dipped closer, licked at her ear, hard and dark, and said, 'Do not look at the man. Do not look at him unless you have to and sometimes you *will* have to because he will be there. Then you can look, but you must never for a moment think that you want to fuck him, to fuck him whole, to fuck him until all his bones are opened up and he can't think and you've loosened away his identity like rusty paint. Don't think you want to blaze right over him like sin. ... Think of your intentions and he will see, because they will leak out in the colour of your eyes and what do you think will happen then?[82]

The passage offers the opportunity of an intertextual reading with the passage in Milton's *Paradise Lost* describing Satan's visitation of Eve in her sleep. The extract from "Original Bliss" makes visible the repudiations performed in the cultural tradition of envisioning women in the image of Eve assailed by sin. In *Paradise Lost*, the angels find Satan

> Squat like a toad, close at the ear of Eve;
> Assaying by his devilish art to reach
> The organs of her fancy, and with them forge
> Illusions as he list, phantasms and dreams,
> Or if, inspiring venom, he might taint
> The animal spirits that from pure blood arise
> Like gentle breaths from rivers pure, thence raise,
> At least distempered, discontented thoughts,
> Vain hopes, vain aims, inordinate desires ... . IV, ll. 800-808[83]

Mrs Brindle's fantasising is constrained by interdictions transmitted through such cultural interpretations of the Christian myth. Her dream

---

[82] Ibid., 200, original italics.
[83] Milton, 269.

"dipped closer, licked at her ear, hard and dark"[84] as if she were assayed by Satan's "devilish art" (IV, l. 801).[85] When, to use Milton's words, "the organs of her fancy" "forge" (IV, l. 802)[86] an image of a sexualised God she "must never for a moment think" of revealing his identity as a locus where, perhaps, the polar opposites sinful vs. pure love, structuring socialisation guidelines derived from the Christian tradition, collapse; where God, "the Patient ... Lover" loves with Satan's "Jealous ... Love."[87] Milton's text repudiates the possibility of conceiving the female body's sexuality as a legitimate kind of ecstasy by showing that "the animal spirits that from pure blood arise" can be "tainted" with the "inspiring venom" of God's inimical angel (IV, ll. 804-5).[88] Thus, to use Milton's words again, Mrs Brindle is troubled because her vision of God may be clouded by "distempered, discontented thoughts, vain hopes" and "vain aims" that make her desires "inordinate" (IV, ll. 807-8).[89] She cannot fantasise, to use Butler's critical metaphor, an interior topography where she can figure herself as woman endowed with a sensuality that embraces also the body's sexuality.[90] This kind of sensuality is repudiated as, to paraphrase Milton's editor, illegitimate sense-data. Mrs Brindle's fall from grace appears to have been caused not by sexual lust, but more likely by her intuition of the revelation of sexuality as life-force, and by her inability to reconcile this intuition with the legitimate practices of a society whose interpretation of the Christian tradition repudiates the passions of the body.

In fantasising an Eden wherein she can place herself as subject, Mrs Brindle conceives a decanted sensuality that draws off spirituality, apparently leaving sexuality undisturbed. Such steadying of the body, however, does not cancel its eroticism, it simply spiritualises it. At first, although sexual desire is not consciously acceptable in Mrs Brindle's fantasising of her identity, its symptoms are registered. They are simply not made sense of, and therefore cannot be used to support a fantasy that

---

[84] Kennedy, "Original Bliss", 200.

[85] Milton, 269.

[86] Ibid.

[87] Kennedy, "Original Bliss", 200, 311.

[88] Milton, 269. Alastair Fowler, the editor of Milton's text used here, thus comments on Milton's understanding of "animal spirits": "Angels could produce apparitions by affecting the mind through the *animal spirits*. So Satan can either manipulate *fancy* directly, or else operate on the animal spirits, source of sense-data from past experiences." Milton, 269, original italics.

[89] Milton, 269.

[90] Butler, "Gender Trouble", 333.

figures Mrs Brindle, to herself, as someone reconciled with the body's eroticism. A passage describing Mrs Brindle's dream in which she recounts her erotic awakening during a school exam, shows a young Helen Brindle struggling with panic as it becomes evident that she will not be able to complete the Chemistry (!) test in time:

> With the fifth and final section of question 14 still undone, her eyes closed without her consent and the proper force of panic began to penetrate. ... She steadied herself against an insistent pressure breaking out between her hips and sucking and diving and sucking and diving and sucking her fast away. Four minutes, three minutes, two. A shudder was visible at her jaw.
>
> And then her breathing seemed much freer and she was perhaps warm, or actually hot, but oddly easy in her mind. She slipped in her final answer, just under the given time ... .[91]

Here Helen gives an account of her body by relying, to use Grosz's words, "on interior, psychical and physiological body-products", i.e. "the sensations, pleasures, pains, sweat and tears of the body-subject."[92] The body's sexual upsurge is pitched against the body-concept obtaining through the disciplinary discourse disseminated in school. As Helen remembers, "[w]omen's orgasms ... had been hinted around in Biology as a relatively pointless sexual extravagance."[93] In the disciplinary discourse of the educational establishment the body "is *named* by being tagged or branded on its surface, creating a particular kind of 'depth-body' or interiority".[94] In the "psychic layer" she identifies as her "(disembodied) core"[95] Helen registers the effect of corrective discursive forces as a "panic" that is "proper". In other words, Helen's fantasising accommodates the idea that it is proper that undisciplined subjects should panic at not knowing their bodies as required.

The passage examines how Helen's "body is internally lived, experienced and acted upon by the subject and the social collectivity".[96] The "proper force of panic" is the effect of power exercised by the social collectivity that, through "checkpoints" such as school exams, verifies that individuals learn to signify themselves (to write on their bodies), and thus

---

[91] Kennedy, "Original Bliss", 199.
[92] Elizabeth Grosz, "Inscriptions and Body Maps: Representations and the Corporeal", *Feminine, Masculine and Representation*, eds. T. Threatgold and A. Cranny-Francis (London: Allen&Unwin, 1990), 62-74, 65.
[93] Kennedy, "Original Bliss", 200.
[94] Grosz, "Inscriptions and Body Maps", 65, original italics.
[95] Ibid.
[96] Ibid.

to identify themselves, as subjects of disciplining discourses such as those of Chemistry and Biology. This force, however, is also shown to open up a space of transgression in Helen's case. Allowing herself to experience the body's eroticism, Helen feels "much freer", "easy in her mind" although "oddly" so. This time Helen's orgasm had not been "pointless" for it "slipped" a clue to the "final answer" to her later confusion of eroticism and spirituality.[97]

This particular narrative event draws attention to the interrelation between the chemistry of the body, the social space wherein the body is deployed, and the figuration through which the body is made sense of. The body figured as actor in fantasised interiority yields the corporeal style of its owner—it is incarnated on the social stage. To apply Grosz's argument in this context, "the messages coded onto the body" "mark the subject", Helen, "by, and as, a series of signs within the collectivity of other signs, signs which bear the marks of a particular social law and organisation, and through a particular constellation of desires and pleasures."[98] But in the above passage, the act of narrating Helen's eroticism (by herself, to herself, in her fantasy, but also by the narrator, to the readers, in the text of "Original Bliss") stimulates "a corporeal resistance to the social" by opening opportunities for more empowering "'intextuation of bodies', which transform the discursive apparatus or social fiction/knowledge regimes, 'correcting' or updating them, rendering them more truthful". At that point in her life, Helen hadn't found the means to intextuate her eroticism, to write it on her body so that it should represent a subversive "*incarnation* of social law in the movements, actions and desires of bodies."[99] This she will do later in life, at a crucial point whose circumstances are narrated toward the end of the novella, when she will have found a way to display the mark of her sexuality that "[brings] her up against the force of Law" in open confrontation.[100] That confrontation between Mrs Brindle's body as text and the dominant discourses whose authority she challenges can be assessed as a discursive strategy or tactic for resisting the disciplining effects of those discourses.[101] In order to understand the value of this strategy, we must first examine how

---

[97] Kennedy, "Original Bliss", 199-200.

[98] Grosz, "Inscriptions and Body Maps", 65.

[99] Ibid., original italics.

[100] Kennedy, "Original Bliss", 197.

[101] For definitions of discursive strategies and discursive tactics see Michel Foucault, *Power/Knowledge: Selected Interviews and Other Writings, 1972-1977*, trans. Colin Gordon (New York: Pantheon, 1980); Michel de Certeau, *The Practice of Everyday Life* (Berkeley: University of California Press, 1984), xiv.

discourses derived from the Judeo-Christian tradition and from pornography affect Mrs Brindle.

For Mrs Brindle, the possibility of reconciling sexual desire and devotion for *her* God, sensually incarnated in the shapes her life had taken, is foreclosed by the myth of Eve's sin, reenacted in social reality by her husband and her lover, albeit in different ways. Her husband represses Mrs Brindle's sexuality, regarding it as sinful if not manifested to please only him; her lover represses Mrs Brindle's spirituality if it diminishes the legitimacy of women's absolute subjection to men that is the "promise" of pornography.

To this is added Mrs Brindle's own repression of her body's desires, even though her religious perceptions of "original bliss" are rather charged with sensuality. Before losing her "original bliss", for Helen, God's presence could be touched, seen, smelled, and tasted: "There wasn't a piece of the world that I could touch and not find Him inside it. All created things—I could see, I could smell that they'd *been* created. I could taste where He'd touched. He was that size of love."[102] Helen's faith in God's immanence, however, is disturbed by her body's sensuality when she is alone with herself. If, having lost religious fervour, Helen would have lost her sensuality of living, God's immanence would have been confirmed. Helen would have been able to think that although she cannot experience God's presence, God nevertheless graces reality in ways she can no longer perceive. However, Mrs Brindle's loss of sensuality is not entirely complete: a "shiver in her blood" persists. Although she does not feel God's touch anymore, "the touch of herself" is experienced as the beginning of the tug of a new awakening. The night after her first meeting with Professor Gluck, Helen Brindle cannot rest because her body doesn't let her: her skin

> felt impossibly naked—the touch of herself, alone with herself, the brush of her arm on her stomach, of her legs against her legs, tugged her awake. … [S]he knew she had a shiver in her blood and whenever she lay down it showed.[103]

This may be so because Mrs Brindle does not know how to locate her body in the pull experienced in her encounter with Gluck, who, unlike God, is just another man. The passage also anticipates Helen's dream-memory of her body's sexual awakening during the Chemistry exam. In the broader context it contributes to developing in narrative the ideas

---

[102] Kennedy, "Original Bliss", 181, original italics.
[103] Ibid., 175.

presented at the beginning as we realise that "instead of dreams" of an Eden of ambiguous sensuality that had "kept her company", Helen begins to acknowledge memories of her body's sexuality, "to say nothing of a real live partner" (whom Gluck will eventually become).[104]

After their second meeting, undressing herself alone in front of the mirror in her hotel room, the intuition of her sexual appeal and what it may lead to makes Mrs Brindle laugh away the idea of sex as sin:

> When she was naked, the mirror stared back at her until she realised she was thinking of the Seven Deadly Finns and of laughing. The mirror smiled and then looked away. Surely to God she hadn't been smiling like that all evening? That wasn't how she'd meant to be. The mirror slipped back to its grin, it didn't mind.[105]

The passage recalls the scene of Eve's fascination with her reflection first time she glimpses herself in the mirror of water, before being led away by God to be given to Adam. Milton's *Paradise Lost* describes the event as leading to Eve's realisation of the vanity of her infatuation with herself, with her bodily beauty, as she learns "How beauty is excelled by manly grace/ And wisdom, which alone is truly fair."[106] But in Kennedy's novella, the Eve in Mrs Brindle belittles the one of the "Seven Deadly Finns" that should forbid her to love her self. The mirror returns perhaps Lilith's wicked smile, endorsing the enjoyment of the sensuality of the flesh, even as Mrs Brindle admonishes herself for such indulgence.

On the other hand, Gluck attempts to shape Helen's subjectivity as a position of independence from moral, social, religious contexts that can provide her with a philosophy for living. Gluck the scientist understands this position of independence as being empowering through the relativism it engenders: "We are both equipped with minds to perceive and alter all possible worlds", he claims.[107] If the kind of "mental cartooning" Gluck advocates may empower one to alter *all* possible worlds, then ultimately no possible world holds true; no world is preferable to another: a splayed reality pared down to its entrances. Here, agency is meaningless, since although one can enter and leave at will, there is nothing to hold will in.

This dissolution of (con)textual authority, echoing strands of postmodern theory, steers the professor towards "a monumental slew of moral and emotional dilemmas", shaping his understanding of Helen's

---

[104] Ibid., 154.
[105] Ibid., 197.
[106] Milton, Book 4, ll. 449-491, ll. 490-91.
[107] Kennedy, "Original Bliss", 179.

body.[108] Mrs Brindle is less of a sinning Eve for Gluck than she is for Mr Brindle, but nevertheless the image of Eve's/Lilith's lust she is. Mrs Brindle understands that he is trying to make her into the image of the women from his pornography collection: "she quite understood; he was making her look like one of the women in his films, like what he must want, a body pared down to its entrances, a splayed personality."[109] What Gluck wants, but his practice of "mental cartooning" does not allow him to get, although promising it, is a real Helen Brindle. In his addiction to pornography, he may be conceiving her as a body suitable for endlessly repeating Eve's sexual corruption, in order to legitimate Eve's gift of knowledge as corruption of God's absolute; a repetition which is ultimately void of any significance as Gluck himself admits when he realises the sameness in difference of pornographic material. While for Gluck Mrs Brindle's ecstasy (the offer of her sensuality) initially provides an object for his masturbatory "mental cartooning", for Mr Brindle his wife's ecstasy translates as sin and is punished through rape and beating.

Thus, while the Judeo-Christian tradition may be empowering for Helen in some ways, it is also disempowering in others. The two subjectivity scenarios that her husband and her lover require her to enact, her subjection, engender both the inscription of her body as the body of a sexual woman ever ready to perform sex, and as the body of a sinning woman. These explorations of the different ways in which the Biblical tradition shapes understandings of the female body suggest that the legitimacy of the myth can never be fruitfully explored except by connecting it with the varied social practices that the tradition inspires. These practices are heterogeneous and dilemmatic.

Eventually, Helen reclaims the power to decide what inscriptions her body should wear: she displays her naked body in front of her husband, letting him see the mark she permitted Gluck to leave. The symbolism of this mark (Gluck had trimmed her pubic hair) may be further analysed. For her husband it is a marking of Helen's body for another's desire, a mark of sin. From a meta-narrative perspective it may be seen as an eidetic reinterpretation of female sexuality that superimposes an image of (Eve's) pre-sexual innocence over an erotic scene of voyeur desire. It thus playfully engages the connections between knowledge, sexuality, and sin established in the myth of Adam and Eve. Unlike, for instance, Milton's Eve, Mrs Brindle is not ashamed. She no longer hides the marks of her body's sexuality. If she were, she would legitimate the voyeur's sin,

---

[108] Ibid., 154.
[109] Ibid., 280.

enjoyed both by the scientist for the revelation that proves the female body's profanity, and by the husband for offering the opportunity to exercise corrective power. But Helen displays herself naked as if she were an Eve attempting to verify whether the myth stands up to the reality of her body. Her gesture suggests Helen's acknowledgment of her sexuality as part of the ecstasy of spiritual experience.

In the terms of Grosz's argument which I discussed earlier, Helen, through displaying the mark of her sexual body in this way, intextuates her body and inserts it as text in the texts through which her husband and her lover had been making sense of her. In Derridean terms, Helen's rewriting of her body introduces the supplement that undoes their texts' claims to decide the version of herself as subject by fantasising sensuality and spirituality as separate domains of femininity.[110] In relation to the Biblical myth of Adam and Eve, this supplement is that which had been covered up and made absent, and in the name of which Eve's conviction could stand (read "conviction" both in the sense of "being convicted" and "being convincing"). All this is made possible by the two-way traffic between reality and fantasy, with "fantasy" understood in the sense theorised by Butler: deploying herself as subject in a topography of confluences between her own and others' fantasies, the subject Mrs Brindle then intextuates her body using elements of these fantasies and inserts this text in social reality. Because this reality is read through narratable fantasies, in this case derived from the Judeo-Christian tradition and pornography, Mrs Brindle's intextuated body is legible in its terms. But this is also precisely why it can change the meanings of those discourses through which social reality is made sense of, thus affecting, to a certain extent, that reality itself, that is, the normative practices derived from discourses that have material effects. In meta-narrative perspective, the text of "Original Bliss" itself can be seen as intervening in the citational chains that constitute the cultural tradition of Adam and Eve, and thus in social reality, because it extends that reality and tradition by offering a subjective position (that of Mrs Brindle) that may engender empowering modes of reading oneself as social actor. Such reading is within the constraints of tradition and social reality, yet it transforms them.

In her analysis of Eve's nativity scene from Milton's *Paradise Lost*, where Eve renounces her self identity glimpsed in the water, Christine Froula argues that Eve's narrative shows that

---

[110] For Derrida's theorisation of the logic of the supplement see Jacques Derrida, *Of Grammatology*, trans Gayatri Spivak (Baltimore, Maryland: Johns Hopkins University Press, 1976).

she has internalized the voices and values of her mentors: her speech reproduces the words of the 'voice' and of Adam and concludes with an assurance that she has indeed been successfully taught to 'see' for herself the superiority of Adam's virtues to her own, limited as far as she knows to the 'beauty' briefly glimpsed in the pool. In this way she becomes a 'Part' not only of Adam but of the cultural economy which inscribes itself in her speech—or, more accurately, which takes over her speech: Eve does not speak patriarchal discourse; it speaks her.[111]

In Kennedy's novella, Mrs Brindle is an Eve who has managed to speak herself, guiltless, within the cultural economy of patriarchal discourses, reiterating its patterns yet remaking them and thus remaking God and rewriting Genesis in terms more truthful to herself as woman.

Thus, through accepting and displaying the mark of her sexual body, Mrs Brindle assumes Eve's sin but derives self-affirming power from it, and at the same time subverts her husband's and Gluck's normative use of the Judeo-Christian tradition and of pornography respectively. Mrs Brindle rejects Eve's fate by using the mark of sin to reclaim faith on equal terms with God: if she is to believe in Him, He must believe in her, body and spirit together. After displaying the mark in front of her husband, he beats her unconscious. Later, Mrs Brindle wakes up in the hospital ward:

As soon as she opened her attention, Something monumental began to pour in. A sense of humour must obviously be amongst the everything that God had—for years she'd needed to hear from Him just a little and now He was determined to be deafening.

'Edward? … I got through. I was taken through. I mean, I'm *alive*, Edward. I believe in Something—or Something believes in me. And I believe in me and I can do any and every living thing a living person does. I am alive.'[112]

Thus, Helen Brindle recuperates agency by reconstructing her identity in ways that legitimate the congruence of experiences of sexuality and spirituality. In her analysis of Eve's nativity scene from *Paradise Lost*, Froula argues that

The reflection is not *of* Eve: according to the voice, it *is* Eve. As the voice interprets her to herself, Eve is not a self, a subject, at all; she is rather a

---

[111] Christine Froula, "When Eve Reads Milton: Undoing the Canonical Economy", *Critical Inquiry* Vol. 10, No. 2 (Dec. 1983): 321-347, 329.

[112] Kennedy, "Original Bliss", 300-301, original italics.

substanceless image, a mere 'shadow' without object until the voice unites
her to Adam ... .[113]

In "Original Bliss", Helen Brindle, as an Eve, has recuperated agency and
confidence in her own voice. She is herself, and the subject through which
she chooses to signify herself is not a substance-less image authored by
others, but it is born out of the passions of her body, of its sensuality. On
equal terms with anybody else, she can do "any and every living thing a
living person does". Her God rewards this kind of love.

This recuperation of the meaning of Genesis undermines the Judeo-
Christian fabula as social myth with a fixed configuration that invariably
renders women as sinners. Unlike the ashamed Eve fearing God's
inspecting eye, "Helen lets herself be. She is here and with Edward as he
folds in around her and she around him and they are one completed motion
under God the Patient, Jealous Lover: the Jealous, Patient Love."[114]
Helen's confusion regarding her repressed sexual desire and desired
spiritual ecstasy is dispelled with the empowering understanding that the
realms of the body and those of the spirit need not be kept separate.

Conclusion

Both texts analysed in this chapter explore questions of authority in the
realm of signification. *Everything You Need* proposes a concept of voice
which endorses the existence of others' voices in the story one tells. This
vision has affinities with Derridean concepts of the subject as always
being formed in an act of citation which echoes other possible subjects.
This is the main idea that we need to keep in mind throughout the analyses
that follow, together with a sense of how women's social identity is
constituted in relation to the authority (and powers of the author) wielded
in stories.

In the analysis of "Original Bliss" I sought to integrate this vision of
the power of words with the vision of the power of fantasising explored in
the novella. From this synthesis we retain the vision of how stories steer
audiences, by steering the realms of fantasy where imagination reigns.
This steering affects one's social identity and conveys prescriptive social
roles. Kennedy's take on the role of fantasy in the relationship between
narrative and reality will be helpful in the coming chapters, especially for
understanding how institutionalised forms of word power derived from

---

[113] Froula, 328, original italics.
[114] Ibid., 311.

myths function, as well as for understanding how agency can be appropriated by those whose identity is constructed through subjection to the myths' normative stories.

It is well to remember at this point that I have defined myth as the reiteration of a story that, through the very reiteration of the same subjectivity construction, engenders norms that yield what counts as legitimate subjects. This process is perhaps nowhere clearer to be seen than in older social rituals whose scenarios are consecrated with a story and which then repeat the roles the story propels whenever it is circulated between the members of a social community. I will therefore begin by focusing on such an older ritual and its associated stories that yielded constructions of femininity which still serve as resource in narratives telling the story of women's social roles in terms of their bodily functions: Persephone's myth explains women's social roles as wives and lovers in terms of their bodies' sexual awakening which signals these bodies' fertility.

CHAPTER SIX

THE PERSEPHONE FIGURE IN LIZ LOCHHEAD'S "LUCY'S DIARY" AND EAVAN BOLAND'S "THE POMEGRANATE"

Myths have always held sway in the realms of our imagination, helping us to define our social identities and social worlds in certain ways. In this chapter, I examine versions of Persephone's story to see how its constitutive elements have been used, on the one hand, to create, and on the other, to challenge a social myth about the transformation of pre-sexual girls into wives or lovers in heterosexual partnerships. I begin by exploring the story of Persephone as rendered in Classical Greek culture, focusing on representations of three experiences that have been used to different effects in Liz Lochhead's poem "Lucy's Diary" and in Eavan Boland's poem "The Pomegranate": ensnarement, enchantment, and anger.[1] In the myth of Persephone, those three experiences are presented as related to young girls' sexual awakening. My discussion, while suggesting avenues for critical investigation, is also aimed at highlighting the three experiences as elements that continue to mesmerise and stir those who find themselves, to various extents, participating in and awoken to the myth through its various literary/narrative versions.

In the previous chapter I used two of Kennedy's texts to define a vision of the disciplinary effects of narrative. I argued that disciplining subjection works through one's voice and through one's fantasising: these processes of expression and definition of identity are constrained by others' voices, sometimes come from the past, and by others' legitimate and illegitimate fantasies that inevitably transform one's perception of oneself if s/he engages with them (as one always does) in forms of social interaction. In this chapter I will explore the validity of this argument beyond the realm of the fictional realities of Kennedy's texts. This time, the voices come

---

[1] Eavan Boland, "The Pomegranate", *In a Time of Violence* (Manchester: Carcanet, 1994), 20-21; Liz Lochhead, "Lucy's Diary", *Bagpipe Muzak* (London: Penguin Books, 1991), 60-62.

from the past, manifested in one's voice, that compel fantasising one's identity, will be seen as being enabled through the power of myth.

In the theoretical introduction of this study I argued in favour of a wider understanding of the concept of myth, defining the latter as a narrative that is part of a chain of narrative reiterations of identities and socialisation scenarios which, through their reiteration, are naturalised as legitimate—a process that also establishes them as normative. This view accounts for the fact that while having normative power, myths also change according to the circumstances that determine a specific narrative reiteration at a given point in time, in a particular place. Furthermore, in this view any narrative can yield a myth, or it can extend an existing myth by altering some of its elements while preserving others, according to how it relates to prior narratives and their investment in myth. In the following chapter, I will explore how Bram Stoker's narrative of *Dracula* (1897) has yielded a myth. But before that, I will give an example of how one's voice and fantasy are affected by myth understood in a more traditional anthropological sense: myth as an "ancient" and prestigious narrative that served to make sense of the social world in traditional communities.

The myth I have selected for this analysis is the Persephone myth. Several reasons prompted this selection. First, the myth offers the opportunity to reflect on how narratives serve to make sense of women's bodies and sexuality in ways that perpetuate male-dominated gender regimes. Second, the main themes of the myth, ensnarement, enchantment, and anger, can also be identified in the Dracula myth developed from Stoker's novel. Because of this, it will be easier to extend the analysis of myth as ancient narrative that legitimates male-dominated gender regimes to analyses of contemporary myths, derived from narratives of comparatively recent date, that fulfil the same purpose (although gender regimes have different configurations across time)—which is the purpose of the next chapter. In this chapter, I will treat Bram Stoker's narrative of *Dracula* as having yielded a myth which shares with the Persephone myth the themes of ensnarement, enchantment and anger. In addition, I will regard the two poems by Boland and Lochhead as reiterations of the Persephone myth (and of the Dracula myth in Lochhead's case) to discern how repeating the stories of both myths challenge their prior patterns and explanatory authority.

Persephone in the Ancient World

In the Homeric Hymn to Demeter, the corn goddess of ancient Greece, her young daughter Persephone or Kore (meaning "young maiden" in Greek) is introduced through a scene of enchantment: the girl is enraptured by a beautiful flower, a narcissus, and seeks to pluck it. The narrator announces that this is the story of how Kore was seized by Aïdoneus as

> ... she frolicked, ... picking flowers across the soft meadow, roses and saffron and lovely violets, iris and hyacinth, and narcissus, that Earth put forth as a snare for the maiden with eyes like buds by the will of Zeus, as a favour to the Hospitable one. It shone wondrously, an awe inspiring thing to see ... . In amazement she reached out with both hands to take the pretty plaything.[2]

The meadow is a paradisal space, yet one that hides dangers. While the narcissus is endowed with wondrous beauty, it is also a snare. On the one hand, Kore's enchantment is possible because of the wondrous beauty of the flower, yet on the other hand, this enchantment is a ruse to ensnare her as Hades' sexual partner. The conspiracy to ensnare Kore is plotted between the male gods, Zeus and Hades, who are brothers. Thus, the hymn posits Kore's enchantment as an ensnarement in two ways which illuminate its meaning. It is narrated in reference to both hypnotising attraction and deadly peril. The narrator posits Kore, however, as unaware of the enchantment's perils, and hence, constructs the pre-sexual girl as innocent and unsuspecting of danger.

In meta-narrative perspective, the story itself is a space of enchantment and ensnarement. It has captivated audiences, readers, and writers throughout the centuries. However, while the story has the power to enchant, it also has the power to ensnare audiences, mobilising their consent to certain configurations of social order and practices. Perhaps its spellbinding power was most effective for the participants in the Eleusinian Mysteries. In ancient Greece, the narrative plot was born(e) through, and enhanced, the rituals of the Mysteries and thus contributed to the legitimation of scenarios of socialisation. In the Pantheon's hierarchy, Zeus and Hades occupy positions of tremendous power, from which they derive authority to plot and transact Kore's fate. In conveying to the audience the authority of Zeus and Hades, the story also conveys faith in the masculine brotherhood whose power was wielded in the social reality.

The Hymn to Demeter relates that when Kore reached out for the narcissus, the earth opened and "the Hospitable Lord [Hades] rushed forth ... . Seizing her by force, he began to drive her off on his golden chariot,

---

[2] *Homeric Hymns. Homeric Apocrypha. Lives of Homer*, trans. Martin West (Cambridge: Harvard University Press, 2003), 33.

with her wailing and screaming ... ."[3] Kore's ensnarement grieves her and provokes her anger. Afflicted by the loss of her daughter, Demeter sets out to search for her and no longer tends to the fertility of the land. This forces Zeus to arrange for Kore's return. When, through her mother's subterfuge, Kore is eventually allowed to leave the underworld, Hades has to perform a trick to insure that she will return to him. He offers her pomegranate seeds, knowing that those who taste of food from the underworld would be chained to that realm forever. When she is reunited with Demeter, Persephone tells her mother that Hades "surreptitiously got a pomegranate seed into me, a honey-sweet food, and made me taste it against my will."[4] It is for this reason that Persephone will have to spend part of the year in Hades' realm and the remainder with her mother.

In Apollodorus' later rendering, Hades' trick is revealed thus: "When Zeus ordered Pluto to send Kore back to earth, Pluto, to prevent her from remaining too long with her mother, gave her a pomegranate seed to eat; and failing to foresee what the consequence could be, she ate it."[5] Here Kore is, again, posited as innocent as she is unable to foresee the consequence of accepting the offering. Apollodorus' version, however, also relates another incident which casts Kore's innocence in an ambiguous light. It relates that "[w]hen Ascalaphos, son of Acheron and Gorgyra, bore witness against her [Persephone], Demeter placed a heavy rock over him in Hades ... ."[6] Even as Ascalaphos' punishment shows Demeter's anger at the testimony which seals her daughter's fate, one may risk asking if Demeter and her daughter didn't attempt to also hide the fact that Kore had tasted the seed willingly. Although both the Homeric hymn and Apollodorus' text posit Kore as innocent, the phrasings employed in this version do not exclude the possibility of conceiving that Kore has been pleased with the enticement. The arguments of this chapter are emphatically concerned with the possibility and potential of this ambiguity, and I will return to it frequently.

The significance of Persephone's acceptance of the pomegranate seed can be explored in relation to her awakening sexuality, and in the context of fertility rites. Summarising the prevailing opinion on the mythical significance of the Homeric Hymn to Demeter, Classics scholar Lars Albinus points out: "the myth of Demeter and Kore has been likened to the myths of Aphrodite/Adonis, Kybele/Attis, Isis/Osiris and Ishtar/Tammuz.

---

[3] Ibid., 33.
[4] Ibid., 65.
[5] Apollodorus, *The Library of Greek Mythology*, trans. Robin Hard (1994. Oxford and New York: Oxford University Press, 1997), 33.
[6] Ibid.

In all of these stories, the motif of the death and resurrection of the beloved victim seems to reflect the cycle of vegetation."[7] If the story were to be regarded as a record of fertility rites, this view would explain how the ancient mind could employ Kore's enchantment in a social sense. The story would allow for the fertility of young women's bodies to be equated with that of nature, while at the same time integrating this fertility with the social function of women as wives and mothers. In this context, Persephone's acceptance of the pomegranate seed can be interpreted as signifying her acceptance of motherhood and an erotic partnership in marriage. The symbolism of the pomegranate seed offers a means to interpret the nature of the young girl's enchantment in a socio-cultural framework: it was only necessary to lure the girl into becoming a wife. The Homeric hymn and Apollodorus' text appear to endorse Persephone's acceptance of her new role in the male-dominated hierarchy, and nothing is said that would allow one to envision Kore as wilful agent, rather than as a mere subject of this enchantment.

To further clarify the significance of Persephone's tasting of Hades' offering, one could attempt to extrapolate it from the information on practices of the Eleusinian Mysteries. According to the Homeric hymn, the Mysteries were given to the mortals by Demeter shortly after her daughter's fate in marriage was decided.[8] Referring to the ritual practices of the Eleusinian cult, Albinus notes that "while the hymn may have influenced the content of the ritual process, the same should be equally probable *vice versa*."[9] This is, therefore, an instance when a story can be derived from series of public performances that hold social significance and credibility in their depictions of marriage, agricultural practices, and mothering. When, in turn, this story is transacted through reiterations, the myth that arises from the reiterations may have contributed to the scripting of those social roles and their performance in society. The correlation between the story and the drawing of a social space is immediately visible. Its performance as ritual gives birth to socialisation patterns that engender specific understandings of women. Therefore, insight into the ritual performance may open up the significance of several important narrative elements that have remained obscure in the Homeric hymn, perhaps due to the limitations inherent in its medium and genre.

According to Albinus "it may be said of the Homeric hymn that it resembles the ritual only insofar as the structure of performances is

---

[7] Lars Albinus, *The House of Hades: Studies in Ancient Greek Eschatology* (Oxford: Aarhus University Press, 2000), 165-6.
[8] *Homeric Hymns*, 70-71.
[9] Albinus, 173.

translatable into a scheme of events that fits the narrative purpose."[10] He then proceeds to extrapolate the significance of the performances of the Eleusinian rites by comparing the Homeric hymn and the Orphic discourse, and by examining archaeological evidence. Cross-referencing renderings of the character of Baubo in the Orphic tradition with the account given by Clement of Alexandria, Albinus asserts:

> In the Orphic context, this 'nightly daemon' ... , as she is called ... , assumes and combines in one person the roles that are divided between Metaneira and Iambe in the Homeric hymn. Being the Queen of Eleusis she receives Demeter as a guest in the palace and offers her a 'draught' ... of wine and meal. When Demeter declines, Baubo teases her by uncovering her 'genitals' ... and revealing thereby the child of Iacchos in her bosom ... . Pleased at the sight, Demeter now accepts the drink, and this—Clements says—is 'the hidden mysteries of the Athenians' ... .[11]

But what has this to do with Kore? Albinus comments that the chthonic sphere was often associated with the female womb or bosom ("thus, 'the bosom of nightly Hades' ... presumably alludes to the bosom of the divine nurse, be it Persephone ... Demeter or Baubo"[12]), that *eskhara*, referring to the hollow altar used in the hero cult, was also a word for the vagina, and that Baubo's spouse, Dysaulus, being "intimately associated with Hades himself", establishes "another implicit association between Baubo and the Queen of the underworld."[13]

Thus, it seems that the rituals of the Eleusinian Mysteries were more emphatically connected with celebrating the fertility of women's bodies. Albinus further relates Kerényi's theory, according to which Demeter and Kore represent two different manifestations of the same goddess.[14] The interpretation outlined by Albinus, suggesting that Demeter is pleased with the opportunity of being able to nurse as a mother would nurse a child, can also be applied to interpreting the figure of Kore: Kore's acceptance of the pomegranate seed can be seen as signifying her acceptance of motherhood within marriage. Such is the story enacted through the rituals of the Eleusinian Mysteries: the girl is pleased with the prospect of fulfilling her body's fertility.

In the ancient world, the vision of Persephone as a cosmic mother consecrates the understanding that women can only master their fertility

---

[10] Ibid., 177.
[11] Ibid., 177-8.
[12] Ibid., 180.
[13] Ibid., 180.
[14] Ibid., 166.

attributes when they transform from an unmarried girl into a wife, just as Kore becomes Queen of the underworld (associated with the female womb) only through marriage with Hades. The tasting of the pomegranate seed seems to mark this transition in femininity. It is possible then to view this same transition as representative of Kore's sexual initiation, although it must be noted that there is no direct evidence of this in the Homeric hymn or in the Orphic texts.

While the emphasis in the Mysteries seems to have been on the celebration of the fertility of women's bodies, the Homeric hymn specifies more emphatically that the girl's sexual awakening, and the potential fertility of her body, must be fulfilled in a certain way: through becoming a wife. The hymn highlights at length the advantages of marriage, for example when it narrates Helios' attempts to convince Demeter that her daughter will fare well as Hades' spouse, as well as in Hades' own "plea" to Persephone that she remain with him before she temporarily returns to her mother.[15] Conversely, the scenario of enchantment and abduction that leads to Persephone's marriage also triggers Demeter's adventures in the human world and occasions her revelation of the Mysteries to the Eleusinians.[16] The Mysteries are related to nursing children, and the revelation of them is preceded by, and metaphorically connected to, the manifestation of Demeter's role as fertility goddess. Thus, the narration of the Homeric hymn emphasises women's fulfilment of the social functions of wives and mothers as envisioned in the myth that inspired both the story and the performance of those social roles in the Eleusinian Mysteries. If the story and the ritual indeed had influenced one another, as Albinus notes, it is arguable that both served the purpose of legitimizing the social "value" of women as wives. In this process, the social meanings of "girl" and "woman" became transcendental and transfixed in a larger and broader vision of gender in the cosmic order: all participants in the Eleusinian Mysteries, men and women alike, must internalise these meanings and no other, because social order must be integrated into cosmic order through this interpretation of nature's cyclical transformations. Persephone's return from the underworld in spring as Hades' Queen signifies the change of seasons on the cosmic level, and the change in any young girl's social status after marriage on the social level. The cosmic and the social are integrated through a common denominator: on the two levels, the changes unlock the fertility potential of nature and of women's bodies. There would be no spring if Persephone did not return,

---

[15] *Homeric Hymns*, 37-8, 61.
[16] Ibid., 41-57.

just as there would be no legitimate manifestation of women's bodies' fertility if they did not accept marriage and consent to rejoin the social order that consecrates it.

In the Homeric hymn, the representation of women's experiences of enchantment, ensnarement, and anger channels patriarchal understandings of the social function of women's sexuality. The narrator portrays Kore as innocent, easily spellbound by the beauty of the narcissus, or, perhaps, by her awakening sexuality. The power of the enchantment that leads to her transformation into a wife is shown as being controlled by Zeus. The narcissus was "put forth as a snare" "by the will of Zeus" "as a favour" to Hades.[17] Hence, enchantment that leads to Kore's sexual initiation and to her subsequent marriage to Hades is narrated in a patriarchal context governed by a transaction settled within the masculine hierarchy of gods. In that patriarchy, Kore is represented as unable to resist being enchanted, or being controlled by its consequences. As long as Kore could be denied control over being enchanted in the mythology of the age, the possibilities of representing her within scenarios that might otherwise enable her to resist or master the power of the enchantment would be suppressed.

Such scenarios would have required the representation of Persephone as being in control of that articulation of her enchantment and associated sexual awakening through her ability to give or withhold consent to becoming Hades' partner. Such ungovernability could not be tolerated, since it would have meant that the authority over the fertility of the land (and that over women's bodies) would have been taken away from the mythical masculine brotherhood of Zeus and Hades (in social reality, from men) and, instead, given to the mythical femininity represented by Demeter and Persephone (in social reality, to mothers and daughters). As such, the sexual control over Persephone through ensnarement by enchantment, by force, and by negotiation, allows one to interpret Zeus and Hades as controlling the function of the fertility of the land and of women's bodies, and simultaneously to envision Demeter and Persephone as "performing" this fertility as nursing mothers and sexual partners.

In meta-narrative perspective, this interpretation also reveals the power of the myth to enchant and ensnare audiences through its narrative expression. Persephone and Demeter may be shown as divine women wielding agency, but their agency is defined by their fertility attributes, and can be seen as being limited by Zeus and Hades' scheming. Although fertility and, indirectly, the female sexual body are celebrated in the figures of Demeter and Persephone, we should not forget that they are also

---

[17] Ibid., 33.

mother and wife, and that Zeus and Hades can always be seen as the patrons of this celebration. To an extent, these identities of male and female gods, and the range of actions they were shown capable of performing, were probably consecrated also through the ritual expression of the myth that enchanted and ensnared the participants through means of subjection that differed from those specific to narrative stories. Through such ensnarement and enchantment, the events and identities conveyed in myth were translated into social identities and scenarios of socialisation in the mundane world.

These interpretations of Persephone's story and its resultant rituals strongly connect Persephone to the rituals of fertility that involve a vision of sexuality and provide hints regarding its social management in a male-dominated gender regime. But Persephone's myth has also created a cultural terrain spanning competing claims between such social myths that propagate and legitimate understandings of sexuality within marriage and understandings of marriage, sexuality, and motherhood that challenge those, especially in reinterpretations by women writers. In the following sections I focus on two examples of how the ethos of the Persephone myth serves contemporary writers. Boland's and Lochhead's poems analysed here exploit the myth for the opportunities it offers to conceive alternative possibilities of cultural expression of women's sexuality and fertility, that do not bind women to the social roles of wives and mothers in a male-dominated gender regime. These opportunities derive from the story of Persephone's enchantment, and from the ambiguity regarding her wilful acceptance of the token of sexual awakening.

Persephone in Eavan Boland's "The Pomegranate"

Eavan Boland's poem "The Pomegranate" was published in the collection *In a Time of Violence* (1994). In his review of the collection, R. T. Smith describes Boland as "an explorer of the terrible beauties Yeats witnessed and ... a creator of language which radiates with both lyrical and intellectual beauty."[18] Like W. B. Yeats, Boland is interested in the otherness of the past as known through myth, which permeates our experience of the present through memory. Yet she has explored myth from a distinctly feminine perspective, as, for instance, Colleen Hynes points out: "[Boland's] efforts to retrieve women's stories from historical silence and record them, beginning in the late 1960s and continuing to the

---

[18] R. T. Smith, Review of *In a Time of Violence*, *Southern Humanities Review* 30, no. 3 (Summer 1996): 304-7, 304.

present, established a new type of poetics in what had previously been a male-dominated field" in Ireland.[19] In reviewing *In a Time of Violence* in the year of its publication, Jan Garden Castro notes that "critics already align [Boland's] ideas with those of Adrienne Rich and Margaret Atwood" and she adds to the list Toni Morrison, Nadine Gordimer, and William Gass.[20] Indeed, the poems of *In a Time of Violence*, as well as those of Boland's earlier collection *Outside History* (1990) show that her writing answered Adrienne Rich's call for revisioning male-dominated traditions.[21] Debrah Raschke argues that in the poems of these collections "the individual moments sustain and heal ... . Boland claims history should be personal and ordinary lest it shift truth ... ."[22] As regards *Violence*'s "The Pomegranate", Raschke notices that, in this poem, "the myth of Ceres and Persephone becomes metaphor for the love and feared loss the mother feels for her child." She explicates: "The myth intensifies an ordinary moment of the mother watching the daughter with a 'can of Coke' and a 'plate of uncut fruit.'"[23] My own analysis of the poem explores the degree to which Boland's use of the Persephone myth to intensify an ordinary experience in the life of a mother serves to change the perception of the social functions of women the myth envisions. I will examine the ways in which the poem suggests that myth and (personal and ordinary) history create each other, or rather, set each other up: myth frames and entraps history and vice versa.

The narrator of the poem grew up as an Irish girl in London, and her perception of the tenseness of Anglo-Irish relations informs her perceptions of masculinity and femininity as belonging within untranslatable domains of experience. History is made personal and ordinary by scepticism about the possibilities of communication and bonding in resonance with relations between the English and Irish, mothers (complicit in masculine arrangements) and daughters, and men and women. This scepticism is

---

[19] Colleen Hynes, "'A song for every child I might have had': Infertility and Maternal Loss in Contemporary Irish Poetry", *The Body and Desire in Contemporary Irish Poetry*, ed. Irene Nordin (Dublin: Irish Academic Press, 2006), 144-59, 149.

[20] Jan Garden Castro, "Mad Ireland Hurts Her Too", *Nation*, June 6 (1994): 798-802, 802.

[21] Eavan Boland, *Outside History: Selected Poems 1980-1990* (New York: Norton, 1990).

[22] Debrah Raschke, "Eavan Boland's *Outside History* and *In a Time of Violence*: Rescuing Women, the Concrete, and Other Things Physical from the Dung Heap", *Colby Quarterly* 32, no. 2 (June 1996): 135-42, 136.

[23] Raschke, 139.

reflected in the poem's use of the Persephone myth to show that traditional versions of the myth legitimate male-dominated gender regimes that alienate women from themselves. However, even as it suggests that the myth is couched in a masculine language of authority, the poem entices us to glimpse an unnameable secret at the heart of its legend—the revelation of which could be empowering for women. The power of myth may yet change historical reality. The following argument will explain how Boland's narrator both longs for and fears this possibility of change.

Boland's narrator's viewpoint is that of a mother who locates her subjectivity in the images of both Persephone and Ceres (Demeter's name in Latin versions of the myth).[24] This is evidenced in the belief of the "I" of the poem that "the best thing about the legend [myth of Persephone] is/ I can enter it anywhere. And have."[25] The narrator's childhood experiences are given meaning, through the myth, as cultural abductions: an Irish girl in London, the narrator finds herself "in exile/ in a city of fogs and strange consonants."[26] London is thus envisioned in parallel with the mythic location of the underworld as a cultural landscape of masculine agency. The narrator not only finds herself in unfamiliar territory but, as young woman, is unable to comprehend the alien, masculine voice of the English. She remembers this voice as inflected by "strange consonants."[27] After she becomes a mother, the myth correlative of the narrator's identity changes from the image of Persephone to that of Ceres, but she finds Persephone again, this time in her daughter:

> Later
> I walked out in a summer twilight
> searching for my daughter at bed-time.
> When she came running I was ready
> to make any bargain to keep her.
> I carried her back past whitebeams
> and wasps and honey-scented buddleias.[28]

The mother's willingness to make any bargain to keep her daughter can be read in reference to Demeter's bond with Persephone in the Greek myth.

---

[24] Boland, "The Pomegranate", 20.

[25] Ibid.

[26] Ibid.

[27] Boland's expression evokes Seamus Heaney's words: "I think of the personal and Irish pieties as vowels, and the literary awarenesses nourished on English as consonants." Seamus Heaney, *Preoccupations: Selected Prose 1968-1978* (London: Faber, 1980), 37.

[28] Boland, "The Pomegranate", 20.

Boland's poem speaks of the daughter as a child, presenting the mother's readiness for the bargain as a memory of the past. However, in relation to the Persephone myth, the bargain referred to is most likely that through which Persephone's faith is transacted between Demeter, Zeus, and Hades. The poem thus suggests that the mother's readiness is characteristic of a maternal figure's anticipation throughout her daughter's childhood of the eventual bargain she will have to make at the time of the daughter's sexual awakening, and hence, alludes to the inevitability of the myth's scenario: for the Ceres inherent in every mother, the myth's patterns are inescapable. The ever-present danger threatening the paradise world of the pre-sexual daughter is suggested by evoking, not only floral adornments, but also the presence of wasps.

As if fated to inhabit the mythic role and to thread the pathways laid out in the mythic story, the narrator fears the meanings she is, hence, myth-bound to read into her own role as mother:

> But I was Ceres then and I knew
> winter was in store for every leaf
> on every tree on that road.
> Was inescapable for each one we passed.
> And for me.[29]

In the second part of the poem, the references to Kore's myth again suggest that a daughter cannot avoid the fate to which she is destined in the myth. When the narrator tells that her daughter is asleep "beside her teen magazines,/ her can of Coke, her plate of uncut fruit", we may imagine her as an innocent Kore who has not yet tasted Hades' offering.[30] The mythic realm of the dead has become the immediate reality, marked by signs of corporate consumerism into which the girl has not yet woken. The story is about to be transformed into reality, and its point of entry into the realm of experience is counterpointed with a questioning of the myth's pattern. Boland records the possibilities of changing the myth's life-shaping stories:

> The pomegranate! How did I forget it?
> She could have come home and been safe
> and ended the story and all
> our heart-broken searching but she reached
> out a hand and plucked a pomegranate.[31]

---

[29] Ibid.
[30] Ibid.
[31] Ibid.

The gesture, signifying the young woman's "hunger",—the awakening of her sexual desire—is seen as being "at the heart of legend". Boland draws the reader's attention to the potential ways in which the words that carry Persephone's myth into a story can signify the young girl's desire:

> She put out her hand and pulled down
> the French sound for apple and
> the noise of stone and the proof
> that even in the place of death,
> at the heart of legend, in the midst
> of rocks full of unshed tears
> ready to be diamonds by the time
> the story was told, a child can be
> hungry.[32]

These verses reflect on the process in the myth through which the girl's desire is rendered. The young girl's hunger is at the heart of the story, contained like a gem in its words. In the lines above, "rocks" and "diamonds" are used to refer to the way the words of Persephone's story function. The words can be like rocks that, instead of awakening women to Kore's fate, rather chain them to it.

This is not the only story that closes off the significance of young girls' sexual awakening by interpreting them only in masculine meaning systems. The rendering of the girl's object of desire as "the French sound for apple" (*pomme*) suggests a reference to the biblical story of Adam and Eve as rendered in Western cultural contexts in which the fruit Eve tasted from the Tree of Knowledge in Eden is an apple. Eve's tasting of the forbidden fruit is widely understood to signify her acknowledgement of her sexuality, which leads to her fall from God's grace. Boland's poem correlates "the French sound for apple" with "the noise of stone". This correlation of *pomme* with a metaphorical rendering of the phonetic expression of "granite", makes up phonetically the "pomegranate"; as such, it suggests that the Eden myth, too, participates in chaining young girls' sexual desire to masculine explanations and legitimisations.

However, the words of Kore's story can also be like diamonds, allowing for a precious gift to shine through the myth. Persephone's story, as we have seen from the analysis of its classical versions, can serve to legitimate constraining social identities for women, but Boland's poem suggests that recrafting the story can uncover the diamonds hidden in the rocks. The narrator is not ready to give up preserving the beauty that she

---

[32] Ibid., 20-21.

perceives lies hidden in the myth—the possibility of transforming rocks into diamonds:

> But what else
> can a mother give her daughter but such
> beautiful rifts in time?[33]

"Rifts" refers to the breaking and remaking of the bond between mother and daughter, the mother's unwilling concession to the girl's transformation into a lover and her draw into the time's becoming. But "rifts" may also suggest the possibility of breaking the materiality of the myth, that is, the myth's manifestation in its timing of a woman's life as daughter and mother, to reveal beneath its cast Ceres' deeper secret: the story of the young girl's hunger can only be given as gift of diamonds by her mother and that outside of the mother-daughter bond the true story of the daughter's hunger remains hidden under barren rocks.

The poem makes us doubt whether "the hidden mysteries of the Athenians", as Clement references the secret of women's fertility, has ever been in fact revealed through the rites and retellings of the myth.[34] Perhaps these rites and retellings of the events of myth have merely covered up the meanings of those events, naturalising across time a mythic experience that benefits men. The ending of the poem retains a sense of the beauty of living through the magic of myth, but also suggests that this magic must be sought beyond the masculine interpretations of the events of Kore's transformation through her sexual awakening. This quest would be a painful working through and within the constraints of myth, which are still perceived as irrevocable:

> If I defer the grief I will diminish the gift.
> The legend will be hers as well as mine.
> She will enter it. As I have.
> She will wake up. She will hold
> the papery flushed skin in her hand.
> And to her lips. I will say nothing.[35]

Boland's poem ambiguously suggests that Persephone's myth, although stifling, yet points towards a specifically women's understanding of its

---

[33] Ibid., 21. Boland adopts a similar position in relation to myths of femininity used in Irish nationalist ideologies, as Edna Longley's arguments show. Longley, "From Cathleen to Anorexia", 187-8.

[34] Albinus, 178.

[35] Boland, "The Pomegranate", 21.

"gift". The myth is used to negotiate the meaning of the rift between the innocent daughter and mother in terms of both inner desire and social constraints. We learn about the making of the girl's "hunger" into a "legend", the "sound" and "noise" of which belong to a masculine voice of "strange consonants". On another level, this voice registers the strange consonance between daughter and mother—strange because the consonance is set up in a myth of masculine agency. Nevertheless it is through this consonance that the mystery of the "gift" is concealed from men, and thus Demeter's true revelation remains the secret of women. The ending line of the poem, in which the mother "will say nothing"—might suggest that nothing of the gift of womanhood will be revealed, or has ever been, in spite of the masculine (narrative) appropriation of the girl's "hunger", that is, of the desire manifested in her sexual awakening.

Boland's poem exploits an idea expressed in W. F. Otto's observation that the relationship between Demeter and Kore differs from the other relationships envisioned in the fertility paradigm as understood in myth studies, for "it does not constitute a liaison between lovers, but the loving bond between mother and daughter."[36] In Boland's poetic interpretation of the myth, this bond is of foremost significance. Boland exploits the possibilities, offered by the myth, that the bond between mother and daughter may be stronger than that between lovers, and thus challenges the myth's traditional meanings.

Noticeably in this poem, the space of myth is integrated with that of the reality of experience. The godly figures of Ceres and Persephone shape the content of human experience, and the mythic location of the underworld is read into the contemporary suburb. The story of Persephone is told as one of personal and social relations, making visible the myth's social functions—i.e., it posits Persephone's myth as a social myth that affects and produces effects in modes of women's socialisation.

R. T. Smith comments that the collection in which "The Pomegranate" appears, *In a Time of Violence*, "employs subversive and disruptive rhetorical strategies to create a distressed beauty, witnessing to the fact that any time is a violent one for those who lack autonomy."[37] "The Pomegranate" reflects a case in point in its emphasis on the inescapability of socialisation patterns designed in male-generated myths, through which women become wives and mothers. However, "The Pomegranate" also suggests that women's own stories of their sexual awakening remain incomprehensible to men, interspaced as they are between the "strange

---

[36] Albinus, 166.
[37] R. T. Smith, 304-7.

consonants" of masculine languages of authority. The poem triggers the intuition that in the tales derived from the myth, their past versions demand an acceptance of masculine abduction as the price for acknowledging young girls' sexual awakening as enchantment. Ceres, the mother, has yet to tell a story that is larger than that maintained in masculine transactions of reality, and hence, the enchantment "at the heart of legend" has yet to be explored on women's terms.[38] Until then, the poem suggests, the enchantment remains only distressingly beautiful.

Reversals: Liz Lochhead's Version of Lucy's Diary

As with Boland in Ireland, Liz Lochhead's poetry responded, in Scotland, to Adrienne Rich's revisionist manifesto, and reacted to the male-dominated literary traditions that govern and constrain the expression of women's subjective identities.[39] Focusing on the oral and performative qualities of discourse, associated in Scotland in the 1970s with the domestic sphere as a women's realm, Lochhead's poetry "offered a radical departure from the forms of previous Scottish poetry" which enabled her "to interrogate accepted social commonplaces with regard to female experience."[40] "Lucy's Diary" was first published in an issue of the series entitled *Writers in Brief* in 1986, and then republished in Lochhead's own 1991 collection *Bagpipe Muzak*.[41] In 1991 Lochhead was an established writer with a significant publication record. Dorothy McMillan suggests that the poems before *Bagpipe Muzak* clear away the myths about women's identities and promise "a story of new woman. But since she has had to endure the agonising struggle of self-conception and self-deliverance,

---

[38] The danger of remythologizing women "on women's terms" in telling such a story should be noted, as Brian Henry suggests when he argues that several poems of *In a Time of Violence*, including "The Pomegranate", transform women into icons so that "Boland's credibility in her essay becomes questionable". Henry refers to Boland's collection of essays *Object Lessons*, in which she denounces male-generated mythologizations of women. Brian Henry, "The Woman as Icon, the Woman as Poet", *Michigan Quarterly Review*, Vol. XXXVI, No. 1 (Winter, 1997): 188-202, 200. Eavan Boland, *Object Lessons: The Life of the Woman and the Poet in Our Time* (Manchester: Carcanet, 1995).

[39] Carol Anderson, "Emma Tennant, Elspeth Barker, Alice Thompson: Gothic Revisited", *Contemporary Scottish Women Writers*, 117-30, 128.

[40] McCulloch, 17.

[41] Liz Lochhead, *Liz Lochhead* (Glasgow: National Book League, 1986), Writers in Brief No. 21. My references will be to the poem as published in *Bagpipe Muzak* (1991).

she faces the danger of solipsism and severance from the past."[42] For McMillan, "the poems of *Bagpipe Muzak* [...] go some way towards tackling this problem, both by recapitulating the strategies of the preceding poems and by going on to provide a new sense of privacy and public meaning."[43] "Lucy's Diary" can be interpreted as a synthesis of Lochhead's play *Dracula*, first published three years after "Lucy's Diary" first appeared. In *Bagpipe Muzak* the poem functions both as a recapitulation of Lochhead's earlier narrative strategies, and as a context for other poems dealing with representations of women's private and public personae.

"Lucy's Diary" is structured in six parts, each an entry narrated in poetry by Lucy. In the note to the title we read: "This Lucy is a version of Bram Stoker's Lucy, Dracula's first and perfect victim", which indicates that the narrative framework used by Lochhead's narrator has been inherited from Bram Stoker's novel by the same name, together with its preordaining scripts.[44]

Lochhead's Lucy, in the poem as in the play, is a young woman who can "enter" Dracula's story "anywhere", to use in a different context the vision of Boland's narrator in "The Pomegranate". Jan McDonald and Jennifer Harvie emphasise that two versions of Lucy are represented in Lochhead's *Dracula*: as fully human, Lucy is "immature, an undeveloped child, not a woman" whereas as vampire she is shown as a sexually mature woman, aware of the power that her body gives her and of its source and means of control.[45] This observation can also be applied to "Lucy's Diary". Thus, Lochhead's retelling uses Dracula's story to reflect on the transformations that accompany young girls' sexual awakening.

In the poem, the narrator might be said to enter Dracula's story as a Lucy inhabiting the threshold between human and vampire state. McDonald and Harvie argue that the poem represents Lucy as anorexic: "This gross flesh I will confine/ in the whalebone of my very own/ hunger."[46] In my view, these lines also suggest that Lucy anticipates favourably Dracula's power in her body. The human, pre-sexual Lucy sees

---

[42] Dorothy McMillan, "Liz Lochhead and the Ungentle Art of Clyping", *Liz Lochhead's Voices*, 17-37, 30.

[43] Ibid.

[44] Lochhead, "Lucy's Diary", 60. But in Stoker's text Lucy is not Dracula's first victim. Perhaps Lochhead wishes to suggest that Lucy's awakening to her body's desires through Dracula can be seen as an initiation experience.

[45] Jan McDonald and Jennifer Harvie, "Putting New Twists to Old Stories: Feminism and Lochhead's Drama", *Liz Lochhead's Voices*, 124-47, 131.

[46] Lochhead, "Lucy's Diary", 62. McDonald and Harvie, 131.

her body as controlled by others and her anorexia can be explained as a manifestation of her refusal of this control. This interpretation is consistent with one of the major thematic concerns of *Bagpipe Muzak*, identified by Lynda Mugglestone as "the refutation of the importance of body image."[47] However, as vampire, and sexual woman, the poem anticipates, the girl's hunger can be identified with Dracula's seductive sensuality and power, and serves to integrate body and self in an identity which Lucy can control, in the whalebone of the girl's own desire.

McDonald and Harvie explain that Lochhead's vision of Lucy's character is derived from *The Wise Wound* by Penelope Shuttle and Peter Redgrove, a text which discusses "the 'benefits' bestowed by Dracula on his women."[48] Based on Shuttle and Redgrove's text, McDonald and Harvie show that Lochhead's Lucy can be characterised as a "chlorotic weak creature" before being turned into vampire, whereas afterwards Lucy can be seen as empowered, sharing the features of vampire women whose "eyes shone" and who "spoke energy with every glance."[49] These insights suggest that Lochhead's reconstruction of a vampiric Lucy envisions an empowerment of the female body that challenges the worldview advocated in Stoker's *Dracula*, in which the corporeal, sexual, woman must be sublimated into the role of the incorporeal "good" wife through a kind of social anorexia determined by the need to govern the body. This need to govern the female body is a reflection of the need to govern the body of nature and the body politic, a government that is threatened by Dracula in his association with wild desires, nature, and anarchy, which is why several members of the gentlemanly elite of late Victorian Britain are set to destroy him. However, while taking this argument into account, my reading of "Lucy's Diary" will focus more emphatically on how the poem offers a background for juxtaposing elements of the Persephone and Dracula myths. In doing so I will explore the valences of the metaphor of Lucy's "hunger", which can be compared to the girl's "hunger" referenced in Boland's poem.

I have defined myth as being engendered by the reiteration of normative stories. This view allows us to conceive that any story can be elevated to the status of myth, so that we may speak of Dracula's and Persephone's myth through the same concepts. We may jostle the two myths in order to see how they corroborate the same norms, yet, at the

---

[47] Lynda Mugglestone, "Lochhead's Language: Style, Status, Gender and Identity", *Liz Lochhead's Voices*, 93-108, 106.

[48] McDonald and Harvie, 131. Penelope Shuttle and Peter Redgrove, *The Wise Wound* (London: Penguin, 1980).

[49] Shuttle and Redgrove, 267.

same time, this jostling may offer opportunities for challenging the norms nestled in the myths. "Lucy's Diary" offers opportunities for such a jostling, which allows us to explore possibilities of representing Persephone's and Lucy's wilfulness in ways that suggest more empowering identities of women as wives and lovers. Exploring these possibilities, I will compare Lochhead's poem and Boland's "The Pomegranate". Through that comparison, I focus on how both poets deal with the themes of enchantment and ensnarement of the pre-sexual girl, as well as with the accompanying theme of anger (suffused with grief in Boland's poem). This comparison will show that young girls' "hunger" has been mythically consolidated in different ways in Lochhead's and Boland's respective voices, with different effects.

In its creation of what has become an archetypal vampire figure, Stoker's narrative represents women's bodily desire and sexuality as demonic by distinguishing between an evil abductor who allows for its unchecked display and the men of good standing of Victorian society. Stoker's text legitimates socialisation modes that require the government of the body through reason in a cultural framework that equates body with nature and women, and reason with society seen as a brotherhood elite's realm of gentlemanly spirit and taste. Within this multi-layered framework, Dracula's story deals with aspects of the interrelation between abduction, desire, and the transformation of young women into wives. This interrelation and transformation renders the text suitable for juxtaposition to Persephone's myth. In the latter, the masculine brotherhood of Jupiter and Hades wins a share in the government of nature that leads to the appropriation of Persephone's body's fertility. The myth provides an explanation for social hierarchies in which women are confined to domestic roles and also legitimises those same roles by connecting a woman's fertility to the fertility of nature. The possible scenarios of erotic encounters between men and women devised in Persephone's and Dracula's myths share similar elements inasmuch as both are concerned with how the realm of the organic, of the body and of its desires, may be governed through masculine agency.

Such common elements are suggested in Lochhead's poem, where entry number 3 reads:

> Yesterday
> the gardener's big lad
> gave me a peach from the greenhouse.
> Unthinking, I bit and sucked
> then suddenly flung it from me
> in a real rage at its beauty.

Something in its furred blush hurt me,
stuck in my throat
like a lump and made me spill,
deliberately,
clouded paint-water all over my watercolour
I'd worked on all morning, spoiling it.[50]

This portion of the poem allows us to compare elements of Persephone's myth with those in the Judeo-Christian tradition myth of Adam and Eve as well as with the elements of Dracula's myth. Lochhead's voice permits envisioning a site of interaction between the meanings of these myths, and thus makes possible an exploration of their tendency to re-create the drama of erotic encounters within frameworks of masculine agency.

As in Boland's poem, elements of Eve's story are interwoven with that of Persephone: "Yesterday/ the gardener's big lad/ gave me a peach from the greenhouse." Reflections on the nature of desire and women's sexuality gather up around this token of enchantment: "Unthinking, I bit and sucked/ then suddenly flung it from me/ in a real rage at its beauty." The young woman's tasting of the fruit is rendered through expressions resonating with those in Dracula's story used to describe the sucking and biting of the vampire. This reveals a framework for reinterpreting Persephone's myth, since the character of Lochhead's poem can be seen as being involved in the overlapping fabulas of several stories.

At first, the young woman of Lochhead's poem appears like an innocent Kore. Like the Kore of Apollodorus' myth who ate the pomegranate seed "failing to foresee what the consequence could be", she accepts the token "unthinking".[51] But, reading Persephone's character through Lochhead's contemporary figure of Lucy, the traditional event in which Persephone accepts food from the deadly abductor is coloured with overtones of sexual lust.

Lochhead's poem invites an interpretation of the Dracula myth through its employment of Persephone's myth, and vice versa. This circular re-interpretation of the myths allows us to challenge the paradigmatic value of the mythical scenarios that explain young women's sexual awakening through using narratives of abduction and temptation. The ancient Persephone myth justifies the abduction of the pre-sexual girl and condones her giving in to temptation by regarding these actions as natural and necessary for the fulfilment of a larger social and cosmic desiderate: the manifestation of nature's fertility that guarantees survival. In Boland's

---

[50] Lochhead, "Lucy's Diary", 61.
[51] Apollodorus, 33.

poem, the tense acknowledgement of the inevitable "cultural" abduction of the pre-sexual girl into a male-dominated social world occasioned by the anticipation of her response to temptation suggests that the girl's transformation into sexual woman will be inevitably made sense of on men's terms, while women's own story of the enchantment of sexual awakening remains accessible only through rifts that open unto alterity, within the bonding relationship between mother and daughter. For Lochhead's Lucy, the temptation signifying a sexual awakening is the occasion of the revelation of both the rage and the beauty that accompanies it. But unlike in Boland's poem, the awakening of Lucy does not trigger the realisation of the impossibility of communicating the experience in a masculine voice, but rather the impulse to challenge this voice: "When Quincey Morris calls me mighty pretty/ it only makes me hate him".[52] As the young woman becomes aware of her "very own hunger" she rejects the matronage of other women figures in her life:

> This gross flesh I will confine
> in the whalebone of my very own hunger. All term
> I would not bleed, not
> for Matron, Mama, Mademoiselle,
> nor my sister Mina.[53]

This Persephone-like Lucy refuses to "bleed" for her mother, an act which reveals her rejection of the notion that she must direct the use of her body's fertility in a manner that fulfils the patriarchal role of the wife. This refusal allows us to reinterpret the significance of Demeter's negotiations as a process in which the mother's consent to Persephone's transformation into a wife is complicit with masculine desire. But the Persephone that Lochhead makes transparent behind Stoker's Lucy is no longer only an innocent: she has assumed the sensuality assigned in Stoker's text to openly sexual women. In Stoker's narrative, Van Helsing's brotherhood deplores Lucy's transformation from an angelic innocent into a sexual predator, and hence proceeds to seal her fate and disenchant her body to underscore her emotions. In Lochhead's poem, Lucy begins to understand and act out the sensuality of the sexual woman by noting: "Despite myself,/ the sea air is giving me an appetite."[54]

It is possible to discern a revised meaning in the ancient myth by re-envisioning it through the prism of Boland's and Lochhead's poems. The

---

[52] Lochhead, "Lucy's Diary", 62.
[53] Ibid.
[54] Ibid.

ancient myth of Kore/ Persephone serves to define both the category of woman (as pre-sexual girl, wife, and mother) and the ritual of erotic encounters that differentiate the roles of men and women in terms of abduction and temptation (to which the girl ambiguously surrenders). Boland's poem underscores a separation between the realms of masculinity and femininity: if femininity has been narrated as abduction and temptation, it has been done by men. Even as women fulfil the social rituals to which the narration subjects them, the loss is men's, for the nature of the enchantment circumscribing women's sexual awakening remains incomprehensible to them.

Lochhead's poem allows us to draw on the myth of Dracula in order to contextualise the sexual connotations of rituals of abduction, enchantment, and temptation that underlie Persephone's story, with those of a modern myth. Here, however, the roles envisioned as socially legitimate in ritual are challenged. The young woman comes to inhabit a masculine position: she becomes an abductress herself but, unlike Stoker's sanitised abductress, whose sexual body was punished to recuperate the angelic incorporeal body, Lochhead's Lucy reclaims the position of both innocent and sexual woman and thus engenders an understanding of "woman" that is irreducible to the categories straitjacketing femininity and masculinity in terms of polarised socially acceptable idealisations.

Conclusion

As noted, Albinus argues that the expression of the Persephone myth in the Homeric Hymn to Demeter may have influenced the content of the ritual practices of the Eleusinian cult, but "the same should be equally probable *vice versa*."[55] Persephone's story is developed from, and in turn served to develop, the practices associated with the Eleusinian Mysteries. The ancient story is derived from a series of events that held public significance in the time in which they were performed and, hence, events that corroborate certain meanings of marriage, agricultural practices, and mothering of cultural significance; in turn, the story contributes to the scripting of such events—in its aesthetic performance. The narrative and ritual expression (the Eleusinian Mysteries) of the myth reinforce each other, scripting and legitimating socialisation patterns for men and women, and also strengthening the desirability of their repetition. Thus, myths become integrated into social rituals that engender forms of socialisation.

---

[55] Albinus, 173.

The ancient myth grants that Persephone, and henceforth every pre-
sexual girl, must be the subject of a transaction between males, be tempted
by their future husbands, and their responses are read only in terms of
giving in to the husband's demands, at least partially. Their marriage is
celebrated, and the terms of this union are legitimated by making it reflect
the cosmic order of seasonal alternation. This corroboration of cosmic and
social order engenders unchallengeable and fixed understandings of
"women".

The recent myth centred on Dracula also defines social rituals of
marriage using the motif of abduction. As in Persephone's myth, the
abductor hails from an "otherworldly" realm, and his victims spend their
existence traversing between this world and his. Their encounters are
eroticised. Here, however, the abduction is not legitimate, for its
legitimation would imply an acceptance of women's sexuality that would
make visible their enchantment, not simply as passive victims, but as
active "predators" themselves. Late nineteenth-century male-generated
understandings of women as innocent would have been undermined if
women were seen to enjoy legitimately an appetite for mastering erotic
encounters. The young woman's abduction is demonised in Bram Stoker's
Dracula so as to qualify negatively her wilful participation in the
abduction; hence, there, wilful women are constructed as archetypical
harlots.

Dracula's myth expresses what Bruno Latour has identified as the
moderns' paradoxes: it carries out both the work of mediation that permits
Nature's intervention "at every point in the fabrication of their societies",
and the work of purification that holds Nature at bay, othered in its
"radical transcendence".[56] The figures of Dracula and Lucy, metonymically
tied to Nature, serve to mediate the social norms that separate masculine
culture and feminine nature and specify the government of the latter by the
former. Although invoking hybrids born through the intersection between
masculine culture and feminine nature, Dracula's myth nevertheless
carries out the work of purification that separates nature from culture.
Kenneth Burke pointed out that as soon as a myth emerges, the need arises
for "specialist" guardians of the myth and supervisors of the correct
fulfilment of rituals.[57] In ancient Greece these would have been the priests
and priestesses who guaranteed the authority attributed to the gods. The
guardians of the cultural order in the society that Dracula haunts are

---

[56] Bruno Latour, *We Have Never Been Modern*, trans. Catherine Porter
(Cambridge, Massachusetts: Harvard University Press, 1993), 32.
[57] Kenneth Burke, "Doing and Saying: Thoughts on Myth, Cult and Archetype",
Salmagundi 7 (1971): 100-119.

representatives of the medical, scientific, and legal professions; their authority is strengthened by narrators such as those enabled in Stoker's text.

It is not my intention to suggest that Dracula's myth is based on Persephone's myth, but only to compare their functioning as social myths in their creation of the meaning of female eroticism and sexual partnership. Persephone of ancient myth is first enchanted with the narcissus' beauty and then enraged at the prospect of living with Hades. Boland's poem suggests a need to preserve the enchantment of the young girl's sexual awakening on feminine, rather than masculine, terms. The Persephone coexisting with Lucy in the narrator of "Lucy's Diary" is both enraged and enchanted, and, as such, she recuperates agency in the cultural space defining sexual encounters between men and women. By making her voice contradictory feelings, Lochhead's poem helps us to understand the ambiguity of Persephone's acceptance of Hades' seed, as well as Lucy's ambiguous status as Dracula's passive victim, as proof of women's wilfulness as erotic partners. Lochhead's young woman both accepts and denies, is enraged at, and longs for, the male's offering. The faithful enchantment of the young woman in the ancient myth has become a dreary enchantment of women's fate in Boland. The faithful disenchantment of the young woman from the demon's grip in Stoker's *Dracula* has inspired Lochhead's re-creation of her as a woman in control of her fate.

CHAPTER SEVEN

STORIES AND MYTHS ABOUT WOMEN IN LIZ LOCHHEAD'S *DRACULA*

Having examined Lochhead's re-creation of Lucy's character in her poem "Lucy's Diary", I will continue with a more extensive analysis of her re-creation of Dracula's story in the play of the same title.[1] Reviewing Lochhead's drama, Jan McDonald and Jennifer Harvie show that

> Although based on historical events, involving 'real' characters, and/or on myths that have become part of common cultural currency, Lochhead's plays do not simply repeat and thus reify 'official' versions of myths and legends or their subversions promulgated, and accepted, by popular culture. Rather, Lochhead's work reconfigures each story, both thematically and structurally, from a feminist standpoint. The plays are thus re-visions as described by Adrienne Rich ... .[2]

In the following analysis of Lochhead's re-creation of Dracula's story, I will explore how its thematic and structural reconfiguration bears on the relation between subjective identity, nature, and myth. This analysis will allow me to extend the understanding of the concept of myth as including not only the corpuses of narratives traditionally recognised by anthropologists as compounding various myths, as is the case with narratives of Persephone's story, but also any set of narratives that has created an ethos which enhances a narrative's assumptions, conferring upon them the same authority and explanatory power that are usually associated with myth. In this perspective, the set of narratives that has created the myth of Dracula includes Stoker's original novel and Lochhead's version of Dracula's story, as well as all the other versions which cite to an extent Stoker's text or other versions. The myth of Dracula is constituted through a chain of narrative reiterations.

---

[1] The play was first performed in Edinburgh at the Lyceum Studio Theatre on 10 August 1987. It was first published by Penguin in 1989.

[2] McDonald and Harvie, 124.

Thus, in my view, the reiteration of a narrative pattern consecrates a narrative as myth. Through this reiteration, an ethos emerges, that is, a set of norms that shapes and forms the identity of those who consent to being signified as subjects through the reiterated narrative at a given point in time. This understanding of myths and their ethos is based on the idea that socialisation processes and social identities are partly determined by how we use narratives to signify ourselves as social actors. In expressing our social identities we cite from others' narratives. Institutional settings are built around and through sets of cited narratives. Citational chains that reiterate the same subjective position over time yield normative constructions of subjective identity. I regard a narrative conveying these norms as the narrative of a social myth. But narrative reiterations may dissolve and reconstruct subjective identity, finding new ways of signifying identities through finding and channelling the voices repudiated in monoglossic discursive regimes. Subjective identity is amenable to the heteroglossic interference of voices come from repudiated realms of otherness. Heteroglossia always leads to desubjection in the sense that its carnivalesque dimension contests norms and authority, allowing new cultural possibilities for signifying the subject to emerge. Normative, monoglossic discourse is often the discourse of a social group, yielding a social myth, and, in the extreme, an ideology, whereas heteroglossic discourse is the discourse of the individual, contesting the dominant narratives and the norms they institutionalise, and which govern one's subjective identity as member of a social group.

In this context, the central concern of my analysis in this chapter is the intertextual relation between the story narrated in Bram Stoker's novel *Dracula* (1897), and its reiteration with a difference in Lochhead's play (first performed in 1987). Cohan and Shires argue that "the term 'narrative' applies to the visual medium of storytelling as well. ... In both cases, the story is mediated by its telling—its medium of communication—so that the two are inseparable."[3] Thus, I regard both versions of Dracula's story as narrative texts. Moreover, the distinction between play and narrative is difficult to make in an analysis of the performative aspects of social identities derived from narrative scripts. Richard Schechner has shown that there exists two-way traffic of performers' identities between aesthetic drama, played by actors on the theatre stage, and social drama, played by social actors in the day-to-day reality.[4] In similar manner, I argue that the subjective identities and actions

---

[3] Cohan and Shires, 2.
[4] Richard Schechner, *Performance Theory* (1977, 2nd ed. 1988. London: Routledge, 2003), esp. 112-169, 125.

of social actors are scripted to a significant extent in narratives prescribing scenarios of events for narrative actors. Our social personae are partly constituted through enacting dramatic scenarios, as well as through narrating ourselves to ourselves and to others in social interaction. Narratives, if reiterated in consecration of a social myth and ethos, of habitual ways of showing ourselves on the social stage, are performative.

The intertextual relation between the two texts, established by Lochhead's narrator/director, forms the background for an exploration of the meanings of feminine bodies enshrined in Stoker's text. I will argue that Lochhead's *Dracula* proposes an alternative view of the feminine body to that afforded by Stoker's novel. Lochhead's play acknowledges, rather than repudiates, the body's organicity, celebrates rather than represses its desires, and uses irony rather than fear to represent the body's relationship to powerful, unbounded, and ungovernable nature. Stoker's narrations about Dracula have yielded, through reiteration in various kinds of texts (literary, cinematic, etc.), a "cult", as opposed to "folkloric", vampire myth.[5] In its original form, the cult myth conveys normative guidelines, rooted in Victorian identity schisms, for the socialisation of feminine bodies. Lochhead's reiteration of the narrative of this myth challenges these guidelines. Many recent vampire narratives derived from Dracula's story bring similar challenges. Lochhead's version is especially interesting because it offers opportunities for reflection on the ethos of the vampire through concepts of the organic. For Lochhead, the organic is a realm of hybridity in which the intersection of the human (the subject) and the non-human (nature) produces new cultural possibilities for conceiving and narrating one's relation to bodily desire. In Stoker's text, the intersections of the human and the non-human provoke horror, and the two realms are eventually separated. The two different ways of envisioning the relation between subjectivity and the organic compel different understandings of one's relation to one's body, reflected in the texts' representations of feminine bodies. My reading will focus not so much on representations of Lucy's and Mina's bodies, which have been thoroughly investigated by criticism, as on another feminine body Lochhead's text represents: that of the commoner Fanny Waller.

---

[5] My comments on vampire folklore are based on a folkloric investigation in the western area of Suceava County, Romania, in which I took part for several weeks in 1992 and 1993. This included a limited exploration of folk beliefs related to *strigoi*, the folklore entity most closely identifiable as a vampire figure. The western part of Suceava County is adjacent to the area surrounding the locality indicated in Stoker's novel as Bistritz, and therefore it is near to the area where Dracula's castle was imagined to be.

In the first section of this chapter I will examine the ways in which the vampire myth in its instantiation in folklore, Stoker's text, and Lochhead's play, permits different ways of envisioning the relation between social persona and the organic. In the second section I will explain how this relation is narrated, and how its narrative reiteration changes various elements of the myth. In the third and final section I will explore what definitions of class and gender can be derived from the two versions of Dracula's story, focusing on how their being part of the same citational chain affects the social value of the vampire myth.

Nature, Society, and the Vampire Myth

In Stoker's text, Lucy's body is metonymically related to nature, that is, Lucy's relation to nature is one of "part for whole". Mina's body can be compared with a palimpsest on which the writing of her character has obscured the expression of her relation to her body to such extent that her body is almost completely absent: she can be said to represent a disembodied version of Lucy, and her body is only metaphorically related to nature. Lochhead's version of *Dracula*, in which Lucy and Mina are sisters, employs a similar vision to different effects. In addition, Lochhead's story introduces a third way of narrating the feminine body, in which the representation of the body is not a cultural metonym or metaphor for nature. In Lochhead's play, Fanny Waller's body represents raw nature, that is, the body as such, without any ties to the social world. The analysis of this representation, and of the ways in which nature inhabits Fanny Waller, offers opportunities for reflection on the cultural paradigms that inform Stoker's text and the vampire myth based on it.

Many interpretations of Stoker's text claim that it is concerned with the management of sexuality: the repudiation of Lucy's wild sexuality is seen as yielding an ideal tame wife, represented by Mina.[6] But other critics suggest that this kind of analysis is aligned with late nineteenth-century discourses of sexuality in legitimating interpretations of Lucy's craving for blood in terms of unclean sexual appetite. For instance, William Hughes points out that the early representations of vampires focused on their sheer violence rather than on their sexual violence, and on their "less than

---

[6] For instance Nina Auerbach, *Our Vampires, Ourselves* (Chicago: University of Chicago Press, 1995), 80; David Pirie, *The Vampire Cinema* (London: Hamlyn, 1977), 30; Carol Davison, "Introduction", *Bram Stoker's Dracula: Sucking Through the Century, 1897-1997*, ed. Carol Davison (Toronto: Dundurn, 1997), 19-40, 27.

human" character.[7] Hughes underlines that Lucy craves blood, not semen, and recommends that critics should focus more on the shift from violence to sexual violence in representations of vampires.[8] Such a shift is reflected in Stoker's *Dracula*, as Hughes shows by analysing Dr Seward's conflicting feelings of horror and fascination vis-à-vis vampirised Lucy.[9] A psychiatrist, Seward is unable to use conventional medical discourse to make sense of the desires affirmed in Lucy's body. As one who is attracted to Lucy, he uses male-generated conventions of women's premarital behaviour to interpret the violence of the body's desires in terms of legitimate versus illegitimate sexuality.

Taking cue from Hughes' argument, the transformation of sheer violence into sexual violence in characterisations of vampires can be assessed in relation to wider cultural frameworks. On the one hand, Seward's understanding of Lucy's craving for blood as sexual can be traced to Enlightenment interpretations of the lived experiences of the body in terms of relationships of government of nature, women, and the body politic, through reason. On the other hand, Stoker's text is partly based on accounts of folklore representations of the need to police the border between nature and the social community. Although they evolved in rural cultural environments, very different from the urban environment of Enlightenment cultures, folklore representations corroborate Enlightenment paradigms to an extent. This assertion remains valid even if one discounts the role of the educated travellers in reshaping the folkloric material in their accounts. The accounts Stoker used would have been inflected by the narrators' Victorian perspectives, but even in its less corrupted forms, folklore material still conveys norms through which the social community may govern nature. However, there are relevant differences between the representation of one's relation to nature in folklore, and the ways in which this relation was represented in those Enlightenment discourses that became dominant in Victorian culture.

In the folklore vampire ethos, the realm of the non-human which vampires inhabit points to the realm of the organic body contiguous with ungovernable nature. The vampires' craving for blood can be seen to signify more generally a desire for legitimating the needs of the organic body, for satisfying the sheer violence of its life force. In Lochhead's

---

[7] William Hughes, "Fictional Vampires in the Nineteenth and Twentieth Centuries", *A Companion to the Gothic*, 143-54, 146.

[8] Hughes, 145. See also Robert Mighall, "Sex, History and the Vampire", *Bram Stoker: History, Psychoanalysis and the Gothic*, eds. William Hughes and Andrew Smith (London: McMillan, 1998), 62-77.

[9] Hughes, "Fictional Vampires", 145.

revision of Stoker's text, the significance of vampires' craving for blood is reinterpreted in terms of this organic life force. When Lochhead's Renfield eats a fly, a gesture through which he attempts to warn Dr Seward of Dracula's thirst for blood, he exclaims: "It's fat with life, strong life, and gives life to me."[10] The representation of the relation between vampires and nature's vitality in Lochhead's play permits the comparison with the folkloric myth, although it is unlikely that Lochhead's sources included versions of the latter. Yet this comparison may help us to elicit an understanding of the body, latent in the vampire ethos, which expresses the needs of the body in terms of its relation with nature's potent life force. The expressions of these needs do not exclude the sexual. However, in folklore, sexuality is perceived as life affirming, and not as destructive. In Stoker's text, the vampires' thirst for blood is used not to signify and acknowledge the life force of the organic, but to condemn it as desire that implies an unwanted transgression of the border that separates the organic body, belonging in the realm of ungovernable nature, from the social persona "worn" on the surface of the body, belonging in the "civilised" social realm.

We may understand this transgression in psychoanalytic terms as representing abjection. Based on the psychoanalytic theory developed by Julia Kristeva, Barbara Creed argues that both male and female vampires represent abjection because they cross "the boundary between the living and dead, the human and animal."[11] But vampires represent abjection also in cultural-historical sense. Located in the realm of the non-human, they inhabit a space that overlaps with the space of nature as understood in Enlightenment discourses.

Enlightenment discourses defined nature as inextricably linked to women's bodies, with both represented as realms of otherness, of the organic, and hence as ungovernable and non-spiritual realms. In Stoker's *Dracula*, representations of transgressions of the border between nature/ organic body and culture/ social persona envisioned in the vampire ethos (such as craving for blood) are used to represent illegitimate transgressions of social and gender norms (such as craving for semen). The ungovernable sexual body is located in the realm of ungovernable nature and is defined as non-human, but also as feminine through an association of ungovernable nature with women's bodies inherited from Enlightenment paradigms. The vampires' craving for blood is filtered in Stoker's text through norms of bodies' socialisation in terms of acceptable or undesirable

---

[10] Lochhead, *Dracula*, 77.
[11] Creed, 61.

sexuality. These norms are part of larger sets of norms defining healthy bodies, legitimate social order, and sound body politic.

Glennis Byron points out that the *fin de siècle* Victorian Gothic evinces

> the desire to identify what is unfixed, transgressive, other and threatening, in the hope that it can be contained, its threat defused; and there is the desire to redefine and fix a 'norm', to reestablish the boundaries that the threatening other seems to disrupt and destabilise.[12]

It has been argued that among the texts of Victorian Gothic, *Dracula* articulates "some of the culture's more harrowing anxieties" about sexuality, gender and racial "others".[13] In my analysis, Dracula's otherness is related to nature's otherness, in relation to which the ungovernability of the organic, feminine, sexually active body, and of the colonised body politic is defined. In Judith Halberstam's words, this is the otherness "that manifests itself as the horror essential to dark, foreign and perverse bodies." As she puts it elsewhere, "Gothic monsters ... transform the fragments of otherness into one body. That body is not female, not Jewish, not homosexual but it bears the mark of the construction of femininity, race, and sexuality."[14] In relation to this use of the vampire figure, Lochhead's play focuses on the marks of femininity that constitute the regulatory ideal of women enshrined in Stoker's story. As Judith Butler puts it, such an ideal

> not only functions as a norm, but is part of a regulatory practice that produces the bodies it governs, that is, whose regulatory force is made clear as a kind of productive power, the power to produce—demarcate, circulate, differentiate—the bodies it controls.[15]

Stoker's representations of ideal/ abject feminine bodies use the regulatory force of the dichotomy reason/ nature in order "to produce—demarcate, circulate, differentiate" the feminine bodies regarded as needing control. Thus, to use Avril Horner's and Sue Zlosnik's words in this context, in

---

[12] Glennis Byron, "Gothic in the 1890s", *A Companion to the Gothic*, 132-42, 133.

[13] Stephen Arata, *Fictions of Loss in the Victorian Fin de Siècle: Identity and Empire* (Cambridge: Cambridge University Press, 1996), 126.

[14] Judith Halberstam, "Technologies of Monstrosity: Bram Stoker's *Dracula*", *Cultural Politics at the* Fin de Siècle, eds. Sally Ledger and Scott McCracken (Cambridge: Cambridge University Press, 1995), 248-266, 248; Judith Halberstam, *Skin Shows: Gothic Horror and the Technology of Monsters* (Durham: Duke University Press, 1995), 92.

[15] Butler, *Bodies That Matter*, 1.

Stoker's *Dracula* "abjection is both temporally and culturally inflected" by late nineteenth-century values.[16] In Lochhead's version, the border demarcating ideal/ abject bodies is rendered fluid and ambivalent by showing the seductive powers of the organic as a realm of abjection. In the scene showing Lucy in conversation with Seward on the night before her complete conversion into vampire, the image of a jar filled with rose petals works as a metaphor representing the ideal as well as the abject body. Lucy recalls how she and Mina used to gather up fallen rose petals and then put them in a jar with rainwater in order to make perfume. But the result was quite the opposite:

> LUCY: But after we left it a week it always festered. Stink and fur! So then we'd turn it into poison. We'd put in...oh, a dead mouse and, and...pee...and poison-pods from off the lupins. It was even better fun making poison than making perfume. Don't you think anyone'd rather?[17]

The references to the organic are straightforward. A little later in the scene Lucy asks Seward to sleep with her. Lucy's sexual desire is underlain by an attraction for the organic, perceived in its manifestations within nature's cycles of transformation. Like Dracula, Lucy begins to inhabit the realm of life-in-death, that is, the repudiated realm of ungovernable organic life that is like death to the subject, for instance Seward, who seeks to govern it through reason. While Seward (and Stoker's text, ultimately), whose "sacred trust"[18] forbids him to acknowledge the desires of the body, is engaged in "making perfume", Lucy is having better fun "making poison". That this is empowering for Lucy is suggested through her recollection of taking poison-pods from off the lupins. The lupins (wolflike) remind us of Dracula's wolves. Indirectly, the passage from Lochhead's play suggests that Lucy might be able to learn how to control the powers of nature, like Dracula does. The possibility of an alliance between the powers manifested in Lucy's body and in nature is perceived by Seward as threatening because, as a member of the medical profession, he is called on to tame and control them.

The discourse of Stoker's novel can be regarded as grounded in a space of conflict between institutionalised (scientific, medical, political) authority and its realms of government: nature contiguous with the realm of the organic body, and perceived as exemplifying an anarchic body-

---

[16] Avril Horner and Sue Zlosnik, "Comic Gothic", *A Companion to the Gothic*, 242-254, 243.

[17] Lochhead, *Dracula*, 110-111.

[18] Ibid., 112.

social. Vampirised Lucy represents the latter paradigm. In Lochhead's play, Seward, witnessing Lucy's apparent death, admits that "There is a kind of animal strength to her and I can't believe she will ever die."[19] Neither human nor animal, but sharing in a powerful life force of nature, manifested in Seward's eyes as unmanageable erotic libido, Lucy's body can be compared to that of the oriental from Richard Marsh's *The Beetle* (1897), first published as a novel in the same year as Stoker's *Dracula*.[20] In Marsh's novel, the stalker is a shape-shifting creature, first encountered by the main protagonist, a British aristocrat, in Egypt. The representation of the creature's body as metamorphic, a body which cannot be classified in any way by scientific authority, indicates an anxiety regarding the ungovernability of the body's desires and the possibility that they exceed what can be known (and thus governed) through scientific method. Kelly Hurley notes that "the villainess of *The Beetle* is ambiguous in bodily identity (both human and animal)".[21] The Beetle, like Dracula, is a creature that transgresses the border between the realm of nature and that of the social world. Embodied through the transmigration of Isis, born neither of God nor man, the figure of The Beetle functions simultaneously as a metonym for ungovernable nature and the Orient.

As Byron points out, Marsh's tale is built on a well known set of opposites: the Orient, a "site of chaos and barbarism" is opposed to the "civilised and ordered world of the West".[22] The tale interprets the conflict between Orient and the West in terms of a conflict between men and nature, augmented by The Beetle's embodiment as female sexual "predator". The conflict is also enacted on her very skin. According to Byron, "the Oriental's apparent hatred of white skins ... only serves to disguise her desire to possess such a white body for herself and consequently confirms the supposed 'superiority' of the white race."[23] But, the novel suggests, such claim to white skin could never be fulfilled if the lecherous priestess of Isis does not renounce the eroticism of her body— depicted as monstrous and alien (literally of a different species than human). This, Byron points out, "reassuringly dispels any doubts about the need for the so-called civilising mission to continue among such a barbarous and dangerous race."[24] Byron points out that the novel was

---

[19] Lochhead, *Dracula*, 121.
[20] Richard Marsh, *The Beetle* (1897. Stroud: Alan Sutton, 1994).
[21] Kelly Hurley, *The Gothic Body: Sexuality, Materialism and Degeneration at the Fin de Siècle* (Cambridge: Cambridge University Press, 1996), 124-40, 24.
[22] Byron, "Gothic in the 1890s", 133.
[23] Ibid.
[24] Ibid., 133-4.

written "at a time of increased British military activity in Egypt."[25] The tale legitimates the configuration of the body politic while also asserting its dependence on the properly managed organic body, whose white skin signifies its taming and government, whereas the non-white body tarnishes the white skin's symbolic cleanliness.

In Lochhead's version of *Dracula*, Florrie, the maid-servant, experiences the effects of the conflict between "civilising" forces and the investment of nature's life force in her body in a particular way. Having received a missive from the Army regarding her lover, who had enlisted, she reacts thus:

> Don't need to read. Telegram from the military, it mean just one thing. Dead. Dead, you bastard. Torn up bits of you all over some patch of dirt other side of world. Bloody generals! Bloody Empire! Dead and me three weeks late.[26]

The passage highlights the ways in which an elite's effort to govern the body politic affects the ways in which the needs of the organic body are tended to in society. Florrie's body's sensuality, manifested in pregnancy, has become subject of anxiety instead of celebration, now that her lover is dead and she may not be able to raise a child on her own. The passage also brings up issues of class. The apparatus through which the Victorian body politic is governed is also an apparatus through which particular social groups are governed, demanding the enlisting of working class males to defend and expand the Empire against "uncivilised nature". But this war against nature, in Florrie's case, is also a war against the manifestation of life affirming nature in the fertility of her body.

The reiteration of normative narrations of nature will always yield a myth which then governs the ways in which we relate to nature, including our bodies. Our subjective identity is born through this relation of government. It is therefore important to see how myths can be challenged. In the following section, I will show how Lochhead's *Dracula* uses discursive strategies that challenge the myth rooted in Stoker's novel. I will then explore in more detail how these strategies challenge the social value of the myth, value deposited in naturalised understandings of class and gender.

---

[25] Ibid., 133.
[26] Lochhead, *Dracula*, 116.

Narrating Nature

Stoker's story of Dracula, like so many texts of late Victorian Gothic, explores to a significant extent the conflict between the desires affirmed in the organic body and nature, and the need for their government. The forces rooted in the organic are perceived as threatening, which leads to their being perceived as abject. In Marsh's novel, the white women victims of the Beetle are subjected "to every variety of outrage of which even the minds of demons could conceive."[27] As Byron puts it, "The Beetle physically violates all her victims with her body".[28] The same could be said about Dracula's violation of his victims. Similar outrages are performed on Lucy's and Mina's bodies by Dracula; but Mina's body is eventually cleaned and re-inscribed as proper through marriage, and Lucy's body is "purified" through staking. In Stoker's *Dracula*, this need of proper inscription of the body reflects the need for legitimising both the government of nature through reason, and the government of the body-social. The regime of government through the "proper" body politic is also a gender regime in which women are governed by men.

Indeed, Stoker's text does bring to the fore the possibility of conceiving an empowering alliance between desiring bodies and nature, and it does politicise the corporeal.[29] However, if the alliance between desiring bodies and nature conceived in Stoker's text were presented as legitimate, it would subvert the social myth whose internalisation guarantees the ruling prerogatives of a masculine elite (Van Helsing's band of brothers), and the socio-political stability of a male-dominated gender regime, which the text eventually endorses. We remember Harker's impressions of Europe's easternmost outpost of (Austro-Hungarian) imperial order, Bistritz, a place he compares to Babel. Beyond that lies the realm of Dracula's arbitrary rule. This realm too is hierarchical, although not in the same way in which imperial order is. Dracula's rule is not based on the idea of taming nature, but rather he channels its force (raising storms, etc.). Dracula does not govern the body but allows its organic, almost animal, empowerment. The body-social under his rule is either repudiated as unworthy of alliance, or it lives through alliance with Dracula, rather than being dominated through institutionalised force. In Stoker's text, the drama of the stabilisation of the body politic is

---

[27] Marsh, 197.

[28] Byron, 140.

[29] As, for instance, Stephen Arata has shown by focusing on the vampire figure as a threat to the legitimate body politic. Stephen Arata, "The Occidental Tourist: *Dracula* and the Anxiety of Reverse Colonization", Bram Stoker, *Dracula*, 462-70.

represented as being enacted in the public sphere where the band of brothers achieve it by destroying Dracula, whose power is associated with that of ungovernable nature, and whose realm is characterised through visions of anarchy. But it is also played out in the domestic sphere when Lucy's adulterous and desiring body is renounced and the legitimacy of kinship rules that ensure men's rights to govern women are thus restored.

In short, Stoker's narrative functions to establish a cultural site for corroborating social practices against forces perceived as threats to a secure social space. It sets up a variety of myths to frame the socially excluded as demonic. On the one hand, it registers a repulsion of the organic body. In Noel Carroll's words, the almost instinctive reactions triggered by Dracula's features that define him as abject are "characteristically the product of perceiving something to be noxious and impure."[30] On the other hand, this repulsion of the organic is signified in social terms. Dracula's figure serves to make sense of the social by pointing out that which endangers what Latour calls the work of purification that maintains the separation between nature and culture.[31] Stoker's vision leads to the creation of a social myth that helps to maintain a social order. Although Stoker's text becomes open to heteroglossic interference through its use of the fantastic, the narrative's heteroglossic dimension is eventually sealed off.[32]

Lochhead's story uses the framework of Stoker's text to re-evaluate the meanings of experiences of embodiment, sexuality, and marriage that Stoker's novel proposes. Her play can be located in the context of feminist rewritings of vampire myths. Gina Wisker points out that

> Contemporary women writers ... have found in the figure of the vampire marvellous potential for radical reappropriation. The status of vampires as cultural indices and metaphors has been revalued ... aligning them with a new feminist carnivalesque. They infuse the age-old figure with new life and new potential to comment on what it means to be human.[33]

---

[30] Noel Carroll, *The Philosophy of Horror* (New York: Routledge, 1990), 28.

[31] Latour, 7, 29-32, 96, 105-9.

[32] Mark Jancovitch points out that "the pleasure offered by the [Gothic] genre is based on the process of narrative closure in which the horrifying or monstrous is destroyed or contained" and thus "the original order is re-established." Mark Jancovitch, *Horror* (London: Batsford, 1992), 9.

[33] Gina Wisker, "Love Bites: Contemporary Women's Vampire Fictions", *Diegesis: Journal of the Association for Research in Popular Fictions* 3 (1998); I am quoting from the version republished in *A Companion to the Gothic*, 167-79, 167.

Lochhead's version of *Dracula* cultivates heteroglossia in order to preserve the story as a space of negotiation, so that her narrator/director may challenge, via elements of Stoker's narrative, the social myths they anchor.

In Stoker's *Dracula*, the introductory statement prepares the reader for a multi-vocal discursive space. But heteroglossia is eventually renounced in favour of a monoglossic discursive regime. The introductory statement evinces an effort to negotiate the legitimacy of contradictory visions of the relationship between narrative and reality: "All needless matters have been eliminated, so that a history almost at variance with the possibilities of later-day belief may stand forth as simple fact."[34] The issues that will be negotiated relate to "possibilities" of "later-day" (i.e. rational) belief, in contradistinction to an alternative "history" "at variance" with these. But eventually, it is quietly signalled, reason will triumph and the alternative "history" will be put forth as "simple fact". That is, the alternative story will be granted a degree of legitimacy by harnessing a professed objectivity to support its verisimilitude.

However, Stoker's story's objectivity works more in the fashion of what Byron calls "many forms of nineteenth-century materialist science" that "attempted to provide tools for identifying and categorising what was decadent, criminal, abnormal within human nature, to establish and distance what was alien and reaffirm the stability of the norm."[35] Thus, to borrow an analysis framework outlined by Gerry Smyth, Stoker's text has both centralising and decentralising effects: it is "organised in such a way as to silence and control the disparate voices of which it is composed."[36] Stoker's collator's claims to objectivity help him, as reason helps his characters, to distance himself (and his readers) from several implications of the content of the accounts. Stoker's narrators' accounts, inasmuch as they suggest an understanding of nature as ungovernable, endowed with agency, and allied with the (feminine) organic body, are never guaranteed authenticity.

Lochhead's *Dracula* endeavours to bring forth the body through narrating its ties with nature, inasmuch as such a narration is possible. In the story of Fanny Waller, narrated by Mina's and Lucy's maid-servant Florrie, we are given a representation of the body at its least degree of removal from nature:

> Poor Fanny Waller in our village as was born not right, with a humpback and a harelip ... so's you'd not have thought a man alive'd been inclined to

---

[34] Stoker, 5.

[35] Byron, 134.

[36] Smyth, *The Novel and the Nation*, 30.

take advantage of her—she went three months and never had to delve in the rag bag till finally her mother made her go to the wise woman to see if she had a growth or an ulcer. Wise woman pressed on her belly—'And can you feel anything?' ... 'No, ... just sometimes, somethin' like li'l bird, flutterin'.' 'Well,' says the wise woman, she says, 'And did you not feel that li'l bird go in?' 'No, mum.' 'Oh well, then, by Christ, and ye'll feel it cam back out again!'[37]

The shifts in subject of narration (from Stoker's angelic or demonic bodies to the body as locus of organic drives and fertility), narrative register (from conventional novelistic to folktale), and narrating agency (the maid-servant is set up as a narrator in her own right, unlike in Stoker's text), lead to a sense of the body's materiality as determined through negotiation of its needs in terms of social contingencies. This is very different from the treatment of materiality in Stoker's novel, where the matter of the body is transacted through answering who has the right to govern nature. Florrie's story of a fellow-villager serves to engender a social space between the maid-servant, Mina, and Lucy, wherein talk about women's bodies leads to the realisation of women's common ground and to a form of solidarity. After Florrie's story:

(LUCY *goes into hysterics of laughter.* FLORRIE *joins in.* MINA *looks disapprovingly but eventually cracks and all three laugh, wiping tears away, hugging each other.*)
[FLORRIE:] Well, us Eve's daughters got to laugh, I reckon, else we'd sit down and cry.[38]

In Lochhead's reinterpretation the things that might have constituted "needless matters" for Stoker's collator are made visible: the possibility of a social space wherein women circulate stories about themselves. In Stoker's text this kind of space is only shown as a men's society: Van Helsing, Seward, Harker, Quincey Morris, a professor, a doctor, a lawyer, and an intrepid adventurer are the only ones credited with the ability to transact knowledge about women. Even the conversations between Lucy and Mina are marked by men's language of authority, for instance when Mina shows her faith in the legitimacy of the attributes of the good Victorian wife.[39]

Drawing on Ricoeur's theorisation of the relation between text and reader, Nicole Ward Jouve notes that narratives serve to define

---

[37] Lochhead, *Dracula*, 105.
[38] Ibid., brackets added.
[39] Stoker, 105.

otherworldly realms as "habitable" places, i.e. places that help us define our ontological status.[40] A central interest of both *Dracula* stories examined here is invested in the body as a habitable or inhabitable place in which the subject relates to nature and the organic. The body as the place of nature and the organic is regarded as otherworldly and uninhabitable in Stoker's novel, while Lochhead's play explores its habitability and worldliness.

In Stoker's novel, the contrast between Mina Harker and Lucy Westenra divides the feminine subject between the legitimate, pure angel, whose purity is not unlike that of reason, and the highly sexual woman, whose ungovernability is not unlike that of a fickle nature, that resists mapping through reason. Neither Mina's nor Lucy's body are habitable. Mina's body is distilled into her representation as perfect wife, into subjectivity, and Lucy's is destroyed for having been given over to nature. In Lochhead's version of *Dracula*, Florrie's story indicates an opening to polyphony that embraces the uninhabitable body through irony. As a storyteller Florrie reminds us of the storytellers of Giambattista Basile's tale of the tales. *The Tale of the Tales* or *The Pentameron* (1634-36) consists of a framing tale and forty-nine stories.[41] The latter are narrated by women, all of whom are from the poorest strata of society. All are afflicted by some blemish drawing attention to their bodily presence and needs. Commenting on these storytellers' work, Jack Zipes notes that their goal "was to make the audience laugh, and laughter itself was a relief and escape for the storyteller who used metaphors to test and perhaps subvert the conventions".[42] In Florrie's story, Fanny Waller's monstrosity is not frightening like that of Lucy turned vampire, because the organic body is not abjected, over-sexualised, and repudiated; rather, as in Basile's tales, the body is "enmeshed in the plot."[43] We may regard Florrie's story as comic Gothic. In Horner and Zlosnik's words, it "recuperates the 'supernatural' Other into the material", translating "the diabolic energy of the Other" into "laughter and sexuality" and accommodating the uncanny

---

[40] Nicole Jouve, *Female Genesis: Creativity, Self and Gender* (Cambridge: Polity, 1998), 187-8.

[41] Nancy Canepa, trans., *Giambattista Basile's "The Tale of Tales, or Entertainment for Little Ones"* (Detroit, MI: Wayne State University Press, 2007).

[42] Zipes, *Why Fairy Tales Stick*, 66.

[43] Ibid., 67. See also Nancy Canepa, *From Court to Forest: Giambattista Basile's Lo cunto de li cunti and the Birth of the Literary Fairy Tale* (Detroit: Wayne State University Press, 1999).

"within a vision of the natural world" which is also the world of the body.[44]

Such discursive strategies destabilise the social myths legitimated through the literary constructions of vampire identity in Stoker's seminal text. Lochhead's use of the folktale register emphasises the social character of narrative to the detriment of its mythologizing function. For Lochhead, social myth is emphatically *social*, whereas Stoker harnesses the mythologizing dimension of social *myth*, extending and adapting mythology to specific socio-historical circumstances. His interpretation of Central-Eastern European folk traditions is based on writings by English travellers or accounts developing these.[45] These accounts of local traditions would have been inflected by Victorian social myths.[46] Stoker's narrative extends and adapts myth (centrally, the vampire myth) to specific socio-historical circumstances in order to legitimate the male-dominated Victorian gender regime.

Stoker's text drains the explanatory power of the folkloric vampire myths that define the interpenetration of human and non-human (nature's) agency, and uses it to channel Victorian values, corroborating Victorian social codes and the social categories these codes interpret and express. Before the scene of Lucy's killing, Seward describes her body lying in the coffin thus:

> She seemed like a nightmare of Lucy as she lay there; the pointed teeth, the bloodstained, voluptuous mouth—which it made one shudder to see—the whole carnal and unspiritual appearance, seeming like a devilish mockery of Lucy's sweet purity.[47]

Seward "shudders to see" Lucy's "voluptuous mouth", her "carnal appearance" which is deemed "unspiritual" in contrast with her former "sweet purity". Shown to favour the spiritual over the carnal, Seward's character is contoured as that of a gentleman of spirit and taste. All the members of the brotherhood instituted under Van Helsing's chairmanship are characterised in similar ways. The social function this brotherhood

---

[44] Horner and Zlosnik, 243.

[45] For instance, Emily de Laszowska Gerard, *The Land Beyond the Forest: Facts, Figures and Fancies from Transylvania* (Brooklyn, New York: AMS, 2001).

[46] See for instance Athena Vrettos, *Imagining Illness in Victorian Culture* (Stanford: Stanford University Press, 1996); Gail Kligman, *The Wedding of the Dead: Ritual, Poetics and Popular Culture in Transylvania* (Berkeley: University of California Press, 1998).

[47] Stoker, 190.

fulfils is to draw the line between the human and the non-human. In this process Lucy's voluptuousness and carnality is ascribed to the non-human. The text constructs Lucy's character through a paradigmatic metaphor: as a stand in for Dracula, she invokes the signified of the vampire figure from folkloric myths, i.e. non-human, ungovernable nature. But Lucy is also a signifier of what Seward desires. Using the mythical vampire figure that explains and institutes a border between the human and the non-human, Stoker's text presents the reader with a way of seeing the non-human in one's own desire via incarnations of women's voluptuous bodies that are posed as that very border.

However, folkloric vampire myths are not concerned with sin discovered in ungovernable sexuality, but with narrating the non-human so that the members of the social community can acknowledge it and learn to live with it. Hijacking the power of myth in order to explain a Victorian dilemma, Stoker endows the myth with particular social value. His *Dracula*, as a literary endeavour, extends a myth by making it work in a specific socio-historical locale. This extension of myth produces a discourse whose deictic force and iterability are used to legitimate cultural frameworks of masculine agency. Representatives of State institutions and of professions that had begun to gain legitimacy through State power (a lawyer, a doctor, etc.) are envisioned as agents with the means and knowledge required to investigate transgressions of normality as understood in late nineteenth-century Britain.

In Lochhead's version, the matter of Lucy's desiring body is first brought up by Renfield:

> RENFIELD: She'll let him in and that'll get you! ... She sewer-whore, her. Seward, you hear? Oh, sweet Lucy in the daylight, so polite, she got it all sewn up, oh no, no sweat. Come night? They're all mad up in Yorkshire you know, set of screw-looses, screw-looses, screw Lucy's, who doesn't? She ride them all ragged round and round and round and round and round ... . Forgot to watch her mouth. Swallow his pride. Virgin bride. She'll let him in. That'll get you![48]

While in Stoker's text Dr Seward is the focalising agent who relays Lucy's unworldly and otherworldly appearance, in Lochhead's version the focalisor is his psychiatric patient. The comparison exposes the fact that should Stoker's Seward have thought what Lochhead's Renfield expresses the former would have been labelled as psychologically diseased. A sense of unease is thus charged on Stoker's Seward and by extension, on the

---

[48] Lochhead, *Dracula*, 106-7.

brotherhood of which he is a member. Its cause might be Lucy's ambiguity voiced by Renfield: is the real Lucy "oh, sweet Lucy in the daylight, so polite" or is she, "sewer-whore", Seward's whore? Lucy's killing in Stoker's *Dracula* might then appear as being driven by fear in the brotherhood of "being got" by women's illegitimate, sexually charged "letting in" of an-other.

Jan McDonald points out that Dracula's victims

> have been interpreted by post-Freudian critics as repressed women who, unable to acknowledge the existence of their sexuality, conjure up a fiendish 'other' who forces them into a physical relationship which they simultaneously loathe and enjoy. ... Lochhead negates this interpretation by positing an alternative, namely, that Dracula liberated his victims from their sexual and psychological repressions induced by a patriarchal culture and its dominant religion, Christianity.[49]

Anne Varty also emphasises that in Lochhead's play "Count Dracula's disruption of patriarchal control is represented as a liberating force for the expression of female sexuality."[50] Lochhead's Lucy and Mina are both enraged and enchanted by Dracula.[51] Stoker's novel reflects the need for decanting their rage and enchantment. For Stoker, Dracula's figure serves as a cultural scapegoat. Through it Lucy's rage is exorcised by being represented as only possible through contamination by the demonic enchanter.

Stoker's Seward recounts in his diary:

> When Lucy—I call the thing that was before us Lucy because it bore her shape—saw us she drew back with an angry snarl ... ; then her eyes ranged over us. Lucy's eyes in form and colour; but Lucy's eyes unclean and full of hell-fire, instead of the pure, gentle orbs we knew.[52]

Once Lucy's rage is demonised, so is her enchantment; purged of sin she can become angelic again. In Stoker's text Lucy's rage and enchantment are relocated to the demonic, non-human otherworld of Dracula. In this way, Lucy can be shown as unaware of her "very own hunger".[53] In

---

[49] Jan McDonald, "Scottish Women Dramatists Since 1945", *A History of Scottish Women's Writing*. 494-513, 497.

[50] Anne Varty, "The Mirror and the Vamp: Liz Lochhead", *A History of Scottish Women's Writing*, 641-658, 653.

[51] See also Lochhead's poem, "Lucy's Diary", 61.

[52] Stoker, 188.

[53] Lochhead, "Lucy's Diary", 62.

Lochhead's versions of Lucy, however, such awareness is restored so that an enraged and enchanted Lucy, both angelic and sensual, can voice what neither the innocent nor the sexual woman as separate kinds of women could: "Despite myself, the sea air is giving me an appetite."[54] Varty notes that Lochhead's use of the relationship between Lucy and Dracula to imagine women's appropriation of the vampire myth as means to express their sexuality is accompanied by the demotion of the brotherhood elite: the men who battle against Dracula "do not acquire the heroic status that is bestowed on them by the novel".[55] The two narratives evince different understandings of women's social roles, based on different ways of understanding and narrating corporeality and desiring bodies. This leads us to a consideration of the effects of narrating nature in terms of class and gender.

Nature, Gender, and Class

I will conclude my analysis with a rereading of Florrie's story about Fanny Waller. This will help us to recapitulate the argument that, unlike Stoker's narrations, which idealise and abject the body, Lochhead's text suggests a view on corporeality that embraces, rather than othering, the ungovernability of the organic body. The recapitulation of the argument will provide a background for an analysis of how these different takes on corporeality are relevant in terms of women's representation across the axes of gender and class.

In Lochhead's *Dracula*, Florrie's story about Fanny Waller is a miniature version of Dracula's myth. Like Lucy, Fanny Waller has been visited by a masculine figure. And as with Stoker's Lucy, she is represented as innocent. Lochhead's *Dracula* suggests that should Lucy have been a mere commoner, "born not right"[56], her story would have been told differently. One suspects a playful allusion in Lochhead's phrase: "born not right" refers not only to Fanny's physical body, but also to her class. The conflation of notions of ungovernable bodies and ungovernable masses in Stoker's text shows that for many Victorians both belonged in the realm of ungovernable nature, a realm of abjection. In order to make Lucy a character that could be rescued from abjected nature, she had to qualify for participation in the legitimate social world, that is, she had to transcend body and class. Transcending her body, Lucy is

---

[54] Ibid.
[55] Varty, 653.
[56] Lochhead, *Dracula*, 105.

attributed a fantasised body, be that demonic or angelic. Fanny Waller's body is not amenable to these fantasies because she is not of the same rank as Stoker's Lucy. If Lucy had been one of the lower classes, rather than referred to as a woman of sweet purity or demonic voluptuousness, she might have been represented as a Fanny Waller: a female body with the sole function of procreating and providing sexual satisfaction to men. Introducing Fanny Waller's story as a mini-version of Dracula's story, Lochhead's play shows the underlying script, the subtext, of Stoker's narrative.

The narrative organisation of events in Stoker's text is guided by a dichotomic relationship between nature and culture that can be traced to Enlightenment paradigms (and further back in time) and which is also implicated in the constitution of the body politic.[57] The Enlightenment paradigms are activated in Stoker's text through the characters traited as gentlemen of spirit and taste, armed with reason, of the Victorian upper class. At the antipode of reason, nature appears wild and unbounded and must be repudiated to make room for culture created through reason, ordered and socio-politically coherent. In this equation wild and unbounded nature is signified through the figure of the vampire. Lucy becomes its correlative in social reality—a woman of unclean and hellish sexuality. In Stoker's text Lucy's demonisation serves to legitimate reason as the apanage of cultural elite. Without this purpose, Stoker's Lucy would appear like Fanny Waller, a body whose corporeality resists idealisation and rationalisation. In order for someone like Fanny Waller to be admitted in Stoker's society as social person, rather than as simply nature, she would have had to enter the process whereby nature is converted into culture through reason, becoming a Lucy or a Mina. Gayle Rubin argues that male-dominated kinship systems, requiring women's marriage to men, transform biological sexuality into products of human activity. Drawing on work by Claude Lévi-Strauss in a Marxist framework, Rubin regards a kinship system as "an imposition of social ends upon a part of the natural world. It is therefore 'production' in the most general sense of the term: a molding, a transformation of objects (in this case, people) to and by a subjective purpose".[58] Borrowing Rubin's words, it can be said that in order to acquire a legitimate social persona Fanny would have had to be represented as undergoing cultural transformation from biological sexual body into a product of human activity: the (angelic) wife.

---

[57] See for instance Adriana Cavarero, *Stately Bodies: Literature, Philosophy and the Question of Gender*, trans. Robert de Lucca and Deanna Shemek (Ann Arbor: University of Michigan Press, 2005), vii-viii.
[58] Rubin, 176.

In Stoker's vision the expression of meaningful social reality depends on defining gender through class. In Stoker's text's ideological "unconscious", women are equated with nature needing to be mastered by a masculine elite using reason. This equation is made invisible by introducing the vampire figure as a metaphor for ungovernable nature and feminine bodies. Thus, while on its "surface" the text indicts the vampire, in subtext, this indictment refers to ungovernable nature and women allied with it. Even though Dracula's figure is drawn as masculine, traits of femininity permeate his design. Dracula not only masters nature's destructive forces. He also shares attributes seen as common to nature and feminine bodies: for instance, he masters the generative force of nature, being able to create new vampires; his victims are reborn with renewed life force. In Stoker's female vampires, ungovernable nature forces blend femininity into the poisonous concoction of the wildly sexual body. Such natural forces, in being located beyond reason, are also perceived as possibly overtaking the lower classes. The stabilisation of these forces bans the corporeal woman, of wild sexuality, that roams the city slums, and yields the incorporeal woman, the tame and devoted wife settled in the aristocratic realms of the gentlemen of spirit and taste.

Byron notes the late nineteenth-century association of London slums with vice, an association which fuelled a fear that the lower classes might invade the aristocratic parts of the city, as well as providing a site for projecting new kinds of abject or exotic otherness.[59] In an analysis of the influence of late nineteenth-century understandings of depravity and decline in Stoker's novel, Laura Sagolla Croley argues that

> Stoker's Count is associated and allied with the poorest of the poor—not the industrious artisan but the vagrant, not the respectable working class but its supposedly shiftless, slum-dwelling underclass—and that the threat of Dracula and vampirism stands in for the late-century threat of the lumpenproletariat.[60]

An illustrative passage in Stoker's text shows Lucy in a motherly posture, mixing her blood with that of a child. In the terms of Croley's argument, this image suggests that Lucy's vampirism represents a corruption of the attributes of the good mother praised by the Victorian gentility. Once infected by the Count, she is transformed into the "bad" mother imagined as belonging to the underclass. Thus, Lucy's monstrous corporeality,

---

[59] Byron, 134.
[60] Croley, Laura Sagolla, "The Rhetoric of Reform in Stoker's *Dracula*: Depravity, Decline, and the Fin-de-Siècle 'Residium'", *Criticism* 37 (1995): 85-108, 85.

gained through her alliance with ungovernable nature, is translated into monstrous liaison with the unemployed of the working-class, whose ungovernability and unreason are perceived as threatening in the same way in which ungovernable and unreasonable vampire-feminine-organic-sexual bodies are perceived as threatening. It is in this passage that Seward first notices how Lucy's purity has transformed into "voluptuous wantonness."[61] In defining illegitimate gender identity through class identity in this way, Stoker's text makes invisible the sublimation of corporeality that yields "acceptable", reasonable women, foregrounding the idea that voluptuous bodies are perhaps like a disease one catches in the city slums, a disease of unreason that also makes one appear unsoundly *unheimliche*.

Lochhead's text draws attention to the equation of women with nature via the othering of lower classes, the equation Stoker's text conceals, and which is one of its sources of horror. In Lochhead's play Florrie speaks with reason, yet reason that does not repudiate the body (nature) but acknowledges its desires and ungovernability. Elizabeth Grosz criticises constructions of desire from Plato to Freud that presuppose a lack (of the body) and argues in favour of conceiving desire as production. Based on Spinoza's writings, Grosz theorises desire as "the force of positive production, the action that creates things, makes alliances, and forges interactions."[62] Florrie's story about Fanny Waller connects desire to bodily instincts and needs, yet these are not regarded as unnameable, buried beneath discourse, but re-producible through it; this acknowledgement of desire forges interaction and a temporary alliance between Lucy, Mina, and Florrie.[63] The women amongst whom Fanny's story circulates form (however temporarily) a social circle in which it is possible to speak about Fanny's corporeality without recourse to dichotomies derived from Enlightenment discourses.

Thus, Fanny's story serves to institute a space of women's solidarity through the acknowledgment of women's corporeality (instead of their male-generated materiality of layered abjection and exoticism) as the foundation of desire and sexuality. But the narrator/director also shows that this common space is problematic. The women's laughter triggered by

---

[61] Stoker, 187.

[62] Elizabeth Grosz, "Refiguring Lesbian Desire", *Space, Time, and Perversion*, 173-85, 179.

[63] However, one notes that Florrie's story may simply be cautionary in respect of the danger of procreation for working-class women, as Aileen Christianson points out. Aileen Christianson, "Liz Lochhead's Poetry and Drama: Forging Ironies", *Contemporary Scottish Women Writers*, 41-52, 48.

the story is awkwardly hysterical (Lucy's), given unwillingly (Mina's), or withheld until it appears permissible (Florrie's). The solidarity between them is sealed with a cliché: "Well, us Eve's daughters got to laugh, I reckon, else we'd sit down and cry."[64] The irony in the following passage suggests a straightforward critical position as regards the tenets of materialist feminism:

> MINA: I hope for you to be happy, Florrie.
> FLORRIE: (*Curtsying*) Yes, miss.
> MINA: Don't 'yes miss' me, that's not very familiar!
> FLORRIE: No, miss. ...
> MINA: Call me Mina! Florrie, we want but one year to a brand new century, times are changing, we'll have no more mistress and servants, I don't believe in them.
> FLORRIE: No, miss. (*Pause.*) You will still pay my wages?
> MINA: Course we will, silly goose...

And later on:

> MINA: ... Florrie! Florrie, look at the mess in there. Things everywhere! Go tidy it up!
> FLORRIE: (*Beginning to go, sharp*) Yes, Mina.[65]

Jan McDonald, highlighting Lochhead's constant preoccupation with the theme of sisterhood in her work, and noting that "Lochhead changes Stoker's characters, Mina and Lucy, from friends to sisters", argues that "Florrie completes the triad of sisters and maid, the prototype of which has been explored in *Blood and Ice*"—another of Lochhead's plays.[66] However, McDonald points out, "Florrie's status as a 'sister' is unstable and depends solely on the whims of Mina, her mistress."[67] Aileen Christianson also notes that

> Between *Blood and Ice*, *Dracula* and *Mary Queen of Scots Got Her Head Chopped Off* run other linking themes of sisterhood, class and blood. All three show both community and difference between women: the sisterhood

---

[64] Lochhead, *Dracula*, 105.
[65] Ibid., 96-7, original italics.
[66] McDonald, 501-2. See also Liz Lochhead, *Blood and Ice* (London: Salamander, 1982).
[67] McDonald, 502.

(true and false) between women, blood, menstrual cycles, birth and bloodsucking, and the resistance and succumbing to victimhood.[68]

According to Christianson, Lochhead "makes clear both women's difference and their mutual position in patriarchy."[69] Thus, sex and gender based solidarity is problematised by interrogating not only axes of social inequality between men and women, but also between women in a position of power and socially disadvantaged women.

Conclusion

Stoker's story of Dracula harnesses the sense-making power of vampire folktales, and thus the power of the myth behind them, in order to spell out a social myth of late Victorian Britain. I argued that the vampire figure of the folk tradition serves to define the threshold between human and non-human as the space which separates man from nature, habitable social space from uninhabitable natural space. At the same time, through the vampire figure, the folk tradition acknowledges that the non-human partakes in the organic nature of the body and communicates an understanding of desire rooted in the needs of the animal body. In an essay on the monstrosity of Grendel in the medieval epic *Beowulf*, James Phillips argues that

> Just as the man-eating predator "animalises" man by claiming for itself the humanness of dominion and by insisting that man is nothing more than a quantum of tissue, man "humanises" certain monsters by imputing to them the possibility of miscegenation with humans: H. Peter Steeves notes that, reinventing the sex act, vampires and werewolves reproduce via the penetration of human bodies and therefore can be said to be close enough in kind to us to interbreed. ... [H]umanity experiences itself in the encounter with the monstrous as both familiar and intolerable.[70]

---

[68] Christianson, 47-8. See also Liz Lochhead, *Mary Queen of Scots Got Her Head Chopped Off, Mary Queen of Scots Got Her Head Chopped Off* and *Dracula*, 7-67.

[69] Christianson, 48.

[70] James Phillips, "In the Company of Predators: *Beowulf* and the Monstrous Descendants of Cain", *Angelaki* 13, No. 3 (December 2008): 41-51, 47. H. Peter Steeves, "The Familiar Other and Feral Selves: Life at the Human/Animal Boundary", *The Animal/Human Boundary: Historical Perspectives*, eds. Angela Creager and William Chester Jordan (Rochester, NY: University of Rochester Press, 2002), 228-64, 264.

In my view, this kind of monstrosity represents an acknowledgement of the ungovernable life force of the organic, familiar in our bodies. Folkloric vampire myths acknowledge that this ungovernability threatens social organisation, and is therefore intolerable to our social persona. However, the monstrous manifestation of the organic is humanised, so that one may understand its needs. Neither the human nor the animal has dominion over the other; rather, they are mutually enthralled. The vampire is seductive but also seduced by its victims. But in Stoker's novel vampires represent the non-human and the organic as that which must be exorcised, rather than accommodated, in order to make sense of our social identities: nature must be governed through rationalising abstraction (Mina's body is governed through the Victorian ideal of the perfect wife) or aggressively repudiated (Lucy's ungovernable body is destroyed). Lochhead's revision of Stoker's text permits a recuperation of the understanding of desires rooted in bodily needs as affirming its life force rather than as being the cause of man's fall from grace. In her script, Lochhead requires one of Harker's female vampire attackers to be played by the actress who plays Lucy, while Lucy's relation to the animal and nature are highlighted throughout the play. This directing strategy draws attention to the equation of life force with erotic libido in Stoker's text. When hypnotised under Van Helsing's and Seward's supervision, Harker describes the Lucy-like vampire as being "like a cat, like a wild, wild animal."[71] He is then shown as being frightened by what he glimpses in the depths of the vampire's body: "Lucy? Not—Lucy. She whispering I am six hundred years old, I am thousands of years old, I'm not just a little girl."[72] Thus Lochhead's narrator/ director reveals the force of primordial nature behind Lucy's desire, and not a demonic force which threatens her angelic, incorporeal social persona.

In Lochhead's text this force is regarded in positive terms. When Van Helsing attempts to convince Seward that Lucy's giving in to Dracula should not be seen as adultery, he emphasises that "the dark kingdom of sleep [opened Lucy] to things sweet daytime reason says she must resist".[73] In the context of the play, "the dark kingdom of sleep" can be interpreted as the kingdom of nature and the body's desires that reason had foreclosed. Lochhead's Lucy is given the freedom to explore this kingdom, rather than being punished for her inability to govern it, yet she is depicted as no less rational than Stoker's men. In Florrie's story of Fanny Waller, the body is shown as "raw" nature, yet in a way that

---

[71] Lochhead, *Dracula*, 128.
[72] Ibid.
[73] Ibid., 130.

circumvents the dichotomy raw nature : cultured social persona. The body is not to be found beyond discourse, but enmeshed in discourse, partaking in discourse as it shapes what can be said about the body, even as it is shaped by what is being said. The body is with reason in its desires and manifestation through discourse. This view of the body in Lochhead's play also allows us to unmask the gender and class hierarchies Stoker's text promotes, and which derive from a view of the organic, the body, nature, and women as partaking in an ungovernable realm that needs to be repudiated in order for Victorian sociality to be constituted within a secure social space.

In their interpretation of Lochhead's plays, McDonald and Harvie argue that

> The audiences are encouraged to see the plays and other forms of representation as representational apparatus which do not merely reflect but construct meaning, and to analyse how that meaning may be ideologically inscribed in ways which denigrate or circumscribe women.[74]

In my analysis I sought to show how Lochhead's reinterpretation of Dracula's myth works to disenchant women from the social fate set in store for them through male-generated abjections and idealisations of their bodies. Her play voices what passes for Stoker as "needless matters" concerning women. Lochhead contests the way in which Stoker uses stories to extend pre-existing social myths which influence our identities and therefore our acts in social reality. Her writing foregrounds ways of women's socialising that have been covered up in the cultural and social practice legitimated by narratives such as Stoker's *Dracula*.

Lochhead's revisionist stance towards male-generated social myths is a characteristic feature of her work. In the following chapter, I will develop my analysis of her vision of narrative as means to unsettle the common-places of these myths as they are found in one of the most familiar places: the stock of household folk and fairy tales.

---

[74] McDonald and Harvie, 144.

CHAPTER EIGHT

TANGLED UP IN BLUE.
LIZ LOCHHEAD'S GRIMM SISTERS TALES

Liz Lochhead's writing is emphatically concerned with the patriarchal inflexions of "cultural memory and legend" and with their role in constructing women's identities and social experiences.[1] Developing subversive narrative strategies that enabled her to explore the relations between traditional stories and myths, and male history, myth, and fantasy, Lochhead's writing answered Adrienne Rich's call for revisioning traditional and patriarchal narrative patterns.[2] In the 1970s, Scotland inherited a field of "old battle-grounds of religion and national identity" and a literary landscape which was dominated by male lyric voices and reflected men's public role as guardians of the cultural heritage.[3] Lochhead's voice found its distinctiveness by exploring the conditions under which women could express their identities and experiences in this cultural environment. The collection of poems *The Grimm Sisters* is an example of such exploration.[4]

The title of the collection reflects its concern with the fairy-tale tradition developed by the Grimm brothers, while also indicating the intention to re-present the tales in a different gender perspective by reprocessing the value of authorship and authority they convey. Lochhead's choice of fairy tales as subject matter for poetry is partly a response to specific cultural patterns of Scotland in the 1970s. It enabled her to focus on the identities and social experiences of women confined to

---

[1] Varty, 644.

[2] McMillan, 17; Crawford, 62; Carol Anderson, 128.

[3] McCulloch, 25; Crawford, 60, 62-3.

[4] The poems were completed in 1978 while Lochhead was in residence at Glendon College in Toronto as a beneficiary of the Scottish Arts Council first Scottish/Canadian Writers' Exchange. See Alison Smith, "Liz Lochhead: Speaking in Her Own Voice", *Liz Lochhead's Voices*, 1-16, 8. *The Grimm Sisters* was first published as a collection in 1981. I am using the edition published by Polygon (Edinburgh) in 1986 in *Dreaming Frankenstein & Collected Poems*, 69-104.

the domestic sphere, midwives of the storytelling tradition, while men, masters of the written word, wielded cultural authority in the public sphere. However, Lochhead's specific choice of the Grimms' tales as the main subject of the collection, tales edited by such male scholars of public distinction, and which, according to Jack Zipes, "are probably the most reprinted and best known in the world and serve as reference points for all kinds of cultural productions", enabled her to also focus on how the male authority of the written word, wielded in the public sphere, permeates and governs women's storytelling voices, even as they are assigned to the domestic.[5] Exploring how this relation of narrative government of women's subjective identity affects women's socialisation, Lochhead's writing engages with larger cultural systems, myths, and ideologies whose power is reflected in Scottish contexts. The result is a multifaceted critique of the power of male curators of the cultural heritage to control women's voices and, thus, the means of expressing their social identities, a critique that is relevant beyond local or national contexts.

My analysis will focus mainly on how Lochhead deals with male-generated narrating agency in fairy-tale representations of women, and on Lochhead's critical view of the class and gender hierarchies this agency engenders. Zipes argues that social contexts and material conditions may demand that certain versions of fairy tales acquire the status and functions of myth.[6] Having become "formative and definitive", "certain fairy-tale texts ... insert themselves into our cognitive processes, enabling us to establish and distinguish patterns of behavior and to reflect upon ethics, gender, morality, and power."[7] However, a defining feature of fairy tales is their amenability to change through retellings which enable "listeners and readers to envision possible solutions to their problems so that they could survive and adapt to their environments."[8] Thus, we distinguish two effects of reiterations of fairy tales. The repetition of fairy-tale patterns fostered by specific social contexts and material conditions over a period of time engenders norms which govern our social orientation in relation to ethics, gender, morality, and hierarchies of power. In this case, fairy tales function as social myths that strengthen dominant ideologies. But reiterations of fairy tales can also be the occasion of heteroglossic intervention whereby narrative patterns and the norms they convey and naturalise are questioned, thus reorienting our bearing in social reality. Lochhead's storytellers narrate the fabulas (series of events) that the male-

---

[5] Zipes, *Why Fairy Tales Stick*, 84.
[6] Zipes, *Fairy Tales*, 11.
[7] Zipes, *Why Fairy Tales Stick*, 26.
[8] Ibid., xii.

dominated fairy-tale canon provides, but they devise competing arrangements of meaning through which the fabulas can be reinterpreted. This enables readers to question the social norms that are naturalised through the process of reiteration that establishes certain fairy tales as social myths.

Alison Smith emphasises Lochhead's conviction that the voices of her poems come from the author's self.[9] The poems of *The Grimm Sisters* suggest that these voices also come from dominant traditions which shape the self's predisposition to channel their expression. With regard to fairy tales, male-generated traditions such as that of the Grimms eclipsed female-generated traditions that developed, for instance, in seventeenth-century France. As Zipes points out, the French term *conte de fée* "indicated the narrative power of women, for the fairies and writers/tellers of those texts are in control of the destinies of all the characters."[10] In *The Grimm Sisters* the very possibility of voice as originating in the subject position of the storyteller is prescribed in the male-controlled tradition which this voice seeks to revise. I will argue that the first poem of the collection is concerned with the construction of the storyteller figure and that it explores problematics related to situating a female storytelling voice in social and material contexts. I will then regard the other poems as they are strategically placed in the collection. Once the storyteller's figure is defined, the following two poems, rendered in this storyteller's voice, are concerned with the genealogy of the fairy-tale feminine in relation to the archetypal father and mother figures used in the tales. This genealogy is further explored in poems where the storyteller focuses on fairy-tale constructions of women's social roles at different stages of social life between pre-sexual girl and elderly woman: the roles of daughter, wife, lover, spinster, seductress, bride, sister, and so forth.

Robert Crawford emphasises that "in *The Grimm Sisters* and elsewhere Lochhead's celebration of and use of orality can be seen as disrupting the fixed, orthodox forms of the written down", revealing a "fluid and dialogic", "particular rather than universalizing" narrative space.[11] The first poem of the collection, titled "1: Storyteller", defines the narrator who will be the teller in subsequent poems by disrupting the traditional discursive position constructed for fairy-tale narrators in the written-down masculine tradition. In doing so, it also explores the boundaries of the place of telling where the woman storyteller is situated. The poem begins by narrating:

---

[9] Alison Smith, 12.
[10] Zipes, *Why Fairy Tales Stick*, 69.
[11] Crawford, 62.

she sat down
at the scoured table
in the swept kitchen
beside the dresser with its cracked delft.
And every last crumb of daylight was salted away.[12]

Here we identify a female character in a scene that recalls the Cap
o'Rushes tale.[13] But this character can also be seen as a storyteller
speaking from the subject position constructed in the male-generated fairy-
tale tradition for the story of Cap o'Rushes. Developing this argument, I
will use this story to provide a meta-perspective on Lochhead's collection
as a whole.

The Cap o'Rushes' tale is classified ATU 510B in the Aarne-
Thompson-Uther tale-type index as a version of Cinderella's story (ATU
510).[14] The main difference between Cap o'Rushes' tale and ATU 510A
versions (closest to the Grimms' Cinderella story) is that the breach
between father and daughter occurs because of the father (there is no
stepmother), who is not satisfied with the daughter's expression of love for
him. The daughter is banned because when her father asks her how much
she loves him, she replies that she loves him as food loves salt.[15]

Several elements suggest that the storyteller in Lochhead's poem is a
version of Cap o'Rushes. She stops to rest after a day's work: the table is
scoured and the kitchen is swept. As in the tale of Cap o'Rushes, there is a
strong allusion to salted food: "And every last crumb of daylight was
salted away." The voice in this poem belongs both to a character
resembling Cap o'Rushes, and to the storyteller whose narration sketches
her tale. But in the male-generated fairy-tale ethos, Cap o'Rushes is never
a narrator, only an actor. Attempting to tell herself into being, Lochhead's
storyteller cannot but convey her voice through the authority that sanctions
what Cap o'Rushes may say in the male-constructed fairy-tale canon. The
disjunctive conjunction of the voice of storyteller and narrative actor
suggests that in the male-generated fairy-tale canon women remain
unrecognised as tellers of stories, being recognisable only through their

---

[12] Lochhead, *The Grimm Sisters*, 70.

[13] A version of the tale can be found in Eveline Camilla Gurdon, *County Folk-
Lore. Printed Extracts No. 2: Suffolk* (London: David Nutt for the Folk-Lore
Society, 1893), 40-43.

[14] See Hans-Jörg Uther, *The Types of International Folktales. A Classification and
Bibliography Based on the System of Antti Aarne and Stith Thompson* (3 vols)
(Helsinki: Suomalainen Tiedeakatemia, 2004). An extensive analysis of Cinderella
stories is offered in Zipes, *Why Fairy Tales Stick*, 107-127.

[15] "I love you as fresh meat loves salt" in Gurdon, 40.

reflections in the stories' characters.[16] However, Lochhead's storytellers/subjects overtake narrating agency so that their subjection through male fantasies becomes itself a subject of narration.[17]

Thus, the poem "Storyteller" begins by introducing a female character similar to Cap o'Rushes who attempts to appropriate the voice of the storyteller that, litera(ri)lly, tells her into being. The last stanza suggests that the night that comes belongs to this storyteller: at first light next morning, "the stories dissolved in the whorl of the ear/ ... till they flew again/ in the storytellers night."[18] The second and third stanzas define the storyteller's work by highlighting the imbricature between realms of fantasy and material spaces where folktales steer social practices. In the context of these stanzas, the phrase "daylight was salted away" suggests that the events of work and social interaction are stored in the stories through which we fantasise reality to taste: stories make the reality of work and social living palatable, richer, and tastier; they "cook" reality.[19] Thus,

---

[16] Valerie Paradiž's analysis of the Grimms' sources shows their frequent recourse to women storytellers, a contribution often left unacknowledged. See Valerie Paradiž, *Clever Maids: The Secret History of the Grimm Fairy Tales* (2004. New York: Basic Books, 2005). On the other hand, Zipes notes that "we have absolutely no proof that women were the 'originators' or prime tellers of tales, the primeval spinners ... both sexes contributed to and continue to contribute to the tale-telling tradition." Lochhead's retellings do not idealise women as storytellers, but she is concerned with the difficulties of women's speaking within the literary tradition of the fairy tale which, although consisting "of appropriated tales from women and men alike, was firmly in the hands of men." Zipes, *Why Fairy Tales Stick*, 54, 55; see also 86.

[17] According to Lochhead, *The Grimm Sisters* relates "familiar stories from another angle" in which women are not treated as simply objects of male fantasies, but as individuals possessing complex subjectivities. Liz Lochhead in an interview conducted by Rebecca Wilson. *Sleeping with Monsters: Conversations with Scottish and Irish Women Poets*, eds. Gillean Somerville-Arjat and Rebecca E. Wilson (Edinburgh: Polygon, 1990), 8-14, 9.

[18] Lochhead, *The Grimm Sisters*, 70. The "night" is not just a period of darkness, but it also metaphorically refers to the dark recesses of the mind as a kernel of creative forces. According to Lochhead, speaking about literary creativity in general, "until an image exists the word is just there, in the night" (approximate quotation from Lochhead's keynote address at a roundtable discussion organised by creative writing students, University of Glasgow, February 2006).

[19] The phrasing is inspired by Lévi-Strauss's *The Raw and the Cooked*. See Claude Lévi-Strauss, *The Raw and the Cooked: Introduction to a Science of Mythology* (London: Pimlico, 1994).

No one could say the stories were useless
for as the tongue clacked
five or forty fingers stitched
corn was grated from the husk
patchwork was pieced
or the darning done.[20]

This stanza offers reflections on the possibilities of realness of the storyteller's place. It is suggested that the telling of stories serves to comfort women working in the domestic sphere, accompanying the "stitching", the "grating of corn", the "piecing of patchwork", and the "darning". But underlying this conventional painting of women as primitive, domestic "common folk", we discover a potentially empowering representation of women storytellers: as "the tongue clacks", perhaps not only cloth is stitched, corn grated, quilt patchwork pieced, or garments darned, but also, as with the clacking of a typewriter, events are joined in narratives, the raw fabula is refined and transformed into a story, patchwork paragraphs are pieced together, and thus reality is mended.

According to Dorothy McMillan, this stanza serves to characterise "the function of both story and teller as useful rather than merely decorative".[21] Storytelling is presented as a material process that intervenes in, and transforms the state of matter: "To tell the stories was her work./ It was like spinning,/ gathering thin air to the singlest strongest/ thread."[22] By highlighting the physical properties of the speaking voice, Lochhead underlines the materiality of the very action of storytelling. At the same time, through the metaphor of spinning, the poem suggests that changing the material reality through storytelling is similar to processing material objects in domestic work to which the storyteller is destined through the tales' scenarios. Thus, storytelling is seen as an activity that shapes material life by transforming the materiality of social locales—that is, by using the vibration of voice to disseminate the significance of material environments in ways that entice us to accept or change set patterns of material life, potentially creating new resonances between individuals and material places, with consequences for the material configuration of one's relation to place. At the same time, storytelling is seen as being shaped in turn by social practices that produce the socialisation scripts mirrored in the tales and by the reality of work environments. The following poems expand this framework to include other cultural forms that are determined

---

[20] Lochhead, *The Grimm Sisters*, 70.
[21] McMillan, 17.
[22] Lochhead, *The Grimm Sisters*, 70.

by, and which determine, the tales' scenarios—for instance marriage, patriarchal authority, or other corpuses of tales and myths. In these poems, as in "Storyteller", the weaving of tales into the texture of reality is seen as having both empowering and disempowering effects.

The metaphor of spinning draws a potentially empowering woman storyteller figure as someone who could change material configurations of social locales, but it is also used to suggest that it locks this storyteller within the world of fairy tales, where spinning often plays an important part in the plot and definition of women characters. Lochhead's storyteller is a woman spinning tales in order to weave a reality in which she may become a different kind of woman than Cap o'Rushes, but the threads of the texture of fairy-tale "reality" she must work with are interwoven with those of the material reality in such ways that the resulting design always yields a Cap o'Rushes. This raises questions regarding the role of narrating agency in creating socialisation scenarios. The woman storyteller figure drawn here is a domestic worker because of the tales that make her show herself to herself as such, because of tales like that of Cap o'Rushes. Suspecting that the voice that tells her into being is not entirely her own, the storyteller proceeds to undo realms of fantasy as masculine dominions and provides instead fantasy scenarios as tools for "spinning", "piecing together", and "darning" a more empowering social reality. The following poems in the collection can be read as tales told by this storyteller, marked by her efforts to reconstruct the male-generated fairy-tale ethos and other elements of cultural memory that reinforce this ethos.

For instance, the poem "Harridan" begins with a reflection on Pieter Bruegel the Elder's painting *Dulle Griet*, also known as *Mad Meg*. The central figure in the painting is a woman depicted running in a scene of nightmarish intensity. In Margaret Sullivan's analysis, "Madness and Folly are the dual—and related—themes of the *Dulle Griet*."[23] In Lochhead's poem the storyteller asks: "Was Meg 'mad' or more the Shakespearean fool?"[24] We are tempted to ask the same question about Cap o'Rushes: was she "mad" to challenge the authority of the father, or the wise fool who teaches a lesson without openly challenging authority? The fairy-tale Cap o'Rushes, although challenging her father, eventually renews patriarchal authority by re-creating her subservience in marriage. Her apparent folly as unmarried daughter is in the end revealed as wisdom, yet wisdom in the service of male authority. Lochhead's poem can be seen as providing a framework for us to interpret Cap o'Rushes' figure in light

---

[23] Margaret A. Sullivan, "Madness and Folly: Peter Bruegel the Elder's *Dulle Griet*", *Art Bulletin* 59 (1977): 55-66, 55.
[24] Lochhead, *The Grimm Sisters*, 74.

of Bruegel's painting. According to S. J. Boyd, Lochhead's reference to the Mad Meg painting "sets the crazy and the grotesque in the most *heimlich* context imaginable".[25] This *heimlich* is the "homely" space of the scullery. The Cap o'Rushes whom we may imagine to inhabit this space, rather than confirming masculine hierarchies, exposes them as conducive of nightmarish madness.

In Lochhead's poem, this madness is further explored with the awareness that it is a male-generated notion that makes sense of women's anger on men's terms.[26] Lochhead's storyteller evokes the figures of Queen Margot and of a virago in Mad Meg's company:

> Mad Meg, Sour-Tongued Margot,
> maddened slut in this mass of misery, a Virago,
> at her wit's end, running past Hell's Mouth, all reason gone,
> she has one mailed glove, one battered breastplate on.
> Oh that kitchen knife, that helmet, that silent shout,
> I know Meg from the inside out.[27]

The poem warns that women like Queen Margot, who placed love and independence before loyalty to family, are often branded as prostitutes. The reference to virago recalls the Latin phrase *femina virilis*—a virile, masculine woman, a reference that implies a remaking of feminine identity to meet expectations of masculinity.[28] We are led to ask to what extent the Cinderella-type figures of banned daughters in the male-generated fairy-tale canon are more similar to viragos, sharing the predicament of a Queen Margot, maddened by their misunderstood anger, "at their wit's end", rather than being witty, wise Shakespearean fools.

In Lochhead's storyteller's voice, the painting of Mad Meg, Queen Margot's history, and the reference to virago all tell a different story of women who reject the law of the father than the story told in Cinderella-type fairy tales. These contrasts suggest that what has not been told about Cap o'Rushes was the story of how her anger was misunderstood as

---

[25] S. J. Boyd, "The Voice of Revelation: Liz Lochhead and Monsters", *Liz Lochhead's Voices*, 38-56, 40.

[26] Sullivan shows that Bruegel's Mad Meg "is based—both formally and iconographically—on [his] earlier engraving of *Ira* from the series of the *Seven Deadly Sins* done in 1558." Sullivan, "Madness and Folly", 55.

[27] Lochhead, *The Grimm Sisters*, 74.

[28] Interviewed by Alison Smith, Lochhead remembers Dalziel High School, where she was a student, as a place where girls were "proxy boys complete with ties and blazers … . The thing about it—there was nothing that actually allowed you to express your *femaleness*". Alison Smith, 4, original italics.

madness and then tamed as mere folly—the unwritten story that lingers in the interstices of male-generated fairy-tale narrative scenarios. This is the story of the "silent shout" of women whose only weapons are "that kitchen knife" and the "mailed glove". In the imagery of the poem, the figure of the housewife is superimposed with that of one of the Furies.[29] As Meg turns into Megaera, we realise that her madness is not shiftless. The figure of Megaera offers an alternative to the women figures obtaining through male-generated versions of Cap o'Rushes' tale, Queen Margot's history, or the virago identity:

> Oh I am wild-eyed, unkempt, hellbent, a harridan.
> My sharp tongue will shrivel any man.
> Should our paths cross
> I'll embarrass you with public tears, accuse you with my loss.[30]

The Furies in Greek mythology are daughters of the night who avenge wrongdoings that escape human public justice. For Lochhead's storyteller, the "storytellers night" could become, as the realm of the Furies, a space where alternative views of social justice may be conceived and legitimated.[31]

Thus, the voice of these poems belongs to a storyteller whose presence is fantasised, for it is someone who cannot escape the spell of myth: she is a Cap o'Rushes of sorts. However, she works to make visible the unthinkable which, in Butler's words, is "fully within culture but excluded from *dominant* culture."[32] If Cap o'Rushes' or Cinderellas were to turn inside out the texture of their sanitised reality, woven in the male-generated fairy-tale canon, madness like that of Megaera, which is conducive of more reasonable social roles, would be released. This "madness" means "not sane" only to the extent that it has been foreclosed in realms of the unthinkable, a foreclosure upon which rests the foundation of the legitimate subject of male-dominated gender regimes.

The ways stories come across in social roles is more pointedly explored in Lochhead's "The Grim Sisters". The poem tells the story of a

---

[29] As Boyd indicates, Lochhead's representations of the Furies can be connected with Mary Daly's celebrations of women as Hag, Spinster, and Fury. Daly writes: "As Furies, women in the tradition of Great Hags reject the curse of compromise." Boyd, 52. Mary Daly, *Gyn/Ecology: The Metaethics of Radical Feminism* (London: Women's Press, 1979), 16.

[30] Lochhead, *The Grimm Sisters*, 75.

[31] Ibid., 70.

[32] Butler, *Gender Trouble*, 77, original italics.

young woman preparing to go out to a ball in the late 1950s, in a rendering that references Cinderella's tale. The dressing-up occurs in a domestic space, where "the grown up girls next door" are called to help:

> I sat at peace passing bobbipins
> from a marshmallow pink cosmetic purse
> embossed with jazzmen,
> girls with pony tails and a November
> topaz lucky birthstone. ...
> [The girls next door] doused my cow's-lick, rollered
> and skewered tightly.
> I expected that to be lovely
> would be worth the hurt.[33]

Examining Lochhead's references to fashion accessories in her poems, Anne Varty finds that Lochhead's technique of evoking "brand names together with more general terms" provides clues regarding the characters' "temporal and social location, asserts the immediately spoken quality of the verse, and at the same time generates a metaphoric gloss about commerce as a means of social control."[34] In "The Grim Sisters", too, fashion is exposed as disciplinary discourse. The public event of the ball is shown as an occasion for demonstrating a kind of femininity that fulfils masculine expectations. In order to become feminine on these terms, the woman's body "must take the social order as [its] productive nucleus", to use Elizabeth Grosz's words, thus becoming the subject of "representations and cultural inscriptions" that "quite literally constitute bodies and help to produce them as such."[35] The social order which subjects the young woman is also a gender regime of masculine dominance whose power is distributed through the interlinked cultural and economic networks that produce fashionable bodies.

According to Grosz, "ritualistically inscribed scars and incisions become the marks of one's social location and position, creating a (provisional) fixity from the flux of the body's experiential intensities." As Grosz suggests, such marks are inscribed on bodies also through using makeup.[36] In "The Grim Sisters", an entire array of cosmetic tools for fashioning women's bodies to please and entice the male is evoked towards the end of the poem:

---

[33] Lochhead, *The Grimm Sisters*, 72-3, brackets mine.

[34] Varty, 645.

[35] Elizabeth Grosz, *Volatile Bodies: Toward a Corporeal Feminism* (Bloomington: Indiana University Press, 1994), x-xi.

[36] Grosz, "Bodies and Knowledges", 34-5.

In those big black mantrap handbags …
were hedgehog hairbrushes,
cottonwool mice and barbed combs to tease.[37]

The issue of women's consent to disciplining their bodies to meet
masculine expectations is problematised with the awareness that the
masculine myths of femininity are transmitted through the very
"sisterhood" that binds women to a common fate. The women next door
are "grown-ups" who transmit "women's wisdom" to their younger sister:

They read my Stars,
tied chiffon scarves to doorhandles, tried
to teach me tight dancesteps[38]

The teaching of "tight dancesteps" suggests a teaching of prescribed
patterns of movement in social spaces. The metaphorical sisters model the
young woman's mind and body to fit the kind of realm of fantasy
instituted through fairy tales of the Cinderella type. They must overcome
the young woman's half-hearted resistance, hinted at, for instance, when
she is shown thinking that "you'd no guarantee/ any partner you might
find would ever be able to/ keep up" with her dance steps. The "tricks of
the trade" the young woman learns from the sisterhood are all tips for
disciplining the body, the failure of which is a grim "disaster".[39]

We are thus offered a rendering of the process whereby women's
fantasising of themselves as "lovely" is conducive of body-markings that
belong in male-generated "maps" of women's bodies. According to
Marina Warner:

the body is still the map on which we mark our meanings; it is chief among
metaphors used to see and present ourselves, and in the contemporary
profusion of imagery … the female body occurs more frequently than any
other; men often appear as themselves, as individuals, but women attest the
identity and value of someone or something else … .[40]

With a critical, ironic eye, the female actors in "The Grim Sisters" are
shown to attest the identity and value of Cinderella-type fairy-tale figures

---

[37] Lochhead, *The Grimm Sisters*, 74.

[38] Ibid., 73.

[39] Ibid.

[40] Marina Warner, *Monuments and Maidens: The Allegory of the Female Form*
(London: Picador, 1985), 331.

and women's socialisation modes enshrined with the fairy tales: "dressed to kill", the young woman must go in search of the lover and the partnership that guarantees future domestic bliss. The use of irony also conveys the grimness of a sisterhood in which the bond between women is materialised only in the domestic sphere while, we infer, in the public domain they compete for men's favours.

Lochhead's story about the Cinderella of the 1950s and the Grimms' fairy tale are disjunctive in relevant points. Both Cinderellas have uncomfortable relationships with their "sisters". In the fairy tale this is clearly because of envy and self-centredness, but in the Cinderella story of the 1950s the metaphorical "grim sisters" do everything in their power to help, instead of preventing, her gaining a lover. However, the poem shows that a mere reversal of the sisters' ethics is unsatisfying, since the grim sisters, while appearing helpful, also discipline the young woman, however benevolently by contrast to the fairy-tale stepsisters' disciplining Cinderella. With this comes the realisation that it is not Cinderella's relationship with her stepsisters that is most damaging, but rather the masculine cultural regime that entices women to fantasise themselves through their competitiveness for winning the male-organised beauty contest. Rereading the fairy tale with this understanding we realise that in the dynamic between Cinderella and her sisters women only hurt women. The condition of the 1950s Cinderella with her hair "skewered tightly", learning uncomfortably "tight dancesteps", may be not so different from the condition of the fairy-tale stepsisters who must cut their toes to meet the body parameters the prince expects. The enmity between the fairy-tale Cinderella and her stepsisters is thus revised to point out a common ground, the realisation of which may inspire a different sisterhood, one that is not divided to suit a male-dominated cultural regime.

Another relevant disjunction is achieved by contrasting the two stories with regard to Cinderella's flight when the clock strikes midnight. In the fairy tale, this only means a postponement of the recognition scene in which Cinderella gains the reward of wedded bliss. But for the 1950s Cinderella the prospect of marriage seems distant. In the absence of the masculine measuring gaze, the young woman appears as a parody of the more "successful" seductresses:

> But when the clock struck they
> stood still, stopped dead.
> And they were left there
> out in the cold with the wrong skirtlength
> and bouffant hair,

dressed to kill[41]

In the contrast between the two stories there emerge questions which challenge the social myths that define women's stance in public spaces (positioning women as competing for winning a male partner); that script their socialisation patterns (i.e., how young women must make their charms available to men in order to gain their company); and that prescribe requirements of bodily beauty and engender female body discipline.

The second poem of the three-piece set "The Furies" offers an image of women for whom the promise of wedded bliss remains unfulfilled in spite of their disciplining themselves for the Cinderella role. According to Varty, the poem "presents from inside the problem of having no obvious function as wife or mother."[42] Titled "Spinster", the poem turns on its head the folktale idea that the young girl's perseverance guarantees fulfilment in marriage. It points out that the alternatives offered by the same society that believes in wedded bliss to Cinderellas who have not secured a prince are void of the sense of fairy-tale marvel. The Cinderellas' perseverance, the anonymous social voice insists, must be invested in resigned acceptance of isolation and of the idea that if women's identity as women cannot be fulfilled as wives, their efforts must be directed toward the traditional womanly concerns with public good and spiritual causes: "Accept./ Support good causes. ... Go to evening classes. ... Try Yoga. Cut your losses./ Accept."[43] If the first poem explores the figure of Megaera, the poem "Spinster" seems to reinterpret the figure of Alecto, who in the sisterhood of the Furies is the one who is unceasing in anger. The voice speaking in this poem seems to belong to a Cinderella for whom unceasing perseverance in satisfying masculine demands turns into unceasing anger, demanding a reconsideration of the social values that the fairy tales corroborate.[44] Indeed, the poem's first line is "This is not a way to go on."

The third poem of the "Furies" set offers yet another disjunctive realm of fantasy. The female identity in "Bawd" is apparently an alternative to that of the subservient 1950s Cinderella. The poem portrays a woman whose night out is not an attempt to please the male gaze but to master it

---

[41] Lochhead, *The Grimm Sisters*, 73.

[42] Varty, 646.

[43] Lochhead, *The Grimm Sisters*, 75. The social pressure on the spinster for resigned acceptance of her outcast status is emphasised in Varty's interpretation (Varty, 646).

[44] In Varty's interpretation, "the spinster is both social aggressor and victim." Varty, 646.

with an assertion of her "fatal dame" sexual power.[45] No longer credulous
and innocent ("I've hauled my heart in off my sleeve"[46]) like the 1950s
Cinderella going out to secure a marriage partner, this woman is more like
the mythic Tisiphone. She sees herself haunting masculine realms of
fantasy with a vengeance. McMillan comments that she seems "to be
reserving a hidden strength rather than protecting a secret fear."[47] Rather
than learning "tight dancesteps", the woman in "Bawd" will

> rouge my cleavage, flaunt myself, my heels
> will be perilously high, oh
> but I won't sway. ...
> There is mayhem in my smile.[48]

However, unlike the wide-eyed 1950s Cinderella, this woman is aware that
the male-generated image of the femme fatale is a fantasy. She adopts it
with theatrical excess in order to subvert it, but eventually we are
uncertain whether such fantasies construct empowering women's
identities: "I'll be frankly fake. ... No one will guess it's not my style."[49]
As Varty puts it,

> the linguistic cast-offs [the woman in this poem] has picked up, together
> with too solid a protestation of bad intent already labelling herself as others
> will, reflect the inauthenticity of the stance and a bitter sense that there is a
> better life (both in terms of pleasure and ethics) than the one she adopts.[50]

The three poems of "The Furies", providing intertextual references
between a wider corpus of myths and fairy tales, supply complexity where
the fairy tales simplify. Varty argues that

> although the three 'furies' do not emerge from any one narrative, they are
> archetypes which lurk in many stories, and stereotypes which figure in
> social attitudes today. In each case Lochhead invites the reader behind the
> scenes, to hear how the woman determines to construct herself according
> to type. The tales ... reveal various kinds of difficulty experienced by the
> single woman in securing her social place.[51]

---

[45] Lochhead, *The Grimm Sisters*, 76.
[46] Ibid.
[47] McMillan, 25.
[48] Lochhead, *The Grimm Sisters*, 76.
[49] Ibid.
[50] Varty, 647.
[51] Ibid., 645.

The sisterhood inspired by the mythological figures of the Furies is empowering by comparison with the divided sisterhood of Cinderella-type tales and with the grim sisterhood of the fifties Cinderella. Yet it paints a troublesome portrait of empowered women: while the "harridan" is "hellbent" and ready to "shrivel any man" by "embarrassing them with public tears" and "accusing them with her loss", she sets out to do so as a Mad Meg, a "maddened slut" Queen Margo and a virago "at her wit's end"; the spinster figure is likewise tense; and the "bawd", in spite of her confident display of female sexuality, is bitterly aware that this is men's style, not hers. We have been given a range of myths and shown how they construct feminine identity in social reality. With this knowledge we may return to Cinderella-type stories to fill in the gaps and flesh out the sketchy contours. The marvel of the ball has been exposed as a bitter occasion of feminine contest to win masculine favours. The banned Cap o'Rushes may now be seen not only as the wisely patient daughter but also more like a Mad Meg at her wit's end. And the alternative to Cinderella's displaying her beauty to lure the prince into marriage is an over-sexualised she-devil behind which we distinguish a woman who is not herself.[52]

The correlation that stories effect between reality and myth is further explored in other poems, by focusing on the roles of father, mother, son, daughter, sister, seductress, seducer, spinster, daughter-in-law, pre-sexual girl, lover, husband, and wife. The poems exploring the father and mother figures of fairy-tale fantasy are the most revelatory in terms of their force to construct social roles. I will therefore focus on these in order to examine their potent influence on the fantasies through which social identity is gained.

---

[52] In this context one notes Varty's argument that the characters of Elizabeth and Mary in Lochhead's play *Mary Queen of Scots Got Her Head Chopped Off* posture "as queenly versions of 'Harridan', 'Spinster' and 'Bawd', each monarch" seemingly "unable to eschew stereotype." Varty, 652. The play, "drawing upon the emblematic aspects of language as a symbol of national identity", is another example of Lochhead's use of elements of the oral tradition, especially ballad material such as "The Twa Corbies", to revise perceptions of historical characters, in this case Elizabeth I and Mary Stuart, as established in male-dominated history discourse and in its ramifications in popular imagination. Mugglestone, 94; Crawford, 61.

Shifty Fathers

The patriarchal authority to define social identities, shared by male curators of the cultural heritage, is disseminated in fairy tales through the figure of the father. Lochhead's poem "II: The Father" focuses on fairy-tale constructions of the image and role of the father in order to highlight his complicity in the legitimation of male-dominated gender regimes, and explores the consequences of daughters' fantasising such father figures in scenarios derived from fairy tales, which they may use in social interaction.

The poem unmasks the father's ineptness through reference to the tale of the Sleeping Beauty—or, in the Grimm brothers' version, the little Briar Rose—and to the tale of Beauty and the Beast: the father, we are told, is "tricked into bartering his beloved daughter/ in exchange for the rose he only/ took to please her".[53] Beauty's tale, like that of the Sleeping Beauty, is an instructional tale. Beauty's compassion and patience, both for her father and for the Beast, are rewarded in marriage. But in the ironic voice of Lochhead's storyteller, the father's attempt to obtain the rose to please his daughter sits uneasily with the idea of bartering. The two tales referred to in Lochhead's poems compound the figure of the father as loving, yet also as in complicity with, and mediating, the social order through which daughters are given into marriage. The father "compounds it all" "by over-protectiveness and suppression".[54] Lochhead's storyteller suggests that the father could have acted in a different way than the classical versions of these tales legitimate, where he is

> (banning
> spinning wheels indeed
> when the sensible thing would have been
> to familiarise her from the cradle
> and explain their power to hurt her).[55]

The passage shows that the classical tales do not serve to familiarise young women with, or explain to them the implications of, the social role of wife. Rather, they serve to trick them into becoming wives through the promise of reward in marriage. A different image of the father than in the classical tales is revealed when we are told that:

---

[53] Lochhead, *The Grimm Sisters*, 71.
[54] Ibid.
[55] Ibid.

> But when she comes,
> the beautiful daughter,
> leading her lover by the sleeve, laughing—
> 'Come and meet my daddy, the King,
> he's absolutely a hundred years behind the times
> but such a dear.'
> and she's (note Redeeming Kiss)
> wide-eyed and aware.
> Stirring, forgiven, full of love and terror,
> her father hears her footstep on the stair.[56]

Here, the young woman's voice is inflected by the conventional voice of the daughter of classical versions of such tales when she refers to the typical fairy-tale character of the King. But we also recognise it as the voice of casual conversation in social reality. This intermingling shows how the voice of the tale permeates and scripts what is spoken in the realm of social reality where social relations are set up and performed (such as the daughter's introducing the lover to her father). The King figure of fairy tales lies behind thinking the "daddy" in the girl's mind.

The final lines of the poem unmask the fathers' wilful ineptness by suggesting their remorse vis-à-vis their hidden complicity in legitimating male-generated myths about women's social roles. Although the father is forgiven, he stirs, "full of love and terror", as he understands that the daughter knows about his taking advantage of her innocence and trust: although "wide-eyed", she is "aware". Unlike the daughters of classical tales, the young woman of Lochhead's storyteller, awoken into a masculine world, may have been credulous, but in time she became suspicious.

Maria Tatar points out the masculine bias of the Grimms' tales by showing that the daughter characters must undergo trials to prove their social worth, while male characters are endowed with qualities that make them fit for social success and are thus in the position to redeem the innocent daughters.[57] Lochhead's storyteller uses cliché as a device in the service of irony to construct the daughter figure as a woman who is aware of the implications of such redeeming (the storyteller insists: "note Redeeming Kiss"). In Lochhead's own words, you cannot use cliché "without acknowledging it to be a cliché. You enter into a relationship with the reader whereby you have the reader join in the game with you, to

---

[56] Ibid.

[57] Maria Tatar, "Born Yesterday: Heroes in the Grimm's Fairy Tales", *Fairy Tales and Society: Illusion, Allusion and Paradigm*, ed. Ruth Bottigheimer (Philadelphia: Pennsylvania University Press, 1986), 95-114, 100-101.

complete the acknowledgement."[58] In "The Father", the suggestion that the young woman is aware of fairy-tale clichéd socialisation scripts, even while she performs the social role of lover and future wife, undermines the fairy tales' construction of young women as innocent and foolish daughters. Quite the contrary, saying about the father that "he's absolutely a hundred years behind the times/ but such a dear" betrays the confidence of a young woman who is aware that it is the father's feigned bungles that lead her into the role of wife, but forgives his scheming.

According to Sellers, fairy tales

> can impact on adult life with all the resonance and force childhood memories produce—whether the emotions stirred by the tales are ones of terror, grandiose dreams of achievement, or puerile satisfaction in justice being dispensed.[59]

In Lochhead's poem we are given a daughter figure whose fantasising identity is shown as being underwritten by the kind of memories that fairy tales produce. Her speech carries echoes of the language employed by the daughters of the classical tale tradition. Her emotions are partly stirred through the recognition in herself, as adult woman, of the fairy-tale figure of the Sleeping Beauty. The poem thus makes visible the interrelation between fairy-tale fantasy and social identity.

"The Father" highlights the difficulties of imagining, in a patriarchal context, how women may exercise agency within the subject positions to which fairy tales confine them, and how they may escape the social roles the tales prescribe. The exploration of these difficulties is continued in the poem that immediately follows "The Father", titled "III: The Mother", which focuses on the mother figure constructed in the Grimms' fairy tales while also invoking tropes of the maternal figure of male-generated myth and legend.

The Witch Mother:
Constructions of the Mother-Daughter Relationship

The poem "III: The Mother" entices readers to reflect on how the Grimms' tales, dovetailing with patriarchal myths, misrepresent women's experiences of the mother-daughter relationship in order to create

---

[58] Colin Nicholson, "Knucklebones of Irony: Liz Lochhead", *Poem, Purpose and Place: Shaping Identity in Contemporary Scottish Verse* (Edinburgh: Polygon, 1992), 201-23, 216.
[59] Sellers, 12.

women's subjective identities that suit male-dominated gender regimes. The poem begins by claiming that the mother "is always two faced."[60] It then explains the statement by first describing the mother figure that fairy tales legitimate as desirable: the "best" mother.

> At best, she wished you
> into being. Yes, it was she
> cried at the seven drops of blood that fell,
> staining the snow—she
> who bargained crazily with Fate
> for that longawaited child
> as red as blood
> as white as snow[61]

These lines highlight the oversimplified portrait of the mother with which male-generated fairy tales operate. The "best" mother is defined in these tales through reduction to the basic biological function of procreation.[62] For instance, the introductory paragraphs of the Grimms' version of Snow White's tale offer an image of the wedded bliss that the Sleeping Beauty or the little Briar Rose might expect: the Queen is found performing domestic tasks, the carrying out of which is disturbed only when, again, she pricks her finger and bleeds.[63] The event marks, perhaps, the woman's access to a new social stage: that of motherhood. As soon as the task of motherhood is performed, the tale summarily disposes of the benevolent mother figure.

This oversimplification of the role assigned to married women as mothers is underlined with irony in Lochhead's poem: "But she's always dying early,/ so often it begins to look deliberate."[64] These lines register anxiety about the stories' reiteration of the best mother's death scenario, and the following lines, investigating its effects, pick up and develop its psychological resonances. For the daughter, "the best" mother's dying means

> abandoning you,
> leaving you to the terrible mercy

[60] Lochhead, *The Grimm Sisters*, 71.

[61] Ibid., 71-2.

[62] Zipes, *Why Fairy Tales Stick*, 132.

[63] Jacob Grimm and Wilhelm Grimm, "Little Snow-white", *Grimm's Fairy Tales* (London: Jonathan Cape, 1972), 48. For an extensive analysis of Snow White tales, see Zipes, *Why Fairy Tales Stick*, 133-9.

[64] Lochhead, *The Grimm Sisters*, 72.

of the Worst Mother, the one who married your father.
She doesn't like you, she
prefers all your sisters, she
loves her sons.
She's jealous of mirrors.
She wants your heart in a casket.[65]

Here, the emphasis on the Worst Mother as being "the one who married your father" suggests that fairy tales demonise the sexually active mother, guarding readers against women whose sexuality is not fully tamed through marriage. Such mother figures threaten patriarchal visions of wedded bliss. In the Grimms' Snow White story, the "worst mother" is a stepmother, but Lochhead's poem suggests that the best and worst mother may be sides of the same woman, albeit mutually exclusive sides: the mother "is always two faced".[66] Lochhead's poem entices us to think that the "worst mother" in the Grimms' tale represents what must be repudiated in order for the good mother to exist. In light of Butler's theorisation of narrative reiterations, we might say that it is the repetition of such talk about the mother in the social space where tales circulate that materialises "the mother" as a social persona, giving her realness.[67]

In the Grimms' tale, the "worst mother" is constructed as envious of the daughter's beauty. On the one hand, the reduction of the mother-daughter relationship to a beauty contest trivialises it. On the other, it constructs the mother-daughter relationship as one of opposition. While the daughter is allowed to use her charms in order to gain a husband, the mother who attempts to preserve her sexual appeal is punished severely through torture and death. This happens at the daughter's wedding. Since the young wife witnesses the punishment, perhaps this is a lesson for her, too, teaching her which ways of socialising her body as wife and future mother are legitimate.[68]

Thus, the masculine fairy-tale tradition convicts mothers when they exceed the social roles to which the tales assign them. These fairy tales also render the relationship between mother and daughter as a split relationship, where mother and daughter compete for the favour of power

---

[65] Ibid.

[66] Ibid., 71.

[67] Butler, *Bodies That Matter*, 129.

[68] For analyses of such corroboration of masculine gender regimes by fairy tales, see, for instance, Sandra Gilbert and Susan Gubar, *Madwoman in the Attic: The Woman Writer and the Nineteenth-Century Literary Imagination* (New Haven, CT: Yale University Press, 1979), 36; Maria Tatar, *The Classic Fairy Tales* (New York: Norton, 1999), 74; Zipes, *Why Fairy Tales Stick*, 15.

implied in their association with a male, be that the father/king or prince/husband/son.[69] The value of the "worst mother" figure as social myth also consists in erasing the mother-daughter bond. This erasure is arranged as a narrative event in such ways that the daughter's availability for exogamous partnership that obtains is seen as reason for celebration, while the repudiated mother's punishment appears rightful. Adrienne Rich argues that

> Matrophobia can be seen as a womanly splitting of the self, in the desire to become purged once and for all of our mothers' bondage, to become individuated and free. ... Our personalities seem dangerously to blur and overlap with our mothers'; and, in a desperate attempt to know where mother ends and daughter begins, we perform radical surgery.[70]

In many classic fairy tales such surgery serves a male-dominated gender regime. In Lochhead's interpretation, the fairy tales' warning against the mother appears damaging, as it also implies a repudiation of the mother's assistance and support during the daughter's sexual awakening:

> Tell me
> what kind of prudent parent
> would send a little child on a foolish errand in the forest
> with a basket jammed with goodies
> and wolf-bait? Don't trust her an inch.[71]

Thus, an alternative way of fantasising the mother is proposed that modifies how audiences perceive the suggestion of distrust carried in folktales. In the realm of fantasy thus opened, "Don't trust her an inch" cannot but sound ironic, undermining the didactic seriousness of male-authored fairy tales such as those of the Grimms.

Reversals of Fairy-Tale Patterns and Roles

Several poems that follow Lochhead's storyteller's reflections on the fairy-tale mother and father figures focus more emphatically on the fairy-tale daughter. A rewriting of the tale of Beauty and the Beast, the second poem of the "Three Twists", highlights the fairy-tale requirement that the

---

[69] See also Marina Warner, *From the Beast to the Blonde: On Fairy Tales and Their Tellers* (New York: Farrar 1995), 213-4.

[70] Adrienne Rich, *Of Woman Born: Motherhood as Experience and Institution* (New York: Norton, 1973), 235-6.

[71] Lochhead, *The Grimm Sisters*, 72.

daughter should show patience in living with a "beastly" companion in order to be rewarded. Translated into a real-life social situation, women's fantasising of the role of patient and understanding wife after the image of Beauty is seen disjunctively as a horror story rather than a story of rewarded endurance. The connotations of rape implied in the description of Beauty's life with the Beast explain the power of "spinning wheels" to hurt the daughter and break the taboo on sexuality in fairy tales by foregrounding the possibility of abuse in the relationship between daughters and their fated husbands:

> Beast
> he was hot
> he grew horns
> he had you
> screaming mammy daddy screaming blue
> murder.
> From one sleepy thought
> of how like a mane his hair…
> next thing
> he's furred & feathered, pig bristled,
> warted like a toad
> puffed & jumping—
> the green cling of those
> froggy fingers
> will make you shudder yet.
> Then his flesh gone
> dead. Scaled as a handbag.
> He was that old crocodile
> you had to kiss[72]

The final stanza points toward realms of fantasy that, in being disjunctive in relation to stories shaped like those of the Grimms, offer a reversal of roles that may be empowering for women:

> Oh, but soon
> (her hair grew lang her breath grew strang)
> you'll
> (little One-Eye for little Three-Eyes, the
> Bearded Lady)
> Yes, sweet Beauty, you'll
> match him
> horror for horror.[73]

---

[72] Ibid., 79-80.

The second line evokes an anonymous medieval Scottish ballad known as "Kemp Owyne", where the test for the male champion ("kemp" is a form of "champion") consists in showing patience and perseverance in wooing the bride, in spite of her turning into a beast: "Her breath grew strang, her hair grew lang,/ And twisted thrice about the tree,/ And all the people, far and near,/ Thought that a savage beast was she."[74] However, the references to the Bearded Lady and to the Grimms' tale of little Two-Eyes render ambiguous the meaning of such matching of the Beast "horror for horror": while the reference to "Kemp Owyne" suggests that the power to horrify the opposite sex into submission is also available to women, we are also reminded of the painful status of women perceived as monstrous. Even though the Grimms' story of little Two-Eyes begins by showing how she is marginalised by her sisters for being the same as everyone else, it is little One-Eye and little Three-Eyes who end up destitute, punished for rejecting normality (a normality which, it turns out, also implies marriage). And the figure of the Bearded Lady is a reminder of the painful practices of Victorian circus parades of women whose features did not conform to norms of femininity. It may be that turning into a beast is not more than turning into a Bearded Lady who performs in the circuslike "wham bam menagerie" of the domestic realm of the home.[75] The third poem of "Three Twists", titled "After Leaving the Castle", reinforces the doubt that simply performing masculine roles is empowering for women.

The poem "Rapunzstiltskin", the first in the "Three Twists" set, merges the Grimms' "Rapunzel" with their "Rumpelstiltskin":

> & just when our maiden had got
> good & used to her isolation,
> stopped daily expecting to be rescued,
> had come to almost love her tower,
> along comes This Prince
> with absolutely
> all the wrong answers.[76]

Here, the range of social meanings associated with the activity of spinning, attribution of skills, and marriage in "Rumpelstiltskin" is brought to bear on the meanings carried in "Rapunzel". Zipes argues that the Grimms'

---

[73] Ibid.

[74] Francis James Child, *The English and Scottish Popular Ballads*, Vol. 1-5 (1882-1898), Vol. 1 (Boston: Houghton, Mifflin, 1882), 306-313, 309.

[75] Lochhead, *The Grimm Sisters*, 80.

[76] Ibid., 78.

version of "Rumpelstiltskin" devalues the female activity of spinning by placing the emphasis on capital accumulation (straw must be turned into gold) in ways that reflect the rise to power of male industrialists.[77] The transference of economic power from the sphere of the home, where women could claim the identity of skilled workers, into the public sphere allows the fantasising of young women as workers who need men's help in order to fulfil the tasks deemed valuable by the capitalist fraternity. In this context, one wonders to what extent the manikin figure in the Grimms' "Rumpelstiltskin" reflects the identity of the anonymous male worker of nineteenth-century industrial society and so to what extent the relationship between him and the miller's daughter, unskilled and unable to prove her worth, reflects divisions of class (the manikin lives in a shabby house and the miller's daughter remains poor, as opposed to the king, who accumulates wealth) and gender (the manikin is skilled while the daughter's skills are worthless) as well as class interests (the tale rewards the daughter, who brings riches to her husband, and punishes the manikin, who threatens to end the passing of wealth to the king's children by claiming the child).

In Lochhead's "Rapunzstiltskin", Rapunzel occupies the position reserved for the manikin in the Grimms' tales, so the poem undermines the class and gender hierarchies envisioned by the latter. Rapunzstiltskin is able to spin straw into gold, but for Lochhead's storyteller this is also a matter of spinning a story. Rapunzstiltskin's strength is her ability to offer a realm of fantasy that departs from clichés and stereotypes of femininity while at the same time speaking from the position of someone excluded through class (as is the position of the manikin figure). Her reaction to the Prince's talk is rendered thus:

> Of course she had not been brought up to look for
> originality or gingerbread
> so at first she was quite undaunted
> by his tendency to talk in strung-together cliché.[78]

The male suitor's inability to escape modes of socialisation scripted through fairy tales is highlighted, while the woman is shown to be aware of, and condescending toward, the persistence of fairy-tale elements in the contemporary narratives of consumer mass culture:

> 'Just hang on and we'll get you out of there'
> he hollered like a fireman in some soap opera

---

[77] Zipes, *Fairy Tales*, 11.
[78] Lochhead, *The Grimm Sisters*, 78.

when she confided her plight (the old
hag inside etc. & how trapped she was);[79]

The young woman is aware of the power of these narratives, when taken
up as socialisation scripts, to shape constraining social experiences for
women:

So there she was ...
throwing him all the usual lifelines
till, soon, he was shimmying in & out
every other day as though
he owned the place, bringing her
the sex manuals & skeins of silk
from which she was meant, eventually,
to weave the means of her own escape.[80]

Rapunzstiltskin realises that the figure of the male rescuer carried through
male-generated myths cannot fulfil the promise of women's escape from
the conditions of a marginalised existence and intuits that this promise
may be forever deferred ("'All very well & good,' she prompted,/ 'but
when exactly?'"[81]) as long as new ways of fantasising women are not
allowed in the stories about them. Rapunzstiltskin appears, on one level, as
a version of the woman storyteller who finds it difficult to escape the
subject position to which the tales she can tell confine her, and on another
level, as the narrative embodiment of a woman whose story remains
unheard because it cannot be rendered in the narrative patterns legitimated
in the masculine tradition of fiction/fantasy. In spite of her efforts to put
new meanings into the masculine voice ("She mouthed at him, hinted,/ she
was keener than a T. V. quizmaster"[82]) he doesn't "get it right":

'I'll do everything in my power' he intoned, 'but
the impossible (she groaned) might
take a little longer.' He grinned.
She pulled her glasses off.
'All the better
to see you with my dear?' he hazarded.
She screamed, cut off her hair.
'Why, you're beautiful?' he guessed tentatively.[83]

---

[79] Ibid.
[80] Ibid., 78-9.
[81] Ibid., 79.
[82] Ibid.
[83] Ibid.

In the male's voice "the impossible" refers to his task, augmenting the identity of rescuer promoted in male-generated traditions of myth and fairy tale. Rapunzstiltskin groans with exasperation when he misses the opportunity to realise that, for her, "the impossible" refers to the inability of his voice to accommodate hers, which would alter the fairy-tale script. He unwittingly hits the mark when he utters the wolf's line from "Little Red Riding Hood" but fails to see the irony about vision which the line carries in the context of the poem. When Rapunzstiltskin, pulling her glasses off, mimes to him to stop seeing her through the lens offered by myths, his use of the fairy tale to hazard a chat line betrays his understanding of her gesture as a call to impersonate the identity of male preying on women which the fairy-tale wolf figure conveys. Finally, assuming the identity of the seducer, he fails to see that by cutting her hair off Rapunzstiltskin invites a subversion of fairy-tale constructions of women, of their beauty, passivity, weakness, and so forth—as referenced in the tale's ascription of metaphoric value to Rapunzel's hair.

The end of the poem offers the opportunity to comment on interweaving gender and class issues. Although by inhabiting the position of the manikin from the Grimms' "Rumpelstiltskin" the Rapunzstiltskin figure subverts traditional associations between gender and skill, she shares the position of class exclusion. However, unlike the manikin, whose name was found out, who could eventually stand forth from anonymity if only to be banned again, Rapunzstiltskin's identity remains unfathomable, because her story is not accommodated in the fairy-tale discourses of the masculine tradition:

> she
> shrieked & stamped her foot so
> hard it sank six cubits through the floorboards.
> 'I love you?' he came up with
> as finally she tore herself in two.[84]

Rapunzstiltskin is torn between two identities constructed in tales which deny her narrating agency—that is, the agency through which she may construct herself. She is assigned subordinate positions in the male-dominated gender regime legitimated by the tales, both in terms of class and gender. Catherine MacKinnon argued that "the organized expropriation of the work of some for the benefit of others defines a class—workers—the organized expropriation of the sexuality of some for

---

[84] Ibid.

the use of others defines the sex, woman."[85] Lochhead's poem suggests
that fairy tales legitimate this organised expropriation, which, although
working along the two coordinates of gender and class, does not permit the
recognition of how both coordinates define the position of women. Such
recognition would show that the gender of the fairy-tale 'woman' is a
function of class hierarchies, and would expose the inequalities of the
partnership of wedded bliss that the tales promote. The lack of this
recognition leaves women, as Lochhead's poem suggests, unnameable,
bracketed between the identities of a Rumpelstiltskin and a Rapunzel, torn
between these identities generated by a masculine narrating agency. The
name "Rapunzstiltskin" as a combination of "Rumpelstiltskin"
(referencing, for Lochhead, class exclusion) and "Rapunzel" (referencing
women's sex as beautified objects in male-generated fantasies) suggests
that gender and class exclusions should be viewed in a framework that
allows us to see how they define each other. But such a story is difficult to
tell unless one views critically the familiar, naturalised women's identities
which are defined through male-generated stories like that of Cap
o'Rushes. The very use of the name "Rapunzstiltskin", as a forced cutting
and pasting together of two different names, invites defamiliarisation and
reflection on how fairy-tale characters convey normative identities.

In "Rapunzstiltskin" the storyteller's failure to tell a different story is
the story that makes a difference. A parody of the recognition scene from
the Cinderella-type tales, the poem conveys a different figure of the young
woman than that of the daughterly, patient character who is rewarded with
wedded bliss: Rapunzstiltskin reminds us of the portraits given in "The
Furies" poems, a Mad Meg seen from a different angle that contributes to
complete the image of the grim sisters.

Such questioning concerning the relationship between narrative and
social reality brings under scrutiny the processes accompanying the
transformation of folktale material into cult fairy tales, of narrative
versions of myths into corporate mythologies that exploit the myths' social
value in order to maintain male-dominated gender regimes. Cult fairy tales
and corporate mythologies fashion human experience, in Hayden White's
words, "into a form assimilable to structures of meaning that are generally
human rather than culture-specific."[86] Lochhead's revision of fairy tales
and myths highlights the contingency of their narrative expression: her

---

[85] Catherine MacKinnon, "Feminism, Marxism, Method, and the State: An Agenda
for Theory", *Signs*, 7, 3 (1982): 515-44, 515.
[86] Hayden White, "The Value of Narrativity in the Representation of Reality", *On
Narrative*, ed. W. Mitchell (Chicago: University of Chicago Press, 1981), 1-23, 1.

narrations introduce elements specific to class, time period, and geographical space.

Conclusion

The poems in *The Grimm Sisters* deal with representations of women at all stages of social life: daughters, young lovers and wives, mothers and elderly women. By disassembling the conjunction between myths and social order whereby a male-dominated gender regime is legitimated, Lochhead's storyteller reconstructs the realms of fantasy wherein identity is forged with disjunctive stories that help re-materialise more empowering identities of women. Offering opportunities of reinterpreting realms of fairy-tale fantasy, the poems are not mere artifices of fancy, for they create an awareness of stories as tools for challenging the sense of social interrelationships established in masculine gender regimes, to the purpose of revisiting the legitimacy of the social goals these regimes enshrine.

The analyses of Lochhead's texts in these three chapters offer examples of how stories derived from myths prescribe social roles by prescribing ways of fantasising subjective identity. The male-generated tradition of Persephone's myth prescribes ways of defining the experience of girls' sexual awakening that prepare them for the role of future wife. But not only ancient myths perform such functions. The vampire myth born in the Gothic genre also serves, among other things, to make sense of women's bodies and sexuality in ways that legitimate male-dominated gender regimes. Derived from myths, but remythologized to fit the requirements of contemporary societies, the male-generated tradition of folk and fairy tale serves similar purposes. We may regard these three different narrative corpuses yielding myths as examples of elements of a cultural network in which discourses discipline subjects to meet the specific needs of the social structure and its hierarchies at a particular historical moment.

In the following chapters, I will examine how the relationship between fantasising, narrative representations derived from myths, and reality, is explored by the Irish writers Angela Bourke and Éilís Ní Dhuibhne, who are also academics, and by the playwright Marina Carr. Although different cultural contexts inform these writings, we will come across familiar themes, the existence of which is owed to the complex connections between British and Irish culture.

CHAPTER NINE

OTHERWORLDLY WOMEN AND NEUROTIC FAIRIES. THE CULTURAL CONSTRUCTION OF WOMEN IN ANGELA BOURKE'S WRITING

This chapter is concerned with the relationship between stories and social reality in Angela Bourke's writing. With this chapter we are shifting the focus to different cultural and political contexts and traditions, and Bourke's work serves as a suitable introduction to the analyses of the following chapters, offering the opportunity to get acquainted with socio-cultural contexts that form the interest of Ní Dhuibhne's and Carr's texts.

Bourke has written a short story collection entitled *By Salt Water* and is an academic working on subjects related to Irish folklore and the mythological tradition.[1] In *The Burning of Bridget Cleary* (1999), Bourke investigates to what extent the events of the social world are scripted through stories derived from myths and folktales, "by disentangling the various strands of narrative which survive about the death of Bridget Cleary."[2] An important focus of her study is the relationship between women's bodies and nature represented in Irish folktales and in metropolitan and nationalist discourses derived from Enlightenment myths. We may regard these three kinds of discourses as major undercurrents shaping feminine identity in nineteenth-century Irish culture. Their echoes are explored by many Irish writers concerned with the constructions of women's social personae.[3]

The subtitle to Bourke's study of the Clearys' case, "A True Story", suggests several points for critical reflection: what is the relationship

---

[1] Angela Bourke, *By Salt Water* (Dublin: New Island Books, 1996).

[2] Angela Bourke, *The Burning of Bridget Cleary: A True Story* (London: Pimlico, 1999), 24.

[3] For instance Éilís Ní Dhuibhne's *The Dancers Dancing*; Kathleen Ferguson, *The Maid's Tale* (Dublin: Poolbeg, 1995); Lia Mills, *Another Alice* (Dublin: Poolbeg, 1996); Emma Donoghue, *Hood* (Harmondsworth: Penguin, 1996).

between stories and reality? How does a story become true? How do stories shape social personae? I shall seek to answer these questions in relation to Bourke's writing and with reference to wider Irish cultural contexts. In answering these questions I will treat Michael Cleary as a character in Bourke's text, even though it is an academic study. This will help me to distinguish between Bourke's Cleary and the historical Cleary. This distinction is necessary in order to add my own analysis of the constitution of the social persona of the historical Michael Cleary. I will begin with a brief examination of the opening story of Bourke's *By Salt Water*, entitled "Deep Down", in order to explain her critical vision through one of its literary manifestations. "Deep Down" shows us that a narrative pattern can serve to constitute different stories carrying different meanings, according to the ways in which they are related to cultural contexts and traditions.

Identities

In "Deep Down" the narrator recalls a medieval text drawn from a manuscript from the Clonmacnois monastery in Ireland.[4] The medieval text tells of a supernatural event in which people gathered around for Mass one day saw "a boat up there in the sky. An ordinary boat, like you'd see on the sea, or on a lake, but it was up above the roof of the church, just hanging in the sky. They were looking at the bottom of it."[5] Its anchor had been caught in the church door. A man swam down to untangle it and, when restrained by the people, he asked them to let go because they were drowning him. Liam, the narrator's collocutor, rejoins with a tale from his grandfather, a fisherman who had once "fished" a young boy from the sea "a live baby, fit and well, with clothes on it."[6] In this tale "a woman came up beside the boat in the water and cursed them up and down for hooking the child out of its cradle down below."[7]

The medieval tale helps its audience to conceive higher realms that mirror the human world. Part of the network of Christian religious

---

[4] Bourke pointed out that the choice of this story was influenced by Seamus Heaney's poem "Lightenings viii". Personal conversation with Angela Bourke, University College Dublin, 17 January 2007. Seamus Heaney, "Lightenings viii", *Seeing Things* (London: Faber, 1991), 62.

[5] Angela Bourke, "Deep Down", *By Salt Water*, 9-18, 9.

[6] Bourke, "Deep Down", 16.

[7] Ibid., 17. Liam's narration is based on a folk story collected from John Henry. John Henry, "A Child from the Bottom of the Sea", *Stories of Sea and Shore*, ed. Séamas Ó Catháin (Dublin: Comhairle Bhéaloideas Éireann, 1983), 55-6.

discourses, the tale corroborates the authority of the Father. Our world is made in the semblance of the higher world of Godly authority. On the other hand, in Liam's version of the tale, the fact that the lost baby is reclaimed by a woman makes possible the reading of the seascape as a womb. The child had been hooked up from the womb's cradle. This tale suggests that perhaps our world too is lodged within a feminine body of nature, allowing for the possibility of a symbiotic relationship between this world and the body of nature.

The two stories narrated in "Deep Down" offer two ways of reading the world through the same narrative pattern: one reading corroborates the masculine authority of the Father, the other maternal authority.[8] "Deep Down" suggests that reiterations of the same narrative pattern may engender mutually exclusive ontological norms. The tale throws into relief the fact that frameworks of knowledge naturalised through the reiteration of a narrative pattern cannot hold meaning on their own, but only in relation to the norms of other texts. Every narrative instantiation of a series of events is always part of a contextual network in which the meanings of tales are assimilated, repudiated, or conflicting. In "Deep Down", the version of the fabula that corroborates the authority of the Father can be installed in the network of religious texts that "fill in", even saturate, the possibilities of expression that the narrative pattern makes available. But in doing so, the possibility of using the narrative pattern to convey norms of maternal authority is repudiated. In Bourke's text the latter possibility is recuperated, but only in order to show that such a loading of the pattern with meaning is competitive, not definitive. To paraphrase Jacques Derrida, Bourke's story shows that every semiotic marking that a tale achieves is also a remarking of (repudiated) possibilities of signification.[9]

In "Deep Down", the first story uses the image of the sea metaphorically to represent a body holding God's creation; this body is also a body-social, a community of people sharing common beliefs. The world hosted in the sea-womb in the second story appears impenetrable by comparison to the sea-world of the first story. The fisherman is alone at sea, aloof from the social community; a feminine figure reclaims the child here. We recognise such themes of the impenetrability of nature and of women's bodies and of their threatening reclamation of authority in Bourke's study of the Cleary case. We may also read its arguments

---

[8] The Christian tale may well have been derived from an older folklore tradition. Zipes points out that the Christian Church exploited "magic and miraculous stories … to codify what would be acceptable for its own interests". Zipes, *Why Fairy Tales Stick*, 53.

[9] Jacques Derrida, "Limited Inc a b c…", *Limited Inc*, 29-110, 70.

through Adriana Cavarero's thesis on the exclusionary relationship through which the (masculine) logos is legitimated by repudiating (feminine) bodies:

> The terrifying nature of the banished body is substantially female. It could not be otherwise within a logocentric ... polis. In the polis, free males reserve the power of the logos for themselves, uprooting themselves from a carnal existence perceived only as the disquieting attachment to a life that is prelogical, prehuman, and nearly animal: therefore female.[10]

Bourke's study points out that late nineteenth-century Irish metropolitan, nationalist, and folklore discourses establish in various ways relations between women's bodies and the body of nature. Through these discourses (but in different ways) Bridget Cleary's identity was marked by visions of her physical existence in a "prelogical, prehuman, and nearly animal" organic integration of body and land. The Bridget Cleary shown to us by Bourke appeared to her husband and to her peers in the rural Irish community as somehow not yet fully born out of the body of nature, an otherworldly woman; on the other hand, representatives of the dominant social institutions of the time, the doctor and the priest who visited her, "reported that she appeared to be in a very nervous state of mind and 'possibly hysterical'".[11] Caught in these two different social strata the perceived association between Bridget and nature is explained in different ways that transform Bridget into an other: she is a fairy and a neurotic woman.

In metropolitan, nationalist, and folklore discourses Bridget Cleary's identity is derived from logocentric frameworks naturalised through citational chains that sometimes cross. These citational chains can be seen as constitutive of social myths. A social myth comes into existence through narrative reiterations that yield consistently similar social imaginaries. Social myths, thus, provide the framework of knowledge instituting an interpretative cultural code that fosters the same story over and over again, compelling its reiteration, in order to naturalise the story's worldview as norm. However, as Marina Warner points out, even though "myths ... are perpetuated through cultural repetition—transmission through a variety of pathways ... this does not mean they will never fade, that they cannot yield to another, more helpful set of images or tales."[12] Developing on this vision, my analysis focuses on several points argued in

---

[10] Cavarero, x.

[11] Bourke, *The Burning of Bridget Cleary*, 69.

[12] Warner, *Managing Monsters*, xiv.

Bourke's study that permit an investigation of the possibilities of subversion of social myths that disempower women's identities.

Stories and Reality

The series of events to which Bourke's study of the Cleary case refers is presented in the form of a chronology preceding her analysis. Bridget Cleary is the wife of a relatively wealthy cooper, Michael Cleary. On 5 March 1895 she falls ill and is confined to bed. In the following days Bridget's father and her husband attempt to summon the doctor, who finally arrives on 13 March. On the same day a priest visits them to administer the last rites for Bridget. After that, Michael Cleary becomes increasingly convinced that his wife is a changeling.[13] He resorts to fairy-lore, using herbs and rituals to attempt to get his wife back from the fairies. On 15 March, after an argument about fairies, while Bridget was sitting by the fire, Michael "knocks his wife to the floor; she burns to death."[14]

Bourke's study is prefaced with a story collected in 1937 from Mrs John Carroll, Assegart, Foulksmills, Co. Wexford, which can be found in the archives of the Department of Irish Folklore, University College Dublin. In this story, a married woman was "*taken by the fairies*"; they left in her place "*another old yoke.*" The husband went to "*a fairyman*" to seek advice:

> *The fairyman told him that they [the fairies] would be passing by the end of his house on a certain night and that he'd see them—he gave him some herbs so that he could see them—and that his wife would be riding on a*

---

[13] In her study, Bourke offers a specialist appraisal of folktales involving changelings. Fairies steal humans (usually children) and leave a changeling in their stead. As Bourke points out, records of many such cases exist in Ireland in which rituals were performed on children thought to be changelings in order to bring back the "real" children from the fairy world. Instances of such rituals being performed on adults are less numerous. Bridget Cleary's fate is the only one known where burning is involved. See "The Wag Chats with Angela Bourke", 31 March 2006: *http://www.thewag.net/interviews/bourkein.htm* ; Bourke, *The Burning of Bridget Cleary*, 4 and 32-4. For another folklorist's account of the narrative patterns of fairy abduction stories, see Katharine Briggs, "Changelings and Midwives", *The Fairies in Tradition and Literature* (1967; London: Routledge, 2002), 136-45. See also, "Fairy Wives and Fairy Lovers", 146-54.

[14] Bourke, *The Burning of Bridget Cleary*, x.

grand grey horse; and when she'd be passing him to seize and hold on to her, that if he missed her he'd never see her again.[15]

The husband obeys and manages to gain his wife back. When they return to their house together, "the other yoke was gone off with herself."[16] Obviously, the story outlines an imaginary world. However, as Bourke indicates, the elements of such fairy stories are connected to reality in manifold ways:

> Viewed as a system of interlocking units of narrative, practice and belief, fairy-legend can be compared to a database: a pre-modern culture's way of storing and retrieving information and knowledge of every kind … . Highly charged and memorable images like that of a woman emerging on a white horse from a fairy dwelling are the retrieval codes for a whole complex of stored information about land and landscape, community relations, gender roles … .[17]

In this perspective, folktales can be seen as offering an imaginary grid for mapping realms of sociality, as well as a stock of social imaginaries interconnecting landscape, human communities, and individual bodies. These social imaginaries help to imagine the social personae that individuals adopt in social interaction. As Zipes puts it, "tales do not only speak to us, they inhabit us".[18]

The tale prefacing Bourke's study can be seen as the vehicle of social imaginaries through which male-dominated hierarchies and gender regimes are legitimized by repudiating alternative possibilities of envisaging the empowering of women's identities. The tale condones the husband's effort to recuperate a woman "gone astray", whom we may imagine as having achieved, at least in a fantasy world, a more empowering status than that of wife. When the tale relates that "his wife would be riding on a grand grey horse", the reader/ audience may imagine her as a confident and independent woman.[19] But the resolution of the events offered in the tale reflects the desired restoration of the male-dominated social order. The legitimating reiteration of female social roles as wives involves the othering of the woman who must have forgotten herself, by blaming her lapse of reason on fairy magic. The otherworldly woman is cast away, and, to use Judith Butler's words in this context, the

---

[15] Ibid., unpaginated, original italics.
[16] Ibid.
[17] Ibid., 29. See also 31, 34-6 and 60.
[18] Zipes, *Why Fairy Tales Stick*, 39.
[19] Bourke, *The Burning of Bridget Cleary*, 38.

"alternative domains of cultural ... possibilities" that the tale had momentarily opened are foreclosed.[20]

Indeed, as Bourke observes, "the overwhelming message of the fairy-legends is that the unexpected may be guarded against by careful observance of society's rules"; the stories establish "the boundaries of normal, acceptable behaviour, ... spelling out the ways in which an individual who breaches them may forfeit his or her position."[21] In the tale opening Bourke's study, significantly, it is the husband who restores the legitimate social hierarchy. While he is cunning and clear-headed, the woman appears flimsy, easily spellbound by such pleasures and passions as have been attributed to the fairy world in the Irish tradition.[22] The collaboration between the husband and a male sage ensures the stability of the legitimate social world defined, against the otherworld of fairy, as a realm of masculinity. The fairy otherworld appears as a realm of fancy, both in the sense that it is a realm where caprice reigns, and in the sense that whatever a woman may think she is in that realm, it is only an illusion. In such tales, the fantasy of women's participation, willingly or helplessly, in the activities of fairies, is used to define femininity by equating it with moodiness, flimsiness, and even an irresponsible craving of luxury. But I am wary of generalising. I must emphasise that it is the world of fairy depicted in late nineteenth-century rural Ireland that is perceived as a realm of femininity. And even for that temporal and socio-cultural configuration one may find that various discourses about fairy creatures made competing claims about the nature of this "other". Indeed, in some stories, the realm of fairy is a masculine realm from which male figures exercise tremendous powers over the people of the "real" world.[23]

Thus, stories fictionalise the social rituals through which society's members consecrate a social order, serving to communicate the socialisation scripts required by that order. Their narrative structures are derived from privileged meaning systems that determine what counts as human. Butler argues that "the construction of the human is a differential operation that produces the more and the less 'human,' the inhuman, the humanly unthinkable."[24] This argument has particular resonance in the

---

[20] Butler, *Gender Trouble*, 145.

[21] Bourke, *The Burning of Bridget Cleary*, 30.

[22] See, for instance, Francesca Wilde, *Ancient Legends, Mystic Charms, and Superstitions of Ireland* (1888; Galway: O'Gorman, 1971), 38.

[23] A literary rendering of the latter case is offered in Éilís Ní Dhuibhne's short story "Midwife to the Fairies". See Éilís Ní Dhuibhne, "Midwife to the Fairies", *Blood and Water* (Dublin: Attic, 1988), 25-34.

[24] Butler, *Bodies That Matter*, 8.

context of Irish folktales, where the construction of the human, social, materially real world is pitched against the otherworld of fairy, inhabited by immaterial shadows and less-than-human men and women. The wife in the folktale prefacing Bourke's study is less "human" due to being in league with the fairies, but also because she is an independent woman. As with Bridget Cleary, this woman conjured through words may acquire inhuman powers in her alliance with the powerful body of nature. She is an impenetrable other caught in the corner of the rational eye. Thus, stories are the work of the imagination, but the imagination is harnessed to producing a range of social imaginaries that, if legitimate, imbue the subject with realness; and if not, the subject they create is imbued with unreality, appearing irrational, perhaps even abject.

How Does a Story Become True?

The occasion of the meeting of people attending to the ill Bridget Cleary the night before her death would have been one of "talking and swapping stories".[25] Gerry Smyth emphasises the import of such occasions, and the

> strong element of *performativity* informing the narrative event. ... The story-teller is not outside or above the story ... but is an active part of it, employing a wide range of skills to collapse the borders between the tale and the telling, while all the time maintaining the audience's investment in the world of the story.[26]

Bridget Cleary's death, as Bourke demonstrates, was partly the result of the belief that she was a changeling, a body left by the fairies instead of the real woman the fairies had abducted. Stories corroborating this "reading" of Bridget had been told and swapped between her peers throughout the time preceding her death.

However, Bourke's study suggests that it is misleading to regard the events surrounding Bridget's death as merely an enactment of the folktales' "changeling scenario". Indeed, such strict tying up of the folktales' scenarios with the events that occurred in the social world would construct the members of the rural Irish community as mere actors, fulfilling an inescapable destiny to which they are condemned by their superstitious, irrational selves.[27] In metropolitan culture, folktales functioned as vehicles by which rational men could express the otherness

---

[25] Bourke, *The Burning of Bridget Cleary*, 3.

[26] Smyth, *The Novel and the Nation*, 39.

[27] Bourke, *The Burning of Bridget Cleary*, 34, 135.

against which they defined social goals and programmes.[28] Folktales threatened to open up a realm of alterity that would have unmasked the inability of Enlightenment consciousness to master wholly the field of meaning.[29] The possibility of this alterity had to be tamed or cast away and foreclosed as a realm of the unthinkable, if reality was to remain governable through reason. In Victorian metropolitan culture, these axioms about consciousness translated into notions of social government. Bourke points out that the interpretation of the events leading to Bridget's death through folktale scenarios served British political interests: as legislation regarding Home Rule for Ireland was being discussed, the relationship between folktale scenarios and the events leading to Bridget's death was used to highlight the ungovernability of the Irish in the absence of a strong civilising authority.[30]

To adapt Derrida's critical insight here, we can say that Bourke's study reveals the iterability of Bridget Cleary's story, which implies that the story

> can always be detached from the chain in which it is inserted or given without causing it to lose all possibility of functioning ... . One can perhaps come to recognise other possibilities in it by inscribing it or *grafting* it onto other chains.[31]

To the extent that Bourke's study points out the iterability of the story in the contexts of widely different cultural discourses each structured by a different code, it also succeeds in showing that the story can disrupt, "in the last analysis", "the authority of the code as a finite system of rules", at the same time subverting "any context as the protocol of code."[32]

---

[28] See for instance Jack Zipes, *Breaking the Magic Spell: Radical Theories of Folk and Fairy Tales*, revised and expanded edition (Lexington, Kentucky: Kentucky University Press, 2002), 3; Zipes, *Why Fairy Tales Stick*, 82.

[29] This perspective is derived from Derrida, "Signature Event Context", 8.

[30] Bourke, *The Burning of Bridget Cleary*, 121-2. The reconstruction of the events surrounding Bridget Cleary's death by Joan Hoff and Marian Yates favours this particular thesis as an encompassing framework of interpretation for the Cleary case. See Joan Hoff and Marian Yates, *The Cooper's Wife is Missing: The Trials of Bridget Cleary* (New York: Basic Books, 2000). See also Henrika Kuklick, *The Savage Within: The Social History of British Anthropology, 1885-1945* (Cambridge: Cambridge University Press, 1991).

[31] Derrida, "Signature Event Context", 9, original italics.

[32] Ibid., 8.

Bourke poses the question "when does a true story end?"[33] Perhaps we may answer by saying that stories pass as true only with the consent of those who adopt the subject positions the stories set up, incorporating them into social imaginaries through which they fantasise their identity as individuals and as members of a social group, nation, or of a legitimate body politic.

The Role of Stories in Shaping Social Personae

Bourke's study of Bridget Cleary's case seeks to point out the partiality and historical specificity of the identities of those involved in ways that also mount a critique of the Enlightenment claim to offer "true" and privileged insight into "the laws of nature". Part of this critique is crucially concerned with what Jane Flax refers to as "widely shared categories of social meaning and explanation" that associate women with nature.[34] Enlightenment constructions of femininity, such as were deployed in metropolitan Victorian culture, are founded on notions of nature made governable through the laws of reason.[35] In her study, Bourke reminds us that metropolitan cultural discourses served to envision Ireland as a feminine realm incapable of self-government. Borrowing Hélène Cixous's words, we may regard the discourses of Victorian metropolitan culture as stemming "from the power relation between a fantasized obligatory virility meant to invade, to colonize, and the consequential phantasm of woman as a 'dark continent' to penetrate and to 'pacify'." Women and nature are "pieced back to the string which leads back ... to the Name-of-the-Father".[36]

On the other hand, notions of women and nature also served, in a different manner, the interests of Irish nationalist circles, in whose discourses Ireland became an idealised feminine body, in need of defence and protection.[37] If in British culture the envisioning of the masculine governance of nature remained connected to Enlightenment paradigms, positing an opposition between "Man" and "Nature", which entitled the

---

[33] Bourke, *The Burning of Bridget Cleary*, 203.

[34] Flax, 41, 43, 44.

[35] See Keller, *Reflections on Gender and Science* and Sandra Harding, *The Science Question in Feminism* (Ithaca: Cornell University Press, 1986).

[36] Cixous, "The Laugh of the Medusa", 362.

[37] See, for instance, Catherine Lynette Innes, *Woman and Nation in Irish Literature and Society 1880-1935* (Athens, GA: University of Georgia Press, 1993), 10 and Margaret Ward, *Unmanageable Revolutionaries* (London: Pluto, 1983), 152.

coloniser to civilise dark, ungovernable realms, for Irish nationalists the legitimacy of the male's right to govern the body of nature depended on an uneasy alliance between "Man" and "Nature". These two ways of envisioning nature as other affected representations of women in the two cultures and their influence can be seen in the representation of Bridget Cleary's relationship with the outside world. Both discourses can be seen to support Bridget's othering and abjection. Although in nationalist discourses the virility and paternal authority of the coloniser were challenged, this only resulted in replacing one manifestation of masculine authority with another whose legitimacy likewise depended on repudiations of women and nature; except this time, women as nature were pieced back "to the place of the phallic-mother", to use Cixous's words in this context.[38] Ireland's sons are one with her land. This investment of phallic power in the earthly mother is, in this instance, regarded by Irish nationalists as beneficial because it provides an origin story for the sons' eventual separation: they will set out to construct a new individuality and history for the primeval Celtic mother. Often, the phallic power of the mother is transmitted to a daughter figure, not fully separated from the mother, but who must acquire masculine features in order to be brought fully into existence in the social realm. Referring to women's identities generated through nationalist discourses, Edna Longley comments that "while Virgin-Ireland gets raped and pitied, Mother Ireland translates pity into a call to arms and vengeance."[39] To apply Cixous's argument here, the sons' separation from the primeval mother is only possible through a repudiation of nature that sublimates the female body into a female figure endowed with masculine power: a virago.[40] In both British metropolitan and Irish nationalist discourses, the feminisation of Ireland produces the fantasy of an elite brotherhood capable of privileged insight into the "laws of nature".

Fantasies of a masculine brotherhood are also conveyed through the patriarchal inflections of folktales, albeit differently. Examining folktale fantasies based on the image of the fairy ring-fort, Bourke explains:

---

[38] Cixous, "The Laugh of the Medusa", 360.

[39] Longley, "From Cathleen to Anorexia", 190. Longley's examples are Maud Gonne and Constance Markievicz.

[40] Longley points out that "to characterise Irish Nationalism (only constructed in the nineteenth century) as archetypally female both gives it a mythic pedigree and exonerates it from aggressive and oppressive intent." Longley, "From Cathleen to Anorexia", 189.

In the narrative maps of oral storytelling, ring-forts function as alternative reference points to places of human habitation and activity. ... [T]hey can serve as metaphors for areas of silence and circumvention in the life of the society which tells stories about them. All the ambivalence attaching to them is contained in the common assertion that forts are where the fairies live.[41]

Throughout her study Bourke suggests that the folktales' referencing of otherworldliness can sometimes serve to corroborate a tolerant social order, open and respectful towards alterity, while at other times the tales may endorse practices of silencing and exclusion. Yet both possibilities are founded upon a dichotomous reading of reality that opposes the body of nature to the body-social.

Bourke shows that the fantasies associating women with nature in Irish folktales are correlated with a mythical geography in which holy wells, fairy raths, and burial mounds represent metaphorically points of access to the inner realms of the body of nature. The body of nature is represented as a powerful feminine body, credited with the ability to punish illicit penetration: many tales contain warnings against transgressing "fairy grounds", and speak of severe punishments that may afflict those who are not welcome to enter. An example of the folkloric rendering of the connections between women's bodies and the body of nature is offered by examining the concept of the *piseóg*, which refers to a kind of black fairy magic. Bourke uses her expertise as folklorist to indicate that

piseóg is a diminutive form of the Irish word for the vulva, *pis* or *pit*. *Piseóg* can also have the very specific meaning of malevolent sympathetic magic, when something organic is hidden and left to rot on another's land. ... [W]omen's sexuality, when not controlled within the orderly progressions of marriage and pregnancy, was seen as horrifically powerful.[42]

Such folkloric beliefs posit an organic relationship between nature and women's bodies that, if not governed, threatens to wreak havoc on the orderly spaces of human culture. In this context, Bourke points out that Bridget Cleary "had accumulated power, both economic and sexual, it seems, far in excess of what was due to a woman of her age and class, and when the balance tipped, all the anger flowed towards her."[43] Thus, Bridget's social status was read as illicit. Her undue empowerment

---

[41] Bourke, *The Burning of Bridget Cleary*, 48.

[42] Ibid., 92-3.

[43] Ibid., 136.

rekindled suspicions about the resurrection of a powerful body of nature upon whose repudiation the patriarchal body-social of rural Ireland was founded. Although folktale fantasies of the female's relationship with nature can be enabling, in nineteenth-century rural Ireland such empowerment would have been eccentric and therefore required discipline in order to reassert a communal repudiation of women who deviated from domestic roles.[44]

Bourke's wider concern with the relationship between human societies and the body of nature emerges in her short story "Le soleil et le vent", first published in *By Salt Water*. The tale is a reflection on the interaction between human technology and nature and thus on the inscription of the dichotomy between culture and nature in material practices. The technological process described in the tale is observed by the narrator in a coastal French town, where a system of canals is used to collect sea water and then its salt. But the narrator describes the technique in words that make us think of a body of nature that is made to sweat, like a slave tamed and harnessed through technological means:

> Behind us were the salt pans: hundreds of them, maybe thousands, lying in perfect flatness, rectangular, with rounded corners, moulded of clay and linked tortuously by channels that brought the sea in twice a day and trapped it there, making it give up its salt.[45]

---

[44] Bourke notes, for instance, the recurrent theme of "cross" women in Irish folklore: "'cross' women—those whose anger or assertiveness made them difficult for men to deal with—were often the ones said to be away with the fairies, as were those 'clever' ones whose special skills set them apart." Bourke, *The Burning of Bridget Cleary*, 175. A more ambiguous treatment of associations between women and nature is encountered in the banshee tradition. Patricia Lysaght traces the banshee figure of Irish folklore tradition to the figures of the sovereignty goddesses who are one with the land, and to the fairy women figures inhabiting fairy mounds. Lysaght points out that the tradition teaches that insulted banshees may be vengeful, and therefore it "warns against being out late hours and indecorous behaviour towards women." However, it is difficult to say to what extent the banshee tradition protects women while also legitimating their confinement to domestic tasks (the banshee is often found beetling at the river). The tradition of Badb, the Irish war goddess in Celtic Ireland, although discernible in the banshee tradition, has not been preserved. All that has been preserved of the sovereignty goddess tradition is the idea that a family who has a banshee is an illustrious family. See Patricia Lysaght, *The Banshee: The Irish Death Messenger* (Boulder, Colorado: Reinhart, 1996), 186, 191-218.

[45] Angela Bourke, "Le Soleil et le Vent", *By Salt Water*, 90-8, 91-2.

The narrator of this short story and the critical voice of the study of Bridget Cleary's case share an interest in the importance of the written word as a mark that endows nature with human bodily features: "Annick wrote the word for the salt-pans ... *oeillet*. Eyelet. Little eye. The local clay is watertight, so they can build banks and make basins that will contain the ocean, and each little salt-rimmed eye ... gazes back at that blue sky".[46] The attribution of anthropomorphic features to the body of nature by the people using technology to harness its power betrays the metaphorical relationships between nature and human bodies. The story shows that these inscriptions accompany practices that change both the geography of the landscape and the social geography of its inhabitants.

Bourke's study of Bridget Cleary's case permits a view of the inscription of the body of nature with feminine features both as the result of colonialist Western discourse that, to use Donna Haraway's words, "structured the world as an object of knowledge in terms of the appropriation by culture of the resources of nature"[47] and of the pre-modern rural folklore that inscribed patriarchal meanings in agricultural work practices and social living tied up with natural cycles. The images in "Le soleil et le vent", reminding us of nature's ungovernability help the narrator to explore her feelings after the loss of her lover. When at the end of the tale the narrator realises that her sadness has begun to subside, we are not sure whether the conversion of an unmanageable, oceanic emotion into calm is after all beneficial, just as we are not sure in Bridget Cleary's story that her association with a wild body of nature should be celebrated. By comparison with the "calmed" woman shown in the short story, Bridget appears wild, eccentric, and passionate. In "Le soleil et le vent" the narrator remarks that "all around me" was "the industrious sea, calmed and regulated, delivering its salt."[48] Bourke's book suggests that Bridget Cleary's body was punished precisely because it threatened to become an incommensurable otherness, unregulated by masculine government, and thus upsetting the social myths that welded the community together in its work and social practices.

The above analyses show that we may suspect that the folktale tradition, the mythologizing tradition of Irish nationalism, and the metropolitan rationalist tradition, although working with different concepts of nature, share an investment in its ungovernability and conceive cultural

---

[46] Ibid., 94.

[47] Donna Haraway, "'Gender' for a Marxist Dictionary: The Sexual Politics of a Word", *Simians, Cyborgs and Women: The Reinvention of Nature* (London: Free Association Books, 1991), 127-48, 134.

[48] Bourke, "Le Soleil", 96.

tropes as a means of conveying the necessity of harnessing the phenomenal world. These cultural practices affect representations of women's bodies and of the body in general as realms of the organic that must be rationalised. Elizabeth Grosz argues that bodies "are the centers of perspective, insight, reflection, desire, agency. ... [T]hey function interactively and productively. They act and react. They generate what is new, surprising, unpredictable."[49] In Irish folktales, representations of feminine bodies are centred on the notion of a common ground between them and nature's body. However, the tales also attempt to regulate the perspectives, insights, reflections, desires, and agency that may emerge in the socialisation of women's bodies through fantasies of this relationship that can take new, surprising, and unpredictable forms. In the following, I will use this framework to analyse the events examined in Bourke's study. I will show that metropolitan and rural folktale discourses, as well as discourses derived from them, rely on readings of women's bodies as ungovernable and that they in turn repudiate such unruliness in order to legitimate male-dominated gender regimes.[50]

Michael Cleary's interpretation of the relationship between Bridget Cleary and the fairy world through folktales rendered Bridget a signifier of impenetrable territories. Bridget's refusal to eat his offered food, which enraged Michael on the night of her death, making him capable of murder, may have been read by him as a refusal of sexual intercourse, as Bourke underlines. Furthermore, this obduracy might have provided for Michael an explanation for the fact that his marriage was childless, casting doubt on his fertility[51] and thus metaphorically revealing an inability to inseminate, and thus master, nature's resources (signified by Bridget's body). Michael might have feared that his conjugal territory was becoming an impenetrable and ungovernable dominion of nature under Bridget's rule, undermining the legitimacy of his position as head of the household. His vision would have been underpinned by a correlative in the landscape: the round enclosure at Kylenagranagh known to the community as a fairy mound, that is an otherworldly realm inhabited by fairy women, with whom Bridget might have been in alliance.

---

[49] Grosz, *Volatile Bodies*, xi.
[50] According to Bourke, in Irish folklore in late nineteenth-century rural communities "nature is engaged with closely" while in metropolitan and bourgeois rural Ireland "nature is perceived across a large chasm, distant." Approximate quotation from personal conversation with Angela Bourke, University College Dublin, 17 January 2007.
[51] Bourke, *The Burning of Bridget Cleary*, 104.

Michael had reasons to believe that his wife had been unfaithful; and she was a capable administrator of various small enterprises, and earned her own money. According to Bourke:

> People were talking about Bridget Cleary; she was an attractive and strong-minded woman, who enjoyed a higher level of personal and economic independence than most of her peers. ... [S]tories about her abduction by fairies could have been a euphemistic way of noting her extra-marital activities. Michael Cleary's success as a cooper, and his economic prosperity, would be of very little use to him if he could not convince his neighbours and his wife's relatives that he was man enough to keep her, and even to control her.[52]

His wife's independence as lover and as a partner in household administration might have helped Michael to find a convenient correlative in folktale imagery for repudiating as illegitimate the identity of independent woman his wife had assumed. The fantasy of the stately woman riding on a grand grey horse could have been read by Michael, consciously or not, as representing an usurper of the masculine right to govern his wife as he rules nature, a worldview conveyed (in different ways) in both metropolitan and rural Irish discourses. Michael used a corpus of narratives derived from mythology to legitimate his attempt to discipline his wife. Several myths were at work in Michael's fantasies about his identity and that of his wife. Examining these will help to establish how myths deployed in social discourses function in complex ways to determine one's acts in reality.

Bourke points out that throughout the period of time after Bridget's death, until her body was discovered, "two competing narratives were at work in the countryside around Ballyvadlea, as some people stuck to their story of fairy abduction while the RIC conducted its methodical search."[53] Michael's confused migration between the two worldviews, the Irish traditional and the British metropolitan perspectives, which these narratives endorsed, is indicative of a larger jostling of cultural norms. Their power lines are in some respects overlapping, yet in other respects disjunctive.[54] Thus, when Michael fantasises that his wife might be at the

---

[52] Ibid., 86. See also 96.

[53] Ibid., 20. Bourke also highlights the ambivalence of expressions that could refer both to landscape surveillance and to bodily interaction. For instance, she notes that "the RIC had penetrated some of the hill's secrets". See Bourke, *The Burning of Bridget Cleary*, 16.

[54] Bourke emphasised that Michael Cleary was from a town, and that he would have found enticing the prospect of joining the rural Irish bourgeois class.

Kylenagranagh fort, riding a grand grey horse, he invests her with the otherness associated in official and vernacular discourses with the ungovernable landscape of nature, consigning her to a zone of the abnormal, the uninhabitable, and the illegitimate.[55] In the meaning systems of metropolitan discourses colluding with the patriarchal meaning systems of folktales, legitimate femininity, the recognisable Bridget, is hardly ever a "woman", but always a "wife"; her body must be permanently available for masculine penetration, physically or metaphorically. Bourke notes, referring to Michael's attempt to force his wife to take the medicine prescribed by the "fairy doctor", that

> the violence meted out to Bridget Cleary before her death has an unmistakeably sexual character. On Thursday, when he used a metal spoon, and again on Friday, when his weapon was a burning stump of wood, Michael Cleary's actions amounted to a kind of oral rape. ... The violence used ... would have been enough to terrify her, and to show her and anyone watching just who was master.[56]

For Bourke, forcing Bridget to eat "was not so very different in significance from the force-feeding of suffragists and other prisoners by state authorities in later years."[57] Bridget's body, like the body of nature, had to be made available for the masculine staking of claims to possession, a requirement of both the Irish patriarchal order and the British/Anglo-Irish Enlightenment culture.

Bourke insistently underlines the significance of the cultural investment through which Irish, British, and Anglo-Irish narratives interpret the landscape of the Kylenagranagh fairy fort differently:

> The fairy legends of oral tradition marked Kylenagranagh as important. The RIC mapped the territory differently, but in both systems Kylenagranagh was a significant reference point: the vernacular map of

---

Representatives of bourgeois rural Ireland would have emulated metropolitan bourgeois identity. Personal conversation with Angela Bourke, University College Dublin, 17 January 2007.

[55] In his appraisal of the theme of madness in Irish writing, Smyth shows that madness "simultaneously resists and reinforces colonial ideology." This seems to be true also with regard to the cultural marking of zones of abnormality, uninhabitability, and illegitimacy. Smyth, *The Novel and the Nation*, 51.

[56] Bourke, *The Burning of Bridget Cleary*, 105-106.

[57] Ibid., 107. See also Rosemary Owens's study of suffragism and nationalism in Ireland. Rosemary Owens, *Smashing Times: A History of the Irish Women's Suffrage Movement 1889-1922* (Dublin: Attic, 1984).

traditional narrative agreed with the police designation of the hill as a place apart from normal habitation and legitimate interests. Anyone seen there could be suspected of being up to no good; anyone desiring privacy might seek it out.[58]

Highlighting the fact that various discourses about the Kylenagranagh ring-fort reassert sometimes conflicting, sometimes colluding norms, Bourke's study shows Irish culture to be a heteroglossic space. It also indicates that the cross-pollination between these discourses is "stress-full" in the sense that, to use the words of Steven Cohan and Linda Shires, their

> paradigmatic, syntagmatic, and semiotic markings … inscribe the text with various stresses … . The markings emphasize certain signifiers over others; they put pressure on the seemingly 'natural' and closed relations between signifiers and signifieds; and they can strain understanding, causing a reader to ask, what does this word, phrase, sentence mean?[59]

The discourses through which Michael Cleary interpreted his identity are examples of such stress-full cross-pollination. In order to achieve the bourgeois metropolitan identity to which he aspired, Michael had to show that he was capable of governing his wife. His conviction was "stressed" through the local folklore tradition. Furthermore, both metropolitan and Irish folklore discourses intersected in Irish nationalist discourses. The latter hijacked the Irish folklore tradition to create a bourgeois identity of Irish, as opposed to British, making. Thus, the heteroglossic aspect of Irish culture can be further investigated by examining intersections between the discursive registers of Irish folklore and Anglo-Irish culture that yielded Irish nationalist stories.[60] Bourke points out that in the first reports of the Cleary case by the correspondent of the newspaper, *The Nationalist*, "the language used … is borrowed from romantic nationalism".[61] She also notes that the newspaper's "first account of Bridget Cleary's disappearance reminds us that in 1895 the Irish Revival was at its height … . New books on fairies … appeared throughout the 1890s to satisfy the appetite of a reading public which was reacting against industrialization and urbanization."[62] Lady Augusta Gregory and W. B. Yeats had begun

---

[58] Bourke, *The Burning of Bridget Cleary*, 17-18.

[59] Cohan and Shires, 21.

[60] Hubert Butler notes that "the Anglo-Irish were … the cruel stepmothers of Gaelic civilisation". Hubert Butler, *Escape from the Anthill* (Mullingar: Lilliput Press, 1985), 157.

[61] Bourke, *The Burning of Bridget Cleary*, 20.

[62] Ibid.

their literary careers and contributed to the philosophy that insisted on the reclamation of the feminised Irish land by the Irish.[63]

This is the cultural atmosphere in which, Bourke notes, the RIC kept the hill at Kylenagranagh under surveillance in connection with National League activities.[64] The National League was set up by Charles Stewart Parnell in the wake of nationalist agitation regarding Home Rule for Ireland. According to the Irish historian Margaret O'Callaghan, the local branches of the League devised regulations that

> drew upon the informal regulatory rituals inherent in the society—or the brutal cruelties of control if one wishes to put it differently—and formalised them. In so doing it attempted to set against the official law of the land a separate, intimately sanctioned behavioural code which defined self and other within rural society. It was a text of inclusion and exclusion, of community and pariah.[65]

The National League had staked their own claims on the body of nature. Their assertion of a right to governance, even though aimed at wresting authority from the British administration, issued similar claims, only this time in the terms of the local culture.

At the same time, Bourke indicates, Irish Republican Brotherhood volunteers trained at the Kylenagranagh fort. Allied with the body of nature, read as a sacred mother/queen who rallies her sons/lovers against the foreign invader, the volunteers would have found spiritual sustenance in the tales of fairy power associated with ring-forts.[66] Speaking of the need, in Irish nationalist circles, of identifying "an *Ur*-epic, an original text from which all Celtic mythology derived", Smyth comments that "sometimes, indeed, the land itself becomes an ideal image of the epic—in the words of the poet Seamus Heaney, a sort of manuscript which Irish people have lost the skill to read"; but, we may add, a skill that nationalist culture pretends to be capable of restoring.[67] We should not forget, however, that ideas of modern Republicanism are Enlightenment ideas, the

---

[63] See Bourke's appraisal of these events; Bourke, *The Burning of Bridget Cleary*, 20.

[64] Ibid., 16-17.

[65] Margaret O'Callaghan, *British High Politics and a Nationalist Ireland: Criminality, Land and the Law under Forster and Balfour* (Cork: Cork University Press, 1994), 9.

[66] Bourke points out that the area is rich in legends about the famous *Fianna* warrior, Fionn MacCumhail.

[67] Smyth, *The Novel and the Nation*, 11, 27. See also Seamus Heaney, "The Sense of Place", *Preoccupations*, 131-49, 132.

kind disseminated by the coloniser, although reassembled creatively by the scholarly Irish nationalist organisations.[68] The nationalist elite glorified the perceived relationship between women's bodies and the body of nature, but at the same time, in the spirit of Enlightenment ideals, they purified, sanitised, and idealised it.[69]

Thus, representations of the relationship between women and nature in late nineteenth-century Ireland intertwine folktales with colonial and nationalist discourses. Strategies of colonial surveillance of the landscape and "the informal regulatory rituals inherent in the society"[70] co-operate in maintaining the otherness of nature and thus of women's bodies. Alternatively the relationship between women and nature envisioned in the

---

[68] According to Joe Cleary, "Irish modernity ... can quite clearly be tracked to ... forces that made Western modernity generally. ... [M]odernity, however, is not a one-way process issuing from metropole to benighted periphery ... . In an Irish context, the United Irishmen, for instance, though certainly adherents to the universal ideals of the Enlightenment, were not simply the crude importers of American or French republicanism." Joe Cleary, "Introduction: Ireland and Modernity", *The Cambridge Companion to Modern Irish Culture*, eds. Joe Cleary and Claire Connoly (Cambridge: Cambridge University Press, 2005), 1-22, 4-5. Fintan O'Toole argues that the cultural revival that had begun in Ireland in the second half of the nineteenth century, "nationalised colonial attitudes, internalising a process which belonged to the colonial mentality and selling it back to the outside world as a reflection of Irish reality." Fintan O'Toole, "Going West: The City Versus the Country in Irish Writing", *The Crane Bag*, 9 (1985): 113. See also Smyth, *The Novel and the Nation*, 15-16; 45; Edna Longley, "'Defending Ireland's Soul': Protestant Writers and Irish Nationalism after Independence", *The Living Stream*, 130-49, 130. See also Declan Kiberd, *Inventing Ireland* (London: Cape, 1995).

[69] Suzanna Chan's comments on the transposition of colonial ideals in nationalist Irish culture through an analysis of constructions of race, help us to understand how the idealisation and purification of nature as other were connected to the paradigms of legitimation/othering or abjection that informed Victorian cultural practices: "In order to establish that the Irish were a European culture worthy of self governance, nationalists stressed a positive identity for the 'Celt-Gael' as white and equal to, yet distinct from the 'Anglo-Saxon', ... eulogising the spirituality and artistry that the Victorians considered characteristics of the 'feminine' (i.e. 'irrational') Celt." Suzanna Chan "Some Notes on Deconstructing Ireland's Whiteness: Immigrants, Emigrants and the Perils of Jazz", *Variant* 22 (2005): 20-21, 20. See also Steve Garner, *Racism in the Irish Experience* (London: Pluto, 2004), 31 and Kavita Philip "Race, Class and the Imperial Politics of Ethnography in India, Ireland and London, 1850-1910", *Irish Studies Review*, 10 (2002): 297-9.

[70] O'Callaghan, 9.

Irish folkloric tradition was used in British and Irish circles to reinforce a vision of Ireland as an abject or as an idealised otherworld, a supplement (in the Derridean sense) of legitimate cultural spaces. Folktales, nationalist tales, and colonial tales share the desideratum of regulating women's bodies which may "generate what is new, surprising, unpredictable"[71] and be potentially subversive of the masculine regime and social order.

In order to contain such illegitimate transgressions, colonial discourse set up superstitious beliefs in fairies as signs of neuroses that extended from individual Irish people to Ireland as a body politic. Bridget Cleary becomes a symbol/symptom of a neurotic society for the coloniser: her dead body stands as proof of a mindless nation; yet in court she is rescued as the pure angelic victim.[72] Her pure soul is rescued by the severance of its ties with a monstrous body of nature, a body contiguous, for instance, with the "body" of the Kylenagranagh ring-fort that withholds secrets from the masculine gaze of the RIC. Bridget's dead body, now available for autopsy, can be seen as the site of an ideal spirit, because, unlike the rest of the "living" Irish, it permits foreclosure (it is dead and not threatening to resurrect ungovernable nature) and inspection (the mind can be satisfied that nature remains outside the metropolis, yet available for probing and surveillance).[73]

On the other hand, traditional Irish beliefs, anchored in the discourse of fairy-legends, also repudiate the feminine body of nature in order to legitimate the shape of the patriarchal body politic of the community. The mound at Kylenagranagh is feared and respected as a feminine otherworld, yet it is desirable that its power does not interfere with the arrangements of the mortals. Thus, in spite of the fact that folklore readings of women's bodies through the symbolism associated with nature seem to offer unique opportunities for constructing women through empowering social imaginaries, that is, by viewing them as other than just wives or domestic

---

[71] Grosz, *Volatile Bodies*, xi.

[72] Bourke's interpretation of the text accompanying Michael's court sentence reads: "Before pronouncing sentence ... the judge indulged in a last romantic and chivalrous reverie on the dead Bridget Cleary as bride. He compared her implicitly to the virgin martyrs of early Christianity, devotion to whom was such a significant feature of middle-class Irish Catholic culture after the Great Famine". This discourse of a representative of British authority can be seen as an example of how metropolitan discourses sanitised and abjected Ireland through using idealised representations of women, while also appealing to the feelings of the Irish bourgeois class. Bourke, *The Burning of Bridget Cleary*, 188.

[73] This perspective is derived from Cavarero's study of Sophocles' *Antigone*. Adriana Cavarero, "On the Body of Antigone", *Stately Bodies*, 13-97.

labourers, these possibilities are often evoked as deviations from the "normal" course of community life.

In his study of new Irish fiction Gerry Smyth finds that its defining feature is an impetus to "challenge established notions regarding the limits and possibilities of Irish identity."[74] This seems to be also the purpose of Bourke's study and the vision of her short stories. Bourke's documentary of the Cleary case indicates that social imaginaries are possible that represent women's control of their bodies and their sharing in the governance of the communities' social spaces. The source of these social imaginaries can be traced to the ethos of women's alliance with an ungovernable realm of nature. Bridget Cleary was able to use this ethos to her advantage, without being less rational or social than the husband who eventually punished her for her independence. Bourke offers evidence that "Bridget Cleary, well versed in fairy-lore, would have found in its stories a language through which to resist her husband's negative assessment of her. A wife who could persuade a violent husband that she was a fairy changeling" could exercise a degree of control over his behaviour; all the more so in Bridget's case, since she "may have taken on some of her mother's role, as possessor of esoteric knowledge, in a way that made her husband nervous."[75] According to Bourke:

> Fairies belong to the margins, and so can serve as reference points and metaphors for all that is marginal in human life. Their underground existence allows them to stand for the unconscious, for the secret, or the unspeakable ... .[76]

In a sense, then, it can be said that Bridget Cleary used the ethos of Irish folktales as "a place from which to speak about [her] own speechlessness", to apply Marina Warner's comments on the role of women in transmitting fairy tales in general.[77] Such use of the Irish mythological tradition involves a challenging of the dominance of the masculine subject who speaks the truths that ward off the unspeakable deeds of the body. Because of that, it also involves a challenge to both Irish nationalist and colonial discourses that idealise or abject, and thus variously other, the fantasy of

---

[74] Smyth, *The Novel and the Nation*, 1.

[75] Bourke, *The Burning of Bridget Cleary*, 67. Referring to charms, Bourke points out that "Like [fairy] stories, charms were a form of symbolic capital, which could enhance the prestige of ... vulnerable people who knew them." Bourke, *The Burning of Bridget Cleary*, 61.

[76] Ibid., 28.

[77] Warner, *From the Beast to the Blonde*, xxv.

the body permitted in folktales, in which women's associations with nature may be envisioned in empowering, productive ways.

These concerns are reflected in Bourke's collection of short stories, where she experiments with the metaphorical valences that tie individuals' bodies to the body of nature. In her literary writing, Bourke is concerned with cultural sites that mythologize the relationship between women and nature. These sites can be the setting of the most casual activities deriving from material practices characteristic of male-dominated gender regimes. In "Dreams of Sailing", exploring the thoughts of a young woman whose summer love adventure is the occasion of her sexual initiation, the narrator shows how gender hierarchies are instilled in the most simple practices, such as sailing a boat for leisure: while her lover, Kevin, is guiding the boat, the woman's role is to "lean in or out to balance us",[78] just as she would be expected to do as wife. Kevin refers to the boat as a "she" and finds it "so responsive", governable.[79] He reads the body of his lover through his fantasy about boats. When on one of their forays the boat capsizes they fall into the sea and, as if awakened from a spell, the woman becomes aware of the phallic geometry of Kevin's fantasy. The scene is loaded with sexual connotations:

> Kevin managed to do something with his feet. He shouted across to me, and up she came.
> The mast and the sail came swinging up against the blue sky, with the sun shining on all the drops of water as they poured off. It looked so beautiful and geometric, very high and white and far away.[80]

Eventually, after it becomes clear that Kevin wasn't interested in a long-term relationship based on equality and mutual respect, the woman realises that the boat "was really only made for one person."[81] We may interpret this story using Foucault's argument that "the body becomes a useful force only if it is both a productive body and a subjected body."[82] Foucault speaks here of the body as a labour resource. In the situation narrated in Bourke's story the young woman's body is seen as a source of pleasure. However, her body is read through an association with nature that we glimpse indirectly through the rich tradition of Irish tales concerning fishing labour that has lent its worldview to the practice of leisure sailing.

---

[78] Angela Bourke, "Dreams of Sailing", *By Salt Water*, 29-38, 34.
[79] Ibid., 32-3.
[80] Ibid., 35.
[81] Ibid., 38.
[82] Michel Foucault, *Discipline and Punish* (London: Allen Lane, 1977), 26.

Regarding nature as a productive body, the Irish cultural tradition of fishing practices endorses nature's subjection. This masculine control of nature also legitimates the appropriation of women's bodies.

Bourke's story entitled "Pinkeens" also explores how the masculine dominance of nature is reflected in socialisation skills and leads to forms of eroticism in which women are abused. The narrator, a pre-sexual girl, is puzzled by the groups of young men whom she sees going fishing every day during the summer. When her older cousin is sent over for the holidays, the two girls are finally allowed to go fishing themselves, on their own. One of the boys offers to show them a place where there would be more fish. When the three get there, he leads the girls to the edge of the water saying

> 'You have to be very quiet and not move.' ... He stood behind us ... . He put his hand on my shoulder and made me lean against him. He was pointing at the water but I couldn't see anything. He kept saying 'Ssh!' and then he said 'There they are!' but he was rubbing my leg with his thumb. It rubbed softly at first, but then really hard, right up inside my shorts. ... I was afraid to move ... .[83]

The passage suggests that the male reads the girl's body as he reads nature: a body in which to fish. The story emphasises the symbolic value of apparently insignificant gestures and phrases to show how they reflect the disciplining of women's bodies as resources for masculine sexual pleasure, just as nature is a resource for the practice of masculine skills. Later, when the two girls return home they carry "jamjars ... full of fish" but they "had to walk very slowly so the water wouldn't all splash out ... ."[84] The text suggests that the girls are "training" for pregnancy, a reading strengthened by the narrator's relating the two experiences through underlining the discomfort they caused: "It was the second time I couldn't move because of the stupid pinkeens."[85] Eventually, the girl decides to empty the jar on the ground and kill the fish. When in the evening her parents ask what she had caught, the girl's reply foreshadows a rejection of social norms that confine women as fertile nature to domestic maternal roles: "'What about you, Una? Did you not catch any pinkeens?' 'I did,' I said, 'I got a whole lot, but I didn't want to carry them.'"[86]

---

[83] Angela Bourke, "Pinkeens", *By Salt Water*, 46-55, 54.

[84] Ibid., 54-5.

[85] Ibid., 55.

[86] Ibid.

Thus, in her short stories as well as in her study of Bridget Cleary's case, Angela Bourke is preoccupied with the empowering as well as with the disempowering ways in which the association between women and nature is represented. Bourke's critical vision conceives of culture as a continuum in which notions of bodies, nature, and body politic are continuously renegotiated.[87]

In the story closing Bourke's collection, "Mayonnaise to the Hills", two women, Lucy and Eithne, discuss the relationship between women and nature. Eithne initiates Lucy into the intimate connection between femininity and nature thus:

> 'Yes. Hills are breasts, and the earth is a woman, and a woman is the earth and all that crap.'
> 'It's a bit pathetic though, isn't it?'
> 'Well, it is. But what I'm trying to say is I think landscape turns everyone on. Or it can—but men think sex belongs to them. ... But the thing is, it's me *with* the land, not me *as* the land. ... I just feel so alive when I come down here. I walk along the road and smell the turf smoke and the salty air and I want to open my mouth and my nose wider and wider to take it in. And then at night the sky is so clean. You feel if you could open wide enough you could swallow the stars. That's what sex is about after all, isn't it? Feeling everything waking up?'[88]

The relationship between women's bodies and nature envisioned here is one of re-appropriation rather than of incorporation. Eithne is allied with nature; she is not taken over by it. In using the Irish folklore tradition to her advantage, Bridget Cleary envisioned an alliance of women with the land, through which she could oppose her husband's incorporative vision of her as a territory to which he could stake a claim.

Irish folkloric discourses offer at least these two possible ways of envisioning women's relationship with nature. In highlighting these possibilities, Bourke's writing underscores the heteroglossic play which the discourses can accommodate. This suggests that the social norms established by the discourses depend on which aspects of the relationship between women and nature are being reiterated until they become naturalised features of bodies and landscapes. Bourke's study of the Cleary case points out that the patriarchal impetus of male-generated social myths in nineteenth-century Ireland resulted from overlapping and

---

[87] Other examples of feminist research adopting this view are Grosz, *Volatile Bodies*; "Refiguring Lesbian Desire" and Gatens, *Imaginary Bodies*.

[88] Angela Bourke, "Mayonnaise to the Hills", *By Salt Water*, 159-68, 166-7, original italics.

disjunctive discourses that emerged in the interaction between Irish rural, Irish nationalist, and British metropolitan cultures. In this context, heteroglossia can be seen as an important concern of Irish women's writing. It can be used to open up various mutually reinforcing social myths that corroborate male-dominated gender regimes through reiterating the otherness of women and landscape.

The analyses of Kennedy's work helped us to define a concept of voice that accommodates other's voices, and the power of fantasising conveyed through these voices. The analyses of Lochhead's texts indicated that often the voices that speak in our voice are come from the past: myths, folk and fairy tales, and canonical tales such as those derived from Stoker's *Dracula* discipline one's fantasising identity. The analysis of Bridget Cleary's case serves as an example of how voices from the past are inflected by the specific contexts of Irish culture, as well as offering the opportunity to examine how women's bodies are affected by the disciplinary discourses of intersecting traditions. In the following two chapters, I turn to the work of another Irish writer, Éilís Ní Dhuibhne. Her stories offer the opportunity to further expand the analysis of the relationship between stories derived from myths and social actors by focusing on the tropes through which bodies are represented as mirroring both the body of nature and the body-social. The body functions like a prism that reflects and refracts the myths through which nature and society are constituted as habitable or uninhabitable places.

CHAPTER TEN

EMBODIMENT AND SUBJECTIVITY IN ÉILÍS NÍ DHUIBHNE'S *THE DANCERS DANCING*

Éilís Ní Dhuibhne's novel *The Dancers Dancing* investigates the constraints tradition places on women's understandings of their bodies.[1] Focusing especially on the ways in which male curators of tradition shape these understandings, the novel explores possibilities of reconstructing the relation between culture, bodies, and feminine identities. The main female characters find ways of resignifying their bodies through new understandings of the relationship between bodies and nature. These possibilities of resignification of feminine bodies are explored in relation to the psycho-social transformations undergone by young girls on the cusp of womanhood. For the purposes of this analysis, I define "womanhood" in Moira Gatens's words as a product of the structuring function of texts and social practices "in so far as they function like texts."[2] "Womanhood" comprises a range of social imaginaries that carry marks of femininity derived from social myths. The transformations undergone by the female characters of Ní Dhuibhne's novel are triggered by negotiations of social imaginaries through which the girls acquire cognitive maps of femininity and corresponding structures of emotional affects.

The main characters of *The Dancers Dancing* are adolescent girls on a summer course of Irish language in Donegal, at an Irish College. In an interview conducted by Nicola Warwick, Ní Dhuibhne points out that "this particular institution is a very interesting one, unique, and quite central to the experience of many Irish adolescents. In reality, as in the novel, it tends to be a rite of passage experience."[3] Indeed, in the novel, the young

---

[1] *The Dancers Dancing* was first published by Blackstaff in 1999.
[2] Gatens, ix.
[3] Éilís Ní Dhuibhne and Nicola Warwick, *Éilís Ní Dhuibhne*. Interview conducted by Nicola Warwick. 26 July 09:
http://www.prairieden.com/front_porch/visiting_authors/dhuibhne.html.

girls' perceptions of femininity are shown to develop through juggling transgressive/legitimate narrative articulations of social locale (including the locale of the body). This juggling allows the girls to move in and out of otherworldly configurations of social spaces and to explore their bodies as sites of feminine subjectivity construction.

In Warwick's interview, Ní Dhuibhne points out that "the wildness of young girls on the brink of adulthood", "their attraction to risk and danger", and "their affinity with the natural world" are central concerns of the novel.[4] *The Dancers Dancing* reflects constructions of feminine subjectivities by focusing on the constitutive difference between "wildness" and "domesticity" that yields legitimate locales (including of the body) through repudiations of ungovernable wildness; on the dangers that await those undertaking risky forays into the repudiated wildness which is figured as an abjected otherworld; and problematises the affinity relationships between the natural world and women's bodies.

In her review for the *Irish Times*, Kathy Cremin notes that

> This novel, like other recent Irish writing, turns west to explore sexual and Irish identities. But rather than being a search for essential origins, Ní Dhuibhne's narrative reveals the contingency of a historical moment. Language and landscape are layered but they cannot fix what is preserved, only muddy it.[5]

In my analysis of the novel I will explore Ní Dhuibhne's take on the role of language in constructing realms of essences, as well as the anchoring of such constructions in historical reality. I will begin by addressing the issue of mappings through the narrator's reflections in the opening chapter. I will then examine how the text addresses the traditions in which feminine subjectivity is constituted through mapping nature's otherness. This examination will use the concepts of abjection, as defined by Judith Butler, and of "imaginary bodies", as developed by Moira Gatens. Before proceeding with my analyses, I will clarify my use of these concepts in relation to Ní Dhuibhne's novel.

In Butler's interpretation the realms of abjection are "excluded sites" that "bound the 'human' as its constitutive outside" and "haunt those boundaries as the persistent possibility of their disruption and rearticulation."[6] Kristeva also defines the "abject" as having to do with "what disturbs identity, system, order. What does not respect borders,

---

[4] Ibid.

[5] Kathy Cremin, Review of *The Dancers Dancing*, *Irish Times*, 7 August 1999.

[6] Butler, *Bodies That Matter*, 8.

positions, rules."[7] Kristeva argues that on the level of individual psycho-social development the realm of the abject is a realm of the mother. It substantiates the rhythms and vibration of speech, it is the matter (mater) of symbolic form.[8] In this Kristevan perspective, the central concern in my analysis is with the marking out of "a precise area of ... culture in order to remove it from the threatening world of animals or animalism, ... imagined as representatives of sex or murder."[9] However, following Butler more closely, my emphasis will be on the social value of the abject in transactions of social imaginaries, even though recognising all the while that this value is deposited in material configurations (of objects, bodies, social environments, nature) delivering the threat of the abject.

In this context, the central female characters of *The Dancers Dancing* can be regarded, in a Derridean perspective, as speaking from a narrative site which establishes "the possibility of parasitism, of a certain fictionality altering at once ... the system of (il- or perlocutionary) intentions"[10] required of these characters by the traditions legitimised at the Irish College. Within the contexts of these traditions, the girls' narratable fantasies are tributary to a social myth. The novel shows how the girls inhabit two worlds: one is the world constructed through the regulatory power of discursive (re)presentations derived from social myths, a power engendered by the reiteration of these discourses in the institutional settings of the Irish College; the other is a repudiated world of alternative fictions, a parasitic world of abjection in relation to which the social myths are legitimated and through which the conditions of their iterability are preserved, and thus, their power to subject is maintained.

Ní Dhuibhne's characters are forced to adopt the legitimate subject positions, but they also discover themselves as abject; they gain realness through becoming subjects constructed through social myths, but they also discover the fictionality of the myths by visiting the "parasitic" world of abjection deflected through discourses derived from the myths. This leads to the awareness that "once this parasitism or fictionality can always add *another* parasitic or fictional structure to whatever has preceded it ... everything becomes possible against the language-police".[11] In my analysis framework, I regard the "language-police" as being mobilised

---

[7] Kristeva, *Powers of Horror*, 4.

[8] Julia Kristeva, *Desire in Language: A Semiotic Approach to Literature and Art*, ed. Leon Roudiez, trans. Thomas Gorz et al. (New York: Columbia University Press, 1980), 134-6.

[9] Kristeva, *Powers of Horror*, 12-13.

[10] Derrida, "Limited Inc a b c...", 99.

[11] Ibid., 99-100, original italics.

through a social myth. The female characters of *The Dancers Dancing* reiterate narratives derived from social myths in defining their identity, but they do so in ways that call up different possible contexts, thus awakening readers to meanings that have been repudiated in the making of the social myths. The characters reiterate (indeed, must learn exactly) the discourses of certain Irish traditions, but they add parasitic fictional structures that emerge from the margins of those traditions. These structures lead to re-evaluations of the relation between legitimate subjects, bodies, and nature.

Ní Dhuibhne's novel, even while deconstructing the masculine conception of an idealised Celtic otherworld, reaches out towards a certain paganism of the earthiness of women's bodies, recollected in visions of a symbiotic relationship between women and nature. However, the narration never quite settles women's bodies in the mythic embrace of nature; the narrator's flair for light irony prevents that. Rather, the narration explores the marginal territories where await the repudiated spectres forced out through monoglossic discourses, the excess which preconditions the iterability of any text.

Elizabeth Grosz's investigation of the relationship between texts and bodies provides insightful arguments for an analysis of representations of bodies and nature in Ní Dhuibhne' novel. Grosz argues that bodies are effectively produced through discourse, in the sense that what can be said about the body determines how it is steered in the social world by being inscribed and read as a particular kind of body suitable for particular modes of socialisation. For Grosz, bodies

> are not only inscribed, marked, engraved, by social pressures external to them but are the products, the direct effects, of the very social constitution of nature itself. It is not simply that the body is represented in a variety of ways according to historical, social, and cultural exigencies while it remains basically the same; these factors actively produce the body as a body of a determinate type.[12]

Although suggesting an empowering alliance between women's bodies and nature, Ní Dhuibhne's text challenges the historical, social, and cultural exigencies that demand the reading of women's bodies as nature that, in being governed through reason or religious faith, needs be subject to masculine government. It challenges the social myths of the governability of bodily passions/women/masses by a masculine social elite. When Orla, the main character of the novel, first discovers the burn and its wildness (which, as we shall see, is associated with the wildness of

---

[12] Grosz, *Volatile Bodies*, x.

women's bodies) she remarks that it is beautiful but that "It's a pity there isn't a bridge across it."[13] That is, she deplores the oppositional casting of mind and body that repudiates nature, denying the possibility of conceiving mind and body as bridgeable, allied territories. It is this bridgeability of mind and body that the novel explores.

In *Gender Trouble*, Butler proposes that the repudiation required for founding the subject in the realm of the symbolic is not definitive. It only lasts through the signifying practices that reiterate the norms which define the legitimate against the abject. The norms are both restrictive and enabling in delimiting realms of abjection as "alternative domains of cultural ... possibilities": "it is only *within* the practices of repetitive signifying that a subversion of identity becomes possible."[14] Ní Dhuibhne's text shows that the rules governing signification are made by a cultural elite, while also showing that the reiteration of texts (signifiers) derived from social myths may be used to subvert the meanings they enshrine.

In their articulation of requirements for progressive feminism, Nancy Fraser and Linda Nicholson highlight the importance of "a practice made up of a patchwork of overlapping alliances, not one circumscribable by an essential definition."[15] The narration of *The Dancers Dancing* is underlain by a similar vision. Orla's quest for feminine identity takes her through mindscapes of imaginary bodies that are empowered through masculinisations of the female body, as well as through realms of nature that seemingly belong in the female body, and through realms of legend where the female body is enchanted in the image of a fairy queen. For instance, Orla's host's daughter, Sava, whom the girls admire, is

> extremely colourful—her hair is black, black as a river at night, not black as a raven's wing. That is Sava's colour, as to hair, and her skin is pearly, a translucent white. Red mouth, needless to add. She is Snow White, she is Étain, she is Deirdre of the Sorrows.[16]

But we should not be misled by this apparent surrendering of Sava to the realm of legend. Her hair is black as a river at night, suggesting her alliance with ungovernable nature, such as Orla will read in the landscape of the burn. This alliance defamiliarises the metaphor for beautiful black

---

[13] Ní Dhuibhne, *The Dancers Dancing*, 44.

[14] Butler, *Gender Trouble*, 145, original italics.

[15] Nancy Fraser and Linda Nicholson, "Social Criticism without Philosophy: An Encounter between Feminism and Postmodernism", *Feminism/Postmodernism*, 19-38, 35.

[16] Ní Dhuibhne, *The Dancers Dancing*, 40.

hair ("as a raven's wing") inherited in the Irish literary tradition from medieval versions of Deirdre's tale.[17] The "needless to add" suggests an ironic reading of the canons of tradition. We are not sure whether the last line reads like praise or a sentencing conviction. The passage suggests a narrative practice of overlapping alliances, including with the dominant tradition. Yet the reiteration that occurs through such alliances is not merely a repetition, but also the occasion of "repetitive signifying" that makes possible "a subversion of identity"[18] through which the dominant discourse is open to heteroglossic encounters with the spectres attending in the shadow of the curtains framing the narrating scene.

The novel is prefaced with the poem "Inversnaid" by Gerard Manley Hopkins, an Englishman who lived in Ireland and in Scotland. On the level of content, "Inversnaid" anticipates the metaphorical investment of Ní Dhuibhne's text in the imagery of nature. The central metaphors of the novel are constructed around the imagery of the burn and its waterfall and are used to explore the awakening of the young girls' bodies to the otherness of nature.

On a formal level, the choice of Hopkins' poem suggests the importance of the rhythms and music of language and the narrator's concern with how different kinds of telling sit differently in one's body and allow different worlds to be embodied and inhabited. We notice that Hopkins' poem maps nature using bodily attributes: it offers an imaginary body of nature. The burn is a "he" in various incarnations, active, an attribute strengthened with the use of alliteration in "His rollrock highroad roaring down". But its bed is feminine, passive (the "brook" "treads" through "the groins of the braes"), or of threatening passivity: the "windpuff-bonnet of fawn-froth" suggests innocent masculinity (in Scots "bonnet" refers to a brimless cap worn by men) sucked in by a "pool so pitchblack", whose "broth" recalls a witches' cauldron that "rounds and rounds despair to drowning." Thus, the rhythms of the body of nature are masculine, while its silent carcass is feminine: a feminine body that pulsates with masculine life force. The assonance in "rounds and rounds despair to drowning" suggests a cavitous nature where the sharpness of "rollrock roaring" tongue may be extinguished in echo. This nature is a passive receptacle contiguous with a sort of echoing body-ness, the *chora*. In Hopkins' poem language is used as vehicle of social imaginaries also

---

[17] See "The Exile of the Sons of Uisliu", *Early Irish Myths and Sagas*, trans. Jeffrey Gantz (Harmondsworth: Penguin Books, 1981), 256-67. See also J. M. Synge, *Deirdre of the Sorrows, The Playboy of the Western World and Other Plays*, ed. Ann Saddlemyer (Oxford: Oxford University Press, 1995), 147-87.

[18] Butler, *Gender Trouble*, 145.

through the manipulation of its formal properties, thus used to corroborate a social myth that makes sense of nature in a certain way. The inclusion of Hopkins' poem indicates that Ní Dhuibhne's text will engage with issues of mapping of social environments, nature, and bodies through the in/formal use of language and, sometimes, of its material qualities (resonances).

On the other hand, the telling of stories is seen as a mapping through representation of material places. In the first chapter of the novel, entitled "The map", we read:

> Imagine you are in an airplane ... . You see what the early map-makers imagined—Giraldus Cambrensis or Abraham Ortelius, Francis Jobson, Richard Bartlett—those whose outrageous ambition it was to visualise and draw on a two-dimensional surface of wood or parchment or vellum or paper or whatever was to hand baronies, counties, countries, continents. Their minds' eyes flew as high as this, and higher: hundreds of thousands of feet above the earth while their bodies remained glued to land. And then the eyes descended, bringing with them the diminished, distorted images from their imagined flight, back to earth, back to the drawing board. This is it, their maps said. This is the earth, the place you live in. This is what it looks like really! See you! Look![19]

The passage connects the act of representation through mapping with a masculine tradition, that of taking in the body of nature as a wildness that needs to be mapped. In order to visualise or draw the body of nature the map-makers' minds fly high, in the austere realms of God, or in the metaphysical spaces of reason. Their visualisation and drawings of the nature's body are preserved on "wood or parchment or vellum or paper"; this suggests a continuity of the tradition of representation that survives through specific historical ages and the tradition's canonical heaviness, its prestige and institutionalisation. The mapmakers mentioned in the passage regard nature as a body suitable for inscriptions of social hierarchies, "baronies, counties, countries, continents" that reflect the identity of social elites, nations, and cultures. The cartographers are ecclesiastics (Giraldus), noblemen (Ortelius), colonist surveyors (Jobson), and soldiers (Bartlett). The body of nature succumbs to the body politic. Ní Dhuibhne's narrator indicts the driving force behind such acts of representation as an "outrageous ambition". The images that this ambition achieves are "diminished" and "distorted".

---

[19] Ní Dhuibhne, *The Dancers Dancing*, 1.

Importantly, the narrator emphasises that the map images are not simply meant for detached contemplation. They engender worldviews and agency. The passage registers their compelling force: "This is the earth, the place you live in. This is what it looks like really! See you! Look!" A map is not just a representation, but always also an image that interpellates the user; it carries an indexical force manifested in an imperative appellation that also enforces a certain kind of realness ("it really looks like this!").

The narrator observes that "after strenuous efforts to be scientifically objective" the "more licentious cartographers"

> gave in at the end to a childish and thoroughly understandable desire to decorate. ... [L]ittle men plough and hunt; wolves and bears and—yes!— unicorns and griffins gambol in the forests. ... And these are the best, the truest, maps: at once guide and picture, instrument and toy ... .[20]

Thus, map-making is also an opportunity to tell a story. Stories, like the best and truest maps, guide readers; they are instruments helping one's (social, political, historical, gender) orientation; but stories can also instigate readers to play with reality. In the next paragraph, this valiant mastery is hinted at in relation to the imagery of Hopkins' poem:

> The burn. ... From your superior angle you see it all, every inch of it, from its source on the side of a low hill, along its eager early course to where it flattens, broad and whorish, drunken and listless and loses itself in the sea.[21]

The passage describes a landscape similar to that of "Inversnaid" and thus points out the iterability of the narrative map of nature offered by Hopkins. But this iteration calls up new contexts: the landscape invested with the sensuality of a human body ("whorish, drunken and listless") gains a "licentious" wildness that escapes the map-maker's (aesthetic) objectivity. The narrator/map-maker can see the burn and "little people on its banks" but as long as the contemplative gaze remains tied-up in its enchantment with the map, it cannot see what is in side of the map, which is the inside of the nature-as-body-place—an otherness—for which the map inscribes its outside, its disembodied presence through conventions of representation.

---

[20] Ibid., 1-2.
[21] Ibid., 2.

> Inside is what you can't see, maker of maps. Behind or below, before or after. ... And the figures on their little journeys, back and forth and up and down and in and out, until they move out of the picture altogether, over the edge, into the infinity of after the story.[22]

The passage suggests that there is an otherness in the map-maker's design/narrator's voice that might threaten the map-maker's/storyteller's assurance of angle by resurrecting a landscape/body s/he cannot recognise (because the map/the voice obstructs it). Perhaps it is necessary to explore the alterity of the storyteller's voice, its echoes in the body it seeks to re-present, in order to find out what this otherworldliness of the map/the narrating voice is (what haunts the map/voice). The following passage considers the limitations of storytelling as mapping:

> What you can't see is what it is better not to see: the sap and the clay and the weeds and the mess. The chthonic puddle and muddle of brain and heart and kitchen and sewer and vein and sinew and ink and stamp and sugar and stew and cloth and stitch and swill and beer and lemonade and tea and soap and nerve and memory and energy and pine and weep and laugh and sneer and say nothing and say something and in between, in between, in between, that is the truth and that is the story.[23]

Stories that are also maps cannot render the "zones of uninhabitability"[24] which, because perceived as such, trigger the need for mapping. That is why stories are never complete, and the bodies they map are never quite achieved (finished off) as required by the social myths which inspire various stories. In side of the finished map, or of the story seeming fully present in the teller's/reader's voice ("saying something"), there, always germinates the possibility of a different story, and so of a different place/body-place (saying, as yet, nothing). The narrator contemplates the "in between" of "say nothing" and "say something" to find what body might be missed by these imperatives.

The first chapter concludes:

> Every picture tells a story.
> A truism. Half true like all truisms. Half false.
> The rest of the story is in the mud. Clear as muddy old mud.[25]

---

[22] Ibid.

[23] Ní Dhuibhne, *The Dancers Dancing*, 2-3.

[24] Butler, *Bodies That Matter*, 3.

[25] Ní Dhuibhne, *The Dancers Dancing*, 3.

Part of the story may be found in the narrative act of representation. But in order for the story to be complete, one must take into account the repudiations enacted in representation. "The mud" talked about here carries connotations of dirtiness, abjection. But the mud may also be what Bridget, a character in Ní Dhuibhne's short story "Gweedore Girl", calls the "soft, hot, smelly stuff" human bodies are made of.[26]

The concept of repudiation that I use in this analysis is similar to that theorised by Judith Butler. Butler writes that abjection presupposes a "casting away" which resonates with the psychoanalytic notion of repudiation (*Verwerfung*), "a foreclosure which founds the subject". But, Butler argues, while in psychoanalysis this foreclosure "produces sociality through a repudiation of a primary signifier which produces an unconscious or, in Lacan's theory, the register of the real," for her "the notion of *abjection* designates a degraded or cast out status within the terms of sociality."[27] In Butler's terms, the constitution of subjectivity presupposes fantasising oneself as belonging to a legitimate social space through fearing the possibility of being a social outcast in zones of uninhabitability. *The Dancers Dancing* explores such zones of uninhabitability on several levels.

On an immediately visible level, the novel uses irony to show that the idealisation of a distinctively Irish Celtic world serves to construct the English as abject. In the passage describing the Tubber Irish College, we read that the college is:

> Not the kind you find in Paris or Louvain, homes from home for priesteens bravely defying the Penal Laws during the eighteenth century and being schooled for ordination in ancient Catholic cities far from the chilly Mass rocks and dark secret byres that await their heroic return, bearers of the sacred mysteries, the magic words, the holy chalice which encloses in its deep gleaming heart the identity of the nation. Our body, our blood. ... Our paradise. ... Everything that is exotic, different, warm, unreal and other. Other but not English.[28]

---

[26] Éilís Ní Dhuibhne, "Gweedore Girl", *The Inland Ice and Other Stories* (Belfast: Blackstaff, 1997), 2-28, 3.

[27] Butler, *Bodies That Matter*, 243, original italics.

[28] Ní Dhuibhne, *The Dancers Dancing*, 18. For notes on the investment of the English, in Irish culture, with "a negative mystique", see John Foster, *Colonial Consequences: Essays in Irish Literature and Culture* (Dublin: Lilliput, 1991), 271; Oliver MacDonagh, *States of Mind: Study of Anglo-Irish Conflict 1780-1980*, (London: Harper, 1983), 119.

The passage refers to several aspects of the differentiating power of social myths. The social myth directly referred to here is the Catholic religious myth. But it is suggested that other social myths are part of the network that legitimises it, and that, in turn, it helps legitimising them. The religious myth is upheld by, and upholds, myths of national identity. As, for instance, Edna Longley points out, in Ireland "nationalism was internalised as God, Nature and Family" thus being "so deeply absorbed as to become unnoticeable".[29] This form of the Catholic religious myth as social myth distinguishes Irish identity from any other, deferring its fulfilment to the moment of an epiphany that transforms the subject into a revolutionary. Such a revolutionary, fighting in the cause of the social myth, turns its differentiating power into social action (for instance, defying British authority by defying the Penal Laws, thus drawing "proper" Irishness in a certain configuration).

The otherworld described in the passage as "exotic, different, warm, unreal and other" is an artifice, a fantasy of the "good", ideal other (the ideal Irish) that serves to delineate the "bad", abject other (the abject English). The ideal other is specified in relation to Catholicism and a sense of belonging to the family that is the Irish nation, as well as in relation to idyllic Irish nature. We are enticed to think that any one term of this triad, family-nature-nation, is formed in relation to the other two, and, indeed, this constitutive relation is one of the central concerns of the novel. In terms of the novel's concern with constructions of femininity through this relation, the pivotal element is nature in its abject otherness, connected to women's bodies, but which is also, contradictorily, the subject of idealised otherness in nationalist discourse, connected with, and constitutive of, Irish identity.

However, as Luke Gibbons pointed out, the exotic "otherness" of the idyllic natural landscape of Ireland is itself an urban construct, disconnected from the realities of agrarian life.[30] Tracing the genealogy of this construct requires reflection on British representations of Ireland. Commenting on the difficulties encountered by contemporary Irish novelists in representing Ireland, Gerry Smyth argues that "the colonial and post-colonial novelist is forced to tread a very precarious line between positive reclamation of the nation on the one hand, and stereotypical

---

[29] Longley, "From Cathleen to Anorexia", 174. See also John Henry Whyte, *Church and State in Modern Ireland 1923-1979* (Dublin: Gill and Macmillan, 1980), 21-3.

[30] Luke Gibbons, *Transformations in Irish Culture* (Cork: Cork University Press, 1996), 169.

reproduction of a received, exotic otherness on the other."[31] Ní Dhuibhne's narrator entices us to apply a similar reflection, not only to the narration of *The Dancers Dancing*—which in fact explores the very constitution of the precarious line between positive reconstruction and stereotypical reproduction of Irish nature—but also to the idealisation of the Celtic otherworld that underlies the ethos of the Irish College. Even though this idealisation reproduces the colonial worldview, its instantiation in the Irish College cultural practices serves an Irish ruling elite that seeks to differentiate itself from a formerly ruling British elite.[32]

Thus, the narrator's reflections in the quoted passage identify two streams of the differentiating power of social myths: one distinguishes Irish identity from any other through conflating Catholic and national identities; the other appropriates a romantic construction of Ireland in order to use its authority to define its authors as abject. The two streams flow into each other in the fantasy correlating the self with the "good" other, compelling one's embodiment according to the legitimate shape of the body politic: "the holy chalice which encloses in its deep gleaming heart the identity of the nation" also encloses "our body, our blood", as well as, we may infer, the contiguous body of nature. One's body is transubstantiated, as is the body of nature, into the body politic.

Another way in which the call for transubstantiation of the body into the body politic is performed is through the policing of bodies during the céilí dances. When we read that the céilí dancers follow the kind of Celtic patterns that can be found "on the crochet tablecloths sold in the souvenir

---

[31] Smyth, *The Novel and the Nation*, 36; see also 60-1.

[32] Smyth points out that "the image of a romantic Celtic fringe was developed in the latter half of the eighteenth century as a foil for England's own pragmatic, progressive identity and to provide a space where the jaded metropolitan imagination could take occasional holidays from the rigours of the imperialist project." Ashis Nandy, focusing on the psychological dimension of colonialism, argues that "the ruled are constantly tempted to fight their rulers within the psychological limits set by the latter." This is partly the case at the Irish College. Smyth, *The Novel and the Nation*, 44; see also 59-60. Ashis Nandy, *The Intimate Enemy: Loss and Recovery of Self under Colonialism* (Delhi: Oxford University Press, 1983), 3. Excellent discussions of the question of the authenticity of Irishness can be found in *Ireland and Cultural Theory: The Mechanics of Authenticity*, eds. Colin Graham and Richard Kirkland (Basingstoke: Macmillan, 1999); Gerry Smyth, *Decolonisation and Criticism: The Construction of Irish Literature* (London: Pluto, 1998); Colin Kidd, "Gaelic Identity and National Identity in Enlightenment Ireland and Scotland", *The English Historical Review*, 434 (1994): 1197-1214; Colin Graham, *Deconstructing Ireland: Identity, Theory, Culture* (Edinburgh: Edinburgh University Press, 2001), esp. 132-3.

shops in Tubber"[33] we realise that the dancing shapes not only the physical performance of the dancers' bodies, but also an identity derived from social and cultural norms, expressed as emblematic designs: a souvenir that replaces the memory of the past with an artefact. The design of this manufactured artefact produces through an artifice the "truth" of a mystic Celtic Ireland, obscuring the reality of the past. The dancers' moves follow "the swirls cut into the stones at Newgrange. In and out, round and round and round, in and out."[34] The power of the artifice derived from social myths can be measured in the intensity that binds body and mythological design. The inscriptions bodies draw in their movements form a text possessed in common by the social group: "by the time the set is over, everyone has danced with everyone else on the floor. It's a metaphor for the life of the parish".[35] Ní Dhuibhne's novel is concerned with how such metaphors "work" in social practices in Ireland, structuring relationships of government of bodies that reflect visions of relationships of government of nature and the body-social/body politic.

When the bus loaded with children enters Donegal

> The tidy hawthorn hedgerows, clipped like crew cuts, have yielded to ragged brambles and bushy fuchsia, dipping and waving and scratching the bus. ... The landscape in the delicate ether of twilight is beginning to look like all the places Irish people go to on their holidays. ... The landscape has stopped being the east and the midlands and the North of Ireland and started being the West.[36]

Here, although taken in as a holiday place, as a marketable Otherworld, an idealised "good" other, the landscape is other also in the sense of being a constitutive outside of culture. There is a perception of nature's resistance to humans' entering: a ragged nature that dips and waves and scratches. This unwieldy nature is the margin of the idealised otherworld marked as "exotic, different, warm, unreal and other". This margin, the possibility of ungovernable nature, must be included in every re-marking of nature tamed through ideals that proclaim its exoticism, difference, warmth, "unreality" in the name of an appropriated otherness.

Such un/governability of nature is subtly echoed in descriptions of the girls' socialisation of their bodies during the traditional céilí dances

---

[33] Ní Dhuibhne, *The Dancers Dancing*, 48.
[34] Ibid.
[35] Ibid.
[36] Ibid., 16-17.

organised nightly at the Irish college. The first narration of such scenes records that:

> All the formalities ... are firmly enacted, even enforced, ... because the male scholars are supposed to be educated to be courteous, gentlemanly, gallant, according to the high standards of the Gaels of yore. ... [T]he invitation formula was drummed into the scholars so thoroughly that even the dimmest and most linguistically clumsy of them can say it perfectly. ... Boys are obliged to ask every time, and girls are required to accept. ... As a system it works with great efficiency.[37]

The passage shows that the manufactured map of an idealised Gaelic otherworld serves to construct scripts of socialisation. These scripts corroborate the fantasised landscape "of the Gaels of yore." The socialisation scripts are formulaic, systemic, and enforced efficiently. The description of the set patterns of traditional Irish dances is used here metaphorically to express the constraining power of social myths of Irishness. Yet the regulatory force of the patterns is thus met by the "older girls", aged fourteen, whom the thirteen year old Orla envies:

> When the music starts their eyes light up, their bodies sway lightly, their long brown arms and legs flex and straighten subtly, poised for action. Orla watches ... Jacqueline and Pauline metamorphose, girls becoming mermaids before their eyes. ... Their corner of the room glows with charm, sexuality, fashion. ... Headmaster Joe glances over at them and quickly turns away again, with an irascible twist of the mouth ... .[38]

Like the body of nature, which "dips" and "waves", the girls' bodies "sway", "flex and straighten subtly", "poised for action." This threatening sexuality to which the girls' bodies awaken endangers the patterned and controlled modes of socialisation the teachers have established, for in the teachers' eyes, it endangers the sanctity of the sanitised otherworld the students are being acquainted with here: that of "the sacred mysteries, the magic words, the holy chalice which encloses in its deep gleaming heart the identity of the nation."[39] When it becomes clear that Pauline begins to like another student, Gerry, Headmaster Joe's thoughts are described thus:

---

[37] Ibid., 47.

[38] Ibid., 50. Unlike the Cinderella-type figures of male-generated fairy tales, evoked subversively in Lochhead's *The Grimm Sisters*, these girls' refuse to conform to prescribed roles, challenging the male designs of self-discipline required for participation at the ball. Lochhead, *The Grimm Sisters*, 72-4.

[39] Ní Dhuibhne, *The Dancers Dancing*, 18.

Gerry seems safe. ... Too subservient to his sacerdotal teachers to put his reputation for purity at risk. But Pauline is fourteen, big for her age, and mad as a hatter. She is the sort of girl who needs watching. Anarchy personified. She is the sort of girl who could lead anyone astray.[40]

Thus, *The Dancers Dancing* highlights different kinds of otherworlds as supplements to the official, sanitised, ideal otherworld. The Celtic otherworld authorised at the Irish College produces an abjected realm of Englishness (this realm may be imagined both as "England" and as anglicised Dublin).[41] But the differentiating power of the myth that produces these realms rests on metaphors that posit nature and bodies/the body as governable (through myth, reason, or spiritual faith). We may speak then of an otherness that circumscribes the relationship between the ideal Celtic otherworld and its ideal abject. This otherness belongs to an otherworld of the ungovernable body of nature understood also as "woman".[42]

---

[40] Ibid., 52.

[41] According to Smyth, "as part of the programme to develop a consistent and coherent resistance to colonialism, identity was structured in terms of similarity (Irishness) and difference (Englishness) during the period leading up to the revolution. This oppositional structure, however, was not modified after the withdrawal of colonial power, but remained the principal device whereby post-revolutionary Irishness was defined and characterised." Smyth, *The Novel and the Nation*, 4.

[42] This point can be explained further by adopting a Derridean perspective. The official discourses setting forth an ideal Celtic world have as their constitutive outside an abjected realm of Englishness. But the very process of othering at work here is one inherited from metropolitan discourses defining Ireland as other. By imagining Ireland as other, metropolitan discourses purified Englishness of its own othernesses, so that metropolitan discourses on Irishness are in fact parasitical fictions of Englishness, banned from the official domain of the proper English subject. This is true both of abject Irishness reflecting abhorred features of the legitimate English subject, and of idealised Irishness reflecting the "improper" impulses of the English subject to lose its identity in an exotic realm of sensuality. In revolutionary and post-revolutionary Irish discourses the tables are turned so that abjection is now sighted in England while what had been the parasitical fiction of an ideal Ireland now defines the realm of the officially legitimate Irish subject. But this spawns yet again the parasitical fiction of the ungovernable nature and the abject ungovernable body, because this fiction attends upon any official discourse that constitutes a subject entitled to government of nature and the body, be that the discourse constituting the proper English subject, nestled in metropolitan discourses, or discourses setting forth proper Irishness, within which the former is grafted and, thus contextualised differently, reconfigured to reflect different

When Orla and Pauline find the burn in their host's garden and travel along it to the waterfall, Pauline has no difficulty in jumping into the pool beneath where she enjoys the embrace of her body within the body of nature, "her brown eyes laughing."[43] But for Orla

> Every time she flexes her body for the leap her fear catches her, like a hand on her shoulder, and pulls her back. ... [T]he hand clutches her and paralyses her. ... Pauline looks up, puzzled. ... Orla waits for her, wishing she could be so reckless, gazing at the black, dark pool. ... It's the jumping she can't cope with, that sensation of free falling, being out of control.[44]

It is not the jump that Orla fears, but what the recognition of the otherness of her body as a powerful body of nature could mean. For Orla, at this stage in the chronology of the events of the story, her body's relation to the body of nature still remains unmapped because she can't cope with "that sensation of free falling, being out of control."

From the analysis to this point we retain the idea that Ní Dhuibhne's novel focuses on such mappings of material places, especially of the place of the body, as can be achieved through the use of language and stories. The Irish College tradition, developed from older Irish anti-colonialist traditions, is an institution where the participants are required to internalise certain cultural maps through internalising the traditions. But this involves a repudiation of the body that implies its sanitisation and purification through the decanting power of abjection and idealisation. In the remaining part of my analysis, I will focus on how the novel presents Orla's recuperation of agency through discovering means of remapping her body in ways that evade the constraining power of myths. I will be using the concept of "imaginary body" as understood by Moira Gatens.

According to Gatens:

> An imaginary body is not simply a product of subjective imagination, fantasy or folklore. The term 'imaginary' [refers] to those images, symbols, metaphors and representations which help construct various forms of subjectivity ... the (often unconscious) imaginaries of a specific culture: those ready-made images and symbols through which we make

---

relations of government. The parasitical fiction of the ungovernable body and nature refers to an otherworld which "corrupts" the horizon of the artificial otherworlds of Irishness and Englishness set up in official metropolitan and official Irish discourses, "contaminating it [the horizon] parasitically, qua limit", to use Jacques Derrida's words in this context. Derrida, "Limited Inc a b c...", 70.

[43] Ní Dhuibhne, *The Dancers Dancing*, 117.

[44] Ibid.

sense of social bodies and which determine, in part, their value, their status and what will be deemed their appropriate treatment.[45]

What Gatens calls "the unconscious imaginaries of a specific culture" are in my terms those images and symbols that belong to a social myth and which structure one's fantasising oneself as a social persona in a specific reality setting. In Ireland, social imaginaries derived from the fantasy of an artificial, sanitised Otherworld, forbid an empowering alliance between women's bodies and the body of nature. These social imaginaries compel women to either enter the legitimate domain of sociality by adopting masculine social personae, as happens with Orla at the beginning, or to remain outcasts whose unmappable otherness remains unintelligible, as with Pauline seen through Killer Jack's eyes as "not all there for you anyway and maybe not all there for herself."[46]

Ungovernable nature is regarded by the authoritarian figures of *The Dancers Dancing* as dangerous. The elderly woman at whose house Orla and Pauline are lodged forbids the girls to go near the burn because "it's deeper and more dangerous than it looks."[47] When it is suspected that the girls are exploring it, Headmaster Joe warns them: "That river is dangerous … . It is full of deep treacherous pools, and strong currents. You can drown in that river … ."[48] But when Orla explores it she finds there an empowering sense of privacy through which she learns that "the reality she is looking for is inside herself, hidden from all eyes."[49] According to Jeanette Shumaker, "the forbidden burn is another symbol of the exotic allure of Donegal. For Orla, the burn is associated with the abject status of her body, class, and nation."[50] In my understanding of the novel, this association is engendered through the social constraints reinforced at the Irish College, and through which ungovernable bodies, outsiders of the nationalist elite, and the less than heroic Irish are relegated to "'unlivable' and 'uninhabitable' zones of social life", to use Butler's phrase.[51] However, it is through the discovery of the burn that Orla begins to realise that she may gain an empowering social persona by understanding her body through understanding the ungovernability of the

---

[45] Gatens, viii.

[46] Ní Dhuibhne, *The Dancers Dancing*, 166.

[47] Ibid., 32.

[48] Ibid., 208.

[49] Ibid., 68.

[50] Jeanette Roberts Shumaker, "Accepting the Grotesque Body: Bildungs by Clare Boylan and Eilís Ní Dhuibhne", *Estudios Irlandeses* 1 (2006): 103-111, 109.

[51] Butler, *Bodies That Matter*, 3.

body of nature. Orla's discovery and then active construction of her relationship with the burn shows that alternative ways of mapping nature and the body's otherness are available in the margin of authorised maps of these, but that in order to discover them one must face the risks of evading the authority that, while subjecting, also protects.

Having discovered, during her explorations of the burn, "a verdant tunnel" with a "high green dome" like "a hidden green cathedral, deeply centred in a vast forest of shrub and bramble", Orla begins to understand (read) the burn and its natural surroundings as a body of nature whose vibrations echo those of her own body.[52] Soon she is both horrified and thrilled:

> There will be otters here, Orla knows. ... Wild, graceful, sly, cunning. The thought of them thrills her and horrifies her. Now that she has allowed that thought into her head, the glaucous cavern seems not enchanted and protective but dangerous—or dangerous at the same time as it is more magically seductive than any place she has ever been.[53]

Here, by taking in the body of nature, Orla becomes acquainted with the desires of her own body as a female sexual body. The danger Orla fears is that of erotic masculinity, "wild, graceful, sly, cunning." Reacting to this intuition, her body becomes, like the body of nature, "dangerous at the same time as it is more magically seductive than any place she has ever been." Further reflection on this awakening determines Orla to retreat from the place, as she remembers that otters may have "possible vindictive purposes"; these are perhaps echoes of cautionary tales that warn young girls against the dangers of men's seductive courtship. On her way back, Orla finds wild berries. The sensations triggered by this finding are related to bodily sensuality. The berries are

> Sweet, tangy, cool, fresh, wild, tinged with an exotic flavour ... that is a perfume from a golden-covered volume of fantastic stories, a flavour that is a confirmation, for her, of the jewel-studded world that awaits exploration ... . That is what the berries seem to be: a taste of a wonderful future, not a residue of a wild world that is past, or passing.[54]

The reference to a "world that is past, or passing" echoes the realm of disembodied essences evoked in W. B. Yeats's poem "Sailing to Byzantium". There, the speaking "I" longs to leave nature behind and join

---

[52] Ní Dhuibhne, *The Dancers Dancing*, 71.
[53] Ibid.
[54] Ibid., 72.

the eternal and ethereal realm of absolutes: "Once out of nature I shall never take/ My bodily form from any natural thing".[55] But Orla wishes to do exactly the opposite; her "wild world" is also a bodily world allied with the body of nature, with its rhythms and currents, in ways that escape control exercised through canonical traditions. Orla begins to recognise her body as a body whose contours she may draw herself, but without repudiating or idealising its ties with nature:

> In the burn, she was part of whatever whole encompassed the water and the weeds and the raspberries and the drooping willows. Her heart beat in time with the babble of the burn down there ... . Babble and rustle, bloodbeat and leaf, eye and water. Orla belonged with the river. ... And completely herself. Orla Herself. Not Orla the Daughter of Elizabeth, Orla the Pride of Rathmines, Orla the Betrayer of Tubber. Just Orla.[56]

Later on, Orla takes Pauline to show her "the glaucous cavern" of the hidden green tunnel. Once there, Orla unexpectedly quotes from Hopkins' poem as if reciting a warning: "'This darksome burn, horseback brown, his rollrock highroad roaring down,' announces Orla suddenly."[57] On subsequent trips to the burn on her own, Orla eventually breaks the taboos that forbid women to speak in a virile voice:

> She has never said fuck before. She did not know before that she could say it, or harboured any wish to do so.
> 'Fucking hell fucking hell fucking hell,' she says, walking down the burn. ... She tries out all the taboo words she knows. ... The very worst words, concerning the devil and sex, were left for the exclusive use of extremely angry or extremely uncivilised men. Still, there is a surprising store of words in Orla's head that have never before emerged into the light of day, into the sound of day. Her own ears. She has hardly ever heard her own voice, listened to her own voice, and it gets louder and louder, clearer and clearer, as she gets used to it.[58]

Orla thus claims the confidence of masculine voices. The morning after, she finds that she has had her first menstruation. This sign of her body's fertility is a source of anxiety for Orla, and part of this anxiety, her dreams indicate, is related to the prospect of having to discipline her body's fertility according to the masculine demands of the twinned bodies of

---

[55] W. B. Yeats, "Sailing to Byzantium", *Collected Works*, 197.
[56] Ní Dhuibhne, *The Dancers Dancing*, 73.
[57] Ibid., 115.
[58] Ibid., 201.

Church and State. Orla dreams about a woman, Nuala Crilly, with whom she partly identifies (Crilly is Orla's surname; also, Nuala looks like Aisling, a girl Orla admires). Nuala has given birth to a baby which she drops over the waterfall familiar to Orla from her trips to the burn. Orla's dream suggests a reclamation of women's right to control their bodies' fertility. Hinting at cases, in Ireland, of newborns abandoned by their mothers, the narrator emphasises the presence of masculine authority in controlling birth and sexuality as, we infer, Nuala had been denied the right to an abortion or became pregnant without being married and attempted to avoid being turned into a subject of public opprobrium. The story shaped in Orla's dream suggests a scene of sacrifice, but it may also be seen as depicting a returning of the baby to the body of feminine nature: the baby "smiles at [Nuala] as he falls like a stone into the black skin of water."[59] In this context, Orla's reading of her body as feminine through the alliance with a powerful body of nature suggests the possibility of recuperating authority over her body and the social spaces it inhabits.

In Ní Dhuibhne's novel, the symbolic load of the imagery of nature, especially of the burn, allows her to investigate the traces of a discourse of femininity from which her characters have been alienated through their socialisation in a male-dominated society. When the students of Irish Gaelic learn this language in an institutionally legitimate setting, they acquire grids for mapping otherness, the landmarks of which are part of the same mapping grill used, for instance, when the rhythms of Hopkins' poem are conferred upon masculinity. This grill helps shaping the body of nature as a passive body electrified by masculine virility. But in this process the passivity of the body of nature, in which women are seen to share, has as its constitutive outside the possibility of its ungovernable strength, an outside that must remain unnameable, incommunicable, indecipherable. The reiterated acts of signifying feminine identity by envisioning women as passive nature guarantee the legitimacy of reason or faith that must govern bodies' passions. The rhythms of Irish, made virile (Headmaster Joe's favourite song from his *Abair Amhrán* is "a rousing Nazi march, but nobody knows this, except maybe the people who compiled the songbook"[60]), come to sit in the students'/readers' bodies governing the bodies' presence and movement, like the patterns of set dances that govern the bodies' dancing. The iterations of such rhythms and patterns mark bodies as feminine or masculine in ways that corroborate male-dominated gender regimes, foreclosing alterity.

---

[59] Ibid., 211.
[60] Ibid., 146.

Ní Dhuibhne's characters seek to articulate this alterity, "the rest of the story".[61] We may define this opening to alterity in terms of Jon Klancher's understanding of the concept of heteroglossia in his introduction to *The Making of English Reading Audiences, 1790-1832*. In this study concerned with the interdependence between texts and institutional settings that legitimate them, Jon Klancher focuses on the social dimension of reading acts. According to Klancher narratives contain traces of socially alien discourses. The possibility of encountering an other's discourse in one's own entails an acceptance of heteroglossia, that is, the possibility of repositioning oneself as member of a differently conceived audience, that audience which the other's voice is seeking. Consequently, as the interlocutor of an other, one learns its language and how to reposition oneself as speaking subject within a differently conceived social group.[62] Such encounters with different possible audiences awaken the subject to alternative ways of conceiving his/her social identity. The characters of Ní Dhuibhne's novel are open to such heteroglossic encounters, and, exploring where they might lead, they begin to reject monoglossic discursive regimes.

Orla's identity is partly determined by the discourses in which she is required to find herself as subject at the Irish College, through which she is situated in the particular social space envisioned as legitimate at this institution. Speaking standardised Irish College Irish, Orla places herself in a certain audience, and is subjected to its power to mediate between her singular voice and her "awareness of belonging to other social formations—class, gender, race—which themselves become conscious by being textually represented", to use Klancher's words in this context.[63] Yet when Orla's subjective space opens to heteroglossia, to different ways of expressing one's awareness of reality, she becomes free to explore the margin of discourse, its constitutive outside, and to find there "alternative domains of cultural ... possibilities".[64]

When Orla re*cites* Hopkins' poem along the banks of the burn, it is because she identifies in it traces of femininity that the poem repudiates in its differential marking; she becomes aware of a remainder which entices her to follow these traces in order to explore the absences created through repudiations, that have made possible the permanence of those social myths of masculinity and femininity which engender constraining social

---

[61] Ibid., 3.

[62] Jon Klancher, *The Making of English Reading Audiences, 1790-1832* (Madison: Wisconsin University Press, 1987), 12.

[63] Ibid.

[64] Butler, *Gender Trouble*, 145.

personae for women. She glimpses the prospect of mastering the rhythms of nature that have been defined on masculine terms. This leads to not merely an appropriation of masculinity, but to a disclosure of nature, as opposed to the foreclosure of nature that is the constitutive schism of the rational masculine subject. As Shumaker puts it, "[Orla] learns to own her body, including its sexuality."[65] This learning process is based on Orla's alliance with the body of nature. This alliance implies the healing of the schism that guarantees rationality through a repudiation of nature. It also implies an awareness of the fantasised character of the schism, and an empowerment of the imagination that is rational in its acknowledgment of the needs of the body, rather than in acknowledging a need for governing the body.

To paraphrase Klancher in this context, the characters of *The Dancers Dancing* read reality by recognising in dominant discourses evidence of a competitive, even antithetic world-view.[66] Theirs is a heteroglot encounter that allows them to recognise an otherness within their own discourse. For Orla, this otherness is signposted by traces, found in dominant discourses, of what can be said about an empowering alliance between the body of nature and her own body, an alliance repudiated in dominant discourses that legitimate the government of nature through reason or faith at the same time as they represent women as passive nature. This heteroglossic interference of a possible voice that finds in Orla an audience conjures up, to use Gatens's words here, different "images, symbols, metaphors and representations" and thus also conjures up different body imaginaries, that call for reconsiderations of the bodies' "value, their status and what will be deemed their appropriate treatment."[67]

The central concern of this chapter has been to show how traditions such as those promoted at the Irish College construct subjectivities through legitimating, as part of the subject's identity, a relation of government of nature, national space, and the body. Through this relation, ungovernable nature, nations, or bodies were constituted as abject. In Ireland, this kind of legitimating practice was inherited from English and European visions of the legitimate body politic which subordinate nature, nation, and the body to a governing elite. This practice took specific forms in Ireland, in accordance with the specific demands of nationalist groups, but it continued to define the ungovernable bodies of women and nature as abject.

---

[65] Shumaker, 109.
[66] Klancher, 12.
[67] Gatens, viii.

The legitimacy of the government of nature, national space, and bodies is partly derived from the subjecting effect of monoglossic discourses which reiterate the necessity of such government. Ní Dhuibhne's novel focuses on the role of the Irish College in repeatedly interpellating subjects in order to position them within legitimate institutional fields created through nationalist discourses, while at the same time investigating the ways in which these discourses are interwoven with discourses of gender and class. The ways in which one uses language to express legitimate and illegitimate identities are central to such investigation, as well as the difficulties of finding a voice to confront the policing exercised through monoglossic discourses.

By learning to read the burn in her own voice, rather than through masculine voices like that of Gerard Manley Hopkins, "Orla learns to love the messiness of nature; she builds upon this love to accept natural passions in herself ... ."[68] On another level, she learns to understand nation as a space of heteroglossia, as opposed to a space of monoglossic idealisations or abjections. These understandings of her body and national identity entail reflections on her situation as woman from a working class background within the class and gender hierarchies of patriarchal Ireland. The overarching idea conveyed in *The Dancers Dancing* is that by learning to narrate oneself through the voice of the other in heteroglot encounters at the margin of official discourses, their legitimating narrative patterns can be reconfigured.

In the interview conducted by Warwick, Ní Dhuibhne underlines the importance of narrating against the value of narrative pattern: "Although I always have a plan, starting off on a novel—I couldn't bear to face the blank page without some sort of map—I rarely stick to it. The ideas flow from the writing. Somehow I think with my pen ... ."[69] This fusion of narrator and narration suggests envisioning the performative dimension of narrating as a setting forth of embodiment. Ní Dhuibhne's novel suggests that we need to examine the making of the stories in the voice that is lent to our bodies, in order to find ways of acquainting ourselves with our bodies that evade their disciplining through social myths: no map is exhaustive.

---

[68] Shumaker, 109.
[69] Ní Dhuibhne and Warwick, *Éilís Ní Dhuibhne.*

CHAPTER ELEVEN

WOMEN'S IDENTITIES AND THE MASCULINE BODY-SOCIAL IN ÉILÍS NÍ DHUIBHNE'S SHORT STORIES

Spectres of the Body. Transubstantiation and the Body-Social

"To tell the stories was her work./ It was like spinning,/ gathering thin air to the singlest strongest/ thread."[1] These verses from the poem "Storyteller", by the Scottish writer Liz Lochhead, could be used to adequately describe the literary vocation of the Irish writer Éilís Ní Dhuibhne. Lochhead's writing often draws on elements of cultural memory, legend, and the folk tradition, finding the strongest thread, and then weaving a new story of contemporary significance around it. In a distinct manner, but achieving a similar effect, Ní Dhuibhne's literary writing creates stories that reveal new aspects of folktale events and characters by filtering them through contemporary con-texts and recent cultural history. Both authors create, to use Marina Warner's words in this context, "newly told stories" that "can sew and weave and knit different patterns into the social fabric"—"a continuous enterprise for everyone to take part in."[2] If, in Lochhead's writing, the Scottish traditions figure prominently, Ní Dhuibhne's stories draw on Irish traditions which she also knows as a specialist with scholarly background in Irish folklore. And, as with Lochhead, Ní Dhuibhne's stories are concerned with storytelling as a means to weave the material of reality out of the invisible vibration of words, that is, with the ways in which stories affect and effect the bearing of our bodies and social personae in social reality.

In this chapter I will focus on Ní Dhuibhne's short stories from several collections, which are concerned with the relationship between bodies and

---

[1] Lochhead, *The Grimm Sisters*, 70.

[2] Warner, *Managing Monsters*, xiv.

the body-social. Here, I define "the body-social" as the body of the social collectivity in which are negotiated the identities of individual bodies in terms of the social roles they are envisioned as playing in that collectivity. This body-social, then, should not be confused with the body social as the social construction of the body in a given society, a definition argued, for instance, by Anthony Synnott.[3] The body is socially constructed but it is also the incarnation of the abstract body-social of a society, functioning both as its metaphor and metonym: the body is the emblem of the body-social, it is emblematic of its norms, while also being contiguous with it. Based on Ní Dhuibhne's stories, I will argue that perceptions of the body are shaped by perceptions of features of the body-social. This shaping is regarded in the stories as an active process of which the characters are often aware only through a kind of faith which they find themselves harbouring. In order to capture this sense of (blind) faith, I will use the term "transubstantiation" to refer to the mirroring of the body-social and of the body in each other.

I use the term "transubstantiation" in order to echo the religious nature of the process in which individual bodies take on the attributes of the body-social. But I use the term outside its Christian context to evoke the religious nature of faith in any social myth. The notion that a social myth provides a religious nature to socialisation processes is derived from the work of the French philosopher Georges Sorel. I retain this notion, even though I use a different understanding of "social myth" than Sorel's. For Sorel, a social myth is "identical with the convictions of a group, being the expression of these convictions in the language of movement; and it is, in consequence, unanalysable into parts which could be placed on the plane of historical descriptions."[4] From this definition I retain the idea that a social myth is identical with the convictions of a group. However, based on Judith Butler's theorisation of normative reiterations[5], I argue that these convictions are formed through narrative reiterations of subjective positions. These reiterations engender patterns which channel the expression of our subjective identities when we present ourselves to ourselves and to others in social interactions. In this view, a social myth is analysable on the plane of historical descriptions. Narrative traditions as sets of narrative reiterations, amongst which myths and fairy tales are the most relevant in this chapter, contribute to creating social myths. The

---

[3] Anthony Synnott, *The Body Social: Symbolism, Self and Society* (London: Routledge, 1993).
[4] Georges Sorel, *Reflections on Violence*, trans. T. E. Hulme and J. Roth (Mineola, New York: Dover, 2004), 50.
[5] Butler, *Bodies That Matter*, 10.

convictions they engender are derived from the norms that obtain in the reiteration of narratives. As regards bodies, these convictions underpin the faith required for the transubstantiation of the body into the body-social. This faith legitimates the social roles attributed to bodies in a social collectivity; social myths define the terms on which bodies can be socialised in acceptable ways.

Judith Butler defines the notion of matter "not as a site or surface, but as *a process of materialization that stabilizes over time to produce the effect of boundary, fixity, and surface we call matter.*"[6] Based on this definition, the materiality of bodies can be seen as partly an effect of narrative reiterations, that is, narrative reiterations are part of the process of materialisation of bodies. Narrations derived from dominant discourses expressing social myths offer scripts for fantasising one's body's identity. The presentations of one's body in social reality are based on these fantasies. Thus, presentations of the body conform to norms of acceptability and desirability that are instituted through the very reiteration of these norms in the fantasy through which one places one's self in the shell of an image of the body. As Butler puts it, in Foucauldian perspective, "the production of a subject—its subjection (*assujetissement*)—is one means of its regulation."[7] The materiality of the body is partly an effect of subjection through using the narratives that yield the social myths which hold together the body-social.

In Ní Dhuibhne's writing, women's bodies are often summoned in order to be convicted or acquitted of misinforming consciousness. This narrative summoning is like the performance of occult magic perhaps, since often spectres of the body are invoked along with material bodies. Thus, women's bodies are often spirited, but they are also spirited away. In "Gweedore Girl", from *The Inland Ice* (1997), a young farmer's daughter imagines her mother's looks as a young woman:

> My mother … was the best-looking girl in the parish. I know this because she has told me so herself—more than once. She does not use the word that means 'pretty' or 'nice' to describe her youthful good looks, but a word that sounds more like 'elegant' or 'gallant'. When she says that word I see her as a girl made of polished, golden wood, like the curved leg of a fine sideboard, and not a woman made of soft, hot, smelly stuff.[8]

---

[6] Ibid., 9, original italics.
[7] Butler, *Bodies That Matter*, 244.
[8] Ní Dhuibhne, "Gweedore Girl", 3.

Two spectres of the mother's body are invoked here. One is rendered metaphorically through reference to a fine piece of furniture. The other image of the body is a repudiated spectre, the "not seen" of mundane "stuff", soft, hot, and smelly, at the expense of which "the best-looking girl in the parish" is brought into the light. Words like "elegant" or "gallant", often found in fairy-tale traditions, are seen as having the power of occult invocation that brings forth the looks of the mother's youthful body. But this bringing forth of the spectre that endows the mother's body with a certain materiality (seemingly "polished, golden"), also implies an occultation through which the actual material body is obscured.

The invocation performed here is the occasion of social spectacles of sorts. By using words that sound like "elegant" or "gallant" to describe herself, the mother fantasises that she belongs to a social realm of higher rank. But to her daughter, such fantasy invests the mother's body with the materiality of "polished, golden wood", objectifying the body. The fairy-tale words that help the mother fantasise herself as "elegant" or "gallant" evoke a social spectacle in which women's bodies are spirited away (the "soft, hot, smelly stuff" women's bodies are made of in the young girl's vision) leaving in their places objectified bodies invested with a fine, polished, golden materiality. The story suggests that the materiality of social personae, their texture, is threaded in the narratives that show one's body to oneself and to the world in a fantasy (in the narrative fancying of bodies).

The concept of materiality used here does not refer solely to the physical body, but to a body that is always also inlaid with text; hence its texture. For instance, the materiality of a statue does not refer only to its physical properties; the statue is always inlaid with the stories of whom or what they represent. In this sense, statues can be flexible, while bodies can be statuesque. In this perspective, the body (as place) can be seen as taking on characteristics of the body-social (as the negotiated social space of the body's presence) and the other way around. Linda McDowell argues in favour of an understanding of bodies as fluid and flexible, according to how their presence is influenced by the various social spaces they may inhabit. According to McDowell,

> While bodies are undoubtedly material, possessing a range of characteristics such as shape and size and so inevitably taking up space, the ways in which bodies are presented to and seen by others vary according to the spaces and places in which they find themselves.[9]

---

[9] McDowell, 34.

In McDowell's view, the flexibility of bodies is determined by the social roles it is appropriate for the body to perform in a given social environment. I understand bodily flexibility also as the ability of bodies to gain different materiality according to the narratives that spun this materiality. Materiality, as defined in this chapter, welds bodies and social roles. Thus, bodies are malleable under the forces that compel their materialisation; these forces are the deictic forces of discourses in which reiterations of certain narratives, that constitute a narrative tradition, ordain the body and the body-social. This body-social is a manifestation of masculine power to the extent that it is held in the gravitational pull of male logocentric authorship that imprints women's bodies as objects in male-generated fantasies. In my analysis I aim to explore how Ní Dhuibhne's texts reflect on the role of male authorship and curatorship of narrative traditions in determining bodily flexibility, presentations/fantasies of women's bodies, and bodies' occupation of space.

The faith which engenders the transubstantiation of the organic body into the body as emblem of the body-social is sustained, for instance, by monuments that honour social ideals, monuments yielded as landmarks of social spaces through the objectification of bodies. Such monuments include, for example, the gold models Bronwyn contemplates in the Uppsala cathedral in the story "How Lovely the Slopes Are":

> This immutable golden woman with deep large eyes, two burnished braids of hair gently smoothed over her breasts, was alive six centuries ago, living with the man whose graven image still lies beside her. They rode on sleighs in the snowy woods, they ate fish and blueberries, they made love. And for six centuries they have been lying here under quiet images of themselves.[10]

Bronwyn's is a longing for the warmth of bodies that are representationally silent, lying "under quiet images of themselves". The reiteration of bodies as artefacts turns "soft, hot, smelly" bodies into dead, if elegant and gallant, statuettes. Their silence is a silence that, Bronwyn notices, "passes into your lungs, into the blood in your body."[11] Bronwyn's body becomes "an ear" for the silence to which time, measured in monuments of tradition, has condemned it.

In Ní Dhuibhne's stories, the silence of such monuments providing epistemological anchoring points originates in an unreachable core of masculinity, of male bodies and of the masculine body-social. In this

---

[10] Éilís Ní Dhuibhne, "How Lovely the Slopes Are", *The Inland Ice*, 238-58, 249.
[11] Ibid., 249.

context, the concept of "masculine body-social" refers to a social collectivity that draws on features of male bodies to define the social function of individual bodies, including women's bodies. In another story from *The Inland Ice*, "Lili Marlene", the narrator is a married woman who meets a lover from her youth, John, now also married. She considers divorcing her husband in order to remarry John. But when she hints to him that they

> should tackle the implications of our relationship in a practical way, he bristled, stiffened his nose and his back, and coughed drily a few times … . His reaction, all this stiffening and sniffing and withdrawing, terrified me physically. I felt squashed underfoot by the sheer force of his disapproval. He is a quiet man but one with a forceful character. That, I think, is what being a forceful character means: having the ability to force people to cringe, shut up, drop everything, go away, with a single twitch of your body.[12]

The passage suggests the woman narrator's intuition that she inhabits a masculine social territory that obtains through the transubstantiation of the male body into the body-social. She is frightened by the masculinity of the social space (potentially making her "to cringe, shut up, drop everything, go away") that is yielded in the conversion of male bodies' attributes into attributes of the body-social. Her male partner "bristled" and "stiffened", words suggesting phallic authority. This is the authority that governs the body-social, "the ability to force people" into subjection "with a single twitch of [the male] body." The masculinity of her partner's body is disseminated into the texture of the reality the woman can narrate in the fantasies through which she defines her identity. In other stories by Ní Dhuibhne, such dissemination of masculinity in the texture of women's reality is seen as being guaranteed by myths. In the following sections I will focus on how the stories represent the role of narratives derived from myths in texturing the materiality of women's bodies.

The Weight of Tradition

In this section I will examine aspects of Ní Dhuibhne's short stories to show how they critique the role of tradition and myth in shaping women's identities. Anthropologist Myra Macdonald argues that

---

[12] Éilís Ní Dhuibhne, "Lili Marlene", *The Inland Ice*, 79-104, 88.

By posing as 'natural' and 'common-sensical', myths obscure their
ideological role in helping to shore up systems of belief that sustain the
power of the powerful. The diversity of real women, potentially
challenging to male authority, is transformed into manageable myths of
'femininity' or 'the feminine'.[13]

A record of male-generated cultural power lines that shape understandings
of femininity is offered by Bernadette, the central woman character of
"Hot Earth" from *The Inland Ice*. The story explores this woman's feelings
after an erotic adventure outside marriage which led to her separation from
both her husband and her lover. Bernadette associates her husband with
the

> flamboyant speculators, high as kites on theories about Saint Bridget and
> Newgrange and the fairies, insistent on the latent spiritual magic lurking in
> every Bronze Age necklace and Celtic cross—certain that magic lurked not
> far under their own aura-blessed skin, an ancient powder waiting to be
> ignited by an expert the like of James.[14]

Unable to see herself through James's reading of the materiality of spaces,
Bernadette summons the mundane materiality of her body only to convict
it: "James was ... wearing his knowledge lightly as a feather. Bernadette
was made of common, denser stuff, delph to his eggshell porcelain,
farmyard duck to his...snowy owl, arctic tern."[15] Confronted with the
power of the masculine body-social, the spirits that animate women's
bodies in Ní Dhuibhne's stories retreat into illegitimate fantasies and
command transformations of women's bodies' physicality into illicit
materiality. Thus, the fantasy that entices Bernadette to commit adultery is
fired by the hot earth she imagines her body has become: "She made
passionate and fulfilling love ... their bodies and the earth ... blissfully at
one. Karma, mandorla, paradise. Daydreams."[16] Eventually, the man who
inspired the fantasy, Kevin, abandons her to marry someone else. This
provokes Bernadette's realisation that the "hot stuff" her body is made of
is a sort of desert in the social world. But even though her heat is
illegitimate, she assumes its otherness. Her body becomes a heart of
darkness: "Bernadette wanted to be black. She wanted to be black in

---

[13] Myra Macdonald, *Representing Women: Myths of Femininity in the Popular
Media* (London: Arnold, 1995), 1-2.
[14] Éilís Ní Dhuibhne, "Hot Earth", *The Inland Ice*, 105-21, 108.
[15] Ibid., 110.
[16] Ibid., 112.

Africa at midday on Midsummer's Day. She wanted to be the Sahara."[17]
This allows Bernadette to feel more real than the figures in the monuments
that mark the social space as male territory, and to defeat the masculine
power that had enchanted her desire:

> Kevin left her mind on that day in Volterra. ... But a few times he has
> returned on flying visits. She sees him flitting across an archway, glancing
> over his shoulder, surprised that she should have finally broken free. She
> sees him grinning from the belly of a gargoyle that coils into a ruby
> window in a church. She sees him and his wife on a bed in Dublin,
> reclining, arm in arm, stern and serious, smiling—accusing, disdainful,
> proud, immutable, stone, marble.
>   Married.[18]

Thus, Ní Dhuibhne's stories suggest, women may reject to partake in the
social rituals that effect the transubstantiation that yields the masculine
body-social. Women may appropriate the narrative tradition that gives the
fantasies through which they show themselves to the world. In "How
Lovely the Slopes Are" Bronwyn acknowledges the power of tradition to
infuse reality with meaning:

> More lines from *Njal's Saga* visit her mind, spontaneously and unbidden,
> as is the habit of proverbs and saws, or any of the old scraps of traditional
> wisdom we have heard and which whirl invisibly in the air around us all
> the time, choosing their own moment to descend to our consciousness, like
> feathers bearing featherlight gifts of truth.[19]

The passage registers the weight of tradition, the narratives of which
"whirl invisibly in the air around us all the time". But Bronwyn also
realises that she can overtake the masculine positions of power such
stories construct. Rather than occupying the subject position of Hallgerdur,
the repudiated wife of the saga, Bronwyn identifies with Hallgerdur's
husband, Gunnar. The story of Gunnar's return home becomes the story of
Bronwyn's return to Ireland after her decision to separate from her
Swedish husband.[20] Bronwyn has overtaken the masculine language of
authority and has thus found room of her own in the body-social.

Elsewhere, Ní Dhuibhne blends stories of the Irish folk tradition in her
own stories in order to reflect on how the tradition engenders masculine

---

[17] Ibid., 119.
[18] Ibid., 121.
[19] Ní Dhuibhne, "How Lovely the Slopes Are", 258.
[20] Ibid.

gender regimes. In the following I will focus on Ní Dhuibhne's use of this narrative technique, thus exploring more emphatically how narrative tradition textures women's bodies' identities. For instance, "Midwife to the Fairies", from *Blood and Water* (1988), is structured through the juxtaposition of a traditional Irish folktale with a tale describing contemporary events.[21] The folktale relates how a handywoman was called out in the middle of the night by one of the fairy people who took her "*in the side of the hill ... to a big house and inside there were lots of people, eating and drinking*".[22] The handywoman sees a woman in labour in a corner of the house, and the story suggests that she had been called to deliver a baby for the fairy people. Some time after this, walking over a bridge by herself in the "real" world, the handywoman meets the man who had led her to the fairy Otherworld, and when he finds out that she can see him, he blinds her.

The series of events forming the contemporary version of this tale relates how a midwife is called to deliver a baby. The dead corpse of the baby is later found in a shoe box, in a rubbish dump its parents had behind their house.[23] The woman decides to inform the police that she delivered that baby, but she is threatened by a man who looks like the one who fetched her. She gives up denouncing what may have been a murder. The effect of the juxtaposition of the events in the folktale with contemporary events (the latter alluding to real cases of abandoned newborns in Ireland) shows how a "benign" folktale may be seen as contributing to legitimate masculine gender regimes. Both in the "contemporary" tale and in the folktale, an elusive but powerful masculine figure, of awesome otherworldliness, controls the fate of women's bodies in their fertility attributes. In the "contemporary" tale, the strangeness of the congregation of people who are aware of the delivery echoes the otherworldliness of the fairy realm in which the handywoman sees a similar scene. The reader's impression is that the motif of the secretive nature of the fairy people may have been used in the folktale in order to justify a male's right to control the circumstances of his wife's pregnancy. Perhaps the folktale formulated a threat and a warning to women in rural communities, showing what may happen when they transgress men's authority on such matters. But Ní Dhuibhne's text suggests that such threats and warnings are not confined to the rural past, or to realms of fantasy. In the contemporary setting of the midwife's tale the group of people who must have been aware of the

---

[21] The story was selected for *The Blackstaff Book of Irish Short Stories* published in 1988.
[22] Ní Dhuibhne, "Midwife to the Fairies", 30, original italics.
[23] Ibid., 32.

delivery, but kept is secret, can be accused of condoning the violence of the newborn's killing.

As in a sort of stereoscopy, the handywoman and the midwife merge into one character, inhabiting two realms: the narrative realm of the fairy tale, and the "meta-narrative" realm of her own tale. This "meta-narrative" realm is not the meta-narrative realm of the reader, but its representation in the text replicates a distinction similar to that between fiction and reality, in order to comment on the relation between the two. This narrative structure allows Ní Dhuibhne's narrator to explore how women's identities as experienced in meta-narrative reality are underpinned by the subjective identity constructed for them in a narrative tradition (the Irish folktales). The matter of who controls women's bodies' fertility is thus presented both as a private question and as subject of public negotiations. Their very treatment in the folktale tradition is evidence of the latter. Folktales can be seen as means to articulate a story whose "truths" become acceptable to all the members of a social community, functioning as means to preserve social order and the unity of the body-social. Ní Dhuibhne's text uses a particular folktale to explore how it conveys masculine authority over certain social practices that engage with women's bodies, and how this authority seeps into the meta-narrative social world. Summarising the growing critical literature on the body, Linda McDowell comments that "questions about the body, its form, meaning and its practices are associated with complicated issues about subjectivity and identity and with social practices often defined both as deeply personal and as subjects of public comment".[24] McDowell concludes that the practices that engage with bodies "are socially constructed and variable, involving changing assumptions about what is or is not 'natural' or 'normal'. They have, in other words, a history and a geography".[25] By jostling a contemporary tale against a tale from the distant past, Ní Dhuibhne uncovers a part of the historical genealogy of contemporary social myths and the social geography in which they are rooted.

A similar strategy is used more extensively in the collection *The Inland Ice*. The collection is structured using a folk story from the manuscript collection of the Department of Irish Folklore, University College Dublin, entitled "The Search for the Lost Husband".[26] Several motifs of the folktale serve as introductions to each of the stories in the collection, so that each story appears as unpacking the motifs' meanings in terms of contemporary social experiences of women as wives and lovers. This

---

[24] McDowell, 36.

[25] Ibid.

[26] See Ní Dhuibhne's acknowledgements note in *The Inland Ice*, unpaginated.

strategy helps to expose the normativity of the folktale while also pointing out the ways in which tales like "The Search for the Lost Husband" interconnect with contemporary discourses to create myths about women that naturalise constraining socialisation patterns.

For instance, the first section of "The Search for the Lost Husband" narrates how a farmer's daughter was visited daily by a goat. Eventually the daughter falls in love with the goat. After the goat stops visiting, the daughter makes enquiries and, learning which road he took, sets off to find him.[27] The story this sequence introduces, "Gweedore Girl", is the story of a young farmer's daughter, Bridget, who sets off to find work in Derry, away from her native village. Bridget fantasises her adventures using fairy-tale scenarios, such as, we infer, may have been transmitted to her by her mother (we recall her mother's keenness to be remembered as a young woman in words like "elegant" or "gallant"—evoking the fairy-tale ethos). But, even though at first Bridget, working as housemaid, sees her employers' house as a place "like the Eastern world, the shining kingdoms I knew about from old stories", she "had to work so hard there that the magic world turned into a nightmare."[28]

This nightmarish atmosphere dominates the intertextual relationship that is created between the folktale and Bridget's story. The farmer's daughter's affair with the goat is reflected in Bridget's affair with a shop boy who delivers to her employers. He promises to marry her and asks her to lend him money to prepare the wedding, but when the marriage date draws near he disappears. Elliot, the boy who woos Bridget, is described in words that remind the figure of a fairy-tale prince, "with his white face, his long fine hands, his mop of angel hair", superior by comparison with the men the young woman sees in the docks, men who "were part of their work and part of the earth, like animals".[29] Her falling in love with Elliot and her subservience to her employers is prescribed in the kind of fantasies about the farmer's daughters' fate enacted with folk stories like "The Search for the Lost Husband".

In the section of the folktale preceding the story "Love, Hate and Friendship"[30], the goat character speaks for the first time to the young farmer's daughter following him, proposing:

---

[27] Éilís Ní Dhuibhne, "The Search for the Lost Husband", *The Inland Ice*, 1. The tale continues on pages 29, 43, 61, 77-8, 103-4, 122-4, 138-9, 163-4, 179-80, 201-2, 218-19, 236-7, 259-62.

[28] Ní Dhuibhne, "Gweedore Girl", 7.

[29] Ibid., 22.

[30] Éilís Ní Dhuibhne, "Love, Hate and Friendship", *The Inland Ice*, 30-42.

'Which would you prefer? Me to be a goat during the night and a man
during the day, or a man at night and a goat during the day?

'I'd like a bit of company at night,' she replied. 'I'd like you to be a
man at night and a goat during the day.' ... They set up home in a big fine
house. And he was a goat by day and a man by night.[31]

Thus, the folktale narrative is exploited by throwing into relief questions
of embodiment and of agency: the male can choose to be embodied as
lover only half the time, a visitor in the realm of the woman's reality, the
texture of which depends on his presence. Without him, the reality
fantasised by the girl as desirable could not be materialised. In "Love,
Hate and Friendship", focusing on the relationship between Fiona, a single
woman, and Edward, a married man, the question of embodiment is right
from the beginning tied up with materialisations of social personae. Fiona
flies from Ireland to attend a conference in France believing that "if she
placed herself in a fresh environment, even for a day or two, she would
change the relationship she was having with the empirical world in
general."[32] The relationship with the world that needs changing is one in
which

Edward colonised her territory. Everywhere she looked in Ireland
reminded her of him. He had taken over every place and every object in
her life.

First he did this systematically. 'I want to know everything about you,
everything!' he said, eagerly. 'Do you have glass in your hall door? Do
you drink red or white? Do you shave under your arms?'[33]

Through her engagement in such dialogical exchanges with Edward, Fiona
surrenders to him the authorship of the fantasy through which she shows
herself to the world. The way she organises her living space, what she
drinks, how she wears her body, in sum, how she knows herself in her
relationship "with the empirical world", is now double-checked by her
partner. The theme of masculine overtaking of women's bodies together
with their social space is also addressed in another tale of masculine
seduction, "The Woman with the Fish".[34] When he visits Anna for the first
time, Michael "wanted to see everything in the house and examined
objects closely, picking up books and ornaments and observing them in the

---

[31] Ní Dhuibhne, "The Search for the Lost Husband", 29.

[32] Ní Dhuibhne, "Love, Hate and Friendship", 30.

[33] Ibid., 36-7.

[34] Éilís Ní Dhuibhne, "The Woman with the Fish", *The Inland Ice*, 220-35.

light."[35] The stories suggest that Michael's and Edward's identities are legitimated with stories like the folktale about the goat.

In "Love, Hate and Friendship", while Fiona lets herself to be known entirely, recognising her identity as that configured in her partner's desire, and thus becoming spectre to herself, Edward, like the goat in the folktale, retains "some hard and masculine characteristic at his centre, some barrier you would have to crack in order to reach him."[36] What Fiona perceives at Edward's centre can be described in Lacanian terms as the power of the phallus through which feminine and masculine desire is constituted in the realm of signification (the phallus is the signifier of desire for the Other). However, in relation to the Other, Edward's position is privileged in Lacanian terms. In the domain of law and language where the relation to the Other is arbitrated, Edward, as male, is permitted to identify himself with the authority that governs signification, whereas Fiona, to use Lacan's words, must reject "an essential part of femininity, namely, all its attributes" in order "to be the phallus—that is, the signifier of the Other's desire".[37] Hence, in a social reality defined by phallic authority, Fiona acquires a hard and polished materiality, that befits the needs of the masculine body-social. At the same time, her identity as woman as is defined by lack (of a phallic referent in her body, her own centre). In other words, as embodied presence, she is spectral to herself.

The story of the affair between Fiona and Edward takes us through the phases of her infatuation in her own recounting of their history together. In the first phase, her desire is shaped according to fairy-tale fantasies, where everything is "exaggerated and crystallised" and objects are "hard" and "polished", a wonderland of reflections—as if through Alice's looking glass—adjusted to Fiona's fantasy of herself as "haughty" fairy-tale "queen":

> First, when he loved her and she did not quite love him, she saw everything exaggerated and crystallised. Objects acquired a hard, polished look; they were like reflections in a highly buffed mirror. She moved through this looking-glass world like a high, haughty queen, letting her hand flutter along surfaces, not condescending to touch anything.[38]

This passage of the story triggers reflection on how folktales like "The Search for the Lost Husband" function to shape women's perception of

---

[35] Ibid., 229.

[36] Ní Dhuibhne, "Love, Hate and Friendship", 37.

[37] Jacques Lacan, "The Signification of the Phallus", *Écrits*, 271-80, 279.

[38] Ní Dhuibhne, "Love, Hate and Friendship", 37-8.

themselves as lovers, and of the social space this faith-full love consecrates. Having acquired a fairy tale-like identity as lover, Fiona distances from the familiar world and enters that of spectral reality, the realm haunted by ideal otherworldly creatures of mythic fantasy. The second phase is described as "the flash-of-lightening phase, the road to Damascus. The gate opens just a chink, but that is enough to eliminate everything that is ugly in the world."[39] But the promised land of fulfilled desire, access to the centre by which all desire is extinguished in blissful fulfilment, is denied. Fiona hits the impenetrable rock of her fantasy enchantment, the masculine place in whose reference the fantasy of her identity is constituted. This is the place of (imagined?) wholeness she is compelled to pursue but which is meant to remain secret if her desire is to be sustained. As soon as she attempts to conquer this centre, to hold and master the reins of desire by staking a claim on this male territory, Fiona's attempts to hold Edward "met with polite but stunning rebuffs: that hard masculine part of him was no longer a secret centre, but a suit of armour which gleamed menacingly".[40]

Fiona is denied access to the revelatory (almost sacral, it is suggested) language of male authority and power in which identity is constituted through the desire that structures her fantasy of fulfilment through erotic partnership. This reflects what happens with the farmer's daughter in the folktale. The desire that structures these women's identity as lovers is maintained by representing absence as the locus of promised revelation, a site that calls for the mythical inscription of ideals. But this is a realm continually deferred. In the folktale, the male is human only half the time, just enough to rekindle the farmer's daughter's desire with the tease that she could know him whole, and thus enter the Eden of married bliss. For Fiona, Edward's "absence was more powerful than his presence. It drained all objects and at the same time invested them with an astonishing potential to inflict pain. Trains, trees, cups and saucers stabbed her."[41] Fiona's longing for Edward may be seen as a longing for the absent male centre, a masculine investment of her desire that cuts through her body ("stabs" her) and disciplines its reality through its "astonishing potential to inflict pain". Fiona's reality is "drained", both channelled and filtered as her desire is regulated through the fantasy of love that she is called to pursue (through the compelling force of stories, we infer, like "The Search for the Lost Husband") but which she is forbidden to (co-)author. In the social reality of women lovers like Fiona, or like that of the farmer's

---

[39] Ibid., 38.
[40] Ibid.
[41] Ibid.

daughter in the folktale, the male partner is "an absentee landlord".[42] Fiona's "imagination has surrendered her places to him, territory which he certainly doesn't want. Half the streets of Dublin are in his fiefdom."[43] Fiona's relationship with herself, with her representationally silent, but not absent, body is metaphorically rendered in the closing passages of the story:

> She walks into the water. It is warm, as she hoped it would be. Not warm like a bath, of course, not even quite lukewarm, but much, much warmer than any natural water in Ireland, or any place she has been before. … It would be lovely to swim, to feel this warm soft water all over her skin, to wallow in the south, in its generosity, its blessedness. But … she has … nothing to wear except that hot grey skirt and starched blouse.[44]

Fiona's fantasy expresses her desire to inhabit her body as her own, rather than as specified through male authorship which imprisons the body in the social persona ("that hot grey skirt and starched blouse"). Fiona's intuition of her body is rendered in the imagery of the lake: the body is a place "much, much warmer" than "any place she has been before". It is akin to the woman's body as the Gweedore girl envisions it, made of "soft, hot, smelly stuff".[45] Fiona longs "to wallow" in this body-place, "in its generosity, its blessedness" but she remains corseted in her social persona.

In these stories, Ní Dhuibhne's use of folktale material in intertextual relationship with stories that depict events in the recognisable social world exposes the former as tales that govern the fantasies through which we texture the materiality of bodies and of the social spaces they inhabit. The social spaces evoked in these stories reflect the texture of masculine bodies in ways that strengthen male authority, because the tales that signify these spaces' materiality service a male-dominated gender regime.

Narrative Reconstructions of Women's Bodies and the Body-Social. Weighing Down the Masculine Tradition

Before concluding this chapter, I will further develop my analysis of the ways in which Ní Dhuibhne's stories challenge male-dominated traditions, this time emphasising the means by which her narrators reconstruct

---

[42] Ibid., 42.
[43] Ibid.
[44] Ibid.
[45] Ní Dhuibhne, "Gweedore Girl", 3.

women's identities, identities of women's bodies, and the identity of the body-social.

Women's searching of tradition for women figures that may challenge the masculine outlook of the body-social yields, as Lennie puts it in "The Flowering", "shadows on the other side of the shadowy looking-glass of the water."[46] In this story from Ní Dhuibhne's second collection *Eating Women is Not Recommended* (1991), Lennie reads about Sally Rua, "a woman who had gone mad because she could not afford to keep up the flowering which she loved". But in Sally Rua's life Lennie finds "the bare bones" of a story that is larger than that of a biography.[47] Lennie

> wants to adopt that woman ... as her ancestor. Because she does not see much difference between history and fiction, between painting and embroidery, between either of them and literature. ... The essential skills of learning to manipulate the raw material, to transform it into something orderly and expressive, to make it, if not better or more beautiful, different from what it was originally and more itself, apply equally to all of these exercises. Exercises that Lennie likes to perform. ... And if someone back there in Wavesend did not, if there was no Sally Rua, at all, at all, where does that leave Lennie?[48]

"The Flowering" challenges readers to think of the possibilities of recuperating the ethos of narrative authority on feminine terms. The overtaking of masculine authorship of women's voices is more pointedly exploited in the short story "The Wife of Bath" where the woman narrator fantasises an encounter with Alisoun, the character from Chaucer's tales.[49] Noting that Alisoun's character is shaped through masculine narrative traditions, the woman narrator indicts her: "you are just a figment of some man's imagination, and he chose to make you a nymphomaniac, a woman exploiting men, a shrew ... !"[50] But in the final scene the two women, now friends, go to swim in the waters of the Bath fountain, and as their bodies dissolve, Alisoun cries: "I was just one man's invention. I'm made of parchment. ... But you, you're real ... You better get out, get out while you have a chance!"[51] A teller of tales herself, Alisoun demands that Ní

---

[46] Éilís Ní Dhuibhne, "The Flowering", *Eating Women is Not Recommended* (Dublin: Attic Press, 1991), 7-23, 8.
[47] Ibid., 22.
[48] Ibid., 23.
[49] Éilís Ní Dhuibhne, "The Wife of Bath", *Eating Women is Not Recommended*, 89-104.
[50] Ibid., 100.
[51] Ibid., 104.

Dhuibhne's narrator reflect on the extent to which women's narrating agency is constrained by the male-generated tradition that figures women as storytellers.

In another story from *Eating Women is Not Recommended*, "Needlework", the woman narrator ponders on the extent to which she is not acceptably feminine because she is not good at knitting. When a needlework inspection takes place at school she is frightened and runs home, preferring the mother's admonishment to being socially exposed and shamed for her shabby work. But rather than admonishing her, her mother takes her on her errands and they

> did what we had never done before: we went into Thompson's Confectionery and Tea Rooms and had coffee and cream slices. Sitting in the warm, fragrant room … my mother said she would turn the heel for me that afternoon. We sipped the coffee, we munched our creamy pastry, we felt the warmth on our chapped faces. We felt comfortable and confident and powerful.[52]

The two women take refuge in a feminine world: domestic images of baking and crocheting predominate. However, this space is also recognised as a subversive social space of women's solidarity and confidence. Mother and daughter plot how to evade the disciplining judgment of the male inspector.

In "Gweedore Girl" the socialisation scenario proposed with tales such as "The Search for the Lost Husband" is reenacted in one of the girl's dreams. In the dream the scenario is denaturalised as the young woman becomes aware of the compelling force of fantasies derived from stories that script women's social roles. She dreams that she is to meet Elliot, the shop boy who, we remember, promised to marry her but disappeared with the wedding money she gave him. But before meeting Elliot, Bridget relates,

> a woman approached me and asked me to walk with her to the corner of the road. The woman was not any woman I know but she was very tall and she looked like someone I knew. My mother maybe, or some woman I see often but do not talk to.[53]

The tall woman, it is suggested, is a spectre of the mother as bearer of the tales that reveal the young daughters' path in life as destiny. Bridget "did

---

[52] Éilís Ní Dhuibhne, "Needlework", *Eating Women is Not Recommended*, 58-70, 69-70.
[53] Ní Dhuibhne, "Gweedore Girl", 27.

not want to disoblige this woman" deciding that she would try to follow her but not too far from the place of the meeting with Elliot. Thus

> I walked halfway down the road with the woman. Then I said, 'Is this far enough?'
> 'No,' she said. 'It's not far enough. You must come the whole way with me.'
> But I didn't.[54]

It is at this point that Bridget disowns the compelling force of tradition, the same force that makes the farmer's daughter follow the goat in "The Search for the Lost Husband". Thus, Bridget gains a new perspective on the archetypal mother:

> I looked at the woman. She was lying on the ground. I picked her up. She had turned into a piece of paper. She was a large cut-out doll, drawn in heavy black ink, with an old ugly face like a witch. She was folded in two on the ground and I opened her up and spread her out and read her.[55]

Here, Bridget is shown as taking charge of the contexts that wall her into her fate as lover. The heavy black ink of so many reiterations of the same story is recognised as contouring the archetypal mother as a witch. Perhaps, as Marina Carr put it, recalling her own childhood representations of the witch figure, the witch "was Time. Time we didn't understand or fully inhabit, and yet we respected and feared her. And fell away humbly under her spells and charms and curses."[56] Not humbled, Bridget frees herself from the spell of time and finds an empowering identity. About her new partner she can say "I know I can marry him any time I want to."[57] But the fairy-tale fantasy still haunts her: "Elliot was gone and I had to run after him, as in all my dreams about him, knowing I could not catch him again that night, but that I would meet him, some other night, in some other dream."[58] Bridget recognises the compelling force of the folk and fairy-tale tradition to shape her longings in her dreams.

The force of male-generated fantasies that form young women's desire for the kind of love prescribed in folk and fairy tales is also felt by Clíona, the main woman character of "Swiss Cheese", when she remembers her first love:

---

[54] Ibid.
[55] Ibid., 27-8.
[56] Marina Carr, "Introduction", *Plays One*, x-xi, x.
[57] Ní Dhuibhne, "Gweedore Girl", 28.
[58] Ibid.

He dived, that night, into her dreams. And there he stayed, all that lovesick summer, and for several years afterwards, a secret hidden in the darkest depths of her imagination, while she studied and played, danced, even dated other boys. She did not think of him constantly, but as the shadowy king of her imagination, he held his sway.[59]

But in another story, "Sweet Sacrament Divine", such fantasies are appropriated as the possible substrate of private rituals of women's initiations, cherished but at the same time cautionary, rituals that may function in the same way as the patriarchal rituals of the Church, but that may obtain a different social world in which being in love is

> not like a marriage. Contracts, property, everyone involved. It's not ceremonious like that, being in love. It's all private and confidential. Like confession.
>   And it's mysterious. Like transubstantiation. And intoxicating. Like Benediction.[60]

The body-social obtaining in this world would be the transubstantiation of an intensely living body, like the one Bronwyn imagines would lie beneath the quiet images of the two lovers in the Uppsala cathedral.

In *The Inland Ice*, the force of tradition that guides women's fantasising their identities is exposed through using the folktale that presents the trials of a farmer's daughter in search of a husband. These trials reflect social imperatives through which the young daughters in a storyteller's audience are disciplined as future wives. This disciplining forms the fantasies through which the daughters must show themselves to themselves and to the world. These fantasies guide their understanding of their presence in the world, shape the ontological mould of their bodies, and offer scripts for their socialisation. *The Inland Ice* is structured using folktale sequences as cues for stories developing and elaborating its motifs in order to investigate how they linger into the fantasies through which we show ourselves to the world. In this process, Ní Dhuibhne's narrators read new meanings into the folktale, challenging its ideological load.

This narrative technique is also used in "The Mermaid Legend" from *Eating Women is Not Recommended*.[61] Here, another Irish folktale is used in juxtaposition with the contemporary story of a woman who marries

---

[59] Éilís Ní Dhuibhne, "Swiss Cheese", *The Inland Ice*, 140-62, 153.
[60] Éilís Ní Dhuibhne, "Sweet Sacrament Divine", *Eating Women is Not Recommended*, 71-88, 87.
[61] Éilís Ní Dhuibhne, "The Mermaid Legend", *Eating Women is Not Recommended*, 169-75.

after an enchanting courtship. In the folktale, the man lures a mermaid into becoming his wife by hiding her cloak. Without her cloak, the mermaid cannot return to the sea—her body place. But one of the couple's children sees where the man hid the cloak and once the mermaid learns where it is she takes it and returns to the sea, never to be seen again. The mermaid's flight is punished through the separation from her children she must endure.[62] In the story of the contemporary married couple, unhappy with a relationship in which the male partner takes her for granted, the woman eventually leaves him and their children. But in the contemporary story, the narrator reclaims authority over her socialisation scripts:

> There is such a thing as access, yes sirree, there is. Even in Ireland, that's legal. It must be. A mother can't be kept from her children. So no more thinking and worrying. ... Action. You're ringing them at eleven thirty sharp and making a definite arrangement.[63]

The ethos of the mermaid legends, widely spread in Ireland, is shown as legitimating masculine authority, and reflects a patriarchal gender regime. Ní Dhuibhne's tale suggests that this ethos may still function to regulate women's identity as wives and mothers in Irish society, and calls for women readers to become aware of the legal mechanisms that they can use to challenge deeply engrained patterns of social life.

In the same spirit of challenge to the regulatory power derived from the folktale tradition, the reconstructed ending of "The Search for the Lost Husband", serving as conclusion to the stories in *The Inland Ice*, reveals a woman empowered to occupy the position of authority that also grants her the rights of authorship over the reality stories materialise. After the farmer's daughter defeats the witch's spell thus saving the goat and his mother, the handsome young man the goat has become announces:

> 'And now ... we can get married, and live happily ever after.'
> The girl looked at him. 'I don't think I want to,' she said. 'You have led me a merry dance, up hill and down dale, and through briars and brambles and bracken and thorns ... I'm tired, running around in circles, chasing you to the ends of the earth.'
> 'But you love me! You can't live without me! You've proved it by your ... dauntless passion!'

---

[62] Ibid., 175.
[63] Ibid., 174.

'I am weary of ardent ways. ... I'm going home ... . And maybe I will find another husband ... . Because it's time for me to try another kind of love. I'm tired of all that fairytale stuff.'[64]

The story ends with the handing over of the voice of authorship to women. Throughout the stories of the collection, we have heard the male-generated voice of the folktale speaking through, and dominating, the voices of the women characters, shaping their perceptions of themselves and of the body-social, of their materiality and texture. At the end, we hear a female voice distinctly articulated, a voice capable of mastering the identity of her self and of her social reality on her own terms. Here as well as in the other stories, Ní Dhuibhne's writing urges us to seek an opening up of reality in ways that break with the familiar horizon of awareness in whose circle women had been hitherto constituted as objects in the orbit of, and subject to the pull of, the male centre. This "breaking orbit" also entails a re-creation of the fantasies which blend bodies into the reality of the social world. Ní Dhuibhne's women may thus write like Emily from the story "Estonia", who "could write in her head, in her blood, in her heart. In her sleep. And she did—it was as necessary as breathing to her, if not as easy."[65]

The analyses of Kennedy's work helped us to understand a concept of voice that acknowledges heteroglossia as a productive means to add to reality through stories, as opposed to understandings of voice as a means to subject reality. This opening to heteroglossia could help us fantasise more empowering identities. The analyses of Lochhead's work showed that this recuperation of narrating agency is not easy to accomplish, as subjects struggle with identity constructions transmitted from the past through myth, folk and fairy tale as well as through traditions that canonise versions of these. These traditions can be disseminated world-wide, or can be specific to a socio-cultural domain. Lochhead's take on themes from the male-generated folk and fairy-tale tradition offers insight into how this tradition functions in Scottish socio-cultural contexts, answering to concerns that stem from local specificities. The analysis of Bourke's work helped us to introduce the specificities of Irish culture, smoothening the passage to the analysis of Ní Dhuibhne's writing. With Bourke, we have also moved on to a more emphatic analysis of how myths affect understandings of women's bodies. Ní Dhuibhne's work offered the opportunity to examine how understandings of features of the body-social are mirrored in one's own understanding of her/his body, and how myths

---

[64] Ní Dhuibhne, "The Search for the Lost Husband", 261-2.
[65] Éilís Ní Dhuibhne, "Estonia", *The Inland Ice*, 181-200, 187.

become incarnated through socialisation. With the analyses of Marina Carr's work, we will return to the concept of voice, to further develop the idea of opening up to heteroglossic interference as a tactic for destabilising monoglossic discursive regimes. The first of the last two chapters will examine to what extent heteroglossia can be productive or as deadening as monoglossic discursive regimes. In the final chapter, we will take this analysis further in order to show the difficulties of transcending the normative and confining subject positions that prescribe not only specific identity configurations, but the very possibility of identity.

CHAPTER TWELVE

HAVOC, BADNESS, AND BLOOD SPILLAGE.
SAMENESS AND DIFFERENCE
IN MARINA CARR'S *LOW IN THE DARK*,
THE MAI, AND *PORTIA COUGHLAN*

In the Introduction to *Plays One*, Marina Carr remembers staging dramatic plays when she "was a scut" and concludes that "we loved the havoc, the badness, the blood spillage, but loved equally restoring some sort of order and harmony. Ignorantly, we had hit upon the first and last principles of dramatic art."[1] In Carr's plays, the representations of a certain order and harmony are wrecked, violated, and taken apart. But although "havoc", "badness", and "blood spillage" certainly occur, sometimes they are eventually resolved into some kind of new order and harmony. In this chapter, I will explore to what extent Carr's plays confront an order and harmony that is characteristic of social myths and of ideologies' dissemination as social myths. I will also explore to what extent the "havoc, badness, and blood spillage" of her plays are effects of opening the order and harmony of the reality stitched together with myth, to heteroglossia. I am interested in how this opening can be seen as a discursive strategy creating conditions for reinterpretations of social myths and raising new awareness of how women's identities and modes of agency as lovers and wives are shaped by social myths.

Low in the Dark opens with a narration by Curtains, whose name and costume (she is completely covered in curtains and rail) suggest an authorial persona. She narrates the first encounter between man and woman in a story that evokes the *illo tempore* of mythic first beginnings:

> **Curtains** Before they ever met the man and woman had a dream. It was the same dream. The woman dreamt she came up from the south to meet the man from the north. It was the same dream. The man dreamt he came

---

[1] Carr, 'Introduction', *Plays One*, ix-x.

down from the north to meet the woman from the south. It was the same
dream with this difference...[2]

The theme of the meeting between man and woman is central to the three
plays examined here. While *Low in the Dark* is more directly concerned
with stereotypes of domestic fulfilment, dreams or fantasies of the meeting
between man and woman derived from the Irish mythological tradition
form the interest of *The Mai*.[3] In *Portia Coughlan* we again find a blend of
both.[4] The main characters of the plays, The Mai, Curtains, and Portia
Coughlan are women "looking for the magic thread" that, as The Mai's
daughter put it, "would stitch us together again".[5] Although Millie, the
storyteller character of *The Mai*, refers specifically to The Mai's situation
as abandoned lover, her words are suggestive of all these women's quest
for a story, "a magic thread", that would "stitch together" an ordered and
harmonious universe where man and woman share the same dream.

Curtains' speech in the above passage, "It was the same dream with
this difference...", suggests a framework of interpretation for the plays in
terms of concepts of sameness and difference. Sameness perhaps
guarantees a harmonious mythic universe while difference wreaks havoc
in the orderly spaces of myth. We can develop this framework using
Cohan and Shires' definition of discourse as telling that is not simply "the
concrete realisation of a master system": "Since discourse is the domain of
actual language use, it stabilizes and conserves the system in which it
operates, but it also continually revises the system to allow for new
conditions by which meanings are produced."[6] This revision, the authors
insist, applies not only as regards grammar, orthography, and vocabulary,
but may also produce "new ways of thinking".[7] Carr's plays engender new
ways of thinking by bringing to the surface of discourse the undercurrents

---

[2] Carr, *Low in the Dark*, 7. *Low in the Dark* premiered on 24 October 1989 at the
Project Arts Centre, Dublin, in the interpretation of the Crooked Sixpence Theatre
Company. It was first published in 1990. I am using the version published in *Plays
One* in 1999. See Marina Carr, *Low in the Dark, The Crack in the Emerald: New
Irish Plays*, ed. David Grant (London: Herne, 1990), 63-140.

[3] *The Mai* premiered on 5 October 1994 at the Peacock Theatre, Dublin. It was first
published in 1995. I am using the version published in *Plays One* in 1999. See
Marina Carr, *The Mai* (Meath: Gallery, 1995).

[4] *Portia Coughlan* premiered on 27 March 1996 at the Peacock Theatre, Dublin. It
was first published in the same year. I am using the version published in *Plays One*
in 1999. See Marina Carr, *Portia Coughlan* (London: Faber, 1996).

[5] Carr, *The Mai*, 111.

[6] Cohan and Shires, 17.

[7] Ibid.

running in the deep of dominant narratives that convey social myths. Social myths stabilise and conserve legitimate sense-making processes, mastering the swirls of contrary impulses and the tendency of their expression to dissolve master meaning systems into an ungovernable, carnivalesque spectacle of signification.[8] I defined social myths as being engendered through successive narrative reiterations of set sense-making patterns, which come to govern one's presentation of oneself to oneself and to others in social spaces. Playing havoc with the "stack" of layered narratives that engender norms, Carr's drama unleashes the regenerative forces of heteroglossia. Thus, heteroglossic havoc is an effect of discursive strategies that make a difference by instigating audiences to rethink the sameness of social myths that script identity and modes of agency.

Sameness

In this section I will show that Carr's plays critique the normative character of myth and cultural tradition by emphasising the sameness of the patterns they legitimate, which filter into the fantasies through which we acquire identity.

In *Low in the Dark*, the first scene of Act One introduces, after Curtains' speech, the characters Bender and her daughter Binder. Bender portrays schematically the role of the mythic mother burdened with the attribute of procreation. Having just given birth she casually remarks: "After the first million you get used to it."[9] This excess (during the scene she gives birth twice) suggests a stereotypical rendering of the archetypal mother, a taking to extreme of the schematic role attributed to her in myth. The ironic juxtaposition of the realms of myth and of social reality foregrounds the impossibility of fulfilling mythic attributes in social roles. However, although Bender and Binder seem capable to reflect in their attitude the irony resulting from this juxtaposition, they are also shown as dreaming to inhabit a realm that obtains through a fusion between mythic and mundane realities. Sarahjane Scaife notes that *Low in the Dark*, as well as the later plays, evince a preoccupation with women who "are

---

[8] I am referring to Bakhtin's "carnivalesque", but with an added ingredient. The phrase "spectacle of signification" contains an allusion to Guy Debord's definition of society as a spectacle understood as "a social relation between people that is mediated by images." In my view, this social relation can be constraining and normative, but also carnivalesque, germinating regenerative potential. Guy Debord, *Society of the Spectacle*, trans. Ken Knabb (Oakland, CA: AKPress, 2005), 7.

[9] Carr, *Low in the Dark*, 9.

obsessed with the artistic or the romantic, the notion of 'the story' that is separate from the here and now."[10] For Bender and Binder, the possibility of fulfilling mythic attributes in social roles is engendered by popular culture. For instance, they are shown as fervent readers of the *True Romance* magazine.[11]

Millie, the storyteller in *The Mai*, also reports the romance clichés circulated in stories about Grandma Fraochlán's life, through which Grandma Fraochlán constructs her identity:

> She was known as the Spanish beauty though she was born and bred on Inis Fraochlán, north of Boffin. She was the result of a brief tryst between an aging island spinster and a Spanish or Moroccan sailor—no one is quite sure—who was never heard of or seen since the night of her conception. There were many stories about him … . Whoever he was, he left Grandma Fraochlán his dark skin and a yearning for all that was exotic and unattainable.[12]

This almost mythical encounter between a man and a woman is often recounted in Grandma Fraochlán's stories. Clare Wallace notes that Grandma Fraochlán's language "is a curious mixture of heavily accented Connemara English tempered with the sentiments of popular romance. In addition, her frequent use of the word 'sublime' is replete with associations with English Romanticism, and coupled with her opium habit, serves to align her with escapism and the imagination."[13] For Anthony Roche, "what Grandma Fraochlán has to offer is stories, drawn from her 'ancient and fantastical memory'."[14] In *The Mai*, the yearning for the exotic and unattainable reality forged in stories haunts not only Grandma Fraochlán, but also her daughter, Ellen, and granddaughter, The Mai. The power of fantasy harnessed to the creation of mythologizing stories about one's identity is a central concern in all the three plays that form the interest of my analysis, with each play offering different lens for examining the manifestations of this power.

---

[10] Sarahjane Scaife, "Mutual Beginnings: Marina Carr's *Low in the Dark*", *The Theatre of Marina Carr: "before rules was made"*, 1-16, 12.

[11] Carr, *Low in the Dark*, 9, 72.

[12] Carr, *The Mai*, 115-6.

[13] Wallace, "Authentic Reproductions", 62.

[14] Anthony Roche, "Woman on the Threshold: J.M. Synge's *The Shadow of the Glen*, Teresa Deevy's *Katie Roche* and Marina Carr's *The Mai*", *The Theatre of Marina Carr*, 17-42, 37-8.

In *Low in the Dark*, Act One, Scene Two, Baxter and Bone, Curtains' and Binder's lovers, rehearse a scene of domestic order and harmony.[15] Their dialogue indicates that the purpose of this rehearsal is to re-enact for Bone a fantasy of his encounters with his lover, Binder. Baxter, acting the woman, knits and cooks buns, Bone's favourite dish. This display of conventional traits of domestic life highlights the stereotypical character of husband and wife identities. But our attention is drawn to the iterability of this scenario, to how it has shaped Bone's expectations of domestic order and harmony, when he is shown to be angered by Baxter's refusal to continue to play the role assigned to the wife:

> **Baxter** (*real Baxter, throws down the knitting*) I'm fed up of this! ...
> **Bone** (*determined to finish the scenario ...*) I do everything to please you!
> *He waits for the response from Baxter. None is forthcoming. He forces the knitting into Baxter's hand, annoyed.*
> Yes you do, darling.
> **Baxter** Yes you do, darling!
> **Bone** And I love you for it!
> **Baxter** And I love you for it.
> **Bone** How would you like some tea?
> **Baxter** How would you like some tea?
> *Bone knocks off Baxter's hat.*
> You always end it like this!
> **Bone** You always force me to! If you'd just say what you're supposed to say.
> **Baxter** (*taking off women's clothes and shoes*) Women don't talk like that!
> **Bone** That one did![16]

In Bone's insistence we see the force of his fantasy of domestic bliss compelling him to reiterate the enactment of a stereotypical social scenario. When the reiteration is challenged Bone attempts to reconstitute it as best he can, frustrated at the prospect of losing control of the deictic force of discourse, of its ordering power.

This ordering power seems to be firmly wielded by Grandma Fraochlán in *The Mai*. Her fantasies of lovers' bliss are expressed using patterns from romance tales derived from the folkloric tradition:

> Remember the Cleggan fair, me nine-fingered fisherman, we went across from Fraochlán in the currach ... Remember, Tomás, remember, and you told me I was the Queen of the ocean and that nothing mattered in the wide

---

[15] Carr, *Low in the Dark*, 16.
[16] Carr, *Low in the Dark*, 19.

world, only me. And we danced at the Cleggan fair and you whispered in me ear—sweet nothins—sweet nothins.[17]

Grandma Fraochlán's memory, haunted by myth, is shown here as the vehicle of forceful reiterations. Reiterating versions of the past, Grandma Fraochlán suggests a few pages later, enables an inescapable force. Revealing her belief that Robert, her granddaughter's husband, will eventually leave her because he left her before and because, in similar circumstances, Robert's father left his mother, she dismisses his attempt to tell a different story by saying "we can't help repeatin', Robert, we repeat and we repeat, the orchestration may be different but the tune is always the same."[18]

Reiterations of prescribed and prescriptive scenarios also occur throughout *Low in the Dark*, but here these scenarios are more emphatically shown as stereotypical. Baxter and Bone re-enact, in Scene Three, a similar scenario to that enacted in Scene Two. Then, when he is with Binder, his lover, Bone attempts to enact the scenario he had been rehearsing, but Binder has a different scenario of married bliss in mind. Eventually, the two versions of married bliss mismatch because each emphasises grossly outlined traits of femininity and masculinity, that is, the kind of stereotypes one finds in magazines like *True Romance*:

Binder ... I want a house with a bath and a man in it and a baby, all together, all for ever, all for me.
Bone I want a permanent relationship for a month or two, and sure who's to say the third month would be the death of us? Are you happy?
Binder No I'm not!
Bone I want a woman who knows how to love. I want laser beams coming out of her eyes when I enter the room. I want her to knit like one possessed. I want her to cook softly.
Binder I want a man who'll wash my underwear, one who'll brush my hair, one who'll talk before, during and after. I want a man who'll make other men look mean.[19]

Thus, both Bone and Binder are looking for a partner designed in the image of soap TV-like transpositions of fairy-tale princesses and princes. Bone seems to dream of a domestic angel perpetually enamoured with him, "laser beams coming out of her eyes" when he enters the room; he also wishes for a woman who knits like one possessed, a modern day

---

[17] Carr, *The Mai*, 121.
[18] Ibid., 123.
[19] Carr, *Low in the Dark*, 48.

Rumpelstiltskin, or perhaps a Cap o'Rushes who knows how "to cook softly". As regards himself, Bone prefers the role of the adventurer, who remains free to move on after a "permanent relationship for a month or two". On the other hand, Binder is seeking a man whom she assembles in her fantasy from such masculine traits as can be found in women's magazines ("one who'll talk before, during and after"), tele-novellas ("a house with a bath and a man in it and a baby, all together, all for ever, all for me") and masculine characters from B-type films ("a man who'll make other men look mean"). Elsewhere we find Binder's mother dreaming of a lover in the image of the stereotyped romantic stranger: "Salvatore… foreign…yes I know it means saviour, and your last name? Di Bella…The Beautiful Saviour…that's lovely, that's really lovely…"[20] Or, when Binder relates her meeting with Bone, she departs from reality and escapes into a realm of fairy-tale fantasy that blends Celtic and Greek motives in an epigonic rendering of the declamatory style of romantic ode:

> **Binder** (*with feeling*) We walk through the trees and the moon…the moon was there … We were looking at it through the lake.
> *Music on at this stage.*
> … Did you know that Fionn MacCumhail hunted on these very mountains?
> … That this lake is called Pallas Lake, named for Pallas Athene who swam here once.[21]

In the meantime, Curtains, who has been striving to find correlatives for her mythic story of the encounter between man and woman in the events of the lives of the other characters that she witnesses, finds it increasingly difficult to recompose a mythic order and harmony. The dream falls apart. As her tale spirals toward disintegration, her voice collects the readymade pieces dropped in the superficial enactments of sketchy outlines of human relationships the other characters' fantasise compelled by forces of the mass culture, of the excessively reproduced cliché, of endless reiteration that turns everything banal. Using these, the characters construct walls to fence out each other's worlds. They wall themselves in into their own fantasies. Bone's obsession with Binder's cooking buns for him is a translation of her fertility into the comfortable geography of kitchen work, displacing the womb with the oven. Again and again, Bone and Binder hang on to their fantasies and their dialogical exchanges end in communication breakdown, poising discursive deictic forces against each other, but failing to inhabit each other's worlds:

---

[20] Ibid., 65.
[21] Ibid., 36.

Binder ... I'd love to get a man pregnant ... He'd arrive home shaking.
'Well, what's up' says I...
Bone Darling, you know when you make buns?...
Binder I'm pregnant,' he says...
Bone The temperature has to be just right...
Binder 'Are you?' says I, giving him a level look...
Bone Has to be 150 degrees...
Binder 'Yes', he whispers, 'must've got caught'...
Bone And you have to pre-heat the oven...
Binder 'And whose the mother,' I'd say, kind of harsh...
Bone For fifteen minutes exactly...
Binder 'Need you ask,' he'd say and the tears would start...
Bone Otherwise they don't taste the way they should.
Binder 'OK! OK,' I'd say, 'I'll stand by you for what it's worth, but I'm
not promising anything, now dry your eyes.' Another bun?[22]

Curtains finds it difficult to tell a story that makes sense of such tensely
intersecting fantasies, a story that could serve to stitch these fantasies
together as shared worldview. Attempting to relate the story of the meeting
between man and woman Curtains manages only a bricolage made up of
commonplace motifs of Irish and world mythic stories, reflecting the
missed encounters she witnesses:

Curtains So the man and woman walked, not speaking unless spoken to,
which was never as neither spoke. Going along the path in this amiable
fashion they came upon a woman singing in a ditch. 'Sing us your song,'
the man said. The woman sang.

In Salamanca I mislaid my daughter,
In Carthage they killed my son,
In Derry I lost my lover,
In this ditch I've lost my mind.

'You've ruined our day,' the man said ... [T]he woman ... turning to the
woman in the ditch ... asked, 'Is there anything we can do except help
you?' The woman did not reply. So the man and woman hit her and moved
on.[23]

In this passage, one (miss)recognises the mythic figure of mother Ireland,
a Cathleen ni Houlihan whose sons and daughters belong not only to the
four provinces of Ireland, as in Yeats's play, but perhaps to the four

---

[22] Ibid., 47.
[23] Ibid., 45.

corners of the world.[24] Yet this is a goddess whose song of loss appears anachronistic: the man and the woman seem exasperated by her grievances when they say "Is there anything we can do except help you?" The encounter with mother Éire fails because it occurs in a realm outwith the orderly harmonious spaces of nationalist myth. The woman in the ditch can also be seen as a reflection of Bender, in her role as mundane version of the mother goddess, who dreams of a Spanish sailor and feels most comfortable in the bathtub, the ditch where she keeps producing offspring mindlessly. Unlike the solemn goddess of the fairy, as Yeats portrayed Cathleen ni Houlihan, Bender is the tragicomic goddess of the house. Her character echoes the stereotypical mistress-of-the-house figure fashioned in soap opera.

In another place, Curtains' story records the man and woman's encounter with three men who crucify three women. A parody of the scene of Jesus' crucifixion, Curtains' rendering portrays the woman on the middle cross frantically asking for vinegar. Her sacrifice goes unrecognised and martyrdom is refused. The woman whose travel Curtains had been tracing is faithlessly ironic when she offers to help: "Would wine do?"[25] This is a universe of death, where the monotony of sterile reiteration of stereotypical scenarios yields but a semblance of life in the characters' insect-like scurrying about, "low in the dark".

A similar kind of death wears out Portia Coughlan; the reiteration of a domestic scenario of stifling banality makes her feel as if living in a coffin:

> **Portia** These days I look at Raphael sittin' opposite me in the armchair. He's always tired, his bad leg up on a stool, addin' up the books from the factory, lost in himself, and I think the pair of us might as well be dead for all the joy we knock out of one another. The kids is asleep, the house creakin' like a coffin ... Sometimes I can't breathe anymore.[26]

Constraining scenarios of domestic life are also explored in *The Mai*. Using a comparative analysis framework, Anthony Roche traces what we may call a chain of reiterations in four different texts, with each text altering the previous (and the original) narrative scripts. The scenario of a tale of an unfaithful wife by the Aran Island storyteller Pat Dirane is reiterated by J. M. Synge in his play *The Shadow of the Glen* (1903), and

---

[24] W. B. Yeats, *Cathleen ni Houlihan, Modern Irish Drama*, ed. John Harrington (New York: Norton, 1991), 3-11.

[25] Carr, *Low in the Dark*, 50.

[26] Carr, *Portia Coughlan*, 207.

can be detected in Teresa Deevy's play *Katie Roche* (1936) and in Carr's *The Mai*.[27] The reiterated scenario is that of an adulterous affair between a woman caught in a stifling marriage and a young man.

Roche explores how each reiteration changes elements of the previous version. If the folktale enlists the audience's sympathy in favour of the cheated husband, reinforcing the legitimacy of a male-dominated gender regime, Synge's play shifts the focus towards the woman's condition, highlighting her limited range of choices and the dullness of a monotonous life controlled by her husband. However, Roche points out, any freedom for this woman remains connected with possibilities of association with a male: she can only escape from her marriage by accepting the protectorate of another man, the Tramp who promises her freedom. Deevy's play develops Synge's emphasis on the social norms that define the identity of wives while at the same time tracing their imbrication with conventional romance paradigms. Both Katie and her older husband, Stan, nourish romantic dreams, but their realms of fantasy are far apart. When at the end of the play Stan, cast as a substitute for Synge's Tramp, announces that he will take Katie away, we realise that she will become a prisoner of his fantasy. As Roche puts it, she is taken "to a life that is the virtual extinction of her person."[28] Thus, Roche concludes, "Deevy's ending resists the romantic allure of 'away'" characteristic of Synge's or Yeats's plays.[29]

Roche goes on to argue that the role of the Tramp in Carr's *The Mai* is fulfilled by Grandma Fraochlán, whose figure offers "a matrilineal line of support and continuity rather than a substitute patriarchy."[30] In my view, this reconstruction of the Tramp figure serves to indicate that the realm The Mai longs for is made possible, to an extent, by the romantic lure of the "away" to which Grandma Fraochlán wholeheartedly surrenders, while at the same time showing that The Mai's longing is governed by conventional romance paradigms, as with Katie Roche in Deevy's play.

For The Mai, the otherworldly "away" is ultimately beyond words; yet words, that is, stories, myths, and legends, including their conventionalised narrative presentation in the Irish folk and literary tradition, are the only means to make otherworlds amenable to the imagination. However,

---

[27] J.M. Synge, *The Shadow of the Glen* in *The Playboy of the Western World and Other Plays*, ed. Ann Saddlemyer, (Oxford: Oxford University Press, 1995), 13-26; Teresa Deevy, *Three Plays: Katie Roche, The King of Spain's Daughter, The Wilde Goose* (London: Macmillan, 1939).

[28] Roche, 35.

[29] Ibid.

[30] Ibid., 38.

otherworlds recede as soon as they are fancied because fantasies are narratable, and otherworlds cannot withstand the sense-making power of discourse. Subjected and consenting to being signified through tales derived from discourses of myth, The Mai gains a social self trough the concrete realisation of her dream of domestic bliss, the house she is building. But at the same time, her ineffable longing for a mythic lover carries her away into the otherworld of a truer self perhaps, an otherworld that has receded with the building of the house that was meant to be its concrete realisation. For The Mai, there is the Robert of her heart's desire, and Robert the mundane (and inadequate) husband. The scenario of Pat Dirane's tale of the adulterous wife is difficult to discern in Carr's play, because the inadequate husband figure and the desired lover figure delineate a single character, even though the lover figure belongs in an otherworld, whereas the husband is of the real world.

Roche observes that The Mai is not "fully contained by the house she has built."[31] At the end of the play, we are left with the impression that she has crossed over into the realm of myth, leaving a changeling in her place. What reality (or materiality) is conferred to this realm through Grandma Fraochlán's stories, or through the stories of any traditions, is but a remarking of its alterity, to employ a Derridean perspective. This remarking makes access to the realm of myth a route through a never ending maze of the imaginary where one may lose one's self, becoming an otherworldly subject; and thus, becoming even more a subject to the power engendered through the stories or realities that invoke the realm of myth. The character of The Mai that we see on stage inhabits the social world held together by a social myth, even though we intuit that her self may be wandering into the otherworld of myth.

On the other hand, since the otherworldly lover and the realm The Mai longs for are, in part, products of folk and literary traditions, when The Mai fades into her otherworld she may be merely exchanging the social prison with a prison of the mind. Thus, Carr's play explores both the stifling conventionalism of domestic life, *and* the role of narrative conventions, and generally of any sense-making structures, in foreclosing the otherworlds which stories and dreams summon to the imagination.

Within the world contoured in the narrative of the play, these conventions are borne through flights of fantasy yielding stories such as those used by Grandma Fraochlán to hold Ellen and The Mai spellbound within the horizon of an unattainable reality. However, at meta-narrative level we become aware that such flights of fantasy take off from folktale

---

[31] Ibid., 40.

scripts; we become aware of the conventions of an established tradition. One tradition, and its conventions, of which we become aware is the folktale tradition; another is the literary tradition in which the use of folktale scripts has become a convention. This convention can hold characters, writers, and audiences spellbound within the cultural horizon dominated by a Yeats or a Synge. Its twilight zone is a threshold where one is compelled to find the realm of one's heart's desire on Yeats's or Synge's terms for instance. In Carr's play, The Mai is compelled to find this realm on Grandma Fraochlán's terms. In the meta-narrative world the audience/readers struggle with the established literary tradition which conditions their response to the otherworlds invoked in the play. On both narrative and meta-narrative levels, the compelling force of tradition that engenders sameness is made perceptible. However, as the audience/readers of the play empathise with The Mai, they, like The Mai, are also compelled to have faith in the difference the realm of heart's desire can make.

In the programme note to *The Mai* presented at the Peacock Theatre in 1994, Tom Mac Intyre writes that the play is "the stuff of romance, story-telling and a mode of survival, and also, story-telling as a mode of escape from demanding imperatives."[32] In my analysis, the demanding imperatives are created through social myths that, yielding conventional patterns and ideologies, engender realms of monoglossic sameness. The afflicting sameness explored through different lens in each of Carr's plays analysed here is the sameness of the stereotype in *Low in the Dark*, the sameness of patterns of the folktale in *The Mai*, and predominantly, the patterns of othering engendered in both the "pagan" folktale tradition and in the Christian tradition in *Portia Coughlan*. However, while the three plays focus on stories and storytelling as means to strengthen the conventionalism of social norms, they also explore how stories and storytelling may be used as means to challenge the imperatives engendered by these norms. In the following section I will explore to what extent the latter may be achieved through enabling stories and storytelling as fields of heteroglossic interferences, intersections, and encounters of voices that speak against the traditions that hitherto confined them within monoglossic domains of discourse.

---

[32] Tom Mac Intyre, "Where Your Treasure Is: *The Mai*", Programme Note, Peacock Theatre, 1994.

Difference

In the following, I will argue that the antidote Carr's plays offer to the sameness that burdens one's fantasising identities is heteroglossia. In *Low in the Dark* the meaning of the encounter between man and woman that Curtains seeks to stabilise through a story reiterating the order and harmony of myth is rendered unstable and unpredictable. Curtains' story moves away from patterns of social myths when she lets it be shaped by the voices of the other characters, taking in their doubts, dilemmas, and mundane commentary, as for instance the following exchange:

> **Curtains** Then the woman turned to the man and said, 'How many lovers have you had?' 'One,' the man answered. ...
> **Bender** The danger has passed.
> **Binder** Really? Only one?
> **Curtains** 'One,' the man answered, 'one and all the rest.'
> **Bender** Let him torture himself a little ... then just when he's beginning to doubt himself, say, you're such a beautiful man darling...
> **Binder** What did he mean by 'one and all the rest'?
> **Curtains** 'Ah yes, one,' the woman replied.
> **Bender** Beautiful man always throws them! ... Let him come to terms with it, there's time. ... Then say it again, you're such a beautiful man darling.
> **Binder** and **Bender** So hairy! ...
> **Curtains** ... 'Ah, yes, one,' the woman said, 'one is all one ever has, the rest come too early or too late.'[33]

Here we see how Curtains' effort to recompose a story of an ordered and harmonious universe of the encounter of man and woman is hindered by Bender and Binder's interventions that cast the encounter as burlesque. They do so by introducing the commonplace "wisdom" they seem to have gathered from the stock of the familiar and conventional hearsay shaped in the cheap romance and thrillers vehiculating to excess the stereotypical renderings of myth.

Here and throughout the play mythic order and harmony are unsettled by heteroglossia. However, the heteroglossia enabled in *Low in the Dark* is not a productive one, that is, one that could provide support for an empowering reconstruction of myth. The opening up of the myth through the invasion of the popular and the carnivalesque produces fantasies that verge on the absurd, because the myth patterns are overloaded with stereotypes. The inoculation of myth with cliché supra-saturates it with

---

[33] Carr, *Low in the Dark*, 33-4.

banality. In an atmosphere that reminds us of James Joyce's "The Dead"[34] the storyteller's voice seems paralysed; having lost the power of myth to provoke epiphanic revelation, Curtains' rendition of the man and woman's story sounds like a typical Irish idyll, a lullaby luring her audience into deadly sleep:

> 'My love,' the man said to the woman, 'let's make hay before we're snowed in altogether.' 'Certainly we'll make hay *a stor mo chroi* [love of my heart]', the woman replied. For the woman loved the man and the man loved the woman.[35]

Myth is dismantled but what is left in its place is no less stifling: the characters find themselves "low in the dark" uncertain if they are dead or alive. When Bone speculates, "suddenly terrified", that the women are out to kill him and Baxter, the latter replies that he thinks they already have.[36]

However, the reiteration of dreams that are not shared, therefore enabling a deadly heteroglossia, need not lead to paralysis of human relationships.[37] In *The Mai*, the eponymous character longs for a realm of lovers' bliss, a longing instilled in her heart and mind by her grandmother. The Mai herself seems somehow unaware that her fantasies govern her social reality. She struggles to re-create in her house an almost mythic space of a mythic lovers' embrace, but her dreams of death reflect her intuition that this could also be a realm extinguished out of reality. When her husband, Robert, who had left her, returns to this house, he suggests that obsessive dreams need not spell out death, but the realisation of the need to challenge the foretold destiny. Robert's understanding that dreams are "coy, elusive things" allows him to recuperate agency[38]. When a different story than that spelled out in dreams derived from myths can be told, a healthy heteroglossia can overturn a myth's proclamation of fate. Matt O'Brien notes that Robert is able to escape, "in his own way, the dangerously impossible world that Mai and Grandma Fraochlán have

---

[34] James Joyce, "The Dead", *Dubliners: Text and Criticism*, eds. Robert Scholes and A. Litz (New York: Penguin, 1996), 175-224.

[35] Carr, *Low in the Dark*, 57-8, original italics and brackets.

[36] Ibid., 98.

[37] In this, Carr's aesthetic can be compared to that of Beckett. According to Melissa Sihra, "Beckett's aesthetic similarly contemplates the journey towards death (as the dominating impulse from the moment of birth), yet it centres around the act of *being*, and how each of us negotiates the journey that is life." Melissa Sihra, "Reflections Across Water: New Stages of Performing Carr", *The Theatre of Marina Carr*, 92-113, 112.

[38] Carr, *The Mai*, 125.

constructed for themselves."[39] This cannot happen for The Mai, whose dreamed fantasy of lovers' bliss is spoken in a voice that shares a social myth of marriage based on fantasies that echo the mythic union of gods and goddesses. Much like Grandma Fraochlán, The Mai fantasises herself in the image of a fairy child or goddess from the Irish stock of folktales, a constraining fantasy:

> I'm a child walking up a golden river and everything is bright and startling. At the bend in the river I see you coming towards me whistling through two leaves of grass—you're a child too—and as you come nearer I smile and wave, so happy to see you ... .[40]

This is perhaps the same kind of dream that animated Grandma Fraochlán's fantasy of lovers' bliss, the same "tune" in spite of a different narrative "orchestration"[41]. It is eventually revealed that Grandma Fraochlán made The Mai's mother, Ellen, marry against her wish. But when Ellen's husband "left her to rot on Fraochlán", Grandma Fraochlán belittled him "till Ellen grew to hate him" and "at the same time she filled the girl's head with all sorts of impossible hope" of personal achievement; "Ellen adored her and looked up to her and believed everything she said, and that's what killed her, not childbirth, no, her spirit was broken."[42] The longing Ellen's (and The Mai's) vision of herself picks up is the same kind of longing that makes Grandma Fraochlán say:

> if you're one of them lucky few whom the gods has blessed, they will send to you a lover with whom you will partake of that most rare and sublime love there is to partake of in this wild and lonely planet. I have been one of them privileged few and I know no higher love in this world or the next.[43]

However, in handing this intense, almost hierophanic, because mythic, vision of love to The Mai, Grandma Fraochlán has also created it as an impossible achievement. Grandma Fraochlán wishes mythic love to materialise as reality and embeds that longing, "always fillin' our heads with stories and more stories", in the fantasies of personal identities and modes of agency of her descendants. But this is also why The Mai is

---

[39] Matt O'Brien, "Never the Groom: The Role of the Fantasy Male in Marina Carr's Plays", *The Theatre of Marina Carr*, 200-214, 211.

[40] Carr, *The Mai*, 126.

[41] Ibid., 123.

[42] Ibid., 145-6.

[43] Ibid., 143.

gradually refined out of concrete reality and into a shadowy realm of myth.

When Millie tells the tale of the Night Hag or Pool of the Dark Witch we realise that The Mai had made herself a character in the tale. The Witch is the old woman who killed Robert in The Mai's dream, Grandma Fraochlán. The story of the missed encounter between Bláth and Coillte is the story of the missed encounter between Robert and The Mai. It is the impossibility to communicate with her lover, under The Witch's spell, that makes Coillte cry until the lake in which she drowns is formed. On another level, it is the impossibility to communicate with a lover fathomed in the depths of myth, and made more real than Robert to the Mai by Grandma Fraochlán's stories (which thus, in a sense, killed him), that drowns The Mai into the otherworld of myth made up of her own longings.

Elsewhere, Millie describes the relationship between The Mai and the princess child that used to visit her during the time The Mai worked in a luxury hairdressing salon in the following words:

> The Mai and the princess were two of a kind, moving towards one another across deserts and fairytales and years till they finally meet in a salon under Marble Arch and waltz around enthralled with one another and their childish impossible world. Two little princesses on the cusp of a dream, one five, the other forty.[44]

Thus, the play suggests two ways of relating to tradition. One way of relating to it is by reducing its heteroglossic dimension to normative, monoglossic discourse, as Grandma Fraochlán does. But this implies a paralysis of dialogue with the myth tradition that forecloses the possibility of the myth's heteroglossic celebration. Eventually, Carr's play suggests that only by listening to heteroglossic voices may the regenerative power of myth be used to recuperate order and harmony that is not necessarily normative.[45] As Millie puts it:

> A tremor runs through me when I recall the legend of Owl Lake. I knew that story as a child. So did The Mai and Robert. But we ... in our blindness moved along with it like sleepwalkers along a precipice and all around gods and mortals called out for us to change our course and, not listening, we walked on and on.[46]

---

[44] Ibid., 153.

[45] Thus, to use Augustine Martin's words in this context, Carr breaks with the conventions of realism "in pursuit of a purer sense of reality." Augustine Martin, *The Genius of Irish Prose* (Cork: Mercier, 1985), 112.

[46] Carr, *The Mai*, 148.

The passage suggests that myths can be both empowering and constraining. If taken in blindly, they can lead to deadening patterns and stereotype. But if one listens to the voices that enable a dialogue between gods and mortals, one can avoid falling into the abyss of loneliness that separates one from one's self and from those others who can instil life in the self through stories that help fantasising it in new configurations.

The staling of human relationships caused by falling under the spells of myths, the reiterated versions of which engender constraining socialisation patterns marked by sameness and stereotype, is also signposted throughout *Low in the Dark*. At one point Curtains' tale registers the communication breakdown between the man and the woman of her story, and the lack of authenticity in their illusory coming together:

> **Curtains** They agreed to be silent. They were ashamed, for the man and woman had become like two people anywhere, walking low in the dark through a dead universe. There seemed no reason to go on. There seemed no reason to stop.[47]

One is reminded of the voice in Beckett's *The Unnamable* trapped in the either/or of "I can't go on, I'll go on."[48] Discussing one actor's initial difficulties in playing Curtains' character, caused by the requirement to be shrouded in curtains, Scaife notes Beckett's influence on Carr's strategies that allow "the actor to create a distance from the words in order for them to exist in the mind of the audience long after the show is over."[49] With reverberating force, Curtains' lines quoted above entice us to ask: is there any hope in this sterile universe? Wreaking havoc in the orderly realms of mythic fantasy by submitting a coherent mythic story to heteroglossic intervention transforms the deictic force of discourse that holds reality in a certain kind of unifying harmony into entropic force. Competing and conflicting discourses transform the monological space of ideological proclamation into dialogical negotiation. Yet what if the dialogue is itself deadened by stereotype? Is this carnival of the absurd profitable? In a crucial sequence of the play we find the characters struggling to give meaning to the encounter of the man and woman, each contributing a piece to a puzzle that may somehow re-create the fantasy of a harmonious and coherent whole:

---

[47] Carr, *Low in the Dark*, 59.

[48] Samuel Beckett, *The Unnamable* (London: Calder, 1958).

[49] Scaife, 15; see also 13-14. For Carr's own comments regarding Beckett's influence on her writing see Marina Carr, "Dealing with the Dead", *Irish University Review* 28 (1998): 190-6, 195.

Curtains Then the man got up one morning and looked out of his window. 'It's time', he said to himself, 'that I started riding.' So he got up on his bicycle...
Bone Can I?
Curtains Certainly you can.
Bone So he got up on his bicycle and he rode all over the Earth, he cycled over the sea...he cycled over the sea... (*Forgets*)
Bender For it was a sturdy bicycle. One evening as he was flying over the highways, he saw the woman in his path.
Bone 'Get out of my road,' he yelled!
Binder But she would not, he said it again, louder this time...[50]

When Curtains stirs everybody to repeat the man's demand, she seems to conduct an experiment in irony: in the power of the chorus thus enabled we recognise a coercive force of pressure akin to that of ideological declamations. Yet Binder insists on her point:

Curtains Everybody.
All 'Get out of my road,' he yelled!
Binder Still the woman would not move.[51]

As the dialogue develops further Baxter summarises metaphorically the recurring themes of the play: will this meeting between the man and the woman be yet another missed encounter, a violent reiteration of guidelines that clears the way for re-creating socially (as Bone does) the patterns and hierarchies of myth? Or will this be a real encounter, a starting point for reconstructing the relationships between men and women, as Binder seems to propose? Baxter suggests both possibilities. When Curtains eagerly enquires what the significance of the contrasting options might be, Bone seems to miss the point; Curtains then suggests a continuation of the story that endorses the scenario of a genuine, rather than missed, encounter. But Bender hijacks the story to make it express the impossibility of fruitful dialogical exchange between the man and the woman, a reflection of her own experience of the male's inability "to give". So Curtains patiently records the resumption of the familiar pattern of missed encounters:

---

[50] Carr, *Low in the Dark*, 26. The imagery of bicycles recalls Flann O'Brien's narrative actors in *The Third Policeman* who ride bicycles in an universe of the dead, low in the dark, but unaware of it. Flann O'Brien, *The Third Policeman* (Champaign, IL: Dalkey Press, 1999).
[51] Carr, *Low in the Dark*, 26-7.

Baxter 'I've two choices,' the man said to himself, 'I can knock her down or I can stop.' In fact he did both.
Curtains Which proves?
Bone Which proves that the bicycle is streets ahead of the human mind.
Curtains 'You!' she said. 'If you have courage get off your bicycle and come with me! I've...'
Bender 'I've nothing to give,' the man said. 'Don't worry,' the woman replied, 'I've learned how to steal.'
Curtains So the man and woman walked. [52]

As this heteroglossia drowns communication in reassertions of stereotypes and soap opera conventions, Curtains can't help but sketch a story of irreconcilable oppositions: men and women have never really met. Towards the very end of the play Curtains thus summarises the story she has found:

Before they ever met the man and woman had a dream. It was the same dream with this difference. The man dreamt he met the woman north by north east. The woman dreamt she met the man south by south west. Long after it was over, the man and woman realized that not only had they never met north by north east or south by south west, much worse, they had never met. And worse still, they never would, they never could, they never can and they never will. [53]

In the overall architecture of the play, the significance of this passage is connected to the idea that language, when it is deadened by patterns and stereotypes derived from myth, cannot serve as vehicle of genuine communication.

While *Low in the Dark* indicts the use of any myth to fantasise identity and agency, *The Mai* challenges only the normative use of tradition, leaving open the possibility of creative engagement with myth and fairy tale. In *Portia Coughlan*, however, the challenge is mounted against the conventionalism derived from corroborating dreams of achieving social status and Christian morality. The Irish Celtic tradition is seen as a means to challenge the ideology of domestic fulfilment that uses the Christian myth to legitimate, for Portia's father, perhaps also for Raphael, their drive for achieving social status through accumulating wealth. Instead of indicting the Irish folktale tradition, this play sees it as a means to achieve the regeneration of a community that can be anywhere in contemporary Ireland, marred by the invasion of mercantilism that trivialises everything.

---

[52] Ibid., 27.
[53] Ibid., 99.

The play indicts a culture that has lost the ability to achieve order and harmony through using myth imaginatively and uses it instead to legitimate constraining norms. The stone troubles the living stream.[54] Fintan dismisses the folktale related to the toponymy of Belmont River:

> **Fintan** … wasn't it about some auld river God be the name of Bel and a mad hoor of a witch as was doin' all sorts of evil around here but they fuckin' put her in her place, by Jaysus they did.
> **Portia** She wasn't a mad hoor of a witch! And she wasn't evil! Just different, is all, and the people round here impaled her on a stake and left her to die. And Bel heard her cries and came down the Belmont Valley and taken her away from here and the river was born.[55]

Portia, who often wanders by the river, haunted by the ghost of her twin brother Gabriel, seems to share the fate of the witch in the tale, punished by the community of people driven by materialistic concerns, imprisoned in the socio-geographic spaces that mimic Christian propriety but thrive on material gain. Dismissing the myth, the community of people here have dismissed the possibility of obtaining a map for spiritual regeneration. Portia is torn between the dullness of this dying world and the vitality of that spelled out in the myth. In his note to the play presented at the Peacock Theatre in 1996, Mac Intyre notes Portia's "mythic force" and her "quest compulsion" for "that which is lost", a force and compulsion that make everything become a sign.[56] In my view, that which is lost, and which Carr's play signposts, is the regenerative power of myth. In a sense, with Portia's suicide by drowning, the play depicts the death of the regeneration goddess, as it indirectly refers to the Celtic festival Beltane, dedicated to the union between the god and the goddess that guarantees the regeneration of nature in spring. When lifted from the river, Portia is shown as a kind of spring goddess, *"dripping water, moss, algae, frogspawn, waterlilies, from the river"*.[57]

A similar suggestion regarding creative, rather than normative uses of myth is made in reference to the Christian tradition. When Portia tells Raphael why she had married him, we realise that Portia has been making

---

[54] See Yeats's poem "Easter, 1916". For the significance of "stone" and "living stream" in Yeats's work see Edna Longley, "The Rising, the Somme and Irish Memory", *The Living Stream*, 69-85, 83; and "Introduction: Revising 'Irish Literature'", 63.

[55] Carr, *Portia Coughlan*, 219.

[56] Tom Mac Intyre, "*Portia Coughlan*", Programme Note, Peacock Theatre, 1996.

[57] Carr, *Portia Coughlan*, 223.

a continuous effort to reconcile feelings for which she had been provided conflicting cultural maps for loving and being loved:

> **Portia** I seen you long before you ever seen me ... and the stillness and sureness that came off of you was a balm to me, and when I asked who ya were and they said that's Raphael Coughlan, I thought, how can anyone with the name like that be so real, and I says to meself, if Raphael Coughlan notices me I will have a chance to enter the world and stay in it, which has always been the battle for me.[58]

The sense of a heteroglossic marriage of mythic traditions is suggested through the ontological flicker this passage provokes. We are not sure if Portia is of this world or that of the fairy, or whether she hasn't been the fairy all along, battling to enter the real world. A certain order and harmony may germinate in this heteroglossic interaction of mythic discourses, an order and harmony that, in answering Portia's ontological doubts, would also provide means for using myth to heal social relationships. In the ambiguous dialogue between Senchil and Portia earlier in the play, "the shadow ones" can equally refer to social "failures" (as Senchil describes himself) and to haunting fairy people:

> **Senchil** ... Never met a body yet as didn't want to leave a mark, some sign, however small, that they was on the earth at a point in time. Be some as leave a good mark, some as leave a bad one, we shadow people leave ne'er a mark at all.
> **Portia** Would ya say I'm one of the shadow ones?
> **Senchil** No—But even if ya were, you'd still be necessary, a necessary backdrop for the giants who walks this world and mayhap the next.[59]

Thus, we infer, the repudiated tradition is a necessary backdrop to the dominant ones through which men and women fancy themselves in the shape of giants who walk this world, "mayhap", with the Christian God on their side. The endorsement of a negotiation between mythic maps is seen as a means to heal social rifts, and give a voice to the "shadow ones"—the alienated "failures" of the social community.

Carr's plays record the missed encounters between the men and the women constrained through the monological rendering of fantasies derived from various myths turned into ideologies through excessive reiteration that ossifies myth. In *Low in the Dark* the various voices give but the illusion of dialogue; they are distorted by cliché and stereotype. In *The*

---

[58] Ibid., 255.
[59] Ibid., 246.

Mai the characters' voices are but alienating monologues of longings inculcated by a storytelling tradition that has become normative and constraining. In *Portia Coughlan* the call for dialogue falls on ears deafened by the loudness of monological proclamations of faith. In her review of the 1996 performance of the play at the Peacock, Medb Ruane finds that "Portia Coughlan is all about speaking the unspoken".[60] In my view, the unspoken is that which has been repudiated through stifling reiterations that consolidate social rituals setting up confining social geographies, especially that of the home, where dialogical exchanges are illusory: they are simply monologues requiring the interlocutor's consent, monologues pitched against each other.

However, Carr's plays also test mythological tales against the forces of imaginative heteroglossia, thus steering the tales away from ideological control and on the terrain where the social myths they convey can be revised. All three plays are concerned with the sameness of the dream derived from myth, but also with how this dream can be dreamed with a difference. In *Low in the Dark*, Curtains manages in the end to shape into a story "the same dream" but with "this difference":

> **Curtains** … One day the man looked out of his window. 'It's time,' he said. So he got up on his bicycle and he rode all over the earth and he cycled all over the sea. One evening as he was flying over the highways he saw the woman in his path. 'Get out of my road,' he yelled, but she would not. 'I've two choices', the man said, 'I can knock her down or I can stop.' He did both. 'You,' she said, 'if you have courage get off your bicycle and come with me.'[61]

We recognise in Curtains' story elements of the myth of the encounter between man and woman that she narrated at the beginning of the play. But after opening that story to heteroglossia, accommodating the divergent, carnivalesque, and burlesque voices through which that myth is vehiculed in expressions of clichéd and stereotyped fantasies, the story looks different; it revises the myth by allowing new conditions for interpreting its meanings. A similar discursive strategy is employed in *The Mai* and *Portia Coughlan* which likewise enable new conditions for meaning production by urging the plays' audiences to assess the heteroglossic potential inherent in dialogical exchanges, through which myths may be revised. There is "the havoc, the badness, the blood spillage" of heteroglossia but there also emerges "some sort of order and

---

[60] Medb Ruane, "Shooting from the Lip", *Sunday Times*, 31 March 1996.
[61] Carr, *Low in the Dark*, 99.

harmony"[62] that belongs in an illuminating, sometimes hopeful, reconstruction of the social myths through which we learn our identities and modes of agency.

---

[62] Carr, "Introduction", x.

CHAPTER THIRTEEN

THE LAND OF WITCH'S HEART'S DESIRE. ONTOLOGICAL FLICKERS IN MARINA CARR'S *BY THE BOG OF CATS...*

In the previous chapter's discussion of the problematics associated with the use of heteroglossia to open up monoglossic discursive regimes, I highlighted the threat that submitting a text to heteroglossic intervention might pose: the entropy of heteroglossia may be as deadening as the force of patterns and stereotypes, if in breaking the latter it does not also recuperate a sense of order and harmony. In this chapter, I will focus on the problematics associated with the deconstruction of the subject. Desirable as the undoing of subjection appears, there are dangers attending one's efforts to transcend subjective identity. I will explore these dangers through the analysis of Carr's play *By the Bog of Cats...*, raising a number of questions and providing partial answers regarding the ontological status of the realm yielded through desubjection.

Brian McHale argues that postmodern historical fiction creates "ontological flickers" between worlds represented through official records of events and apocryphal versions of these: "one moment, the official version seems to be eclipsed by the apocryphal version; the next moment, it is the apocryphal version that seems mirage-like."[1] We are no longer sure which world is the subject's ontological "home".

Marina Carr's *By the Bog of Cats...* is centrally concerned with the characters' struggle to find a "home". Hester Swane, a traveller woman, and her lover from the settled community, Carthage Kilbride, had been living together in a caravan, nourishing hopes to join the settled community.[2] But although they built a farm next to the caravan site together, Carthage decides to leave Hester and marry Caroline, the

---

[1] Brian McHale, *Postmodernist Fiction* (New York: Methuen, 1987), 90.
[2] *By the Bog of Cats...* premiered on 7 October 1998 at the Abbey Theatre, Dublin. It was first published in the same year. I am using the version published in *Plays One* in 1999. See Marina Carr, *By the Bog of Cats...* (Meath: Gallery, 1998).

daughter of wealthy farmer Xavier Cassidy. However, Hester's and Carthage's efforts are not only directed toward acquiring a physical home; they are also invested in a struggle to settle ontological domains through competing definitions of subjective identities—the homes of the self. These definitions are derived from histories legitimated with canonical myths that evoke "official" versions of Irish identities, but also from apocryphal versions of these. The superimposition of the two discursive registers yields a carnivalesque world of heteroglossic entropy. In the following analysis I will show that Carr's play provokes ontological flickers that unravel the texture of realities whose threads are citational chains: reiterations of discourses that become normative and constraining.[3] These chains stabilise the subject's ontological domain, but this domain can be unsettled through provoking ontological flickers that make regulatory discourses amenable to heteroglossic intervention. This unchaining is costly: the subject becomes ontologically homeless. In this context, I will argue that the subject position constructed for the main character of the play, Hester Swane, is a projection in the world of the text of the narrator/director's position: both are chained through the reiterative force of discourses channelling the power of various myths; both break these chains, but then find themselves ontologically homeless.

Rosi Braidotti, theorising the concept of nomadic subjectivity, explains that:

> The nomad does not stand for homelessness, or compulsive displacement; it is rather a figuration for the kind of subject who has relinquished all idea, desire, or nostalgia for fixity. This figuration expresses the desire for an identity made of transitions, successive shifts, and coordinated changes, without and against an essential unity.[4]

However, Braidotti explains, "the nomadic subject ... is not altogether devoid of unity; his/her mode is one of definite, seasonal patterns of movement through rather fixed routes. It is a cohesion engendered by repetitions, cyclical moves, rhythmical displacement."[5] This kind of unity might provide an alternative ontological plane as a "home" for nomadic

---

[3] According to Derrida, the textual formulations of utterances are "identifiable as *conforming* with an iterable model", "identifiable in some way as a 'citation'". Derrida, "Signature Event Context", 18, original italics. Judith Butler emphasises the normative and constraining character of citational chains. Butler, *Bodies That Matter*, esp. 1-4 and 12-16.

[4] Rosi Braidotti, *Nomadic Subjects* (New York: Columbia University Press, 1994), 22.

[5] Ibid.

subjects. In Carr's play this is precisely the kind of "home" Hester seeks. But such transcendence of fixity cannot be disconnected from the painful ontological homelessness that befalls a subject daring its internal prescribed unity. Indeed, exploring Hester's fate, Carr's play shows that "home" is also a dimension of interiority provided through various traditions through which one may know one's self.[6] The subject's fixity is not only the property of an external position that one may choose to occupy by consenting to be signified as subject; this fixity is also the subject's internal condition of existence.

Judith Butler argues that a subject is constituted "through the force of exclusion and abjection, one which produces a constitutive outside to the subject, an abjected outside, which is, after all, 'inside' the subject as its own founding repudiation". Butler's argument points out that in order for a subject to become legitimate, it must be defined against a fantasy of the abject that is seen as "the defining limit of the subject's domain." According to Butler,

> The abject designates here precisely those 'unlivable' and 'uninhabitable' zones of social life which are nevertheless densely populated by those who do not enjoy the status of the subject, but whose living under the sign of the 'unlivable' is required to circumscribe the domain of the subject.[7]

In Carr's play, the realms where the Swane women wander are seen as uninhabitable zones of social life by those who need to define those realms as unlivable in order to gain the status of legitimate subjects. But, more emphatically, Carr's play explores the otherness at the heart of the subject, how the "abjected outside" is "after all, 'inside' the subject as its own founding repudiation."[8] Hester's ontological homelessness is connected to the (un)inhabitability of one's own self; it points towards a subject whose interior domain is not/no longer homely.

---

[6] Frank McGuinness points out that Carr is "a writer haunted by memories she could not possibly possess, but they seem determined to possess her." *The Dazzling Dark: New Irish Plays*, ed. Frank McGuinness (London: Faber, 1996), ix. Wallace comments on Carr's "engagement with origins and ontology" arguing that, in her plays, "destiny is articulated and implied on multiple levels through naming, genealogy, memory and storytelling." Wallace, "Authentic Reproductions", 60. See also Clare Wallace, "Tragic Destiny and Abjection in Marina Carr's *The Mai, Portia Coughlan* and *By the Bog of Cats...*", *Irish University Review* 31 (2000): 432-49.

[7] Butler, *Bodies That Matter*, 3.

[8] Ibid.

Hester's ontological fantasies cause her to drop in and out of reality, alternatively enchanted and disenchanted by the spells of myth seething in the vibration of her fantasies. Various traditions bespeak themselves through Hester (as well as through the narrator/director), compelling their citation and reiteration.[9] Hester's (and the narrator/director's) predicament is that she must sometimes struggle with them in order to free herself; but at other times she celebrates them for the same reason. Through these ontological flickers between legitimate and illegitimate realms of the subject, Carr's play unsettles ontological domains in ways that expose the repudiations through which legitimate identities and social locales are constituted, while also highlighting the imbrication between these internal and external domains of the subject.

In the following section, I will focus on the "otherworlds" and on the social worlds Carr's play evokes, in whose realities Hester's (and the narrator's) ways are threaded. In the final section, I will explore how the intersections of the two bring into relief, as in a curious stereoscopy, the otherworldly space of homeless subjects.

Otherworlds

The opening scene of Act One is a telling introduction of the character Hester Swane in conversation with a Ghost Fancier. In the opening sequence, he watches Hester trailing "*the corpse of a black swan after her, leaving a trail of blood in the snow.*"[10] The imagery of the scene references elements of Celtic mythology: the black swan leaving the red mark of blood on the white snow reminds us of Deirdre's story.[11] During her imprisonment in the king's castle, Deirdre sees a black raven drinking the blood of a slain calf on the white snow and wishes for a lover with black hair, red cheeks, and white skin. Imprinted in such imagery, patterns

---

[9] Scaife asks "Do we just, as seems an overriding theme in Marina's work, keep repeating the appalling patterns of human behaviour despite our attempts to the contrary?" Scaife, 13.

[10] Carr, *By the Bog of Cats*, 265.

[11] For a translation of the medieval Gaelic version, see "The Exile of the Sons of Uisliu". Swan figures are central in the Celtic tradition. See "The Dream of Óengus", a continuation of the opening episode of another story, "The Wooing of Étaín". In "The Dream of Óengus", a fairy bride is wooed by Óengus, himself the child of a powerful god of the Síde race (or fairy people). Their union is only possible when they both assume the shape of swans. See "The Exile of the Sons of Uisliu", "The Dream of Óengus", and "The Wooing of Étaín" in *Early Irish Myths and Sagas*, 257-67, 108-112, and 39-59 respectively.

of myth reverberate in the play's themes of longing, suicide, and sexual desire.

We also find references to Yeats's re-creation of the ethos of Classical myth. Yeats's "Leda and the Swan" envisions Leda's rape as an event leading to the violent birth of civilisation.[12] In Carr's play, Hester, like Yeats's Leda, is "mastered by the brute blood of the air", but Jupiter's role is fulfilled by her mother, symbolically constructed as a swan with the powers of a goddess. Like Jupiter in Yeats's poem, the mother-goddess figure both subjects and empowers Hester. The world of the settled community Hester enters through her union with Carthage can be seen as inaugurated by "a shudder in the loins" that is not a powerful male's doing, but her own. Regarding Carthage, Hester claims: "It was in my bed he slowly turned from a slavish pup to a man and no frigid little Daddy's girl is goin' to take him from me."[13] Here, and throughout the play, Hester is shown as challenging the masculine gender regime of the settled community farmers. But, unlike Yeats's Leda, she is the black swan of Greek myth, a Medea who also avenges Leda.[14]

However, such revisions of feminine identity are not necessarily seen as empowering in Carr's play. When Hester tells that she found the swan "frozen in a bog hole last night, had to rip her from the ice, left half her underbelly"[15], she sounds as if she is describing yet another rape, by herself, on herself. The bog field can be compared to the field of meaning of a tradition (that of song and tale where Hester's mother belongs, and to where Hester must disappear if she wants to follow her) that imprisons its subjects in frozen stances. Using the swan-goddess powers given to her by her mother's tradition is, in the end, also a kind of subjection. To exercise the powers of the swan goddess is to reiterate the symbolic rape which produces the subject of cultural memory and legend (albeit in a different configuration than that envisioned by Yeats). In meta-narrative perspective, the Ghost Fancier may be read as a surrealistic representation of the narrator or storyteller who creates subjective identities through conveying the power of a tradition in his/her tale, be that a narrator like Yeats or like Hester's mother (or like Marina Carr). When she is visited by the ghost of her brother, whom she had killed, or when she conjures up her

---

[12] W.B. Yeats, "Leda and the Swan", *Collected Works*, 218.

[13] Carr, *By the Bog of Cats*, 266.

[14] For a detailed analysis of Carr's use of the Medea figure, and of Greek tradition in general, see Wallace, "Authentic Reproductions", 58-60.

[15] Carr, *By the Bog of Cats*, 266.

mother's image, we are tempted to see Hester herself as a Ghost Fancier.[16] We can also read the introductory passage of the play as referencing the Anglo-Irish revivalist "love affair" with ghosts of the Celtic past, while providing sarcastic commentary voiced by a character who might be a revivalist ghostly construction herself.

Thus, the play's introductory scene uses elements of mythic interest that have been central in the Irish literary tradition. The representation of the swan provides opportunities for establishing references to various stories derived from myths, from retellings of the medieval story of "The Dream of Óengus" to Yeats's interpretation of Greek myth. But the story Carr's play assembles out of these stories destabilises the narrative patterns derived from myths through interpolations between mythic scripts. The ensuing heteroglossia causes the ontological harmony and order of myths to flicker: myth is thus returned to the ground zero of the carnivalesque and the absurd. Only in this space of polyphonic voices can the myth's social value be transacted and remade. Whereas canonical writers like Yeats would have ideologised myth, Carr's play restores the myth to its social function as a negotiation of ontological horizons.

What are we to make of Hester in this topsy-turvy world? We can read her in many ways: as a wanderer on the Bog of Cats, she may even be cast as a tutelary goddess of the land. When Hester describes her bond with Carthage we sense an invocation of the strength of the sovereignty goddess figure: "Love is for fools and children. Our bond is harder, like two rocks we are, grindin' off of wan another and maybe all the closer for that." And "Carthage Kilbride is mine for always or until I say he is no longer mine."[17] In this reading, Carthage appears, ironically, as fulfilling the part of a sovereign who repudiates Hester's otherworldliness for the worldly arrangements that guarantee him a wealthy farmer's royalties. However, Hester's composure as subject of myth derived from ancient traditions or of new myths of personal fulfilment through accumulation of wealth legitimated by the inheritors of these traditions, who have used

---

[16] Yeats's words from "To Ireland in the Coming Times", where he fantasises himself as a conjuror of ghosts, could equally characterise Hester: *"the elemental creatures go/ About my table to and fro,/ That hurry from unmeasured mind/ To rant and rage in flood and wind;"*. W. B. Yeats, "To Ireland in the Coming Times", Collected Works, 46, original italics.

[17] Carr, *By the Bog of Cats*, 269. According to Celtic traditions, a king could not be instituted as sovereign without the ritual union with the tutelary goddess of the land. See, for instance, Gantz's analysis of the Gaelic word "feis". Gantz notes that this word, which designates a "feast", is derived from the root of a verb meaning "to sleep with". *Early Irish Myths and Sagas*, 269.

them politically and then decanted them to obtain a purer vision of legitimate social order on their own terms, is disrupted through heteroglossia and polyphony. Because of such disruptions, Hester's ontology flickers between different fantasies of reality. As she puts it, she lives "in a house, though I've never felt at home in it".[18] Hester is homeless, migrating between subjective (and subjecting) worlds; not only a traveller in terms of social categories, she is, in mythic terms, a wandering goddess left homeless because outcast from people's fantasies, now structured around dreams of material gain.

At the same time, Hester Swane often mocks the mythic worlds where we are enticed to place her. Thus, her character is neither revealed fully as that of a goddess nor decidedly shown as that of a mortal woman. We may glimpse her as the wandering ghost of the women figures myths construct. In Carr's play, the ontological solidity of women, established through myths, is dissolved through the reiteration of their construction in different contexts so that canonical ways of women's narrative presentations are uprooted from their legitimating contexts. The authority of myth is thus undermined, and with it the ontological stability of the locale delineated through discourses derived from myths.

The citational force of myth is rendered in the play with the suggestion of inescapable circularity of fate. Both Hester's mother and her daughter bear the same name (Josie Swane) and in Act One, Scene Two we hear little Josie singing Hester's mother's song, as if rehearsing her life's scenario. However, when Hester kills little Josie, at the end of the play, we may understand the tragic dimension of this drama not only as a resumption of the condemning pattern of fate, but perhaps also as a liberation from it through the resurrection of an alterity hitherto denied. On a meta-narrative level, the condemning pattern of fate is the citational chain of discourse that constrains the possibilities of narrative expression. In its otherworldliness, Carr's carnival of voices challenges these constraints, producing a narrative of insubordinate transgressions and appropriations.

Locked in otherworlds of sorts, the Swane women share the shadow nature of the goddesses of fairy realms. This sharing both empowers their opposition to the constraining identity patterns conveyed in the myths of the settled community and disempowers their ability of staking a claim on the social territories defined through these myths. In *By the Bog of Cats...* we become acquainted with two kinds of communities: the community of travellers, to which Hester belongs, and the community of settled people,

---

[18]Carr, *By the Bog of Cats*, 266.

in which Carthage was born. In both communities their members' identities appear to be shaped through disciplinary modes of self-knowledge.

Hester's identity is partly shaped by a tradition of folk and fairy tale that would have constituted a dominant medium of socialisation in the travellers' community. Indeed, Hester is shown to be a close acquaintance of the Catwoman, with whom she visits regularly. The Catwoman is introduced in Act One, Scene Three, as "*a woman in her late fifties, stained a streaky brown from the bog, a coat of cat fur that reaches to the ground, studded with cats' eyes and cats' paws. She is blind and carries a stick.*"[19] The passage contains a reference to Teiresias, the blind prophet of Sophocles' tragic drama *King Oedipus*, the significance of which I will come back to shortly.[20] I will comment on the significance of this reference shortly. The Catwoman character shares several features with cats represented in traditional Irish folktales.

In her studies on representations of fairies in tradition and literature, Katharine Briggs invokes evidence from a wide range of sources, including Lady Wilde's highly popular folktales collection *Ancient Legends, Mystic Charms, and Superstitions of Ireland* (1888), to show that cats "in Ireland at least, are regarded almost as fairies in their own right".[21] Indeed, in Carr's play, we hear the Catwoman speaking the words of a spirit of the land when she says: "I know everythin' that happens on this bog. I'm the Keeper of the Bog of Cats in case ya forgotten. I own this bog."[22] The opening to myth occasioned by these lines is challenged in Hester's ironic reply: "Ya own nothin', Catwoman, except your little house of turf and your hundred-odd mousetraps and anythin' ya can rob and I'm missin' a garden chair so ya better bring it back."[23] Hester refuses to let herself be disciplined through the authority of the folktale tradition. Yet it is in the register of folktale that Hester's fate is foretold by the Catwoman when she recounts a vision in which the black swan "puts her wing on me cheek and I knew this was farewell."[24] Later, the Catwoman's story of Hester's fated relation to the swan clearly reflects folktale patterns:

---

[19] Ibid., 271.
[20] Sophocles, *King Oedipus*, *The Theban Plays*, trans. E. Watling (London: Penguin, 1974), 23-68.
[21] Briggs, 85-88.
[22] Carr, *By the Bog of Cats*, 271.
[23] Ibid.
[24] Ibid., 272.

Sure the night ya were born she took ya over to the black swan's lair, auld
Black Wing ya've just buried there, and laid ya in the nest alongside her.
And when I axed her why she'd do a thing like that with snow and ice
everywhere, ya know what she says, 'Swane means swan.' ... 'That child,'
says Josie Swane, 'will live as long as this black swan, not a day more, not
a day less.'[25]

In spite of Hester's repeated rejection of tradition and superstition, her fate
remains connected to the otherworldly swan. The reiteration of this
connection reveals the permanence of certain contexts through which the
self may be fantasised. The context referred to through the use of the swan
figure is that provided by the Irish folktales' tradition. However, another
context is evoked with the reference to the blind prophet whose role is
here fulfilled by the Catwoman: the context provided by Greek myth and
its sense of tragedy. Two contextual iterative forces are thus blended so
that Hester is positioned at the intersection between the register of Irish
folktales and that of Greek tragedies.

The two discursive registers coerce the narrator/director's discourse
through the imposition of dominant narrative patterns. How can Hester's
story be told to an audience educated, in Revivalist spirit, to regard highly
Greek tragedy and Irish drama based on folktale without recourse to these
legitimate patterns? Carr's play, thus, offers opportunities for reflecting on
the disciplinary effects of reiterable narrative patterns rooted in contexts
that can't be done away with, challenging audiences' holding on to
patterned ontologies. With the ironic employment of an Irish folktale
character (the Catwoman) for the role of a character in a prestigious
dramatic tradition (the blind prophet) both patterns are defamiliarised in
ways that expose, on the one hand, the iterability, and, on the other, the
arbitrariness, of legitimising traditions.

Summing up research in feminist theory and cultural studies on the
universalising effects of narrative acts, Janice Carlisle concludes that "if
acts of narration exert their power by creating patterns of 'order' and
'shape', such power is often exerted only at great cost to those excluded
from or deformed by the construction of such meanings."[26] In Carr's play
we find traces of the exclusionary and distorting force of patterns of order
and shape on two levels. Within the fictional world set up through
narrating, mythic patterns of order and shape are exposed as distorting
Hester's character by interfering with her attempts to home herself
ontologically. Narratives of the self that echo the Celtic mythic tradition

---

[25] Ibid., 275.
[26] Janice Carlisle, "Introduction", *Narrative and Culture*, 1-12, 4.

and narratives of self devised in myths of social success through economic wealth, interfere with each other and hinder Hester's attempt to construct a coherent ontological schema. Being denied an ontological schema through which she may grasp the connectedness between self and world, Hester becomes, in various ways, an impossibility. On a meta-narrative level it is the distorting force of literary traditions that the play's narrator/director confronts, attempting to find an ontological angle for narrating the universe of meanings taking off from the margins of these traditions.

But even though, in both the narrative and meta-narrative worlds, things seem to be falling apart, a certain kind of harmony is achieved in this discursive fugue when the polyphony of voices enabling the play's contrapuntal structure renders the same theme. For instance, we hear the Catwoman say to Hester:

> **Catwoman** You're my match in witchery, Hester, same as your mother was, it may even be ya surpass us both and the way ya go on as if God only gave ya a little frog of a brain instead of the gift of seein' things as they are, not as they should be, but exactly as they are.[27]

A statement of the role of the narrator's voice can be deduced from this passage, as someone who should see things as they are, rather then seeing things as patterns of order and shape make them out to be. The Catwoman speaks from an otherworldly location, such as would have been taken in, ideologically, in Gaelic Revival writing, or would have been repudiated through new ideologies connecting wealth and social fulfilment. As we have seen, the social world based on the latter is not a home for Hester. But neither is one constituted through the myths of the Celtic tradition. Perhaps this is because Hester indeed sees "things as they are", not "as they should be". Both possible social worlds are otherworlds for Hester. In between them, she stands homeless, like the narrator/director who cannot settle the score with constraints of literary traditions if she wishes to present "things as they are" rather than representing them "as they should be". In the Catwoman's otherworldly voice quoted above we distinguish a narrator's voice nestled in Hester's characterisation. Hester (and the narrator/director) inhabit a different kind of otherworld than that of myth or that of the (social) other, they inhabit the in-between of thresholds. Their witchery consists in the attempt to splice their identity as women by

---

[27] Carr, *By the Bog of Cats*, 273-4.

visiting the con-texts and the inter-texts that disjoint and scatter them across (un/inhabitable) time.[28]

Hester's dynamic relationship with world and otherworld as fantasies for gaining an ontological schema for self-perception provides opportunities for commentary on the various "ontological homes" she wanders into. Such commentary is illuminating of those worlds as spaces of socialisation. Thus, for instance, when Hester longs for her mother Josie, and for the otherworldly realms she imagines as her mother's, the Catwoman provides an enticing description of Josie Swane along with a warning of what should befall those who renounce the folktale tradition:

> **Catwoman** Ya'd often hear her voice coming over the bog at night. She was the greatest song stitcher ever to have passed through this place and we've had plenty pass through but none like Josie Swane. But somewhere along the way she lost the weave of song and in so doin' became small and bitter and mean.[29]

The closing lines of Catwoman's speech ambiguously refer both to the community of the settled people and to Hester's bitterness and her own kind of meanness and smallness. Yet the people of the settled community reject the song of the Irish mythic tradition from different reasons than does Hester.[30] They attempt to appropriate the Bog of Cats for its market value as farm land. The shift in mythical paradigms through which the Bog as a socio-cultural locale is defined reflects a shift in Irish politics and culture from the Revival nationalist Ireland, Yeats's realm of the Rose[31], to the Ireland of Eamon De Valera's idealism of a marriage between material and spiritual wealth, an Ireland fantasised as an idyllic land of farms and villages rather than as a realm of ancient sages and heroes.[32] On the other hand, Hester does remain enchanted to a realm of the Rose fashioned in her heart's desire. If she repudiates it, it is in order to break the citational chain that has instilled in her a destructive longing for a mother that is more than her parent in being a spirit of the land. Perhaps

---

[28] As Carr puts it, referring to the witch character from plays staged in childhood, maybe The Witch "was Time. Time we didn't understand or fully inhabit". Carr, "Introduction", x.

[29] Carr, *By the Bog of Cats*, 275.

[30] See also Sihra's comments. Melissa Sihra, "A Cautionary Tale: Marina Carr's *By the Bog of Cats...*", *Theatre Stuff*, ed. Eamonn Jordan (Dublin: Carysfort, 2000), 265.

[31] W. B. Yeats, "To the Rose upon the Rood of Time", *Collected Works*, 27.

[32] Tim Pat Coogan, *Ireland Since the Rising* (New York: Praeger, 1966), 72.

Josie Swane shares more with Yeats's Cathleen Ni Houlihan than is apparent.

From meta-narrative perspective, the representation of both kinds of repudiations indicate the narrator's/director's thrust to create a play in whose performativity is challenged "the reiterative and citational practice by which discourse produces the effects that it names."[33] In the metaphorical encodings of the play, the narrator's warning, regarding the danger of becoming a prisoner of traditions engendered by discursive reiterations, filters into the Catwoman's voice when she demands of Hester to leave the Bog: "Lave this place now or ya never will."[34]

As regards the community of settled people, a similar warning sounds when they are shown unable to see Hester's struggle with the myths as a struggle to free herself from the reiterative citational practice that embeds mythic visions into the "home" that the self is. Even though they rejected the mythic tradition as a tradition of witches and demons, they remain blindly attached to their own myths based on ideals of wealth and respectability.

Carthage's mother describes Hester to her granddaughter, little Josie Swane, as being "thick and stubborn and dangerous wrong-headed and backwards to top it all."[35] Hester's longing for the past she sees in dreams and fantasies based on the Irish folktale tradition is regarded as backwardness; her view of the settled people and their myths is "wrong-headed"; her challenge is a sign of her "thickness" and "stubbornness". For all this, Hester is dangerous. She threatens to destroy the harmony and coherence of the social world legitimated through myths by offering a discursive position whence one may at least start to think of devising a map of the way out of the maze to which the mythic imaginary confines us. The kind of social action that the settled community requires in situations like this is best summarised by Mrs Kilbride when she addresses Hester's daughter thus:

> **Mrs Kilbride** ... I'll break your spirit yet and then glue ya back the way I want ya. ... Don't you worry, child, we'll get ya off of her yet. Me and your daddy has plans. We'll batter ya into the semblance of legitimacy yet ... .[36]

---

[33] Butler, *Bodies That Matter*, 2.
[34] Carr, *By the Bog of Cats*, 276.
[35] Ibid., 277.
[36] Ibid., 279-281.

Hester's and little Josie Swane's situation throughout the play reminds us of the situation of Hester Prynne and her daughter from Nathaniel Hawthorne's *The Scarlet Letter*.[37] Both mother characters are, by the standards of the community of settled people, "thick and stubborn and dangerous wrong-headed". But whereas Hester Prynne remains silent and compliant, Hester Swane is vocal and uproarious. When she meets Caroline, Carthage's new fiancé, Hester firmly asserts her desire as a right to the man she has allowed as her partner:

> **Hester** ... Caroline, there's two Hester's Swanes, one that is decent and very fond of ya ... . And the other Hester, well, she could slide a knife down your face, carve ya up and not bat an eyelid.
> (*Grabs her hair suddenly and viciously.*)
> ... Carthage Kilbride is mine and only mine. He's been mine since he was sixteen. You think you can take him from me? Wrong. All wrong.[38]

What is "all wrong" from Hester's perspective is connected to Caroline's surrender of agency, for it is not Caroline who "takes" Carthage away from Hester. Caroline's marriage with Carthage is arranged to suit the machinations of her father who treats it as one more business opportunity, and to satisfy Carthage's ambition to enter the social circles of the middle-class elite. But Hester Swane, unlike Hester Prynne and Caroline, appropriates masculine roles and agency. In intertextual reading with Yeats's "Leda and the Swan" we may recognise Caroline posed as Leda and Hester Swane as the Swan—an appropriation of masculine roles constructed in Ireland's literary tradition. This appropriation also happens when it is related how Hester recounts her murder of her brother: we are tempted to think of Christie's tale from Synge's *The Playboy of the Western World*.[39] But this time the crime is not made up, although it is done in order to fulfil a similar function to Christie's imagined deed: murdering her brother, Hester robs him in order to insure a successful start of her concubinage with Carthage (later Joseph's ghost reveals that the money he was carrying was meant for her anyway).[40] Such reversal of roles shows Hester usurping a masculine position as this position would have been cited in fictional discourse. The narrative pattern in which the

---

[37] Nathaniel Hawthorne, *The Scarlet Letter* (London: Penguin, 1994).

[38] Carr, *By the Bog of Cats*, 285.

[39] J. M. Synge, *The Playboy of the Western World*, *The Playboy of the Western World and Other Plays*, 95-146.

[40] In Synge's play Christie's posturing as a murderer provides him with a tale which he uses to attract women; he uses the tale as his "capital" with which to start erotic partnerships.

man behaves "manly" in order to gain a female partner appears distorted when a woman is presented as performing a "manly" deed in order to gain a male partner.

Revising traditional narrative patterns, Carr's play offers images of carnivalesque social worlds. The stability of the patterns is challenged through role reversals and unexpected denouements. This undermines the citational force of discourse through which reiterative narrative acts solidify myths. Carr's social otherworlds also undermine the dualist dialectic of repudiations through which social worlds are legitimated against abject otherworlds. The realness derived from the ideological naturalisation of fantasies offered in myths begins to flicker as its ontological schema falls apart. Hester Swane's world is a social otherworld of flickering ontologies; perhaps the only kind of realm available to Braidotti's nomadic subject, before it can shake off the chains of tradition.

Social Otherworlds

In the previous section I focused on the effects of Carr's play through which a distinction between legitimate worlds and repudiated otherworlds is blurred so that we may rather speak of worldly otherworlds and otherworldly worlds. My aim was to suggest that worlds and otherworlds cannot be easily decanted. Their interwoven threads form the texture of social spaces. In this section, I will restate this argument in order to claim in the end that Carr's play wears thin the texture of social spaces, so that we may see their unworldliness, while glimpsing through their rarefied texture the truly otherworldly space of homeless subjects. This is a different kind of otherworld, not necessarily one of legend or of social *indesirables*, although it may partake in these two as well. It is a realm whose otherworldliness derives from the fact that it is enabled through heteroglossic voices that cannot hold subjects spellbound. This otherworld is shown in Carr's play, to use Frank McGuinness's words in this context, as a country of the imagination with imagination "crossing the border always between the living and the dead."[41] Hester enters this world by dying. Yet at the end of the play, we are left with the strange feeling that it is the world of those who survive Hester that may be dead or deadly.

In her proud response to the ultimatum given by the community of settled people Hester asserts that she has "as much right to [the Bog of

---

[41] Frank McGuinness, "Writing in Greek: *By the Bog of Cats...*", Programme Note, Abbey Theatre, 1998.

Cats] as any of yees, more, for it holds me to it in ways it has never held
yees."[42] The Bog of Cats holds Hester to it through a fiction of her mother,
whose return Hester is still expecting. Significantly, Hester's mother
abandoned her on the day of her Communion. Hester recounts:

> Ya know the last time I seen me mother I was wearing me Communion
> dress too, down by the caravan, a beautiful summer's night and the bog
> like a furnace. I wouldn't go to bed though she kept tellin' me to. I don't
> know why I wouldn't, I always done what she tould me. I think now—
> maybe I knew. And she says, 'I'm goin' walkin' the bog, you're to stay
> here, Hetty. And I says, 'No,' I'd go along with her and made to folly her.
> And she says, 'No, Hetty, you wait here, I'll be back in a while.' And again
> I made to folly her and again she stopped me. And I watched her walk
> away from me across the Bog of Cats. And across the Bog of Cats I'll
> watch her return. [43]

We may interpret big Josie Swane's leaving as a repudiation on her part of
the Christian myth. Seeing that her daughter is wearing the symbols of
Holy Communion, she may have regarded her as belonging to another
world, no longer hers. However, we notice the folktale patterns of the
story: there is premonition and testing of the heroine's (Hester's) powers
to elucidate a secret meaning. Because the story resembles those of the
folktale tradition we begin wondering whether it is true. When Hester
enquires about her mother, of her brother's ghost, she says: "What was she
like, Joseph? Every day I forget more and more till I'm startin' to think I
made her up out of the air. If it wasn't for this auld caravan I'd swear I
only dreamt her."[44] Perhaps the ontology of the place that "holds her to it"
is for Hester linked to a fantasy bred in myths of Celtic otherworlds.
Hester's mother can be interpreted as symbolising the hold the Irish
folktale tradition can have upon people's imagination. This tradition has
been repudiated in the community of settled people. But their own values
are shown as also growing out of myths, even though of a different kind
from Hester's. Their myths are derived from the Christian tradition which
they use to legitimate the social goal of prosperity. Yet their behaviour is
marked by greed. One need only think of Carthage's mother, whose
obsession with money and winning is rendered hilarious when she is
depicted as cheating little Josie at a game of cards.

Thus, neither Hester's mother's otherworld nor Hester's alienated
lover's world seem ordered and coherent. On the contrary, they are

---

[42] Carr, *By the Bog of Cats*, 289.

[43] Ibid., 297.

[44] Ibid., 320.

rendered contradictory, as realms where ghosts intermingle with humans as a matter of course. Homeless in this flickering realm of unstable, conflicting ontologies, Hester takes pride in being a wanderer. From meta-narrative perspective this pride can be read as condoning nomadic subjectivity: a kind of subjectivity that rejects the "inbred, underbred" subjectivity sustained in various traditions through reciprocally corroborating narratives.[45] This reciprocal corroboration transforms myth into ideology.

Dominant ideologies of twentieth-century Ireland are echoed throughout Carr's play. Strangely though, a marriage of the mutually exclusive traditions of Christianity and folk belief rooted in Celtic mythology, while seeming awkward when suggested in the play, is enticing. The odd couple of the priest and the Catwoman make the carnival complete: "*The Catwoman and Father Willow have entered, linking arms, both with their sticks. Father Willow has his snuff on hand, pyjamas showing under his shirt and trousers, hat on, adores the Catwoman.*"[46] Father Willow's character is reminiscent of Maria Edgeworth's slovenly but witty male characters and evokes her reconciliatory narrations of carnivalesque benevolence.[47] But, in Carr's play, the carnivalesque is only rarely entertaining. Instead, her carnival is the occasion of uneasy ontological meltdown.

No reconciliation of conflicting realities is offered by the end of the play, although some sort of catharsis is achieved. When Hester sets on fire the house and stock she and Carthage had shared, we may think of Yeats's world born out of Leda's rape:

A shudder in the loins engenders there
The broken wall, the burning roof and tower
And Agamemnon dead.[48]

But in Carr's play there is no violent union that centres reality through the logocentric spell of myth. In the world depicted through male-dominated traditions women cannot last, even though they appropriate symbols of phallic power, or perhaps precisely because of that. Wielding a knife Hester kills little Josie and then herself as she and the Ghost Fancier "*go into a death dance with the fishing knife, which ends plunged into Hester's*

---

[45] Ibid., 289.
[46] Ibid., 306.
[47] Maria Edgeworth, *Castle Rackrent* (Oxford: Oxford University Press, 1999).
[48] Yeats, "Leda and the Swan", 218.

heart. ... Exit Ghost Fancier with knife."[49] In the deadly dance of rewriting tradition played by Carr's narrator/director, the woman-swan remains in the shadow of the god Swan. The narrative cut out here cannot survive in the realm of heart's desire shaped through ideological interpretations of myth. Hester's epitaph by her nearest friend is a fitting closing: "Hester—She's gone—Hester—She's cut her heart out—it's lying there on top of her chest like some dark feathered bird."[50] Hester must leave, and metaphorically, women's presence in the masculine domains of myth and tradition is relocated to the spectral realm of ghosts wandering in between male centred worlds. Yet although Hester exits these male-dominated worlds, we remain with the strange feeling that her exit is an entering into a realm where myths have no hold upon the self, because there, instead of ideological forms of social myths, we encounter the heteroglossia of voices in which the meanings of these myths are creatively renegotiated. Thus, Marina Carr's play is an invitation to reconstruct current social realities as dialogical spaces in which women's voices confront constraining traditions.

---

[49] Carr, *By the Bog of Cats*, 341.
[50] Ibid.

CONCLUSION

Elizabeth Grosz, working from Foucauldian theory, argues that discourses become inscribed on bodies through "'voluntary' procedures, life-styles, habits, and behaviors".[1] As McDowell remarks, "voluntary" expresses here the idea of "compliance with disciplinary power", but also that of "taking pleasure in bodily inscription and in subverting dominant discourses."[2] One way to achieve this subversion is by taking charge of the processes of discursive construction of subjectivity that also define one's bodily space.

In this study, I have argued that the narrative content of a text often filters into one's fantasy, into the interior space where one sees oneself as a certain kind of subject. Since this fantasy is eventually worn on the body, the kind of subject we become through fantasising disciplines how we present ourselves in the material world. In order to challenge this disciplining force we must reconfigure naturalised narratives that engender constraining worldviews. These reconfigurations may change how one fantasises one's identity, and therefore how one expresses oneself and acts in the social world. In the texts I have analysed, representations of women's place, including the body as women's place, have tactical value. They are used to unsettle the common-places of naturalised gender and social hierarchies.

However, when foregrounding such challenging representations we struggle with citational chains. Sometimes, like Mary and Nathan in *Everything You Need*, we hear voices not our own speaking inside us. With some of these voices, like those of fairy tales, we have been acquainted since childhood, as Liz Lochhead's reinterpretation of the Grimms' tales suggests. Other voices are channelled through various institutions and, as with Helen in "Original Bliss", they come to govern and discipline our bodies. For women, challenging these voices can be deadly, as it was for Bridget Cleary whose fate is discussed in Bourke's study. Not raising the challenge can lead to texturing women with the materiality of statuettes, as it happens with Ní Dhuibhne's women

---

[1] Grosz, *Volatile Bodies*, 142.
[2] McDowell, 51.

characters, not all there for themselves. Or it can leave women straddling across impossible ontological spaces, as with Marina Carr's characters.

Such entanglement between our selves and narratives, I have argued, is mediated by the fantasies through which we negotiate our social and gender identity. But narratives are always, to an extent, vehicles of social myths, be they ideological or subversive of ideologies. Therefore, our fantasies and the narrative expression of our identities are constrained by the norms social myths establish. Can we challenge and change these? Indeed, I hope to have shown that this is possible. Narratives are both enabling and constraining as regards agency. Readers surrender agency by allowing themselves to be signified as subjects in discourse. But this surrender can be wilful. This wilfulness seems to characterise the subject positions the texts examined here produce. The construction of such subject positions, which, when occupied, allow one to be a wilful subject, instead of a subjected subject, imply working with the norms of social myths conveyed through narratives, norms that constrain, via tradition or "common sense" (consensual sharing of naturalised representations and meanings by the members of a society), what can be narrated, or how certain aspects of experience can be narrated. The texts analysed here provide means of evading, challenging, and re-creating the norms.

Speaking about contemporary theories of identity, Linda McDowell argues that

> identities are a fluid amalgam of memories of places and origins, constructed by and through fragments and nuances, journeys and rests, of movements between. Thus, the 'in-between' is itself a process or a dynamic, not just a stage on the way to a more final identity.[3]

The women's identities we encounter in the texts I have analysed in this study arise from fragments of memories (perhaps the kind that "hung themselves upside down/ in the sleeping heads of children"[4]) filtered through the experience of journeys and rests that constitute the dynamics of women's socialisation in a masculine world. These women's realms of fantasy are born out from complex ramifications of elements of myths into contemporary discourses; their narrative expression reflects back on the intertextual web in which myths hold social meaning. These reflections make visible the un/inhabitability of narrative agency, and therefore the power to transform the symbolic order enshrined with various myths as a masculine domain.

---

[3] Ibid., 215.
[4] Lochhead, *The Grimm Sisters*, 70.

The narrators and the characters of the texts analysed point out possibilities of re-signifying the identity deadlock into which social myths ensnare women's self. In Kennedy's "Original Bliss", Helen is at first unable to relate intimately to her partners except through their fantasies. However, she eventually becomes capable of fantasising a sensuality of love that she can use to heal her self. Nathan's healing in *Everything You Need* implies giving up his fantasy of Maura as otherworldly muse and goddess, which in turn implies giving up the position of mastery of reality through word power that Nathan sought as writer. Liz Lochhead's re-significations of the characters Lucy and Mina from Stoker's famous text deconstruct paradigms that, in separating nature from culture while gendering these as feminine and masculine, have created constraining social roles for women. Lochhead also shows in *The Grimm Sisters* and elsewhere that most male-generated myths achieve similar effects: a Persephone-like Lucy struggles to understand the rage and enchantment that accompanies her sexual initiation as not necessarily tied up with il/legitimate social roles. The storyteller of *The Grimm Sisters* struggles with her realness, as she can only tell fairy tales from narrating positions enshrined through masculine canonisations of the genre. Bridget Cleary, Bourke's study shows, is perceived as not fully human, or less than human. The young girls in Ní Dhuibhne's *The Dancers Dancing* find it difficult to relate to artificial, male-generated visions of nature's otherness, or otherworldliness. The women in Ní Dhuibhne's short stories become aware of a confining materiality, spun in male-generated stories compelling the male body's transubstantiation into the body-social. In *By the Bog of Cats...*, Hester's otherworldliness points toward a liberatory space outwith constraining traditions, a space "before rules was made", where one must travel in order to begin renewing them.[5] Such awarenesses and challenges are offered, in various ways, in all the texts studied here. They point out ways of fantasising that challenge norms derived from various traditions, enshrined through social ritual, and delivered in fantasies of the self's identity that have become prescriptive and constraining.

In an interview conducted by Neil Badmington, commenting on the role of cultural critics in contemporary society, Catherine Belsey points out that deviations from the order and harmony of received cultural patterns may unlock alternative worldviews:

> Meanings, unstable, unpredictable, might display their own uncertainty or limitations in an elusive phrase, a surprising brush stroke, a jump cut, the transgression of a rhyme scheme, a hiatus in the narrative or an unexpected

---

[5] Marina Carr, *On Raftery's Hill* (Loughcrew: Gallery, 2000), 56.

deviation from genre. And these meanings and betrayals of meaning give access to alternative perceptions of the world, which unsettle the accounts we too readily take for granted.[6]

Such unsettling often occurs in the texts I have analysed, especially when they explore the embedding of social myths in the characters' personal histories. Situated at crossroads of memory and experience, the women characters in these texts reshape the stories derived from mythic fabulas and thus discover avenues for developing more empowering perspectives of themselves. The characters' memories and experiences are indeed constituted by citing in their fantasies discourses derived from social myths; these citations are visible in the narratives through which they present themselves to themselves and to others. I sought to point out how this citing places subjectivities at a crossroads where the generation of subjective experience as devoid of agency may be steered towards enabling possibilities of recuperating agency. Based on this unravelling of the citational force mobilised by social myths, I explored how fantasies of the self become narrated in ways that depart from reiterative stories. The writers studied here exploit the regenerative effects of the force of narrative reiterations. Their narrators use this force to decant possibilities of reconstructing the narratives that make up myths. They are thus able to identify lines of resistance on the interface between conforming constraints and nonconformist desires. It is on the interface between the idiosyncratic and the private, on the one hand, and the socially normative or the public, on the other, where women's identities are reconstituted as empowering, challenging the dissemination of masculine authority in the body-social. In this process, they break the citational chains whereby discourses of identity come to constitute a personal sense of self in the service of a social persona who acts according to the patterns prescribed with social myths.

Throughout the present study, I emphasised the role of deixis and heteroglossia in exercising agency through narrative: despite losing autonomy through being signified as subjects, readers/audiences are endowed with the power to re-create subjectivity by establishing novel intertextual connections between narratives and by using narratives to express multiple identities in discursive interaction, through the various voices that narratives make available. Thus, the deictic forces of discourses can be manipulated in order to open a text to heteroglossic intervention, because they imply constant reference to other texts or

---

[6] Belsey and Badmington, 2.

collocutors' voices, and thus offer the opportunity to jostle the meanings of a text against those of another text.

The concept of social myth I have used, which I distinguish from the concept of ideology, allowed me to focus on the constraining role of narrative in shaping identities while also allowing me to preserve a dynamic view of the social imaginaries the texts construct. Judith Butler argues that narrative reiterations yield normative frameworks of self-presentation.[7] This normative force of narrative, established through a citational chain, constitutes in time a dominant narrative that I called social myth. However, because the norms of this narrative can be challenged using a discourse's deictic force to reconfigure social imaginaries, the text is not immune to the intervention of the subjects it nurses into being.

This take on the value and functions of myth, although partly inspired by the texts analysed, has, I believe, wider applicability. The concept of social myth theorised here can be used not only to investigate texts produced in cultures whose past is perceived as having been (and perhaps as still being) immersed in myth. Irrespective of our social, geographical, and political situation, we come across the force of social myth at every step. Preexisting narrative patterns infiltrate, through the citational force engendered by myth, in our innermost recesses, scripting our fantasies of ourselves and thus shaping our perceptions of ourselves. These in turn underlie our presentations of ourselves to others in social reality, and our social acts, moulding our presence and how we make sense of our lived experiences. I feel that it is important to interrogate those patterns (and writers are in the best position to do so) in order to find out why they are constraining. And if they are, we need to know how they can be changed. Such reconstructions and revisions are indeed ways of steering ourselves and our world, helping us to re-create ourselves and our world in more empowering configurations.

---

[7] Butler, *Gender Trouble*, 140, 145, 226; and *Bodies That Matter*, 1-29, 124-40, 187-9.

BIBLIOGRAPHY

Primary Sources

Apollodorus. *The Library of Greek Mythology*. Trans. Robin Hard. Oxford: Oxford University Press, 1997.

Beckett, Samuel. *The Unnamable*. London: Calder, 1958.

Belsey, Catherine and Neil Badmington. "From *Critical Practice* to Cultural Criticism: An Interview with Catherine Belsey". *Textual Practice* 19 (2005): 1-12.

Boland, Eavan. *Outside History: Selected Poems 1980-1990*. New York: Norton, 1990.

—. *In a Time of Violence*. Manchester: Carcanet, 1994.

—. *Object Lessons: The Life of the Woman and the Poet in Our Time*. Manchester: Carcanet, 1995.

Bourke, Angela. *By Salt Water*. Dublin: New Island Books, 1996.

—. *The Burning of Bridget Cleary: A True Story*. London: Pimlico, 1999.

Calvino, Italo. *If on a winter's night a traveller*. Trans. William Weaver. Orlando, Florida: Harcourt, 1981.

Canepa, Nancy, trans. *Giambattista Basile's "The Tale of Tales, or Entertainment for Little Ones"*. Detroit, MI: Wayne State University Press, 2007.

Carr, Marina. *Low in the Dark. The Crack in the Emerald: New Irish Plays*. Ed. David Grant. London: Herne, 1990. 63-140.

—. *The Mai*. Meath: Gallery, 1995.

—. *Portia Coughlan*. London: Faber, 1996.

—. *By the Bog of Cats...* .Meath: Gallery, 1998.

—. *Plays One*. London: Faber, 1999.

—. *On Raftery's Hill*. Loughcrew: Gallery, 2000.

Castro, Jan. "Mad Ireland Hurts Her Too". *Nation* 6 (1994): 798-802.

Charles, Ron. "No Man—or Writer—Is an Island". *Christian Science Monitor* 164 (2001): 18-19.

Craig, Amanda. "Passion & Physics". *New Statesman* 435 (10 January 1997): 47.

Crow, Christine. *Miss X or the Wolf Woman*. London: Women's Press, 1990.

Deevy, Teresa. *Three Plays: Katie Roche, The King of Spain's Daughter, The Wilde Goose*. London: Macmillan, 1939.

Donoghue, Emma. *Hood*. Harmondsworth: Penguin, 1996.

—. *Kissing the Witch: Old Tales in New Skins*. New York: Harper, 1997.

Edgeworth, Maria. *Castle Rackrent*. Oxford: Oxford University Press, 1999.

Ferguson, Kathleen. *The Maid's Tale*. Dublin: Poolbeg, 1995.

Gantz, Jeffrey, trans. *Early Irish Myths and Sagas*. Harmondsworth: Penguin, 1981.

Gerard, Emily de Laszowska. *The Land Beyond the Forest: Facts, Figures and Fancies from Transylvania*. Brooklyn, NY: AMS, 2001.

Grant, Katie. "More Four-Letter Words Than You Need". *Spectator* 8912 (29 May 1999): 40-1.

Gurdon, Eveline Camilla. *County Folk-Lore. Printed Extracts No. 2: Suffolk*. London: David Nutt for the Folk-Lore Society, 1893.

Hawthorne, Nathaniel. *The Scarlet Letter*. London: Penguin, 1994.

Heaney, Seamus. *Preoccupations: Selected Prose 1968-1978*. London: Faber, 1980.

—. *Seeing Things*. London: Faber, 1991.

Henry, John. *Stories of Sea and Shore*. Ed. Séamas Ó Catháin. Dublin: Comhairle Bhéaloideas Éireann, 1983.

Joyce, James. "The Dead". *Dubliners: Text and Criticism*. Eds. Robert Scholes and A. Litz. New York: Penguin, 1996. 175-224.

Kennedy, A. L. *Night Geometry and the Garscadden Trains*. London: Phoenix, 1993.

—. *So I Am Glad*. London: Vintage, 1996.

—. *Original Bliss*. London: Jonathan Cape, 1997.

—. *Original Bliss*. London: Vintage, 1998.

—. *Original Bliss*. New York: Knopf, 1999.

—. *Everything You Need*. London: Vintage, 2000.

Kennedy, A. L. and Yvonne Nolan. "A Dream Not Her Own". *Publishers Weekly* 248 (23 July 2001): 43, 46.

Knapp, Mona. Review of *Everything You Need*, by A. L. Kennedy. *World Literature Today* 76 (2002): 151.

Lochhead, Liz. *Blood and Ice*, London: Salamander, 1982.

—. *The Grimm Sisters*. London: Next Editions, 1981.

—. *Liz Lochhead*. Glasgow: National Book League, 1986. Writers in Brief No. 21.

—. *The Grimm Sisters. Dreaming Frankenstein & Collected Poems*. Edinburgh: Polygon, 1986. 69-104.

—. *Mary Queen of Scots Got Her Head Chopped Off* and *Dracula*. London: Penguin, 1989.

—. *Bagpipe Muzak*. London: Penguin, 1991.

Lochhead, Liz and Rebecca Wilson, Interview with Rebecca Wilson. *Sleeping with Monsters: Conversations with Scottish and Irish Women Poets*. Eds. Gillean Somerville-Arjat and Rebecca Wilson. Edinburgh: Polygon, 1990. 8-14.

Mac Intyre, Tom. "Where Your Treasure Is: *The Mai*". Programme Note, Peacock Theatre, 1994.

—. "*Portia Coughlan*". Programme Note, Peacock Theatre, 1996.

Marsh, Richard. *The Beetle*, Stroud: Alan Sutton, 1994.

McDermid, Val. "The Sorcerer's Apprentice". *Los Angeles Times* (26 August 2001): 5.

McGuinness, Frank. "Writing in Greek: *By the Bog of Cats...*", Programme Note, Abbey Theatre, 1998.

Mills, Lia. *Another Alice*. Dublin: Poolbeg, 1996.

Milton, John. *Paradise Lost*. Ed. Alastair Fowler. London: Longman, 1998.

Mundy, Toby. "Novel of the Week". *New Statesman* 4437 (24 May 1999): 49.

Ní Dhuibhne, Éilís. *Blood and Water*. Dublin: Attic, 1988.

—. *Eating Women is Not Recommended*. Dublin: Attic, 1991.

—. *The Inland Ice and Other Stories*. Belfast: Blackstaff, 1997.

—. *The Dancers Dancing*. Belfast: Blackstaff, 1999.

Ní Dhuibhne, Éilís and Nicola Warwick, *Éilís Ní Dhuibhne*. Interview conducted by Nicola Warwick. 26 July 09: http://www.prairieden.com/front_porch/visiting_authors/dhuibhne.html.

O'Brien, Flann. *The Third Policeman*. Champaign, IL: Dalkey, 1999.

Petro, Pamela. "School of Wales". *Women's Review of Books* 18 (2001): 30.

Ruane, Medb. "Shooting from the Lip". *Sunday Times* (31 March 1996).

Smith, R. Review of *In a Time of Violence*. *Southern Humanities Review* 30 (1996): 304-7.

Sophocles. *King Oedipus*. *The Theban Plays*. Trans. E. Watling. London: Penguin, 1974. 23-68.

Stoker, Bram. *Dracula*. Eds. Nina Auerbach and David Skal. New York: Norton, 1997.

Synge, J.M. *The Playboy of the Western World and Other Plays*. Ed. Ann Saddlemyer. Oxford: Oxford University Press, 1995.

Waugh, Teresa. "This Small Masterpiece". *Spectator* 8790 (18 January 1997): 35-6.

Wall, Eamonn. Review of *Original Bliss,* by A. L. Kennedy. *Review of Contemporary Fiction* 19 (1999): 161.

West, Martin, ed., trans. *Homeric Hymns. Homeric Apocrypha. Lives of Homer.* Cambridge, Massachusetts: Harvard University Press, 2003.

Wilde, Francesca. *Ancient Legends, Mystic Charms, and Superstitions of Ireland.* Galway: O'Gorman, 1971.

Yeats, W. B. *Cathleen ni Houlihan. Modern Irish Drama.* Ed. John Harrington. New York: Norton, 1991. 3-11.

—. *The Collected Works of W. B. Yeats, Volume I: The Poems.* Ed. Richard Finneran. New York: Simon&Schuster, 1997.

Secondary Sources

Albinus, Lars. *The House of Hades: Studies in Ancient Greek Eschatology.* Oxford: Aarhus University Press, 2000.

Alsop, Rachel et al. *Theorizing Gender.* Cambridge: Polity, 2002.

Althusser, Louis. *For Marx.* Trans. Ben Brewster. London: Allen Lane, 1969.

—. *Lenin and Philosophy and Other Essays.* Trans. Ben Brewster. New York: Monthly Review, 1978.

Anderson, Carol. "Emma Tennant, Elspeth Barker, Alice Thompson: Gothic Revisited". *Contemporary Scottish Women Writers.* Eds. Aileen Christianson and Alison Lumsden. Edinburgh: Edinburgh University Press, 2000. 117-130.

Arata, Stephen. *Fictions of Loss in the Victorian Fin de Siécle: Identity and Empire.* Cambridge: Cambridge University Press, 1996.

—. "The Occidental Tourist: *Dracula* and the Anxiety of Reverse Colonization". *Dracula.* Eds. Nina Auerbach and David Skal. New York: Norton, 1997. 462-70.

Attridge, Derek, ed. and Jacques Derrida. "'This Strange Institution Called Literature': An Interview with Jacques Derrida". *Jacques Derrida: Acts of Literature.* Trans. Nicholas Royle. London: Routledge, 1992. 33-75.

Austin, John Langshaw. *How to Do Things with Words.* Eds. James Urmson and Marina Sbisà. Cambridge: Harvard University Press, 1975.

Bakhtin, Mikhail. *The Dialogic Imagination.* Ed. M. Holquist. Trans. C. Emerson and M. Holquist. Austin: University of Texas Press, 1981.

—. *Problems of Dostoevsky's Poetics.* Ed. Caryl Emerson. Minneapolis: University of Minnesota Press, 1984.

—. *Speech Genres and Other Late Essays*. Trans. Vern McGee. Eds. Caryl Emerson and Michael Holquist. Austin: University of Texas Press, 1986.

Bal, Mieke. *Narratology: Introduction to the Theory of Narrative*. Toronto: University of Toronto Press, 1997.

Barthes, Roland. *Mythologies*. Trans. Annette Lavers. New York: Hill&Wang, 1983.

Benveniste, Emile. *Problems in General Linguistics*. Trans. Mary Meek. Coral Gables: University of Miami Press, 1971.

Boje, David. "Stories of the Storytelling Organization: A Postmodern Analysis of Disney as "Tamara-Land"". *Academy of Management Journal* 38 (1994): 997-1035.

Boone, Joseph. "Of Me(n) and Feminism: Who(se) is the Sex That Writes?". *Engendering Men: The Question of Male Feminist Criticism*. Eds. Joseph Boone and Michael Cadden. New York: Routledge, 1990. 11-25.

Bourdieu, Pierre. *Distinction: A Social Critique of the Judgement of Taste*. Trans. Richard Nice. London: Routledge, 1984.

Boyd, S. J. "The Voice of Revelation: Liz Lochhead and Monsters". *Liz Lochhead's Voices*. Eds. Robert Crawford and Anne Varty. Edinburgh: Edinburgh University Press, 1993. 38-56.

Braidotti, Rosi. *Nomadic Subjects*. New York: Columbia University Press, 1994.

Briggs, Katharine. *The Fairies in Tradition and Literature*. London: Routledge, 2002.

Burke, Kenneth. "Doing and Saying: Thoughts on Myth, Cult and Archetype". *Salmagundi* 7 (1971): 100-119.

—. "Revolutionary Symbolism in America". *The Legacy of Kenneth Burke*. Eds. Herbert Simons and Trevor Melia. Madison: University of Wisconsin Press, 1989.

Butler, Hubert. *Escape from the Anthill*. Mullingar: Lilliput, 1985.

Butler, Judith. "Gender Trouble, Feminist Theory, and Psychoanalytic Discourse". *Feminism/Postmodernism*. Ed. Linda Nicholson. New York: Routledge, 1990. 324-40.

—. *Gender Trouble: Feminism and the Subversion of Identity*. New York: Routledge, 1990.

—. *Bodies That Matter: On the Discursive Limits of "Sex"*. New York: Routledge, 1993.

—. *The Psychic Life of Power*. Stanford: Stanford University Press, 1997.

—. *Undoing Gender*. New York: Routledge, 2004.

Butler, Marilyn. *Romantic, Rebels and Reactionaries: English Literature and Its Background 1760-1830*. Oxford: Oxford University Press, 1982.

Byron, Glennis. "Gothic in the 1890s". *A Companion to the Gothic*. Ed. David Punter. Oxford: Blackwell, 2000. 132-142.

Campbell, John. "The Body Image and Self-Consciousness". *The Body and the Self*. Eds. José Bermúdez et al. Cambridge, Massachusetts: MIT Press, 2001. 29-42.

Canepa, Nancy. *From Court to Forest: Giambattista Basile's* Lo cunto de li cunti *and the Birth of the Literary Fairy Tale*. Detroit: Wayne State University Press, 1999.

Carlisle, Janice. "Introduction". *Narrative and Culture*. Eds. Janice Carlisle and Daniel Schwarz. Athens: University of Georgia Press, 1994. 1-12.

Carr, Marina. "Dealing with the Dead". *Irish University Review* 28 (1998): 190-6.

Carroll, Noel. *The Philosophy of Horror*. New York: Routledge, 1990.

Carter, Angela. "Notes from the Front Line". *Shaking a Leg: Collected Journalism and Writings*. London: Vintage, 1998. 36-43.

Castoriadis, Cornelius. *The Imaginary Institution of Society*. Michigan: MIT Press, 1998.

Cavarero, Adriana. *Stately Bodies: Literature, Philosophy and the Question of Gender*. Trans. Robert de Lucca and Deanna Shemek. Ann Arbor: University of Michigan Press, 2005.

Chan, Suzanna. "Some Notes on Deconstructing Ireland's Whiteness: Immigrants, Emigrants and the Perils of Jazz". *Variant* 22 (2005): 20-21.

Child, Francis. "Kemp Owyne". *The English and Scottish Popular Ballads*. 5 vols. 1882-1898. Vol. 1. Boston: Houghton, Mifflin, 1882. 306-313.

—. *The English and Scottish Popular Ballads*. 5 vols. 1882-1898. Vol. 1. Boston: Houghton, Mifflin, 1882.

Christianson, Aileen. "Liz Lochhead's Poetry and Drama: Forging Ironies". *Contemporary Scottish Women Writers*. 41-52.

Cixous, Hélène. "Sorties: Out and Out: Attacks/Ways Out/Forays". *The Newly Born Woman*, with Catherine Clément. Trans. Betsy Wing. London: Tauris, 1996. 63-132.

—. "The Laugh of the Medusa". *Feminisms: An Anthology of Literary Theory and Criticism*. Eds. Robin Warhol and Diane Herndl. (New Brunswick: Rutgers University Press, 1997. 347-62.

Clayton, Jay. "The Narrative Turn in Minority Fiction". *Narrative and Culture*. 58-76.

Cleary, Joe. "Introduction: Ireland and Modernity". *The Cambridge Companion to Modern Irish Culture*. Eds. Joe Cleary and Claire Connoly. Cambridge: Cambridge University Press, 2005. 1-22.

Cohan, Steven and Linda Shires. *Telling Stories: A Theoretical Analysis of Narrative Fiction*. London: Routledge, 1988.

Collins, Randall. "On the Microfoundations of Macrosociology". *American Journal of Sociology* 86 (1981): 984-1013.

Coogan, Tim Pat. *Ireland Since the Rising*. New York: Praeger, 1966.

Cornis-Pope, Marcel. "Narrative Innovation and Cultural Rewriting: The Pynchon-Morrison-Sukenick Connection". *Narrative and Culture*. 216-37.

Cowie, Elizabeth. "Fantasia". *m/f* 9 (1984): 70-105.

Crawford, Robert. "The Two-faced Language of Lochhead's Poetry". *Liz Lochhead's Voices*. 57-74.

Creed, Barbara. *The Monstrous Feminine: Film, Feminism, Psychoanalysis*. London: Routledge, 1993.

Cremin, Kathy. Review of *The Dancers Dancing*. *Irish Times* (7 August 1999).

Croley, Laura Sagolla. "The Rhetoric of Reform in Stoker's *Dracula*: Depravity, Decline, and the Fin-de-Siècle 'Residium'". *Criticism* 37 (1995). 85-108.

Daly, Mary. *Gyn/Ecology: The Metaethics of Radical Feminism*. London: Women's Press, 1979.

Davison, Carol. "Introduction". *Bram Stoker's Dracula: Sucking Through the Century, 1897-1997*. Ed. Carol Davison. Toronto: Dundurn, 1997. 19-40.

De Certeau, Michel. *The Practice of Everyday Life*. Berkeley: University of California Press, 1984.

De Man, Paul. *The Resistance to Theory*. Minneapolis: University of Minnesota Press, 1986.

De Troyes, Chrètien. *The Complete Romances of Chrètien de Troyes*. Trans. David Staines. Bloomington: University of Indiana Press, 1990.

Debord, Guy. *Society of the Spectacle*. Trans. Ken Knabb. Oakland, CA: AKPress, 2005.

Derrida, Jacques. *Of Grammatology*. Trans. Gayatri Spivak. Baltimore, Maryland: Johns Hopkins University Press, 1976.

Derrida, Jacques. *Signéponge/Signsponge*. Trans. Richard Rand. New York: Columbia University Press, 1984.

——. *Limited Inc.* Ed. Gerald Graff. Evanston: Northwestern University Press, 1988.

Dunnigan, Sarah. "A. L. Kennedy's Longer Fiction: Articulate Grace". *Contemporary Scottish Women Writers.* 144-55.

Eagleton, Terry. *Ideology: An Introduction.* London: Verso, 1991.

Eliade, Mircea. *The Sacred and the Profane: The Nature of Religion.* Trans. Willard Trask. New York: Harcourt, 1957.

Federman, Raymond. "Surfiction—Four Propositions in Form of an Introduction". *Surfiction: Fiction Now...and Tomorrow.* Ed. Raymond Federman. Chicago: Swallow, 1975. 5-15.

Flax, Jane. "Postmodernism and Gender Relations in Feminist Theory". *Feminism/Postmodernism.* 39-62.

Foster, John Wilson. *Colonial Consequences: Essays in Irish Literature and Culture.* Dublin: Lilliput, 1991.

Foucault, Michel. *Discipline and Punish.* London: Allen Lane, 1977.

——. *Power/Knowledge: Selected Interviews and Other Writings, 1972-1977.* Trans. Colin Gordon. New York: Pantheon, 1980.

Fraser, Nancy and Linda Nicholson. "Social Criticism without Philosophy: An Encounter between Feminism and Postmodernism". *Feminism/Postmodernism.* 19-38.

Frazer, James. *The Golden Bough: A Study in Magic and Religion.* Hertfordshire: Wordsworth, 1993.

Froula, Christine. "When Eve Reads Milton: Undoing the Canonical Economy". *Critical Inquiry* Vol. 10, No. 2 (Dec. 1983): 321-347.

Frye, Northrop. *Anatomy of Criticism: Four Essays.* Princeton: Princeton University Press, 1957.

——. *The Critical Path: An Essay on the Social Context of Literary Criticism.* Bloomington: Indiana University Press, 1971.

——. *The Secular Scripture: A Study of the Structure of Romance.* Cambridge, Massachusetts: Harvard University Press, 1976.

——. *Words with Power: Being a Second Study of The Bible and Literature.* New York: Harcourt, 1990.

——. *Myth and Metaphor: Selected Essays, 1974-1988.* Ed. Robert Denham. Charlottesville: University of Virginia Press, 1990.

Garner, Steve. *Racism in the Irish Experience.* London: Pluto, 2004.

Gatens, Moira. *Imaginary Bodies: Ethics, Power and Corporeality.* London: Routledge, 1996.

Genette, Gérard. *Narrative Discourse: An Essay in Method.* Trans. Jane Lewin. Ithaca: Cornell University Press, 1980.

Gibbons, Luke. *Transformations in Irish Culture.* Cork: Cork University Press, 1996.

Gifford, Douglas. "At Last—the Real Scottish Literary Renaissance?". *Books in Scotland* 34 (1990): 1-4.

Gilbert, Sandra and Susan Gubar. *Madwoman in the Attic: The Woman Writer and the Nineteenth-Century Literary Imagination.* New Haven, CT: Yale University Press, 1979.

Goering, Joseph. *The Virgin and the Grail: Origins of a Legend.* New Haven, CT: Yale University Press, 2005.

Graham, Colin and Richard Kirkland, eds. *Ireland and Cultural Theory: The Mechanics of Authenticity.* Basingstoke: Macmillan, 1999.

Graham, Colin. *Deconstructing Ireland: Identity, Theory, Culture.* Edinburgh: Edinburgh University Press, 2001.

Gray, John. *The Krt Text in the Literature of Ras Shamra: A Social Myth of Ancient Canaan.* Leiden: Brill, 1964.

Grimm, Jacob and Wilhelm Grimm. *Grimms' Fairy Tales.* London: Cape, 1962.

Grosz, Elizabeth. "Inscriptions and Body Maps: Representations and the Corporeal". *Feminine, Masculine and Representation.* Eds. T. Threatgold and A. Cranny-Francis. London: Allen&Unwin, 1990. 62-74.

—. *Volatile Bodies: Toward a Corporeal Feminism.* Bloomington: Indiana University Press, 1994.

—. *Space, Time, and Perversion: Essays on the Politics of Bodies.* New York: Routledge, 1995.

Hagemann, Susanne. "Women and Nation". *A History of Scottish Women's Writing.* Eds. Douglas Gifford and Dorothy McMillan. Edinburgh: Edinburgh University Press, 1997. 316-328.

Halberstam, Judith. "Technologies of Monstrosity: Bram Stoker's *Dracula*". *Cultural Politics at the Fin de Siécle.* Eds. Sally Ledger and Scott McCracken. Cambridge: Cambridge University Press, 1995. 248-266.

—. *Skin Shows: Gothic Horror and the Technology of Monsters.* Durham: Duke University Press, 1995.

Haraway, Donna. *Simians, Cyborgs and Women: The Reinvention of Nature.* London: Free Association, 1991.

—. *Modest_Witness @ Second_Millenium: FemaleMan ©_Meets_OncoMouse™.* London: Routledge, 1997.

Harding, Sandra. *The Science Question in Feminism.* Ithaca: Cornell University Press, 1986.

Hayles, Katherine. *How We Became Posthuman: Virtual Bodies in Cybernetics, Literature, and Informatics.* Chicago: University of Chicago Press, 1999.

Heath, Stephen. "Male Feminism". *Men in Feminism*. Eds. Alice Jardine and Paul Smith. New York: Methuen, 1987. 1-32.

Henry, Brian. "The Woman as Icon, the Woman as Poet". *Michigan Quarterly Review* 36 (1997): 188-202.

Hoff, Joan and Marian Yates. *The Cooper's Wife is Missing: The Trials of Bridget Cleary*. New York: Basic, 2000.

Horner, Avril and Sue Zlosnik. "Comic Gothic". *A Companion to the Gothic*. 242-254.

Hughes, William. "Fictional Vampires in the Nineteenth and Twentieth Centuries". *A Companion to the Gothic*. 143-154.

Hurley, Kelly. *The Gothic Body: Sexuality, Materialism and Degeneration at the* Fin de Siècle. Cambridge: Cambridge University Press, 1996.

Hyman, Stanley. "The Ritual View of Myth and the Mythic". *Myth: A Symposium*. Ed. Thomas Sebeok. Bloomington: Indiana University Press, 1965. 136-53.

Hynes, Colleen. "'A song for every child I might have had': Infertility and Maternal Loss in Contemporary Irish Poetry". *The Body and Desire in Contemporary Irish Poetry*. Ed Irene Nordin. Dublin: Irish Academic Press, 2006. 144-59.

Innes, Catherine Lynette. *Woman and Nation in Irish Literature and Society 1880-1935*. Athens: University of Georgia Press, 1993.

Irigaray, Luce. *Elemental Passions*. Trans. Joanne Collie and Judith Still. New York: Routledge, 1992.

Jancovitch, Mark. *Horror*. London: Batsford, 1992.

Jouve, Nicole. *Female Genesis: Creativity, Self and Gender*. Cambridge: Polity, 1998.

Kavita, Philip. "Race, Class and the Imperial Politics of Ethnography in India, Ireland and London, 1850-1910". *Irish Studies Review* 10 (2002): 297-9.

Keller, Evelyn Fox. *Reflections on Gender and Science*. New Haven, CT: Yale University Press, 1985.

—. "Secrets of God, Nature, and Life". *The Gender/Sexuality Reader: Culture, History, Political Economy*. Eds. Roger Lancaster and Micaela di Leonardo. New York: Routledge, 1997. 209-218.

Kiberd, Declan. *Inventing Ireland*. London: Cape, 1995.

Kidd, Colin. "Gaelic Identity and National Identity in Enlightenment Ireland and Scotland". *The English Historical Review* 434 (1994): 1197-1214.

Klancher, Jon. *The Making of English Reading Audiences, 1790-1832*. Madison: University of Wisconsin Press, 1987.

Kligman, Gail. *The Wedding of the Dead: Ritual, Poetics and Popular Culture in Transylvania*. Berkeley: University of California Press, 1998.

Kress, Gunther. "The Social Production of Language: History and Structures of Domination". *Discourse in Society: Systemic Functional Perspectives*. Eds. Peter Fries and Michael Gregory. Norwood, NJ: Ablex, 1995. 115-40.

Kristeva, Julia. *Desire in Language: A Semiotic Approach to Literature and Art*. Ed. Leon Roudiez. Trans. Thomas Gorz et al. New York: Columbia University Press, 1980.

—. *Powers of Horror: An Essay on Abjection*. Trans. Leon Roudiez. New York: Columbia University Press, 1982.

Kuklick, Henrika. *The Savage Within: The Social History of British Anthropology, 1885-1945*. Cambridge: Cambridge University Press, 1991.

Lacan, Jacques. *The Seminar of Jacques Lacan, Book III: The Psychoses 1955-1956*. Ed. Jacques-Allain Miller. Trans. Russell Grigg. New York: Norton, 1993.

—. *Écrits: A Selection*. Trans. Bruce Fink et al. New York: Norton, 2004.

Laplanche, Jean and Jean-Bertrand Pontalis. "Fantasy and the Origins of Sexuality". *Formations of Fantasy*. Ed. Victor Burgin et al. London and New York: Routledge, 1986. 5-34.

Latour, Bruno. *We Have Never Been Modern*. Trans. Catherine Porter. Cambridge, Massachusetts: Harvard University Press, 1993.

Levinson, Stephen. *Pragmatics*. Cambridge: Cambridge University Press, 1983.

Lévi-Strauss, Claude. *Structural Anthropology*. Trans. Monique Layton, 2 vols. Chicago: University of Chicago Press, 1976.

—. *The Raw and the Cooked: Introduction to a Science of Mythology*. London: Pimlico, 1994.

Lincoln, Bruce. *Theorizing Myth: Narrative, Ideology and Scholarship*. Chicago: University of Chicago Press, 1999.

Lord Raglan. "Myth and Ritual". *Myth: A Symposium*. 122-35.

Lumsden, Alison. "Scottish Women's Short Stories: 'Repositories of Life Swiftly Apprehended'". *Contemporary Scottish Women Writers*. 156-69.

Lumsden, Alison and Aileen Christianson. "Introduction". *Contemporary Scottish Women Writers*, 1-7.

Longley, Edna. *The Living Stream: Literature and Revisionism in Ireland*. Newcastle-upon-Tyne: Bloodaxe, 1994.

Lysaght, Patricia. *The Banshee: The Irish Death Messenger*. Boulder, Colorado: Reinhart, 1996.

Macdonald, Myra. *Representing Women: Myths of Femininity in the Popular Media*. London: Arnold, 1995.

Mack, Phyllis. *Visionary Women: Ecstatic Prophecy in Seventeenth-Century England*. Berkeley: University of California Press, 1992.

Martin, Augustine. *The Genius of Irish Prose*. Cork: Mercier, 1985.

Martin, Biddy. "Sexuality without Gender and Other Queer Utopias". *Diacritics* 24 (1994): 104-121.

Massé, Michelle. "Psychoanalysis and the Gothic". *A Companion to the Gothic*. 229-41.

Massey, Doreen. "Masculinity, Dualisms and High Technology". *Transactions of the Institute of British Geographers* 20 (1995): 487-99.

MacKinnon, Catherine. "Feminism, Marxism, Method, and the State: An Agenda for Theory", *Signs*, 7, 3 (1982): 515-44.

McClintock, Anne. *Imperial Leather: Race, Gender and Sexuality in the Colonial Contest*. London: Routledge, 1995.

McCulloch, Margery. "Scottish Women's Poetry 1972-1999: Transforming Traditions". *Contemporary Scottish Women Writers*. 11-26.

McDonald, Jan and Jennifer Harvie. "Putting New Twists to Old Stories: Feminism and Lochhead's Drama". *Liz Lochhead's Voices*. 124-47.

McDonald, Jan. "Scottish Women Dramatists Since 1945". *A History of Scottish Women's Writing*. 494-513.

McDowell, Linda. *Gender, Identity and Place: Understanding Feminist Geographies*. Cambridge: Polity, 2005.

McGann, Jerome. *Romantic Ideology: A Critical Investigation*. Chicago: University of Chicago Press, 1983.

McGuinness, Frank, ed. *The Dazzling Dark: New Irish Plays*. London: Faber, 1996.

McHale, Brian. *Postmodernist Fiction*. New York: Methuen, 1987.

McMillan, Dorothy. "Liz Lochhead and the Ungentle Art of Clyping". *Liz Lochhead's Voices*. 17-37.

Mighall, Robert. "Sex, History and the Vampire". *Bram Stoker: History, Psychoanalysis and the Gothic*. Eds. William Hughes and Andrew Smith. London: McMillan, 1998. 62-77.

Mugglestone, Lynda. "Lochhead's Language: Styles, Status, Gender and Identity". *Liz Lochhead's Voices*. 93-108.

Mumby, Dennis, ed. *Narrative and Social Control: Critical Perspectives*. Newbury Park, CA: Sage, 1993.

Nandy, Ashis. *The Intimate Enemy: Loss and Recovery of Self under Colonialism*. Delhi: Oxford University Press, 1983.

Nicholson, Colin. "Knucklebones of Irony: Liz Lochhead". *Poem, Purpose and Place: Shaping Identity in Contemporary Scottish Verse.* Edinburgh: Polygon, 1992. 201-23.

O'Brien, Matt. "Never the Groom: The Role of the Fantasy Male in Marina Carr's Plays". *The Theatre of Marina Carr: "before rules was made".* Eds. Cathy Leeney and Anna McMullan. Dublin: Carysfort, 2003. 200-214.

O'Callaghan, Margaret. *British High Politics and a Nationalist Ireland: Criminality, Land and the Law under Forster and Balfour.* Cork: Cork University Press, 1994.

O'Grady, Jean. "Northrop Frye at Home and Abroad". *Northrop Frye Newsletter* 8 (1999): 22-32.

O'Toole, Fintan. "Going West: The City Versus the Country in Irish Writing". *The Crane Bag* 9 (1985).

Owens, Rosemary. *Smashing Times: A History of the Irish Women's Suffrage Movement 1889-1922.* Dublin: Attic, 1984.

Paradiž, Valerie. *Clever Maids: The Secret History of the Grimm Fairy Tales.* New York: Basic, 2005.

Phillips, James. "In the Company of Predators: *Beowulf* and the Monstrous Descendants of Cain". *Angelaki* 13, No. 3 (December 2008): 41-51.

Phillips, Nelson and Cynthia Hardy. *Discourse Analysis: Investigating Processes of Social Construction.* Thousands Oaks: Sage, 2002.

Pirie, David. *The Vampire Cinema.* London: Hamlyn, 1977.

Raschke, Debrah. "Eavan Boland's *Outside History* and *In a Time of Violence*: Rescuing Women, the Concrete, and Other Things Physical from the Dung Heap". *Colby Quarterly* 32 (1996): 135-42.

Rich, Adrienne. *Of Woman Born: Motherhood as Experience and Institution.* New York: Norton, 1973.

—. "Toward a More Feminist Criticism". *Gender.* Ed. Anna Tripp. Houndmills: Palgrave, 2000. 42-50.

Roche, Anthony. "Woman on the Threshold: J.M. Synge's *The Shadow of the Glen*, Teresa Deevy's *Katie Roche* and Marina Carr's *The Mai*". *The Theatre of Marina Carr.* 17-42.

Rubin, Gayle. "The Traffic in Women: Notes on the Political Economy of Sex". *Toward an Anthropology of Women.* Ed. Rayna Reiter. New York: Monthly Review Press, 1975. 157-210.

Scaife, Sarahjane. "Mutual Beginnings: Marina Carr's *Low in the Dark*". *The Theatre of Marina Carr.* 1-16.

Schaffer, Roy. *A New Language for Psychoanalysis.* New Haven, CT: Yale University Press, 1976.

Schechner, Richard. *Performance Theory.* 1977, 2nd ed. 1988. London: Routledge, 2003.

Schelling, Friedrich. *System of Transcendentalism.* Trans. Peter Heath. Charlottesville: University of Virginia Press, 1978.

Sellers, Susan. *Myth and Fairy Tale in Contemporary Women's Fiction.* Houndmills: Palgrave, 2001.

Shumaker, Jeanette Roberts. "Accepting the Grotesque Body: Bildungs by Clare Boylan and Eilis Ni Dhuibhne". *Estudios Irlandeses* 1 (2006): 103-111.

Shuttle, Penelope and Peter Redgrove. *The Wise Wound.* London: Penguin, 1980.

Sihra, Melissa. "A Cautionary Tale: Marina Carr's *By the Bog of Cats...*". *Theatre Stuff.* Ed. Eamonn Jordan. Dublin: Carysfort, 2000.

—. "Reflections Across Water: New Stages of Performing Carr". *The Theatre of Marina Carr.* 92-113.

Smith, Alison. "Liz Lochhead: Speaking in Her Own Voice". *Liz Lochhead's Voices.* 1-16.

Smyth, Gerry. *The Novel and the Nation: Studies in the New Irish Fiction.* London: Pluto, 1997.

—. *Decolonisation and Criticism: The Construction of Irish Literature.* London: Pluto, 1998.

Sorel, Georges. *Reflections on Violence.* Trans. T. E. Hulme and J. Roth. Mineola, New York: Dover, 2004.

Steeves, H. Peter. "The Familiar Other and Feral Selves: Life at the Human/Animal Boundary". *The Animal/Human Boundary: Historical Perspectives.* Eds. Angela Creager and William Chester Jordan. Rochester, NY: University of Rochester Press, 2002. 228-64.

Sukenick, Ronald. *In Form: Digressions on the Act of Fiction.* Carbondale: Southern Illinois University Press, 1985.

Sullivan, Margaret A. "Madness and Folly: Peter Bruegel the Elder's *Dulle Griet*". *Art Bulletin* 59 (1977): 55-66.

Synnott, Anthony. *The Body Social: Symbolism, Self and Society.* London: Routledge, 1993.

Tatar, Maria. "Born Yesterday: Heroes in the Grimm's Fairy Tales". *Fairy Tales and Society: Illusion, Allusion and Paradigm.* Ed. Ruth Bottigheimer. Philadelphia: University of Pennsylvania Press, 1986. 95-114.

—. *The Classic Fairy Tales.* New York: Norton, 1999.

Todorov, Tsvetan. *Theories of the Symbol.* Trans. Catherine Porter. Ithaca: Cornell University Press, 1982.

Unterecker, John. "Introduction". *Yeats: A Collection of Critical Essays.* Ed. John Unterecker. Englewood Cliffs, NJ: Prentice Hall, 1963. 1-6.

Uther, Hans-Jörg. *The Types of International Folktales. A Classification and Bibliography Based on the System of Antti Aarne and Stith Thompson* (3 vols). Helsinki: Suomalainen Tiedeakatemia, 2004.

Varty, Anne. "The Mirror and the Vamp: Liz Lochhead". *A History of Scottish Women's Writing.* 641-658.

Vernant, Jean-Pierre. *Myth and Society in Ancient Greece.* London: Methuen, 1982.

Von Hendy, Andrew. *The Modern Construction of Myth.* Bloomington: Indiana University Press, 2002.

Vrettos, Athena. *Imagining Illness in Victorian Culture.* Stanford: Stanford University Press, 1996.

Walby, Sylvia. *Gender Transformations.* London: Routledge, 1997.

Wallace, Clare. "Authentic Reproductions: Marina Carr and the Inevitable". *The Theatre of Marina Carr.* 43-64.

—. "Tragic Destiny and Abjection in Marina Carr's *The Mai, Portia Coughlan* and *By the Bog of Cats...*". *Irish University Review* 31 (2000): 432-49.

Ward, Margaret. *Unmanageable Revolutionaries.* London: Pluto, 1983.

Warner, Marina. *Monuments and Maidens: The Allegory of the Female Form.* London: Picador, 1985.

—. *Managing Monsters: Six Myths of Our Time (The 1994 Reith Lectures).* London: Vintage, 1994.

—. *From the Beast to the Blonde: On Fairy Tales and their Tellers.* New York: Farrar, 1995.

Weissenborn, Juergen and Wolfgang Klein. "Introduction". *Here and There: Cross-linguistic Studies on Deixis and Demonstration (Pragmatics& Beyond III: 2-3).* Eds. Juergen Weissenborn and Wolfgang Klein. Amsterdam: Benjamins, 1982.

Wellek, René. *Concepts of Criticism.* New Haven, CT: Yale University Press, 1963.

White, Hayden. "The Value of Narrativity in the Representation of Reality". *On Narrative.* Ed. W. Mitchell. Chicago: University of Chicago Press, 1981. 1-23.

Whyte, John Henry. *Church and State in Modern Ireland 1923-1979.* Dublin: Gill&Macmillan, 1980.

Wisker, Gina. "Love Bites: Contemporary Women's Vampire Fictions", *Diegesis: Journal of the Association for Research in Popular Fictions* 3 (1998). Republished in *A Companion to the Gothic.* 167-79.

Yorke, Liz. *Impertinent Voices: Subversive Strategies in Contemporary Women's Poetry*. London: Routledge, 1991.

Zipes, Jack. *Fairy Tales and the Art of Subversion*. New York: Routledge, 1991.

—. *Breaking the Magic Spell: Radical Theories of Folk and Fairy Tales*. Lexington: University of Kentucky Press, 2002.

—. *Why Fairy Tales Stick: The Evolution and Relevance of a Genre*. New York: Routledge, 2006.

INDEX